THE GREAT BRITISH COOK BOOK

200 CHEFS
200 RECIPES
10 REGIONS

Copyright © The Great British Cookbook
www.thegreatbritishcookbook.co.uk
PROJECT DIRECTOR | ALL ABOUT TOURISM | GARY ALLEN
FOUNDERS – ANDY WHYLES AND GARY ALLEN
www.allabouttourism.co.uk

PHOTOGRAPHY | PETRA MEDLEY & WARREN TAIT
www.petramedley.com

DEVELOPMENT AND DESIGN | MARK JOYNER & TERRY SUMMERFIELD
www.gossama.com

First Published 2014 by All About Tourism Ltd
Copyright © All About Tourism Ltd

30 Woolpack Lane – Lace Market – Nottingham – NG1 1GA
A CIP catalogue record of this book is available from the British Library

ISB: 978-1-5262-0501-8. This ISBN is unique to All About Tourism Ltd.
This ISBN has been assigned to:
"The Great British Cookbook"
Binding/Format: hardback

200 CHEFS | 200 RECIPES | 10 REGIONS

In 2012 we began a nationwide search of Great Britain to find two hundred chefs to create extraordinary dishes. This unique book captures a snap shot of what these chefs are cooking for millions of customers each year. The essential ethos of the book is to feature recipes by inspirational local Chefs who are passionate about using local sustainable produce to create wonderfully divine dishes.

The Great British Cookbook will take you on a journey through some of the UK's most prestigious Pubs, Guest Houses, Hotels, Michelin Starred and AA Rosette restaurants.

We have highlighted some of the industries brightest stars of the future, alongside some of Britain's most well respected chefs and celebrity chefs.

The book is sleek, stylish and reflects the amazing talent of the phenomenal chefs on display. This awe-inspiring compendium of mouth-watering recipes will have every foodie salivating.

Bon appetite!

CONTENTS

MARKS
VEGGIE
PLOT

Mark and Jane Willis live in Hampshire, although Jane is originally from Lancashire and Mark was born and raised in Malaysia but his family roots are in Cornwall. They met at university where they soon realised they both share a passion for good food. They quickly learnt to cook for themselves as the alternative was mass produced college food. After they married, Mark's job as an Officer in the Brigade of Gurkhas took them to Brunei, Hong Kong and Germany. They loved to explore the local markets and restaurants, learning to cook many exotic dishes, learning from the Nepalese people who they lived and worked among.

Army life meant frequent house moves so there was never an opportunity to establish a proper garden, although there were always pots of herbs on the balcony. Now they have settled in their Hampshire home for over 20 years, the garden reflects the diversity of foods from all over the world that they love to cook and eat. They still love to travel and always try to visit local shops and markets to find out what the REAL local food is like, rather than that served to tourists. A holiday souvenir is more likely to be a bottle of olive oil or a pack of salad seeds than a straw donkey or fake designer t-shirt!

Mark says:

For me, gardening has been more-or-less a lifelong hobby. I inherited my love of it from my father and set up my own garden at the earliest opportunity. To my mind a property without a garden is incomplete, even when we lived in a 5th –floor flat I somehow contrived to have a balcony full of plants. Our two daughters have continued the family tradition too, raising their own children with the same love of plants – especially edible ones. When the grandchildren visit us they always want a tour of the garden and like nothing better than to eat a few of Grandpa's tomatoes or blueberries straight from the plant.

The plot after which my blog "Mark's Veg Plot" is named is the back garden of our house, an area of roughly 10 metres by 10 metres. Most of my vegetables are grown in rectangular raised beds but I have an ever-increasing number of miscellaneous pots and containers. People are always amazed to see how much produce I can squeeze out of this modest space, one friend even calls my plot the "Tardis Garden"! In the Spring, the garden 'expands indoors' in a manner of speaking, since every windowsill in the house gets lined with trays of seedlings being started off in the warmth, prior to hardening-off in one of my several plastic mini-greenhouses and eventual planting out when the weather allows.

Our 'temperate' British climate lends itself to the growing of a very wide range of plants, I like to grow as many different vegetables as possible – potatoes, beans, tomatoes, lettuces, etc. This means that if one of them fails to do well for any reason, something else is bound to do better! As well as the routine 'staples,' I do like to try growing a few unusual things too. One year I had a bumper crop of tomatillos, a fruit a bit like a tomato, which is almost impossible to buy in the UK. With my upbringing in Malaysia and my Army Service with the Brigade of Gurkhas, I suppose it was inevitable that I should gravitate towards growing chillies. We are not keen on the throat-searing super-hot varieties but we do like a bit of a spicy tang in our food, so chillies have become a constant feature of my veg plot. The only vegetable that has definitely beaten me is the celeriac. I tried to grow it three years in a row but the biggest bulb I got was hardly bigger than a tennis-ball.

Despite the occasional glut of something (runner beans for example), and a few gifts to family members, most of the vegetables grown in my garden are consumed by me and my wife Jane, and eaten fresh too because we are not particularly keen on frozen veg. Over the years I have learned to grow what we like best and also what is best when it is home-grown. For instance, purple sprouting broccoli (PSB) is often limp and tired-looking when you buy it but is perky and vibrant when it comes straight from the plot to the kitchen, and what can compare with the pleasure of eating new potatoes cooked just minutes after harvesting? These days, I grow several varieties of potato in large pots and containers because I can't afford the space in the raised beds. I always choose early varieties rather than main crops, so that I can harvest them before the dreaded Blight becomes an issue. Watering the pots can be a bit of a chore but I assure you that the result is definitely worth it!

With limited space available, you quickly learn to use it efficiently so I grow lots of herbs. Herbs are expensive in the shops and many of them don't keep well, so it makes sense to grow your own. Our style of cooking calls for lots of fresh herbs and it is so convenient to be able to quickly pop into the garden and grab a few sprigs of something when you need them. In spring this might be winter savory to flavour broad beans; in summer time, parsley for tabbouleh or mint for with some lamb chops; and in the cooler weather thyme and rosemary appear frequently in roast meat dishes and sage of course is vital for the sage and onion stuffing in the Christmas turkey. A recent discovery is leaf celery, this produces really pungent leaves which add a delicious savoury flavour to soups, stews and stock.

Even the smallest garden can accommodate some fruit trees and bushes. There are plenty of varieties bred specially to be small and suitable for growing in containers. I have a couple of apple trees and a conference pear grown in the very slim 'Minarette' form, as well as several potted blueberry bushes and some strawberry plants grown in plastic crates so that I can shift them around when required. Oh, and a row of raspberries against a fence. Home-grown raspberries and blueberries with Cornish clotted cream – now that's a proper treat!

The most significant challenge is to keep the harvests coming throughout the year which is much easier said than done! The vegetable calendar starts for me with the PSB harvest in March/April followed soon after by the arrival of delicious asparagus in May and June giving way to a rush of lettuce, radishes, beetroot, peas and runner beans in June and July. High spot of the year comes in August and September because this is the time for squashes, tomatoes and my beloved chillis. In the autumn it's cabbages, parsnips and leeks, and then the old Christmas-time favourite the brussels sprout – in our house usually served with foraged chestnuts. With a bit of ingenuity and a few cloches, I can usually manage to produce something (even if it's just a few leaves of landcress or a single head of radicchio) every week of the year.

Let's not forget that the whole point of growing fruit, veg and herbs is to eat them. My wife Jane and I are both keen cooks and we eat loads of fruit and veg, so few things give me more pleasure than to see home-grown produce appearing on the dinner-table!

Jane says:

When you think about British food, foods associated with special occasion's spring to mind – brussels sprouts with Christmas dinner, strawberries while watching Wimbledon, roast lamb at Easter, bobbing for apples and carving pumpkin lanterns at Halloween. Certain foods have become associated with particular events because of our great tradition of feasting, and any feast needs to have the very best foodstuffs. Which means food that is at the peak of perfection. When a food, be it fruit or vegetable, animal or fish is in season that is when it is going to look and taste its absolute best. It will have travelled less distance, spent less time in storage, and be perfectly suited to the climate of the season and therefore ideal for the banquet table! Most of our food traditions were established long before refrigerated storage and processed foods were invented so they make the very best of what is in season.

Of course if you grow your own, the fruit and veg you have available naturally change with the seasons, but not everyone is lucky enough to be able to do that. So, how can you tell what is in season when you are shopping? Here are some pointers to look out for:

The price – out of season produce costs more to produce, ship and store, so almost all foods are cheaper in season. When crops are at their peak supermarkets will often have bargain offers to clear stocks quickly so seasonal eating can save you a lot of money.

The country of origin. Apart from things like apples, that store well, food produced in Britain is more likely to be seasonal than imported food. For items that need a hotter climate than ours such as citrus fruits, look out for produce grown in Europe or around the Mediterranean where the seasons, although warmer, are still synchronised with ours. I've never really seen the point of buying something like a swede that has travelled all the way from New Zealand!

The things that are growing around you. Even if you don't have a vegetable patch yourself look out of the car or train window as you travel to see what's in the fields, gardens and allotments. A field of sweet corn means that cobs of corn will soon be in the shops, while the bright red splash of the flowers on a row of beans means the runner beans are almost ready for picking. Apple cores thrown from car windows over the years mean that many of our roadside verges have apple trees growing there. When those apples look ripe, British apples will be at their best in the shops.

Tradition – as already mentioned, traditional foods for a special occasion nearly always work with the seasons. And what we don't eat is also dictated by tradition – for instance the fasting of Lent coincides with what many gardeners call "the hungry gap." This is when little fresh produce is available and before the advent of freezing and canning, people had to rely on foods that stored for a long time. Another tradition that is based on seasonality is that of not eating shellfish, especially oysters, when there is no 'R' in the month – this helps to protect the stocks during the breeding season and in the days before refrigeration also helped to keep people safe from eating shellfish that had gone bad.

The law – many game meats are not allowed to be caught for food during their breeding season. This protects future stocks, but also means you only get the rich, dark heavy meats in the colder months when the warming meals you can make with them are more welcome. You can buy some farmed game meats all year round but would you really fancy a rich venison casserole on a hot summer day?

You'll find "What's in season, when" guides in many recipe books and all over the internet, but use them with care! Of course you need to check that they are intended for your own country but you also need to remember that weather conditions mean that seasons can move slightly every year, and the kind of spring that makes one vegetable appear early and in abundance can make another one arrive, rather reluctantly, a month late. So if you use a chart, use it in conjunction with the above tips to help you to develop your own instincts as you learn to shop and eat with the seasons.

London and South

Starter
Main
Dessert

MEDLAR RESTAURANT

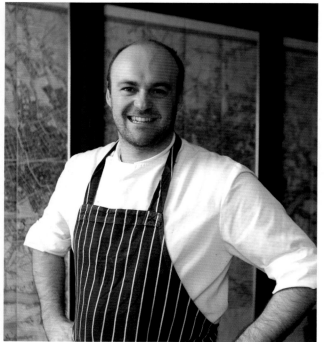

BIOGRAPHY

After attending Eton and Oxford University, Joe embarked upon his culinary career. He first attended Leith's School of Food and Wine in 2001, only deciding afterwards to make cooking his profession. Roles at Carluccio's, The Savoy Grill and Chez Bruce followed, along with a spell in Sydney working at Neil Perry's Rockpool.

Joe launched Medlar Restaurant along with business partner David O'Connor in 5th April 2011 on the Kings Road in Chelsea, London.

At Medlar Joe aims to cook seasonal ingredients from the British Isles and Europe accurately and simply. The style is French based but takes inspiration from all over. A love of food drives Joe to the kitchen, and he strives to cook food that is first and foremost satisfying to eat, without overelaboration or pretension.

'My ethos is simple; cook what you like to eat and be generous with it'

Duck Egg Tart

with red wine sauce, turnip purée, lardons, young sorrel and sautéed duck heart

INGREDIENTS

Rough Puff Pastry

250g Cold butter

250g Flour

125g Water

2.5g Salt

Red Wine Sauce

1 ½ bottles of Red wine

½ bottle Port

½ bottle Madeira

2 litres of Veal stock

Salt (large pinch)

8 Shallots

5 Bay leaf

½ (bunch) Thyme

1 Head of garlic cut in half

Turnip Purée

1kg Turnip

50g Butter

50ml Water

250ml Double cream

Salt

METHOD

Rough Puff Pastry

Finely dice the butter keeping it cold. In a large bowl work the diced butter into the flour/salt with your fingers until it is almost at the breadcrumb stage but still keeping a few lumps of butter there. Add the water and bring the pastry together. Form into a block and refrigerate for an hour. Roll the pastry out until the thickness of a one pound coin or use a pasta machine set to 5. Cook the sheets of puff pastry between two heavy metal trays lined with greaseproof paper at 160°C for 20 minutes or until golden brown. Use a large round cutter to carefully cut discs of the pastry out.

Red Wine Sauce

Briefly sweat off the sliced shallots in a little vegetable oil and add the red wine and reduce to a syrup. Add the port and Madeira and reduce again by two thirds. Finally mix in the veal stock and herbs and cook on the stove gently for three hours. Add salt to taste.

Turnip Purée

Peel and dice the turnip and place in a pan with the butter and water. Cook with a lid on a low heat until soft. Add the cream and bring to the boil. Remove from the heat and using a high speed blender, blend until smooth. Season to taste.

To Assemble The Dish

Sauté a duck heart, keeping it very pink and leave this to one side.
Cook some mushrooms, any firm variety will do, and some bacon lardons.
Steam a small amount of spinach and keep warm.
Warm some turnip puree.
Place into a small pan of the gently heated red wine sauce the mushrooms, lardons and duck heart which you have sliced in half.
Gently fry a duck egg using a little vegetable oil. Cut out the egg using the same cutter used to cut the pastry.

Place the spinach in the centre of a warmed plate. Place the disc of puff pastry on top.
Spread some turnip purée onto the pastry and drip three small spoonfuls around.
Lay the fried duck egg on top.
Finally spoon the red wine sauce with the sautéed duck heart, mushrooms and lardons around the egg. Garnish with the sorrel on top.

LEVI ROOTS

BIOGRAPHY

Charismatic Sauce-man and Entrepreneur, Levi Roots first shot to fame on BBC2's Dragon's Den in 2007, when defying the odds with his spirited Reggae Reggae Sauce song, he charmed dragons Peter Jones and Richard Farleigh into investment in his tangy homemade Reggae Reggae Sauce. With a speedy launch at Sainsbury's only a few weeks later, the sauce flew off the shelves, outselling even Heinz Tomato Ketchup and it's been a whirlwind ever since.

As well as his wide range of products, Levi has released a 6 cookbooks and a business book. Levi's sixth and most recent book, Grill it with Levi, is a collection of his BBQ recipes. The Levi Roots Brand continues to blaze a trail while Levi's warm and infectious ethos of Caribbean Sunshine continues to put music into food, and life everywhere across the nation.

Levi Roots was nominated for a MOBO award in 1998 for his 'Free Your Mind album'. He sang 'Happy Birthday' to Nelson Mandela when the South African icon visited Brixton and used to play football with Bob Marley every Sunday in Battersea Park. Levi's last album "Red Hot" was launched in autumn 2009 by Sound Box Media and he is currently getting ready to release his new album, due for release this summer.

His latest EP 'SoundBox' is out now and includes the hugely popular 'Rice And Peas'.

Lime Marmalade, Rum & Chilli Poussins

INGREDIENTS

For The Marinade

6 Garlic cloves, crushed

1 Chilli, halved, seeded and finely chopped

1 tbsp Fresh thyme leaves

Grated zest and juice of 4 limes

Sea salt flakes

Freshly ground black pepper

2 tsp Ground allspice

100ml Dark or light rum

2 tbsp Olive oil

4 Poussins

For The Glaze

150g Lime marmalade

2 Red chillis, halved, seeded and chopped

2 Garlic cloves, crushed

3 tbsp Clear honey

Juice of 1 lime

Salt and pepper

METHOD

First make the marinade. Pound the garlic, chilli, thyme, lime zest, salt and pepper and allspice together with a mortar and pestle. Add the wet ingredients and combine well. Make slits in the birds in places where they won't be seen – between the legs and the body, for example – and coat well with the marinade. Make sure the insides of the birds are coated as well. Cover with clingfilm and chill for about 6 hours, turning the birds every so often.

Preheat the oven to 180°C/350°F/Gas 4. Lift the poussins out of the marinade and transfer them to a roasting tin. Season with salt and pepper, and roast for 30 minutes. Remove the poussins from the oven and leave them to cool a little – if you put the glaze on while they're hot it will just run off.

Meanwhile, make the glaze by vigorously stirring everything together. You need to use some elbow grease here to break down the marmalade. Spread the glaze all over the birds, inside and out, and barbecue for 10 minutes, turning every so often and brushing with more glaze. Check for doneness – the juices between the legs and body should run clear, with no trace of pink. Brush with a final coat of glaze and serve immediately.

PETRICHOR @ THE CAVENDISH LONDON

BIOGRAPHY

Nitin Padwal, born in India from a holy pilgrimage city of Nashik. Since his childhood Nitin was inspired and has developed a passion for cooking watching his mother cook.

Having developed a passion for cooking at a young age he has spent the last 16 years working away from the family in Mumbai, Indore, Yorkshire and finally settled in London honing his skills and developing his cooking style.

Nitin has been working at The Cavendish London hotel (Petrichor restaurant) for over 9 years and have achieved 2 AA rosettes for his cooking. He changes the menus every quarterly by getting the team engaging them in coming up with fresh ideas and refining them. Nitin also takes great pride in sourcing the local British produce for his menus and committed to source 100% British or sustainable produce wherever it's possible.

Pan Fried Quail Breast
quail eggs, confit leg croquette, braised onion & grape must mustard, truffle foam, puff pastry

INGREDIENTS

4 whole Quail plucked and cleaned

1 sprig Thyme

1 sprig Rosemary

250gm Goose fat

1 clove Garlic

10gm Baby spinach

1 large White onion

Butter for cooking

16 Quail egg whole

1 Egg beaten

10gm Flour

100gm Breadcrumbs

100ml Milk

10gm Lecithin

10ml White truffle oil

100gm Black truffle paste

5gm Pink peppercorns

5gm Cumin seeds

5 gm mixed Black & white sesame seeds

10gm Grapemust mustard

Oil & butter for frying

METHOD

For the Quail-

Clean the quail breast form the excess hair and blow torch lightly to burn any hair that cannot be plucked. Season with salt & pepper

For the croquette-

Fill a heavy bottom tray with goose fat, rosemary, garlic & thyme then place in the oven at 70 degrees. Separate the meat and the bones.

Shape the leg meat in round croquette and coat with beaten egg, flour & panko breadcrumbs

Braised onion -

In a heavy bottom pan add clarified butter and sliced onions. Cook till nicely colour and caramelised and soft add grapemust mustard to it in the end and drain off excess fat.

Truffle foam –

In a pan add milk, double cream, lecithin, truffle paste & truffle oil. Boil once and simmer for 5 minutes.

For Assembly-

Pan fry quail breast till the skin is nice and crisp and meat is juicy in the centre.

Cut puff pastry in circle and cut another 2cm circle in the centre, egg wash and sprinkle the pink peppercorns and cumin seeds before baking in the oven at 190 degrees for 15 minutes.

On a plate place braised onion and buttered baby spinach. Place 3 diced and fried potato cubes as a base to hold the puff pastry ring. Place the quail croquette & breast on top of the braised onion. Align the pastry ring on top and on the pastry put pan fried quail egg. Finish with truffle foam.

TRINITY RESTAURANT

BIOGRAPHY

Since it's opening in 2006, Trinity has won the ' Time Out Best New Restaurant ', the AA's prestigious 'London Restaurant of the Year' as well as holding three AA rosettes for 9 years, Trinity was voted in the top ten restaurants in London by both Hardens and Zagat in both 2010 and 2011 and has been listed in the Times Top 100 Restaurants in the UK for the past two years. It is regarded as " as close to an absolutely perfect experience of eating out as it is possible to have " – Giles Coren, The Times.

In 2012, Adam and Angus opened a sister restaurant to Trinity in Clapham: Bistro Union is a quintessentially British bistro, providing all day dining in a relaxed environment. Adam has recently overseen the extensive refurbishment of Trinity, including a new dining room on the first floor of the restaurant, Upstairs, providing contemporary, relaxed dining. Meanwhile, Trinity will continue its neighbourhood fine dining offering in a new, stylish setting.

Big Eye Tuna Carpaccio
avocado, sesame and lime

INGREDIENTS

6 x 80g portions of
mid-loin Yellowfin tuna

1 Carrot

1 Red onion

1 Cucumber

1 Chilli

20g fresh Ginger

180ml Soy sauce

90ml Sesame oil

10g Caster sugar

4 Limes

2 Ripe hass avocados

100ml Double cream

3 Radishes

2 Baby turnips

10g Coriander cress

METHOD

Place the one tuna portion between two pieces of plastic and flatten it with the base of a heavy pan until it forms a circle 15cm in diameter. Repeat with the remaining 5 tuna portions.

Cut the carrot, red onion, cucumber and chilli into a fine brunoise.

For the vinaigrette; in a large bowl, mix the soy sauce, sesame oil, caster sugar and the juice of 2 limes. Combine this with the diced vegetables and reserve for later.

For the avocado mousse; remove the flesh from the avocadoes and place into a blender. Add the juice of the 2 remaining limes and blend until smooth.

In a medium-sized bowl, lightly whip in the double cream until it reaches the ribbon stage. Fold in the pureed avocado and season to taste. Reserved chilled for later

Thinly slice the radishes and turnips on a mandolin and reserve in ice water for later.

Lay the tuna onto the centre of a large, flat, cold plate and remove the plastic. Season with salt and pepper. Drizzle the vinaigrette liberally around the plate. Place a quenelle of avocado into the centre of the plate. Garnish with sliced radish, turnips, and coriander cress. Serve immediately.

CORINTHIA HOTEL LONDON

BIOGRAPHY

The Northall showcases the very best of British cuisine with a focus on seasonal produce from artisanal suppliers who provide the restaurant with the finest ingredients from around the British Isles.

The light and airy 185 cover restaurant is designed by GA Design. The Northall is arranged across four stunning and distinct areas, offering a private dining room for intimate dinners. It encapsulates quintessential British hospitality – both past and present – with a comfortable and relaxed eating environment, whilst offering views over Whitehall Gardens towards the River Thames.

The all day menu incorporates dishes such as mouth-watering Goosnaugh Chicken with white bean and parsley cassoulet and wild mushrooms, and roast butternut squash risotto with Harbourne blue goat's cheese.

Warm Asparagus
with orange confit hollandaise sauce, red sorrel cress

INGREDIENTS

24 pieces Asparagus

2 Oranges

100ml White wine vinegar

100gm Castor sugar

50g Red sorrel cress

Hollandaise

250g clarified Butter

3 Egg yolks

1 Lemon

Reduction

200ml White wine vinegar

12 White pepper corns

2 sprigs Tarragon

2 Shallots

METHOD

Lightly peel the asparagus and place into iced water.

Cook the asparagus with plenty of boiling salted water until just cooked, then refresh into ice water. Remove and place onto kitchen paper to drain and then cover with damp kitchen paper.

To make the hollandaise reduction, place all the ingredients into a pan and quickly reduce by two thirds, stain and cool

Now place the egg yolks and reduction into a bowl. Whisk until creamy and soft peaks are formed over a pan of simmering water.

Slowly add the warm clarified butter to the eggs, continually whisking. The sauce should now start to thicken and emulsify.

Add a few drops of lemon and season accordingly. Pass the sauce through muslin cloth and keep in a warm

To prepare the oranges, firstly remove the zest with a peeler and cut into thin strips.

Blanch into boiling water for a few seconds and then refresh into ice water, remove.

Now add the sugar and vinegar to a pan and simmer, remove and cool.

Place the blanched zest into the mix and set to one side.

Segment the oranges and cut into a neat dice.

Retain all the juices from the oranges, place into a pan and reduce quickly to a syrup, and then add to the hollandaise.

Gently warm the asparagus, brush with a little butter, season and arrange onto a plate all facing the same way.

Drizzle over the orange infused hollandaise and neatly arrange the diced orange and zest over the asparagus.

Finish the dish with the red sorrel cress

RACHEL KHOO

BIOGRAPHY

Rachel's unconventional food background has helped formulate her unique culinary touch. She graduated with a Bachelors degree in Art & Design from the renowned Central Saint Martins College of Art and Design in London. Thereafter she worked for a luxury fashion brand, doing PR and e-marketing. Ultimately, her passion for pâtisserie lured her to Paris, where she studied at Le Cordon Bleu and obtained a pastry degree.

She put her skills to excellent use at the delightful Paris culinary bookstore and tea salon, La Cocotte. There Rachel concocted delicious sweet treats, regularly providing catering for culinary book launches and hosting cookery classes on site. Following the success of her edible endeavours at La Cocotte, she now works on culinary projects throughout the world. Her role as an international food creative has spanned six-course dinners and workshops in places as far-flung as London, Paris, Berlin, Milan, Melbourne, Sydney and Buenos Aires.

She is also a food writer with books "Barres à céréales, Granola et Muesli faites maison" and "Pâtes à tartiner" published by Marabout. "Barres à céréales, Granola et Muesli faites maison" has also been published in Dutch, Italian and most recently in English – "Pâtes à tartiner" has also been published in English. Her third cookbook (her first English book) "The Little Paris Kitchen" was published by Penguin on March the 15th 2012.

Ratatouille
with herb and gruyère cobbler

The herb and Gruyère cobbler on top will make ratatouille purists blanch, but some rules are made for breaking. It may not be one for your French granny, but my little twist on the medley of Mediterranean veg makes a great one-pot supper for friends.

INGREDIENTS

6 tbsp Olive oil

1 Onion, peeled and finely chopped

1 Garlic clove, peeled and sliced

1 Aubergine, cut into rough chunks

2 Medium courgettes, cut into 2cm rounds

1 Red pepper, deseeded and finely sliced

1 Yellow pepper, deseeded and finely sliced

2 Tins whole cherry tomatoes

1 tbsp Balsamic vinegar

250g Self-raising flour

85g Cold butter, cubed

60g Gruyère, grated

10g Fresh herbs (such as sage, marjoram, chives), finely chopped

1 Egg

3 tbsp Milk

1 Beaten egg, for brushing

10 Basil leaves, to garnish

METHOD

Preheat the oven to 180C. Heat 2 tbsp of the olive oil in a medium ovenproof casserole dish. Add the onion and garlic, plus a pinch of sea salt, and sweat for 10 minutes over a low heat. Put a large sauté pan or wok on a high heat with 2 tbsp olive oil and add the aubergine, tossing every so often.

After around 5 minutes, remove from the pan and set aside. Add the remaining oil and the courgettes and peppers and cook for 4-5 minutes. Remove from the pan and set aside with the aubergine.

Add the tomatoes to the casserole, then stir in the aubergine, courgettes and peppers. Season with black pepper and add the vinegar.

Leave to simmer on a low heat while you make the cobbler. Mix the flour, butter and Gruyère in a food processor. Add the herbs, egg and enough milk to bring it together to a smooth dough. Season well with sea salt and black pepper. Roll out to a 1.5cm thickness and use a 7cm cookie cutter to cut out 7-8 rounds. Take the ratatouille off the heat.

Arrange the dough rounds across the top and brush with the beaten egg. Place in the oven for 40-45 minutes or until golden and cooked through. Scatter with the basil leaves and serve immediately.

CITY
SOCIAL

BIOGRAPHY

Originally from Aldershot in Hampshire, Paul Walsh has spent the last 12 years working alongside many of the UK's most respected and well-known talents in some of London's most demanding kitchens.

Paul began his training with a catering course at Westminster Kingsway College. His first role, in 2000, was as a Commis Chef at the Savoy Hotel under Anton Edelmann, where he stayed for two and a half years, working his way up to Chef de Partie. From there, Paul moved to the Savoy Grill when it reopened under the direction of Marcus Wareing, and helped it to achieve a Michelin star, the first in its 100 year history. Here he was promoted to Junior Sous Chef.

In 2005, Paul moved to Restaurant Gordon Ramsay on Royal Hospital Road, where he was to spend five years, finishing as Senior Sous Chef. During this time, he worked with some of the biggest names from the Ramsay stable, including Simone Zanoni, Mark Askew and Clare Smyth. Paul was one of the longest serving chefs in this challenging environment, and credits it with shaping the way he cooks today.

In June 2010, Paul left Gordon Ramsay Holdings to launch the first 28-50 Wine Workshop and Kitchen, a venture from Icelandic chef Agnar Sverrisson and French master sommelier Xavier Rousset. Paul launched two further 28-50 sites before leaving to work with Jason Atherton, taking the head chef position at City Social in April 2014.

Six months after opening, City Social was awarded a coveted Michelin star in the 2015 Michelin Guide. In October 2014, City Social won the BMW Square Meal Award for Best New Restaurant. The celebrations continued into early 2015, with the restaurant winning the accolade of three AA Rosettes; Paul Walsh's food was described as "inventive, detailed and bursting with entertaining combinations of taste and texture".

Lincolnshire Rabbit Saddle & Sausage,
pommery mustard mash, morels, garlic.

INGREDIENTS

Rabbit saddle
1 Rabbit saddle 160g
boneless
2 slices of Parma ham

Rabbit Sausage
200g Rabbit meat (minced)
200g Pork mince
100g Pork fat
5g chopped Garlic
2g ground Ginger
5g chopped Parsley
Salt
Sausage skins

**Rabbit leg beignet (makes
one terrine) serves 20**
12 Rabbit legs
6 Rabbit kidneys
4 Rabbit livers
250ml Rabbit sauce
(reduced to 100ml)
Pommery mustard 50g
20g Tarragon

Rabbit Sauce
5Kg Rabbit bones
12 lrg Banana shallots
(sliced)
1 head of Garlic
5g Thyme
2g Rock salt
12 White peppercorns
crushed
20ml of Sherry vinegar
2l of reduced Veal stock
2l of white Chicken stock

Pommery mustard mush
250g Ratte Potatoes
50g Milk
50g Butter
20g Pommery mustard

Parlsey oil
50g picked Flat parsley
100ml Olive oil
Bowl of iced water

Garnish
50g Morels
30g St george mushrooms
4 stems of White or purple
sprouting broccoli
4 cloves of Garlic

METHOD

Rabbit saddle
Remove the fillets & place where the back bone used to be, then thin out
the bellies with a knife trimming away any fat & sinew, season and roll,
place the roll on the Parma ham and wrap it around. Roll tightly in cling
film to make a ballotine, sous vide, and then cook at 65oc for 20 minutes,
remove from cling film and roast for 4 minutes in a frying pan until the
Parma ham is crispy.

Rabbit Sausage
Mix all the ingredients together and pipe the mix into the sausages skins,
tie them off at 5cms. Fry for 2 minutes.

Rabbit leg beignet (makes one terrine) serves 20
Sous vide all the rabbit legs with butter, thyme, garlic & salt, cook at 75oc
for 4 hours, once cooked pick all the meat from the bones. Finely chopped
the livers, kidneys and tarragon and mix all the ingredients together with
picked leg meat, and adjust seasoning, then set mix into a terrine mould
and press over night.
Once set slice 1cm thick and trim it into pieces 3cm by 6cm, pané with
flour, eggs & panko breadcrumbs, deep fry for 3 minutes.

Rabbit Sauce
Roast all the bones into a large pan until golden, strain the bones into
a colander, in the same pan put fresh oil and roast off the shallots until
golden, add thyme, peppercorns & rock salt, deglaze with sherry vinegar.
Then return the bones back into the pan & pour in both the veal stock and
the chicken stock, bring this up to the boil and keep it at a low simmer for
90 minutes, skimming off any fat with a ladle. Pass though muslin cloth.

Pommery mustard mush
Boil the potatoes in skins in lightly salted water for 20 minutes until soft,
peel and pass though a ricer or simply mash, beat in the butter whilst hot,
add the milk, mustard adjust seasoning with salt.

Parlsey oil
Place the parsley into a metal bowl then heat the oil to 140oc and pour over
the parsley, place this bowl directly on ice water and stir until cold. Once
cold blitz in food processor until smooth.

Garnish
Thinly slice the garlic on a mandolin, blanch in boiling water for 5 seconds
then chill in iced water, repeat this twice then dry slices on a paper towel.
Once dry deep fry at 140oc until golden, season with salt once fried.
Cook the broccoli in boiling salted water until tender.
Fry the St George & morel mushrooms in butter for 2 minutes.

ALAIN DUCASSE AT THE DORCHESTER

BIOGRAPHY

Born in Nice, in the South of France, Jean-Philippe Blondet has been working alongside Alain Ducasse for several years. His first role with Alain Ducasse was interestingly at Spoon at Sanderson in London from 2004 to 2006, where he progressed to become a Chef de Partie. Following this experience, he joined the 3-Michelin star Le Louis XV Alain Ducasse at the Hotel de Paris in Monaco, Alain Ducasse's iconic restaurant by the Riviera.

Before returning to London and joining Alain Ducasse at The Dorchester, Jean-Philippe held the position of Sous-Chef at Spoon in Hong Kong, a 2-Michelin star Alain Ducasse restaurant, further adding to his international experience and satisfying his curiosity and interest in cuisines of the world.

In September 2013, he joined the team at Alain Ducasse at The Dorchester as Sous-Chef with Jocelyn Herland to quickly progress to Head Chef within 2 years. Jean-Philippe Blondet became Executive Chef at Alain Ducasse at The Dorchester in January 2016.

Jean-Philippe interprets Alain Ducasse's cuisine in London in a contemporary and refined way. In keeping with Alain Ducasse's philosophy, the ingredients are the key elements. Jean-Philippe only uses the freshest and most seasonal produce, strictly sourced for their quality and provenance.

Cookpot of Leek
agria potatoes and truffle

INGREDIENTS

Leek condiment
Olive oil

Butter

Leeks (white part)

Truffle jus

Black truffle (finely chopped)

Parmentier Sauce
360gr Agria potatoes (diced)

240gr Leeks (white part, sliced)

300gr Unsalted butter

700gr Water

60gr White wine

40gr Olive oil

7gr Salt

1gr White pepper (ground)

Shallot/Madeira Confit
10 Peeled shallots

1 Bottle of Madeira (750ml)

Preparation of the Cookpot
6gr Leek condiment

135gr Agria potatoes

7gr Black truffles

25gr Unsalted butter

1gr Olive oil

15gr Truffle jus

3gr Shallot/Madeira confit

1gr Pepper

2gr Salt

METHOD

Leek condiment
Wash and cut the leeks in half lengthwise, then cut into small segments. Sweat the cut leeks in a pan with some olive oil and butter. Deglaze the pan with a bit of truffle jus and add the finely chopped truffle.

Season with salt and pepper to taste.

When the leeks are tender and thoroughly cooked, cool down in a blast chiller.

Parmentier Sauce
Sweat the sliced leeks gently in olive oil.

Add the butter and finish cooking the leeks.

Deglaze with white wine, and then add the diced potatoes, water and seasoning.

Simmer the potatoes until they are completely cooked (30/40 minutes).

Blitz the potatoes, leeks and cooking liquid in the thermomixer for 8 minutes, and then strain through a fine sieve.

Shallot/Madeira Confit
Chop the shallots into fine dice (brunoise) and leave them to simmer in a pan with the Madeira until the liquid is reduced and the shallots are thoroughly cooked.

Preparation of the Cookpot
Wash and peel the potatoes.

Slice the potatoes with the Japanese turning slicer, until you have a long ribbon.

Cut the potato ribbons to the same height of the cookpot, but leave them long.

In a big bowl season the ribbons with truffle jus, chopped black truffle, olive oil, shallot/Madeira confit, and salt and pepper.

On the bottom of the cookpot, spoon in the leek condiment, and arrange the potato ribbons on top to form roses.

Scatter small pieces of butter on top of the potato roses.

With the lid on, bake the Cookpot at 150°C in the oven for 30 minutes.

After 30 minutes, remove the lid and continue to bake at 180°C for a further 15 minutes to colour and crisp the potatoes.

Remove the Cookpot from the oven and cool down in the blast chiller.

When the Cookpot is cold, close the lid and stick the puff pastry around the cookpot with egg yolk. Tightly wrap the puff pastry around the vessel to seal it.

Once sealed, bake in the oven at 180°C for 5 minutes until the pastry is puffed and golden in colour.

To open the Cookpot, cut through the pastry between the lid and base using a sharp knife keeping the pastry on the lid and base intact.

To finish, shave some black truffle over the top and serve.

ATUL KOCHHAR

BIOGRAPHY

Atul Kochhar's unique talent as a twice Michelin starred chef has changed the way people perceive and experience Indian cuisine. Taking inspiration from his native India, while continuously researching regional dishes, Atul has managed to combine his heritage with his love of British ingredients to create a unique and innovative modern Indian cuisine.

As the very first Indian chef to receive a Michelin star, accomplished during his tenure as Head Chef at Tamarind in 2001, he then went on to open the highly acclaimed Benares Restaurant & Bar for which he was awarded second Michelin star in 2007.

Extract taken from Atul's Curries of the World by Atul Kochhar (Absolute Press, £20)

Photography © Mike Cooper

Tulsi Ka Tikka Aur Timater
basil chicken tikka with tomatoes

INGREDIENTS

4 x 180g Boneless, skinless chicken supremes, each cut into 3 pieces

15g butter

1 tablespoon Sunflower oil

Sea salt

Basil cress sprigs, to garnish

Edible purple flowers, to garnish

Mint and coriander chutney, to serve

Red and yellow baby tomatoes, halved, to serve

For the tomato paste

1 tablespoon Sunflower oil

2 Green cardamom pods, bruised

½ teaspoon Cumin seeds

1 teaspoon peeled and finely chopped fresh Ginger

2 Garlic cloves, chopped

½ Onion, chopped

3 large Tomatoes, chopped

1 teaspoon Ground coriander

½ teaspoon Red chilli powder

½ teaspoon Garam masala

2 tablespoons Dark brown sugar

2 tablespoons White wine vinegar

1–2 tablespoons Water (optional)

For the basil marinade

50g Basil leaves, plus extra to garnish

30g Coriander leaves

30g Baby spinach leaves

2 small Green chillies, chopped

4 tablespoons Greek-style yogurt

2 tablespoons Lemon juice

2 tablespoons Olive oil

2 tablespoons Single cream

15g fresh Ginger, peeled and finely chopped

1½ teaspoons Garam masala

1 teaspoon Chaat masala

½ teaspoon Red chilli powder

1 tablespoon grated Cheddar cheese

1 tablespoon Gram flour roux

For the curried mayonnaise

5 tablespoons Mayonnaise

2 teaspoons Benares curry powder

1 teaspoon Lime juice

finely grated zest of 1 Lime

METHOD

First make the tomato paste, which will keep for up to 2 weeks in a covered container in the fridge. Heat the oil in a large saucepan, add the cardamom pods and cumin seeds and sauté over a medium heat until the spices crackle. Add the ginger, garlic and onion and sauté for a further 3–5 minutes until the onion is translucent. Add the tomatoes and ground spices and stir for 4–5 minutes until the tomatoes start to break down. Sir in the sugar, vinegar and salt to taste, and simmer for 10–12 minutes until the tomatoes are cooked and the flavours blended. Remove the pan from the heat and leave the tomato mixture to cool completely, then purée in a blender or food processor. Cover and chill until required, then loosen with the water, if necessary. Remove it from the fridge in enough time for it to reach room temperature before serving.

Put all the marinade ingredients in a clean blender or food processor and blend to a fine paste. Rub the paste all over the chicken pieces, then set aside to marinate in the fridge for 2 hours.

Meanwhile, mix all the ingredients for the curried mayonnaise together, cover and chill until required.

After the chicken has marinated, preheat the oven to 200°C/Fan 180°C/Gas 6. Place the chicken pieces with their marinade, butter and oil in a roasting tray lined with a non-stick oven mat, and roast for 10 minutes, basting twice with the butter and oil mixture, or until the pieces are cooked through and the juices run clear when they are pierced with the tip of a knife. Leave to rest for 5 minutes, covered with kitchen foil.

Arrange the chicken pieces, tomato paste, curried mayonnaise, chutney and halved baby tomatoes on the plates in an abstract presentation. Garnish and serve immediately.

ADAM SIMMONDS

BIOGRAPHY

Over a 28 year span, Adam has built himself a remarkable reputation leading some of Britain's finest kitchens. In 2001, he accepted his first head chef position in 2001 at The Greenway in Cheltenham, spending a year honing his skills before moving to Ynyshir Hall in Wales; the previous home of her majesty, Queen Victoria. Here his determination, hard work and isolation in the Welsh hills resulted in his first Michelin star in 2006.

After 6 years in Wales, Adam joined Danesfield House Hotel near Marlow in Buckinghamshire. Numerous awards and accolades were bestowed on 'Adam Simmonds at Danesfield House' during his seven years as Executive Chef, including a coveted Michelin star, four rosettes in the AA Restaurant Guide, a Catey Award for 'Hotel Chef of the Year' and a consistent 8/10 in the Good Food Guide, placing Adam's restaurant as 12 th in the country.

Adam has made several appearances on television including the BBC2 show, 'The Great British Menu' in 2013 and 2014 representing the South East. In 2014, Adam won the starter course and went on to cook for the D-Day veterans at the banquet in St Paul's Cathedral commemorating 70 years since the war.

Alongside cooking, Adam is passionate about giving his time to charity. An ambassador for Clink, Adam also cooks at various dinners throughout the year to raise money for Macmillan, Cancer Research UK, and the Luton ad Dunstable Neonatal unit. He also ran the Royal Parks Half Marathon for the Roy Castle Lung Cancer Foundation in memory of his father.

At present, Adam is working as a Consultant Chef; opening, improving and implementing changes to a number of quality establishments around the UK, providing him with a wealth of knowledge in preparation for his very own restaurant, due to open in Central London soon. To follow his progress, visit www.adamsimmonds.com where further details will be released in due course.

Slow Cooked Loin Of Lamb Belly, Onion, Curd And Thyme

INGREDIENTS

2 loins of Lamb

200g Sweetbreads

4 griotte Onions

6 springs of Sea purslane

Thyme Oil

18g Thyme (bruised)

90g Grapeseed oil

Goats Milk Curd

500ml Goats Milk

1g Salt

10g Water

5no Drops of Rennet

Pickling Liqueur For Shallots

26g Water

9g Vinegar

1g Salt

Pinch of Sugar

Shallot Rings

15g finely sliced Shallots

10g Pickling liquor

METHOD

Lamb

Take 2 loins of Lamb, remove the sinew and place into a Vac Pac bag. Seal and cook in a water bath that is set to 62°c. Cook until the core temperature is 55°c, then remove and allow to rest. Once rested, season and quickly seal in foaming butter until a little colour is achieved. Divide equally between four plates.

Sweetbreads

Take 200g of Lamb sweetbreads and place under running water. Remove the membrane and dry well. Place a pan on the stove and add a little grapeseed oil. Add the sweetbreads and cook quickly, allowing them to colour. Once the colour is achieved, add a knob of butter and season. Cook for a few minutes further and drain.

Onions

Take four griotte onions and remove the tops, leaving the bottom of the onion to blanch in boiling salted water. When they are ¾ cooked, remove and place into iced water. Once cold, drain, cut in half, season and colour in a pan with a little oil.

Thyme oil

Rub the thyme to release its flavour and place in a pan.

In another pan, bring the grapeseed oil up to 70°C and pour over the thyme.

Clingfilm and infuse in a warm place for 6 – 8 hours.

Pass.

Sea Purslane

Blanch in salted boiling water.

Goats milk curd

Mix the water with the rennet and allow to stand.

Place the salt and milk in a Vac Pac bag and drop into the water bath at 40°C for 20 minutes.

Pour into a large pan and stir to make a whirlpool.

Drop the rennet in slowly so it is dispersed evenly, taste and add more salt if required.

Pour evenly into trays about 1cm deep.

Place the trays where the temperature is about 30°C for around 2 hours or until set.

After 2 hours the curd should be shiny and soft to the touch.

Pickling liqueur for shallots

Place all the ingredients in a pan and bring to the boil. Allow to cool before use.

Shallot Rings

Blanch very quickly in boiling, salted water.

Refresh in iced water and drain well.

Place into a Vac Pac bag with the liquor.

Seal and keep for two days before using.

To plate

Take a spoon of the puree and place on the plate. Position the lamb next to the puree and the sweetbread next to the Lamb. Follow this with one piece of Lamb belly and two halves of the griotte onions, followed by a spoon of curd. Finish the dish with the pickled shallot rings, cooked sea purslane and thyme oil.

BABYLON AT THE ROOF GARDENS

BIOGRAPHY

Ian Howard has been Head Chef of Babylon for six years; he is responsible for creating a unique menu that is best described as contemporary British and regularly changes to ensure only the freshest seasonal ingredients are used.

Ian's early career began in a number of London restaurants including the Savoy working for Anton Edelmann, W1 Brassiere working for Gary Rhodes and the Cumberland. Ian then moved slightly out of the city to take up the position of Head Chef of the Woodlands Park Hotel in Cobham, Surrey; it was here that Ian really developed his talent for creating dishes using fresh and in-season produce.

Ian's passion for producing sustainable dishes has contributed towards Babylon achieving a three-star rating with the Sustainable Restaurant Association (SRA) over three consecutive years, and winning 'Most Sustainable Business' at the SRA Awards.

"It is very important to us in Babylon to use as many local and sustainable ingredients as possible. Our menu regularly changes to reflect the British seasons, so we are able to make the most of quality local ingredients; even those grown by our very own Head Gardener here at The Roof Gardens! I think it is important for the team to meet our suppliers and understand where our produce has come from, so I'll take them across the country to understand the journey from source to plate. We also have a map in our kitchen with our food pinned to it so all the team know exactly where it has come from and can tell our guests."

Ovation Welsh Saltmarsh Lamb Loin
white polenta, English peas and broad beans, asparagus, courgette flower, madeira jus and edible flowers

INGREDIENTS

Lamb Loin For 4 Portions
1 short Saddle of lamb

Olive oil

4 Stalks of thyme

Vacuum pak bag

White Polenta
100g White polenta

200ml Water

200ml Whole organic milk

1 tablespoon Rosemary (picked and finely chopped)

2 Cloves garlic (crushed)

50g Butter

Parmesan to season

Peas, Asparagus & Broad Beans
300g fresh English peas (in the pod)

400g fresh English broad beans (in the pod)

1 bunch of medium English asparagus

Baby Courgette Flower
4 Flowers with the courgette attached

Madeira Lamb Jus
Lamb bones and trimmings from the saddle with excess fat removed

1 litre Veal jus

1 litre Chicken stock or lamb stock

3 roughly Chopped shallots

2 Cloves of garlic peeled and chopped

3 sticks of Thyme

350ml Madeira wine

2 sticks of Rosemary

METHOD

Lamb Loin
Remove the loins from the saddle. Leave the fat on top of the loin but remove the bark. This will give you two loins. Set aside the lamb bones and trimmings for the Madeira lamb jus

Place the loins into the vac pak bag with 2 tablespoons of olive oil and 4 stalks of thyme. Seal the bag and place in the fridge until you are ready to cook

To cook place the sealed bag in a water bath at 58°C for 22 minutes

Remove the lamb from the bag and colour all over in a hot pan with butter

Leave to drain and then carve each loin in half giving 4 portions

Madeira Lamb Jus
Chop the lamb bones and lamb trimmings down to an even small size

Place the bones and trimmings into a solid base saucepan and sauté until brown in colour

Add the shallots, rosemary, garlic and thyme and continue to sauté until the shallots are lightly browned

Deglaze the pan with the Madeira wine and scrape the bottom of the pan to release the caramelisation

Add the veal jus and chicken stock and gently bring to the boil, skimming the impurities as it simmers

Cook out for 1.5 hours and then pass through muslin cloth

Return the lamb jus to a pan and reduce to a coating consistency adding salt and pepper to season

White Polenta
Bring the water and milk to the boil and rain in the polenta in a steady stream, continue to stir on a low heat until the polenta has cooked out

Add the butter to a hot pan and bring to a golden brown colour then add the crushed garlic and rosemary. Remove from the heat and add to the polenta

Continue to cook for a further 2-3 minutes very gently and then season and adjust consistency as required

Peas, Asparagus & Broad Beans
Pod the peas and the broad beans and place in a pan of boiling salted water for only a few seconds. Drain and roll in melted butter salt and pepper

Remove the scales from the asparagus stick and remove the woody tail end. As with the peas and broad beans place the asparagus in a pan of boiling salted water for only a few seconds. Season and roll in melted butter

Baby Courgette Flower
Remove the stamens from the flower

Snap the flower away from the courgette and tear the flower along the natural lines

Cut the baby courgette in half and place in a pan of boiling salted water for only a few seconds, season and roll in melted butter

The Build
Spread the polenta on the bottom of the plate

Place the peas and broad beans

Cut the lamb loins in half and trim the end, season with Maldon sea salt

Add the courgette and its flowers along with pea shoots and edible flowers

Dress the plate with extra virgin rapeseed oil and a little Madeira jus

39

HIT TRAINING

BIOGRAPHY

Karlis Pumpurins

I have been working for BaxterStorey for 1 ½ years. It took some time to get used to, as this was my first contract catering job. Before this I was working in various restaurants for 5 years. I started from the bottom washing pots but I knew food was my passion so I worked hard and now I cover the head chef in his absence. I enrolled in the HIT and Chef Academy training as soon as I found out about it. It has been a great journey of knowledge and it has improved my confidence in the kitchen dramatically. I would like thank my mentor Executive Chef for TFL, John White and all the guys from HIT and The BaxterStorey Chef Academy. Without their support I would not be able to do what I do.

Caribbean Inspired Jerk Pork Belly
with coconut-infused sweet potato dauphinoise

INGREDIENTS

2.5kg Thick cut pork belly

Marinade
3 Large scotch bonnet peppers
1/2 Bunch thyme
6 Cloves garlic
1 Bunch spring onions
1tsp Ground cumin
500g Tinned mandarin segments
1L Pineapple juice
60ml Dark soy sauce
Salt and pepper to taste
(Blend everything in food processor until smooth, pass through a chinois, then reduce by half)

Dauphinoise
1,5kg Sweet potatoes
1.5kg White potatoes
6 Cloves of garlic, finely chopped and lightly roasted
500ml Coconut milk
500ml Double cream
Salt and pepper to taste
(Cream, coconut milk, salt, pepper and garlic mixed together)

Sweet potato crisps
1 Large sweet potato (cut 2cm wide and make long slices using a peeler)

Salad
300g Red kidney beans
1 Large carrot, julienned
1 Head of frisee, picked
100g Spring onion julienne, only green part
Thyme leaves for garnish
Lemon juice and olive oil to dress
(Put the carrots and spring onion in cold water in the fridge. This will give them a nice shape and a firm texture.)
Micro coriander and violets for garnish.

METHOD

Remove the skin, score to make a fine diamond pattern then marinade the pork belly for 24hours in a fridge. Score the skin the same way and put in freezer.

Make the crackling by slicing long triangle shapes of the skin while it is still frozen. Then put it in a gastro tray on parchment paper, oil it and salt it. Cover with another piece of parchment and press another tray on top of it. Roast in the oven at 180C for 45minutes.

Drain the marinade through a chinois in a saucepan and put the pork on a cooling rack on top of a gastro tray and pour some water in the tray. (This will prevent smoking whilst the pork is cooking) Cook the pork in the oven at 180C for 45 minutes. Then cover it with parchment and tinfoil, turn down the heat to 160C and cook for another 1hour and 10minutes.

In a half size gastro tray layer the sweet potatoes and white potatoes evenly adding the cream mixture in between layers. First sweet, then white until seven layers are made. Top with 250g of melted clarified butter and a cartouche. Cook in oven at 180C for 50 minutes. Then rest.

Take the pork out and let it rest for 20minutes. Then square it off and cut into 12 even pieces.

Reduce the marinade again by 1/3 to make the sauce. Adjust seasoning if needed.

Turn out the dauphinoise on a chopping board. With a 10cm ring cutter cut out 6 discs. Use a blowtorch to give the potatoes a dark charred edge.

Mix the salad and dress it with the lemon juice and olive oil.

Bake the sweet potato strips in an oven at 180C for 9minutes. Season with salt.

Serve as presented in the pictures below:

Put the potatoes on one side of the plate and stack two pieces of pork next to it.

Pour a couple of table spoons of the sauce over the pork.

Put the salad on the other side of the plate and stick a few crisps and crackling between the pork and the potatoes.

Garnish with violet flowers, micro coriander and thyme leaves.

BRASSERIE JOEL

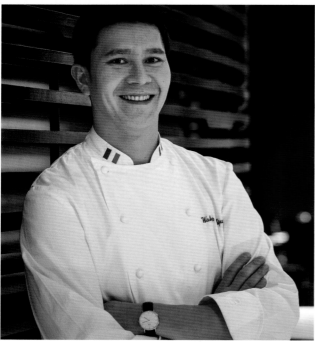

BIOGRAPHY

Brasserie Joel is located at Park Plaza Westminster Bridge London, near the London Eye, Houses of Parliament, National Theatre, OXO Tower and Royal Festival Hall.

Chef Walter Ishizuka has sourced only the highest quality, freshest ingredients, and his team create classic brasserie dishes to delight the palate. Brasserie Joel also holds 2 AA rosettes for culinary excellence.

Chef Walter's father travelled from Japan to Lyon in the 1960's, to learn the art of French cooking – he remains to this day one of Chef Walter's biggest inspirations. He had the opportunity to work at some of France's most famous restaurants and was a role model for the young Chef Walter with his approach to cooking. Modesty and rigour have been qualities of his that Walter has brought into his own style of cooking.

Chef Walter first trained in the French city of Lyon, renowned for its gastronomic heritage. He worked for three years at Lyon's infamous three Michelin starred Paul Bocuse Restaurant, then three and a half years at Paris Ritz's two Michelin starred restaurant: L'Espadon. He brings his own blend of creativity and passion for food to London. Walter's menus blend classic French fare with a delicate approach to flavour and texture derived from his Japanese heritage – his dishes feature bold, simple flavours cooked using only the very finest ingredients.

Chef Walter has been at the helm of Brasserie Joel since 2011, imbibing each dish and new menu with his enthusiasm for fresh, seasonal ingredients and the wealth of quality British produce that he often goes to select himself at London's many famous foodie markets such as Billingsgate, or Borough Market. Whilst he remains true to the culinary legacy of great French cuisine, he brings a modern and innovative approach to Brasserie Joel.

Fillet of French Barbary Duck
beetroot purée and raspberry sauce

INGREDIENTS

4 Barbary duck fillets

200g Cooked beetroot

100g Mashed potato

50g Unsalted butter

Small handful of pine nuts

12 Baby beetroots

125g Fresh raspberries

50g Shallots

50ml Pouring cream

Teaspoon of raspberry vinegar

50ml Duck stock (or chicken stock)

Peashoots to garnish

Salt, pepper

METHOD

To make the sauce peel and slice the shallot coarsely. Place in a small pot with a knob of the butter, cook until starting to caramelise then deglaze with the raspberry vinegar. Reduce the sauce by a third. Once reduced, add the duck stock and cook slowly until you obtain a glossy texture.

Pass the sauce through a fine sieve or muslin bag and reserve to one side.

Pre-heat your oven at 180 degrees.

For the puree, place the cooked beetroot in a blender. Blend until you obtain a smooth texture. Mix in the mash potato until even in colour and finish with some butter and cream until you are happy with the consistency.

Heat a frying pan until smoking hot. Pan-fry the seasoned duck fillets skin-side down until browned and crispy. Turn and cook for a further minute on the other side. Place the fillets onto a roasting tray and cook in the oven at 180 degrees for 10 minutes (pink).

Peel and blanche the baby beetroots for one minute in simmering water. Remove and put to one side.

To serve, place a couple of generous spoonfuls of mash into the centre of the plate. Top with the sliced fillets. Dot the baby beetroots around. Drizzle over the duck sauce and top with peashoots and toasted pine nuts.

TOM AIKENS

BIOGRAPHY

Tom Aikens is one of the UK's most acclaimed and inspirational British chefs. His remarkable career took him to David Cavalier's in Battersea, Pierre Koffman's La Tante Claire, Pied-à-Terre and Joel Robuchon in Paris to name a few. At 26, Tom became the youngest British chef ever to be awarded two Michelin stars.

The celebrated chef is dedicated to serving only the highest quality, ethically sourced ingredients and continually supports The Environmental Justice Foundation to raise awareness of illegal 'pirate' fishing and diminishing fish stocks.

Tom has written three books; Cooking (2006), Fish (2008), and Easy (2011), and has made several appearances on television, reaching the final banquet of 2013's Great British Menu on BBC2 in aid of Comic Relief.

Tom works closely with various charities including: the Great Ormond Street Hospital Children's Campaign, Royal Marsden Cancer Campaign and School Food Matters, where he teaches young children basic cooking skills.

Seven Hour-Braised Shoulder Of Lamb
with onions, thyme & balsamic

This hearty lamb shoulder recipe, with its creamy mashed potato pairing, makes a wonderful and rustic lamb dinner.
Slowly braising the lamb in a rich sauce ensures that the meat's full, immense flavour is drawn out.
You can either slice or shred the meat from the bone to serve.

INGREDIENTS

Braised Shoulder of Lamb
1 Shoulder of lamb, around 2.5kg in weight

150ml Olive oil

20g Fresh thyme

2 Garlic bulbs, peeled cloves

Sea salt and black pepper

8 Medium onions, peeled

350ml Balsamic vinegar

Mashed Potato
2l Water

12g Salt

200g Butter

150ml Milk

600g Peeled potato, cut in 1/4's

12 Turns of milled black pepper

METHOD

Place a large casserole pot onto a medium gas, adding the oil.

Season the lamb and place the shoulder into the pot once the oil is hot (be careful adding the lamb as it could spit). Colour for 3-4 minutes each side until nicely caramelised and then remove the lamb and put to one side.

Add the onions and colour for 4-5 minutes still on a medium heat, stirring now and again. Add the garlic and thyme then place the lamb back on top.

Place into the oven at 110°c and cover with a lid cooking for 2-2.5 hours, then take out the onions once they are soft. Carry on cooking the lamb for another 2.5-3 hours.

Add the vinegar and carry on cooking without the lid so the vinegar reduces as the lamb cooks, basting the lamb every 30 minutes, being careful not to reduce it too much.

Cook for a total of 6-7 hours until the lamb is nice and tender then add the onions and garlic back at the end and reduce the vinegar to a nice thick consistency.

Place the cut potato into the cold water with 10g salt in a pan, place on to the heat and bring to a simmer turn the heat down and simmer for 30 minutes then tip the potatoes into a colander to drain really well.

Place the potato back in the pan and dry out on a low heat for 1 minute then add the butter, salt, pepper and the warm milk while you mash the potato.

THE
PAINTED
HERON

BIOGRAPHY

Legendary Yogesh Datta is one of the UK's top Indian chefs. Having trained in classical Indian cooking, Yogesh worked his cooking magic for the Taj Group and Sheraton Hotels in India.

After moving to London, Yogesh began to develop his innovative, award winning techniques first of all at Tabla in Canary Wharf.

Then he launched fine dining Indian cuisine at The Painted Heron in Chelsea. Since then Yogesh has gone on to win numerous awards including the Remy Martin Award, Best Restaurant and Best Chef by the Curry Club Guide.

In 2012 The Painted Heron celebrated 10 years as London's finest Indian restaurant.

Rabbit Biryani
with onion, tomato, cucumber relish

INGREDIENTS

Rabbit on the bone - 1kg

Basmati rice – 500gms

Butter / ghee / oil – 200 gms

Low fat yoghurt – 500ml

Kashmiri chilli powder – 3 heaped tea spoons

Turmeric – 2 heaped tea spoons

Ginger/ garlic paste – 3 table spoons

Onions – 2 – chopped

Tomatoes -2 – chopped

Juice of 1 lemon

Asafoetida – commercial variety, mixed with flour (optional) – 2 teaspoons

Special garam masala powdered – black cardamom seeds, black cumin seeds (kala jeera), coriander seeds, cumin seeds, mace flowers(javitri) and grated nutmeg. – 50 gms

Bouquette garni- cinnamon sticks, cloves, green cardamom, bay leaves

Saffron – 1pinch

Salt – to taste

Kewda water (optional) – 10ml

Milk – half a cup

Fresh mint – 1 bunch

Fresh coriander – ½ a bunch.

Prunes pitted – 50gms

Fried cashewnuts – 100gms (optional)

Paneer grated (optional) – 100gms

Fried brown onions (optional) – 50gms

Onion / Tomato / Cucumber Relish

Sliced red onions, tomato juliennes and cucumber juliennes

Greek yoghurt, cream, salt, pepper, chopped garlic and chopped coriander, salt to taste

METHOD

Wash and soak rice in cold water and set aside. Wash the rabbit in running water as well. Chop onions and tomatoes.

Wash mint and coriander bunches, chop the leaves and stems and keep separately.

Pat dry the meat and marinate in yoghurt, one table spoon of ginger/garlic paste, juice of one lemon, red chilli powder and salt and set aside for half an hour.

Heat ghee/ butter/ oil in a deep heavy bottom pan add asafoetida, turmeric, followed immediately by the chopped onions. When the onions begin to colour, add rest of the ginger/ garlic paste. Cook over low flame until the mixture begins to stick to the bottom of the pan. Add the chopped stems of coriander and mint followed by chopped tomatoes.

Add the rabbit meat along with all the marinate into the pan and cook.

In another pan add lots of water along with salt and bouquette garni- cinnamon sticks, cloves, green cardamom, bay leaves. Cook the rice until 3/4th cooked, throw away excess water and allow rice to cool to room temperature.

Soak saffron in warm milk in a small bowl

In a deep heavy bottom pan, to layer the biryani, start with one fourth of the rice. Next add half of the cooked rabbit, half of coriander and mint, half of the special garam masala and half of the prunes and cashewnuts. Follow this with another layer of half of the remaining rice, followed by rest of the rabbit, garam masala, purnes, cashewnuts and half of the remaining mint and coriander. Top this up with all the remaining rice, mint, coriander, drizzle all the saffron milk around the pot along with the kewda water.

Finish with fried onions and grated paneer. Cover the pot with a tight lid and cook again over low flame for 10 minutes. Serve hot with onion, tomato and cucumber relish

CORRIGANS OF MAYFAIR

BIOGRAPHY

Richard is the Michelin star chef/owner of Corrigan Restaurants, which operates Bentley's Oyster Bar & Grill, Corrigan's Mayfair in London and Bentley's Sea Grill in Harrods, London. In addition to wowing the London food scene, Richard has cooked for the Queen twice, British Airways Concorde and is the Chef's Alliance Spokesperson of the Slow Food Movement. Lauded as one of the greatest chefs of his generation (having won 3 AA restaurant of the year awards), he has received praise from some of the fiercest food and restaurants critics in the land. Richard's culinary career, in brief, spans several years in the Netherlands, head chef of Mulligan's in Mayfair in London and his first Michelin star, awarded to him when he was head chef of Fulham Road in Fulham in 1994, also in London. Richard went on to open Lindsay House in Soho, London, and won a Michelin star there in 1997. He then bought and refurbished Bentley's in 2005, an oyster and seafood restaurant just off Piccadilly. He went on to open Corrigan's Mayfair in 2008, Bentley's Sea Grill at Harrod's was his next venture in 2012 and most recently, in 2013 the Virginia Park Lodge. On screen, Richard is known for being crowned winner of the Great British Menu, no less than three times. He also won the Great British Waste Menu, and was one of the 3 chefs who have appeared on Great British Budget Menu. Richard is the author of three books: The Richard Corrigan Cookbook: From the Waters and the Wild; The Clatter of Forks and Spoons; and Cookery School (which accompanied the Channel 4 television programme of the same name). He is currently writing his next book, due for publication in Spring 2016.

Honey & Stout Tart

INGREDIENTS

250g Plain flour
Pinch of salt

125g Cutter, cut into small cubes, and some more for greasing

50g Caster sugar

3 Eggs (one of them beaten, for eggwash)

Cream to serve

Filling

4 Bramley apples

330ml bottle of Stout, such as Guinness

200g Rolled oats

250g Golden syrup

250g Honey

250g Stale breadcrumbs

6 Eggs, beaten

4tsp Lemon juice

Zest of 1 lemon and 1 orange

METHOD

Start by making the pastry. In a bowl, combine the flour and the salt, then rub in the butter with your fingers; if you do it properly the mixture will look like fine breadcrumbs. Add the sugar and mix in well. Then, add the beaten eggs a little at a time and work it together until you have a dough. Alternatively, you can use a food processor in which case put the flour, salt, butter and sugar into the blender and pulse until you get the fine breadcrumbs texture.

Add the egg mixture and pulse until they are combined. Then, turn it out onto a work surface or into a bowl and mould into a ball. It is important not to work the dough anymore than it takes to form a ball.

Cover the pastry with cling film and chill in the fridge for about 20 minutes to make it easier to roll. And chill in the fridge for about 20 minutes, which will make it easier to roll.

Pre-heat the oven to 150C/gas mark 2 and prepare a 25cm loose-bottomed flan tin by greasing it with a little butter.

Roll out the pastry on a floured surface until it forms a circle about 5cm bigger than your tart tin. Roll the pastry loosely around your rolling pin, then drape it carefully over the tin and press it gently in. Trim off the excess pastry with a knife.

Now you need to bake the pastry case 'blind' by lining it with greaseproof paper, over which you scatter some dried beans (or ceramic 'beans') which will stop the pastry from rising too much. Bake for about 45 minutes until the pastry is pale golden, then remove and turn the oven up to 180C/gas mark 4.

Don't delay. Remove the greaseproof paper right away and while the pastry case is still hot, brush it generously with eggwash to seal it. Even if the pastry seems to crack a little as it cools, the eggwash should keep it pretty well sealed.

Pour the stout into a saucepan with the peeled and grated apples and bring to the boil, then reduce the heat and let the volume of the liquid reduce by about half. The apple will go brown, but that's the way it's meant to be. Take off the heat and allow it to cool.

When the stout and apple mixture is cool, add the other filling ingredients and mix thoroughly. Then pour into the pastry case and bake in the oven for 20-25 minutes until set.

Preheat the oven to 150 degrees Celsius/ gas 2. Have ready a 25 cm, loose-bottomed flat in, greased with a little butter. On a floured surface, roll out the pastry into a circle about 5 cm bigger than your tart tin. Roll the pastry loosely round your rolling pin, then drape it over the in and gently press it in. Trim carefully around the edge with a knife. To bake 'blind', line the pastry with greaseproof paper and scatter over a layer of dried beans and brush (or ceramic baking beans)- this will stop the pastry from rising up. Bake in the oven for about 45 minutes until pale and golden, then remove and turn up the oven to 180 degrees/ gas 4.

Immediately after taking the tart tin out of the oven, remove the greaseproof paper and beans and brush the whole of the inside of the pastry case with egg wash. This will seal it and prevent it from cracking as it cools- It may still crack a little, but don't worry. Peel and grate the apples. Pour the stout into a saucepan, add the apple, bring to the boil, then turn down the heat and let the liquid reduce by about half. The apple will go brown but its natural. Take off the heat and allow to cool until just warm.

Serve with cream.

STOKE PARK

BIOGRAPHY

Originally from Swanage in Dorset, Chris Wheeler is Executive Chef at Stoke Park Hotel and Country Club in Buckinghamshire.

Chris joined Stoke Park in 2003 and has been building up the culinary reputation for 12 years now with his fine-dining restaurant Humphry's achieving 3 AA Rosettes.

From recreating the Olympic Torch as an exquisite cake in celebration of London 2012 to cooking at Stoke Park's annual Boodles Tennis event, Chris' flexibility as a Chef is legendary. Chris and his team plate up just short of 9000 delicious three-course lunches and afternoon teas over the five-day Boodles event each year.

Chris previously worked with celebrated Chef, Jean Christophe-Novelli, who spotted his talent early on and hired him at a young age. Chris worked his way through the ranks with Novelli for 10 years to become Group Head Chef and right-hand man to Jean Christophe.

If Chris isn't in the kitchens, he can be found out and about doing fantastic things for the local community, running the marathon for charity, hosting a pop-up charity restaurant or getting stuck in at cake sales.

Chris is also a familiar face and voice to our screens and radios; he appeared on Great British Menu 2016, Hell's Kitchen 2, BBC1's Saturday Kitchen and Channel 4's Sunday Brunch, Capital FM, BBC Berkshire and Chef Radio with more television and radio appearances planned.

Gingerbread Soufflé
poached english rhubarb accompanied by a rhubarb and ginger sorbet

INGREDIENTS

Gingerbread
140g Golden Syrup
140g Black Treacle
115g Light Brown Sugar
115g Butter
225g Self Raising Flour
1 tsp Mixed Spice
1 tsp Ground Ginger
2 Eggs
2 tbsp Milk

Poached Rhubarb
2 sticks of English Rhubarb
1 Vanilla Pod (Seeds only)
½ a Lemon (Juice Only)
50g Sugar
Caramel Sauce
250g Caster Sugar
250ml Double cream
50g Butter

Sorbet
500g English Rhubarb
(Peeled)
190g Sugar
1 Vanilla Pod (Seeds only)
1 lemon (juice only)
50ml Sweet White Wine
10ml Grenadine
250ml Water
40g Fresh Ginger (Peeled)

Soufflé Base
450ml of Milk
5 Egg Yolks
80g Caster Sugar
45g Strong Flour
100g of Crumbled
Gingerbread

Soufflé
200g of the above base
160g Egg Whites
60g Caster Sugar

METHOD

Gingerbread
Melt the Syrups, Brown Sugar and Butter together
Stir in all dry ingredients, add Eggs and Milk and mix well
Pour into a loaf tin, bake at 160°C for 30-40minutes

Poached English Rhubarb
Peel Rhubarb, cut into batons
Place in an ovenproof dish with the Vanilla, Sugar and Lemon Juice
Cover with Foil, place in oven and poach for 15minutes

Caramel Sauce
Melt the Sugar in a pan until it forms a Caramel
Add the Cream, then the Butter - stir until all has dissolved

Sorbet
Bring all the ingredients to boil
Simmer for 10 minutes
Blend
Churn in an Ice Cream Machine

Soufflé Base
Make a Crème Pâtissière by boiling the Milk
In a separate bowl whisk the Yolks and Sugar together
Add Flour and mix until smooth
Pour the mixture into boiling Milk, whisk until thickened
Add crumbled Gingerbread

Soufflé
Pre-heat the oven to 180°C
In a clean bowl whisk the Egg Whites to form soft peaks
Slowly add the Caster Sugar and whisk for 1 minute. Fold the Egg Whites into the Soufflé Base
Pipe mixture into buttered and sugared ramekins and bake in the oven for 12 minutes
Serve immediately!

To Serve
Place a small amount of Gingerbread crumb on the plate
Finish with one scoop of Rhubarb and Ginger Sorbet
Place the cooked Soufflé next to it and arrange the poached Rhubarb around the plate
Serve with the warm Caramel Sauce on the side

Chefs Tip
Make sure you fold the Soufflé mixture – do not whip it

THE STONEMASONS ARMS

BIOGRAPHY

Fifteen years of cooking have given Gavin what he needs to push boundaries on food that inspires his customers. Perseverance and strength of character are the qualities necessary to endure professional kitchens, Gavin's feels his nan has always inspired this in him. His experience has come with time and with that, a wealth of knowledge from various establishments he has worked in.

For the last three years, Gavin has been working for Fuller, Smith & Turner. Paul Dickinson, head of Fullers food, has played an important role supporting Gavin's development in becoming an exemplar chef for the company. Gavin began his Fuller's journey as Head Chef at the renowned Wykeham Arms in Winchester. More recently, he has taken the reins of the kitchen at The Stonemason's Arms in Hammersmith. His passion and skills he has picked up along the way are playing their part in making Fuller's famous for food.

Lemon Curd
meringue, lemon verbena ice cream and caramelised white chocolate

INGREDIENTS

Lemon curd
Zest & juice 5 lemons
224g Caster sugar
9 whole Eggs
250g Double cream

Meringue
4 Egg whites
225g Sugar
6 tbsp Water

Lemon Verbena Ice-cream
20g Lemon verbena leaves, rinsed & dried
375 ml Semi skimmed milk
375ml heavy Cream
150g Caster sugar
10g liquid Glucose
6 large Egg yolks

Garnish
200g Sugar
100g Water
Peel of 3 Lemons
300g White chocolate

METHOD

Lemon Curd

Place all ingredients in a heatproof bowl on top of simmering water.

Whisk the mixture until it thickens & starts to hold itself creating ribbons.

Set aside to cool in a container.

Meringue

Whisk four egg whites until they form stiff peaks (an electric mixer is best)

In a pan, stir sugar & water together over a medium heat, Once sugar is dissolved bring to a fast boil until you reach 120C/250F.

Pour the syrup onto the egg whites in a thin steady stream as you whisk, continue to whisk until cool, place in a disposable piping bag.

Lemon Verbena Ice Cream

Warm the lemon leaves with milk, cream & glucose.

Once warm remove from heat cover with clingfilm, infuse for 1 hour. Strain, squeeze the cream for maximum flavour.

In a bowl whisk the eggs & caster sugar. Re-warm the verbena-infused cream, slowly pour the infusion over the eggs & sugar whisking constantly.

Transfer the mix to a pan, cook on a low heat stirring continuously until the custard leaves a trail on the spatula when you draw your finger across it.

Chill thoroughly in fridge, then churn in ice cream machine according to manufacturer instructions. Place in airtight container and freeze.

Garnish

Candied lemon: peel three lemons with a peeler, removing any bitter white pith. Slice the peel very thinly, place into a pan covered with cold water. Bring to the boil, then strain. Repeat this process three times.

Make a syrup by heating the sugar & water together, add the lemon peel, bring to a simmer. Remove from stove, allow to cool, refrigerate.

Caramelised white chocolate: melt the chocolate in a pan on a very low heat mixing continuously. The chocolate should start to change colour as the sugars caramelise. Do not overheat or it will become grainy. Once a light caramel colour has been achieved, pour onto a silicone mat and set in fridge.

Assembly
Pipe the meringue onto the plate in little peaks & blow torch.
Pipe the lemon curd along the plate.
Stack up the shards of white chocolate.
Place a scoop of the ice cream on the plate.
Scatter the candied lemon across.

LE CORDON BLEU

BIOGRAPHY

With more than 35 schools in 20 countries, Le Cordon Bleu is the world's leading network of Culinary Arts and Hotel Management institutes. Its role is to teach a whole range of technical and University training programs for working in the restaurant, hotel and tourism industry. The story began 120 years ago thanks to the initiative of a journalist Marthe Distel and it is now the largest network of culinary institutes. Every year it welcomes over 20 000 students of more than 100 different nationalities across its institutes.

It all began when Marthe Distel founded the first weekly culinary magazine entitled La cuisinière Cordon Bleu, while inviting subscribers to take part in cuisine lessons. The magazine reflected French cuisine of that time and openness to International cuisines as it was published in several languages. The first lesson was taught at Le Cordon Bleu Paris on October 15, 1895.

After more than a century of culinary education, Le Cordon Bleu has learned the secret to success in the kitchen is more than just a recipe, but a solid understanding of ingredients, techniques and processes.

Le Cordon Bleu has a comprehensive team of Master Chefs from a variety of backgrounds, some from Michelin starred establishments, all dedicated to share their expertise. Selected for their skills and professionalism, they can often be found developing recipes, as part of judging panels or competing at international level in their own right.

In its current state-of- the-art location, Le Cordon Bleu London provides students with the most innovative opportunities in culinary and hospitality education. From Diplomas to short courses, Le Cordon Bleu London offers a range of programmes for aspiring or experienced professionals and food enthusiasts.

Le Cordon Bleu London prides itself on staying ahead of the curve when it comes to culinary education and trends by developing its academic programmes to include Wine, nutrition and management Diplomas.

Fruit Macaroon Crown
with rosewater infused fruits and lychee cream

INGREDIENTS

Macaroon

70g ground Almonds

110g Icing sugar

60g Egg whites

30g Caster sugar

Pink food colouring

Rosewater infused raspberries

250g Raspberries

50g Sugar

40ml Water

10g Organic natural rosewater

Lychee cream

175g canned Lychee in syrup or lychee purée

150ml Double cream

15ml Kwai Feh lychee liqueur or muscadet wine

Decoration

1 punnet of Raspberries

10 Strawberries

2 Red plums

1 punnet Redcurrant's

1 punnet Blueberries

Optional plating decorations

reserved Lychee syrup

pulled Sugar spirals

Crystallised rose petals

METHOD

Macaroon: Preheat the oven to 140ºC. Sieve ground almonds and icing sugar. Make a stiff peak meringue with the egg whites and the caster sugar; add in the pink food colour. Add the dry mix over the meringue in 2 inclusions and 'macaronner' the mixture until smooth and shinny. Line a baking tray with baking paper and using a piping bag with a number 10 nozzle pipe the macaroon base approximately 7 cm in diameter. For the top 'crown' shape pipe or spread using a 'doughnut' template a shape that is also 7 cm in diameter and has a centre hole measuring 3 cm. Set aside at room temperature for 20 to 30 minutes until a skin has formed. Cook for 10 minutes then reduce oven to 120°C for approximately 4 minutes. Once baked, allow to cool on the tray undisturbed.

Rosewater infused raspberries: Place raspberries in a bowl. Heat the sugar and water to make a syrup. Allow to boil until slightly thickened, about 2 minutes, remove from the heat and then add the rosewater. Immediately pour rose flavour syrup over the fruits. Allow to cool at room temperature until required.

Lychee cream: If using canned lychees drain off the syrup and reserve. Place into a food processor and blend until smooth. Add only enough of the reserved syrup to adjust the consistency and aid the blending of ingredients. Place into a pan and cook slowly, stirring continually until the volume has reduced by approximately half. Allow to cool completely before proceeding. Whisk cream until a firm peak is achieved and then whip in the wine/liqueur. Blend cold purée and cream to smooth but firm consistency. Place into a piping bag for assembly. Chill until required.

To serve: Sort the macaroons into pairs; one base and one ring per person. Pipe lychee cream onto the base macaroon layer. Drain rosewater infused raspberries, reserving the syrup and place into the centre of the piped cream. Place the top ring of macaroon onto the cream and press lightly to secure. Decorate with a selection of finely cut fresh fruits spilling out of the centre of the macaroon. Place assembled macaroon on to the plate and use reserved rosewater syrup to accompany. Decorate the plate with any of the additional optional plating decorations if desired.

GREAT FOSTERS

BIOGRAPHY

Douglas Balish

Head Chef of The Tudor Room at Great Fosters, Douglas Balish was born in Scotland and began his career in Ayrshire working part time in the kitchen of his local pub. Realising he didn't want to do anything other than cook, he ventured to Jersey to work at Bohemia, a Michelin starred restaurant, ranked in the top twenty UK best restaurants. Four years later and keen to progress, his next position was at Whatley Manor which held 4 AA rosettes and 2 Michelin stars. Ambition then led him to Sydney where he worked at Quay, ranked 48th best restaurant in the world for a year before returning to the UK to take up the much sought after position that he now holds.

The Tudor Room at Great Fosters is a lavishly decorated, sophisticated dining room with the intimacy of only 24 covers. Set within an historic, Grade one listed building which has been sympathetically converted to a luxury hotel, the service is attentive, yet unobtrusive. A showcase for Dougie's inspiration and aspirations, his style is classic but with a modern twist and his love of fresh, seasonal ingredients, sourced locally where possible shines through in the dishes he creates .

Chocolate Pudding
with passion fruit yogurt

INGREDIENTS

Coffee and chocolate sponge
(bottom layer)

235g Caster sugar

90g Butter

230g beaten Egg

65g Cocoa powder

20g Coffee granules

Passion fruit yogurt mix
(2nd layer)

250g Greek yogurt

25g Yogurt powder

200ml Milk

150ml Whipping cream

3 Gelatine leaves

110g Caster sugar

65g Passion fruit seeds and
pulp

Passion fruit jelly
(3rd layer)

150g Passion fruit purée

100ml Sugar syrup

2 Gelatine leaves

Chocolate mousse
(4th layer)

125g Egg yolks

1 whole Egg

75ml Water

75g Caster sugar

260g Dark chocolate

500ml Whipping cream
(whipped)

METHOD

Coffee and chocolate sponge (bottom layer)

Cream the sugar and butter in a mixing bowl and slowly add the eggs.

Fold in the cocoa powder and coffee granules.

Once mixed, spread onto a tray lined with greaseproof paper and bake at 180°C for 10 minutes.

Allow to cool.

Passion fruit yogurt mix (2nd layer)

Heat the milk, sugar and cream to 60°C, add the gelatine leaves and stir to dissolve.

Allow the mixture to cool to room temperature.

Combine the yogurt and yogurt powder with the passionfruit seeds.

Mix all the ingredients thoroughly.

Passion fruit jelly (3rd layer)

Warm the sugar syrup in a pan.

Add the gelatine leaves and stir in the passion fruit purée.

Set aside to cool.

Chocolate mousse (4th layer)

Whisk the egg yolks and whole egg together until it creates ribbons.

Boil the water and sugar to 118°C.

Melt the chocolate to 35°C in a bowl over some simmering water or in the microwave.

Add the sugar syrup to the eggs and whisk for 2 minutes.

Add the melted chocolate to the mix and then fold in the whipped cream.

THE BUILD

You will need eight 7cm cooking rings.

Cut out a circle of sponge using one of the rings and place inside each of the 8 rings before placing them on a tray.

Warm the passion fruit yogurt mix and divide between the 8 rings forming the second layer.

Cool in the fridge until set.

Warm the passion fruit jelly and pour on top of the yogurt layer and allow to cool.

Finally spoon in the chocolate mousse and smooth off the top with a palate knife or spatula.

Chill in the fridge until ready to serve.

Carefully remove the rings (with the aid of a blow torch, if available) and decorate with chocolate shavings.

Serve with passion fruit sorbet.

South West

Starter
Main
Dessert

MICHAEL CAINES

Michael Caines

BIOGRAPHY

Michael Caines is one of Britain's most acclaimed chefs. AA Chef's Chef of the Year in 2007, and awarded an MBE in 2006 for services to the hospitality industry, Michael is the Executive Chef at Gidleigh Park, the acclaimed and prestigious country house hotel which was voted the number one restaurant by Sunday Times Food List in 2013. Gidleigh Park is located on the edge of Dartmoor at Chagford, Devon, where Michael has earned his reputation - as well as two Michelin stars - serving distinctive modern European cuisine utilising the finest local and regional produce and ingredients. Amongst numerous other accolades, Michael has cooked in 10 Downing Street for the Prime Minister.

Michael was born in Exeter in 1969 and adopted into a large and loving family. He gained his passion for food from his mother who he used to enjoy helping in the kitchen.

Quail Egg Tartlets
with summer truffles, button onion confit, wild mushrooms and a chive butter sauce

INGREDIENTS

375g Puff pastry

15 Quail eggs

50ml Vegetable stock/nage

100g Unsalted butter

Chopped fresh chive

100g Mixed wild mushrooms

1 Large summer truffle, sliced thinly into 12

For the Onion Confit

50g Butter

200g Button onions, peeled and thinly sliced

50g Smoked bacon, cut into fine lardons

100ml Double cream

10g Garlic puree

METHOD

Planning Ahead
This dish is all about having everything ready before you start to assemble it.
You will need to make the vegetable nage the day before to allow the flavours to infuse.
The puff pastry can be baked in advance and kept in a sealed container in the fridge.
The quail's eggs can be fried, put on a plate and stored in the fridge, covered with clingfilm.

Pastry
Roll out the puff pastry thinly and cut out 4 rectangles, 4cm x 13cm. Place them on a baking tray lined with baking parchment and then, using a fork, prick the pastry all over. Put into the fridge for 20 minutes. Preheat the oven to 180°c/gas mark 4. Place another piece of baking parchment over the top of the pastry and place a second baking tray on top to keep the pastry flat. Bake for approximately 20 minutes, until golden brown and cooked through. Leave to cool.
Rub the butter and the flour until the mixture resembles fine grains of sand. Mix the remaining ingredients together and add progressively. Blend until mixed, shape into a ball, wrap in cling film and refrigerate.

Roll out the pastry and take four, buttered Broche Moulds and Line. Rest in the fridge for 15 minutes before baking, then bake at 160°c. Leave to cool then remove from the moulds.

Onion Confit
Melt the butter in a heavy-based pan and add the sliced onions. Season with salt and pepper and cook slowly until soft and tender, roughly 30-40 minutes. Leave to drain in a sieve. Pan-fry the lardons in a little oil and strain off the excess fat. Mix the onions and lardons together. Put the cream into a small pan and simmer until reduced by a third, then add to the onions and lardons. Finally add the garlic puree and season with salt and pepper. Place in container and cover with clingfilm and keep warm in a bain-marie.

Quail Eggs
Carefully crack the eggs on to a plate, 5 at a time, being careful not to damage them. Rub a large non-stick pan with unsalted butter and put it on a medium heat. When it's hot, add the quail's eggs, Cook gently until the whites have formed, then remove from the heat. Using a 25-30mm cutter, cut out the eggs, place them on a plate. Repeat with the rest of the eggs, then cover them with a piece of oiled clingfilm, oiled side down, and place in the fridge until needed.

Sauce
Heat the vegetable nage and whisk in the butter. Season with salt and pepper and add the chives at the last minute before serving.

To Finish
Preheat the oven to 180°c/gas mark 4 again if it is not still on. Pan-fry the wild mushrooms in butter and season with salt and pepper. Take the puff pastry sheets place them on a tray and spoon 1 tablespoon of onion confit onto each and spread down the centre. Alternate the quail's eggs with the slices of summer truffle, it's thee quails eggs per potion and 2 truffle. Now put back into the oven for about 1 minute to heat the eggs through. Place the remaining onion confit on each plate, then carefully, using a palette knife, lift the tartlets on to the confit. Spoon the mushrooms around the tartlets and finish with the sauce, adding the chives at last minute.

THE JETTY

BIOGRAPHY

Having opened his first restaurant, Le Poussin, in 1983, Alex Aitken taught himself to cook – a fact that Gordon Ramsey noted when he named Le Poussin one of his top 11 favourite places to eat in The Times. Alex's culinary journey began on the seas where he worked as a trawler man, giving him unparalleled knowledge of fish and seafood and how to make the most of the ocean's bounty. Championing simple, seasonal and local produce from the very beginning – Alex has received multiple awards and accolades to support this philosophy, most recently a prestigious Michelin Bib Gourmand for The Kings Arms in Christchurch.

Chef Patron for Harbour Hotels, Alex heads up three of the group's restaurants in Christchurch, Dorset – The Jetty, on the water's edge in Mudeford, Upper Deck Bar & Restaurant and The Kings Arms. Alex was thrilled to represent Dorset on BBC's recent 'Taste of Britain' show, as Janet Street Porter and Brian Turner joined him at The Jetty for an afternoon of cooking and filming. Alex chatted to Brian and Janet about the restaurant's unique location and prepared his (now famous) Mudeford Crab Croquettes. Brian Turner described them as "a clever combination of seaside flavours" and Janet Street Porter was left speechless ("I can't speak; I'm enjoying these so much")

Mudeford Crab Croquettes

INGREDIENTS

Brown Crab

110g Brown crab meat

110g soft Butter

Pinch of Cayenne pepper

A pinch of Salt

Juice 1/2 of a Lemon

1 tbsp chopped Chives

1 tsp chopped Tarragon

White Crab Brandade

225g White crab meat

225g dry mashed Potato (allowed to cool)

2 tbsp chopped Chives

Salt and pepper

Tartar Butter Sauce

1 Shallot (finely chopped)

150g Butter

30ml White wine vinegar

75ml White wine

10ml Cream

30ml tock

Salt and pinch of sugar

Juice of 1/2 a Lemon

METHOD

Brown Crab Butter

Place the brown crab meat into a food processor and blitz until smooth then pass through a sieve.

Mix the crab meat with the softened butter, the chopped herbs and spices and season with salt, cayenne pepper (not too much pepper, it's nice and hot) and lemon juice.

Place the softened mixture into a piping bag and pipe into a cylindrical shape onto parchment paper. Freeze.

White Crab Brandade

Mix all together and season with salt and pepper.

To Make The Croquettes

Remove the brown crab butter from the freezer and cut into finger length pieces.

Carefully wrap them in the white crab brandade mixture so they resemble sausages and return to the freezer.

Whilst the croquettes are freezing, you can start to prepare the breadcrumbs.

In three separate bowls you will need some plain flour, some dried breadcrumbs and 2 beaten eggs let down with a dash of cold water.

Place the frozen croquettes first into the flour to give them a light coating, then dip into the beaten egg shaking off the excess then roll in the bread crumbs to coat. For best results do this twice.

The croquettes can now be placed into the fridge ready for deep frying

Heat a large pan of oil to 170°C and carefully place the croquettes inside, turning occasionally to achieve an even golden brown colour. Alternatively use an electric deep fat fryer.

Tartar Butter Sauce

Add shallot, vinegar and wines to a pan and reduce until dry. Add stock and cream and simmer.

Remove the pan from the heat and whisk in the diced butter a little at a time, waiting until the butter has melted and been incorporated before adding any more.

Season and add and lemon juice, adjust the consistency with a dash of water if necessary.

Pass through a sieve.

Garnish

Garnish the butter sauce with chopped capers, chopped baby gherkins, chopped parsley and finely diced shallots.

12/7/95

✓ # IDLE ROCKS

BIOGRAPHY

Guy Owen, Head Chef of the Idle Rocks Hotel

The Hampshire born chef developed his culinary expertise with some of London's leading chefs, including Gordon Ramsay at his Michelin starred restaurant at Claridge's, Jerome Tauvron at L'Etranger and James Bennington and Bruce Poole at Michelin starred La Trompette.

Guy moved to South East Cornwall at the age of eight and throughout his school years began helping in the kitchens of local restaurants after lessons and at weekends. More recently, having returned to the West Country in 2009, Guy worked at leading hotels Gidleigh Park, under Michael Caines, and the Driftwood hotel, where he became sous chef under Chris Eden.

It was Cornish produce that fuelled Guy's passion for food. The menu at The Idle Rocks reflects the hotel's ethos of re-engaging with the simple pleasures in life and uses only the best ingredients with a mix of classical and modern cooking methods. Guy is totally focused on sustainability, and promoting local businesses. Whether that be a local day boat fisherman like Danny Phillips of Cadgwith, who catches their monkfish, or Ross Geech of Padstow kitchen garden who grows their vegetables.

The Idle Rocks is a privately owned 19 bedroomed waterfront Relais & Chateaux hotel in the picturesque village of St. Mawes, Cornwall.

Mackerel Rillettes

INGREDIENTS

10 Mackerel fillets

250g Crème fraiche

zest of 1 Lime

juice of half a Lemon

two good pinches chopped Parsley

1 good pinch chopped Dill

Salt

White pepper

Cucumber Salsa

2 Cucumbers – skin off

¼ bunch chopped Dill

20 ml Chardonnay vinegar

1 minced Banana shallot

pinch of Castor sugar

Sea salt (to taste)

**Cucumber gel
(See Method)**

Dill Pickled Celery

thin peelings of Celery/ribbons

150g White wine

150g Castor sugar

150g White wine vinegar

Dill stalks

10 Coriander seeds

4 White peppercorns

Chervil puree

1 bunch of Chervil (picked down)

big handful of Baby leaf spinach

Salt

METHOD

Mackerel Rillettes

Vacuum pack and cook the mackerel at 85 degrees for 7 minutes. Take out of the bath and plunge into ice-water and leave to cool for 5 minutes.
Flake the mackerel into a bowl, removing the skin and discarding it.
In a separate bowl add together all of the other ingredients, except the seasoning. Beat this together until fully incorporated, you may need to loosen the mixture a little with a splash of milk.
Fold all the ingredients together and season to taste. Store in a container, shelf life 3 days.

Cucumber Salsa

Finely brunoise the cucumber, remembering to not allow any seeds into the mix. Keep the seedy centres for the gel later.
Very finely brunoise/mince the banana shallot, add this to the diced cucumber.
Add the chopped dill, vinegar, cucumber gel (enough to bind it all together) sugar and salt to taste.

Cucumber Gel

Make the cucumber gel by, blending the seeded centres, and add 1 more whole cucumber with the skin on. Pass the blended mix through a chinois. Weigh the liquid required, and divide the overall weight by 10. Eg. 500 ml of cucumber liquid / 10 = 50ml

When you have the correct number, weigh this amount out in vegegel.
Have a container ready at the side, pour the liquid into a pan, heat it up to just below boiling, add the vegegel and whisk it hard until all powder is full incorporated, then pour quickly into the container and leave it to set and cool down.
Once it has cooled down, blend it in the blender to form the gel, season it a little with some salt, and pass it through a chinois. Vacuum the air out of it, and keep it in a bottle.

Dill Pickled Celery

Bring all the ingredients together, except the celery, and bring to the boil.
Once boiled leave it all to infuse in the fridge until cold.
Strain through a chinois.
Pour over the celery ribbons and vacuum pack down for at least 24 hours.

Chervil puree

Heat a pan of boiling water, make sure it is at a rolling boil. Add the chervil with a good pinch of salt and boil for roughly 2 minutes. Then add the spinach to the same water with the chervil and continue to cook for a further minute. After the minute is up you need to gently lift a singular leaf out of the boil water with a spoon, place the leaf between your thumb and index finger, and rub together quite firmly. If the leaf breaks down and starts turning into a paste then it is ready to be taken out, if it feels rubbery and doesn't want to break down then it must be cooked for another 30 seconds or so until it does start to break down. Once the leaves are cooked. Transfer them quickly to the ice water. This will preserve that beautiful, deep green colour. And then simply blend in a good quality liquidiser. Add your salt and maybe a little water to loosen. Once smooth, cool down over ice water, in a metal bowl. It's so important to cool green purees like this down quickly, as this will prevent them from discolouring and turning brown.

To Garnish

To garnish the plate, we use beetroot crisps and foraged sea cress, like rock samphire, sea beet etc.

STAR CASTLE

BIOGRAPHY

The Star Castle Hotel is situated 28 miles off the coast of Lands End, Cornwall, on the island of St Mary's, the largest of the inhabited islands of the Isles of Scilly.

Head chef Billy Littlejohn, originally from Scotland, began working at the hotel in 2001, where he has worked his way up to head chef, after settling on the islands by marrying and having a family.

Billy and his team cook the freshest local produce, including freshly caught brill and lobster, home grown vegetables and foraged samphire from the shore that is a stones throw from the hotel.

Local Brill

samphire, saffron potatoes, lobster and sauce vierge

INGREDIENTS

Brill

4 Brill fillets

Olive oil

Seasoning

20g Butter

Saffron Potatoes

2 large Potatoes (diced)

large pinch of Saffron

Sauce Vierge

150ml Olive oil

3 Tomatoes, concasse

juice of 1 Lemon

I minced Garlic glove

6 Coriander seeds

1 small bunch of shredded Basil

1 small bunch of shredded Chervil

100g Samphire

20g Butter

1-1.5 kg cooked Lobster

METHOD

Dice potatoes, cover with water and add saffron.
Leave until potatoes have took on colour. Cook for 6 minutes and refresh. Re heat when required.

Gently cook the shallot and garlic in olive oil.
Remove from heat. Skin, de-seed and dice the tomatoes and add with the remainder of the ingredients.
Leave to infuse.

Season the brill, cook skin side down for 2 minutes,

flip over and add a knob of butter, cook for a further 1 minute. Rest before serving.
While resting cook samphire in butter, do not season, add lobster and cook for 1 minute.

Place reheated saffron potatoes around the plate.
Put samphire sand lobster in middle of plate, top with brill and drizzle with sauce vierge.

THE MASON ARMS

BIOGRAPHY

Having spent 12 years at the three Michelin starred The Waterside Inn, Bray as Michel Roux's Head Chef and 3 years as Executive Chef at Cliveden, Taplow, Mark decided to spread his wings to Devon. He and his wife Sarah bought the 13th Century Masons Arms, Knowstone in 2005 and the accolades have followed, including a Michelin Star, first awarded in 2006, six months after opening and retained since. In 2008 the Masons Arms was named as North Devon's Best Restaurant, in September 2009 Michelin chose it to be it's 2010 Pub of the Year and in 2011 it was named as North Devon's Best Pub. 10 years on the pub has gone from strength to strength and now with the help of the internet has become a global local! it is no surprise that the food has a modern take on British and French classics with a certain complexity to the cooking. An à la carte menu and seasonal lunchtime specialities are served in relaxed surroundings overlooking the rolling foothills of Exmoor. Real Ale on draught and Champagne by the glass. Mark and Sarah's philosophy is simple "to create the kind of pub that they would love to find whilst on holiday or visiting the area".

Breasts of Wood Pigeon
with blueberry Jus

INGREDIENTS

8 skinned Wood pigeon breasts

2 raw Beetroots (300g)

50g soft Dark brown sugar (half for the purée and half for the sauce)

200ml Double cream

100ml Red wine vinegar (half for the purée and half for the sauce)

50gCaster sugar

100ml Dark chicken or veal stock

100g Picked salad leaves

50gBlueberries

1 large Potato

METHOD

The Beetroot Purée

In a pan cook the beetroot on a low heat, covering them with water, add a pinch of salt, and leave to cook until soft, this could take up to two hours, you will need to top up the water. When soft, drain well and return to the pan, stir them round to evaporate the last of the liquid. Cook a little with the soft dark brown sugar and then pour in the red wine vinegar, cook further until the liquid is a nice caramel colour and then add the double cream, leave to cook and thicken. Place the mixture into a blender and blend until smooth, season to taste, reserve and keep hot.

The Sauce

Put to one side 20 blueberries and then put the others in a pan and reduce together with 50g of Caster Sugar and 50g of Red Wine Vinegar. Crush the blueberries with a fork. When the liquid is syrupy add the stock and cook further until a syrupy sauce consistency. Pass and then add the reserved blueberries.

Crisps

Peel and then slice the potatoes thinly, criss-cross or plain. Rinse them in water, pat them dry and then fry them in hot oil until golden. Drain on absorbent paper, season and reserve until serving.

Cooking & Serving

In a hot pan cook the pigeon breasts, a couple of minutes on each side will leave them pink. Leave them to rest before slicing. Place the purée onto the plate and then some salad leaves. Slice the pigeon and place on the plate on top of the pigeon place the potatoes. Pour on the sauce and serve immediately.

CRAB HOUSE

BIOGRAPHY

"We're devotees of the early 21st century shack school of architecture," says Nigel Bloxham of

his nationally-famous seaside restaurant. But then you don't visit the Crab House Café in search of grandeur. Just a stone's throw from Dorset's Chesil Beach, it has earned a world-class reputation for its delicious seafood. Nigel's menus are built on the freshest fish and shellfish harvested from the surrounding coast – including the Crab House's own oyster beds, just yards from the dining tables.

As a champion of foodie causes, including the Slow Food movement and The Fishermen's Mission, Nigel is dedicated to helping people eat well, in every sense. With a lifetime of experience in sourcing, preparing and cooking good seafood, it's his continued passion whichkeeps him at the top of his game.

Sparkling Portland Pearl Oysters

INGREDIENTS

12 large Portland pearl oysters or whichever variety you prefer

2 Tomatoes

2 Banana shallots or red onions

Flour, to dust the oysters

1 tbsp Oil

Salt, to season

Sugar, to season

METHOD

Boil a kettle full of water and pour into a bowl. Also fill a separate bowl with cold or iced water. Take the little core out from the top of the tomatoes – you can actually get a little gadget that does this for you now, and even as a chef I admit they're good!

Nick the skin by putting a cut with a knife in the side, about 1 centimetre in. Put the tomatoes in a bowl of boiling water until you see the skin start to peel o3, then take them out and plunge them into the cold or iced water. Take them out and peel them. They should peel really easily. Cut them in half, get rid of all the seeds then roughly chop.

Finely dice the banana shallots by cutting them into strips one way then holding them in place and cutting them into dice the other way, take your time.

Mix the tomatoes and the shallots to make a concasse. Season with salt and sugar. You'll find that this will actually flavour the tomato and pull some of the water out.

Meanwhile, open your oysters and take the meat out of its shell and roll it in flour. Put them on a plate ready for frying.

Set up your oyster shells ready to serve.

In a non-stick pan, heat 1 tablespoon of oil over a high heat. Put the floured oysters in the pan. Take them off once the flour is cooked, not necessarily the oysters – they may still be quite moist, but the protein in them has firmed up and tightened. This will probably take less than a minute.

To serve:

Put a spoonful of the concasse into each oyster shell.

Serve the oysters as soon as they are cooked.

You can garnish with a sprig of herb. I like fennel, parsley and chive – anything green would show up really nice.

Serve, enjoy, pour the wine. This is a good one for a nice buttery Chablis!

WEST BEACH

BIOGRAPHY

WestBeach, one of Bournemouth's most prestigious and busiest restaurants, is proud to have Head Chef, Nick Hewitt, at the helm of this popular beachside eatery. Nick joined the team in 2011 and comes to WestBeach with outstanding pedigree, having trained at Claridges in London. Nick is proud to have been Sous Chef at 5 star hotel, the Chewton Glen and Head Chef at the popular Bournemouth brasserie, The Print Room. Nick's great passion is working with fresh, seasonal and locally sourced ingredients. He loves the thrill of working with seafood, freshly caught and delivered from WestBeach's very own fishing boats because, in his words, "you never know what you're going to get!". His stand- out signature dish, that is the talk of the town, is his wild sea bass with buttered cabbage, cherry tomatoes, tiger prawns, courgettes, mini fondant potatoes and delicious herb butter sauce. WestBeach, which boasts 2 AA rosettes, has been named Bournemouth's only recommended restaurant in The Good Food Guide 2015.

Sea Bass

with curried crème fraîche, quinoa, mango & brown shrimp salsa

INGREDIENTS

2 x 140g Sea bass fillet

1 tsp of Mild flavoured oil such as vegetable

For The Crème Fraîche

100g Crème fraîche

1 tsp Curry powder

Salt & pepper to taste

For The Quinoa

100g of Quinoa

zest of 1 Lime

chopped Coriander

For The Mango & Brown Shrimp Salsa

1/2 Mango cut into 1/2 cm cubes

2 tbsp of Brown shrimps

1 tsp Capers

100ml of Olive oil or more if needed to bind

For The Garnish

3 tips of Asparagus

micro Coriander Cress

METHOD

Start by preparing the accompaniments so that you can put them to one side and give your full attention to the sea bass. To prepare the Curried Crème Fraîche simply toast the curry powder in a pan until you can smell the spices. Allow the spices to cool and then mix thoroughly with the crème fraîche and season to taste.

For the salsa, mix all of the salsa ingredients together and season to taste. Simple. Next get the Quinoa started by adding to salted boiling water and allow to simmer for 12 mins or as per the instructions on the packet. When cooked, the quinoa will be lighter in colour and have a fluffy texture, stir in the lime zest and chopped coriander.

Once you've got the quinoa on the go start a second pan of water boiling ready for your asparagus later Now start cooking the sea bass. Heat the oil in a pan and cook the fish until the skin is crispy and the sea bass is white all the way through. This will take roughly 3-4 mins on each side. Finally, while the fish is cooking, boil the asparagus for 2 mins or until you can cut easily with a sharp knife.

Plate all of the ingredients and enjoy.

GUYERS HOUSE

BIOGRAPHY

Chef Matt Gillard joined Guyers House Hotel December 2015, after spending 10 years working in some of the south west's finest Hotels and Restaurant's. Matt brings passion, desire and a natural ability Paired with flair to Guyers house hotel's two rosette restaurant and dining Experience's in Corsham.

His Ethos is to take classic British and French Cuisine and turn it on its head, with modern techniques, foraging and sourcing all of his ingredients locally. Most notably by paring with suppliers such as Terry and sons Butchers in Bath and Total Produce.

"for me cooking is about taking something classic and raw and reinventing it and this process produces a journey filled with fun and history with a unique and stunning result"

Roast fillet of Beef

smoke ox tail tortellini, carrots, baby onions and girolles

INGREDIENTS

Beef fillet

4 x 6 oz Beef fillets

Carrot puree

2 large Carrots peeled

Carrot juice

Pasta

140g 'oo' Flour

1 Egg

1 Egg yolk

Baby onions

x20 Baby onions

Thyme

Braised ox Tail

1kg Ox tail

1 Carrot

1 Onion

1 Celery

Smoked garlic

2 Shallots

1 bunch Parsley

200ml Red wine

Carrots

1 each purple, yellow, orange carrot

Girolles

50g Girolles

METHOD

Pasta

Place the flour in a food processor and pulse it. Add the whole egg and egg yolk and keep blending until the mixture resembles fine breadcrumbs. This takes 2-3 minutes.

Tip out the dough and knead to form into a ball shape. Knead it briskly for 1 minute, it should be quite stiff and hard to knead. Wrap in cling film and leave to rest in a cool place for 1 hour before using.

Now cut the dough into 2 pieces. For each piece, flatten with a rolling pin to about 5mm/¼ in) thickness. Fold over the dough and pass it through the pasta machine at its widest setting, refolding and rolling 7 times (not changing the setting) until you have a rectangular shape 7.5x18cm/3x7 in. It is important to work the dough until it is nice and shiny, as this gives it the "al dente" texture.

Now you are ready to roll out. Start with the pasta machine at its widest setting, pass the dough through the rollers. Do not fold but repeat this process, decreasing the roller setting down grade by grade with each pass. For most uses, I take the pasta down to the penultimate setting – once is rolled cut in to 8 cm circles, line a small try with Clingfilm and place the pasta on and cover and refrigerate.

Braised ox tail,

Sear the ox tail in a deep hot pan caramelizing all over, roughly chop the carrot, celery, smoked garlic and onion until the vegetables are coloured add the red wine and fill with water cover and braise at a medium heat for 4 hours.

Carrot puree, peel and slice the carrot then add to salted boiling water until soft, transfer to a blender and using the carrot juice blend until a smooth puree is achieved

baby onions, blanch the baby onions in boiling water for 2 mins, drain and set aside

carrots, peel and roughly cut, blanch in boiling water and once cooked drain and set aside

Girolles, trim and scrape the stalks then brush excess dirt off

Tortellini

Once the ox tail is cooked and the meat is flaking off the bone pick all the meat off the bone and add to a clean bowl (reserving the cooking liquor) finely slice the shallots and the parsley add this to the ox tail and season to taste, take the pasta from the fridge and place a small amount of the ox tail in the middle of the pasta and fold over using egg wash to seal then place in-between your little finger and forefinger and pull the edges around to meet and squeeze together continue until all the pasta is used up.

To build

Get a frying pan hot and add a little oil once hot add the fillet steak and sear all around then add the girolles, baby onions and carrot to the pan and some garlic and thyme, place in the oven for 3-4 minutes. Once out of the over add a knob of butter and baste, remove and rest in a warm place.

Add 50mls red wine to the pan and reduce once reduced add the cooking liquor from the ox tail and reduce until is a sauce like consistency.

Put your tortellini in salted boiling water for 4-5 minutes and once cooked at to the beef Sauce. Then warm your carrot puree.

The dish is now ready to be plated and serves 4 people

ELLENBOROUGH PARK

BIOGRAPHY

David Kelman is the executive head chef at Gloucestershire's only Five Star hotel Ellenborough Park and a contestant in The BBC Great British Menu 2014.

Aside from his golden TV appearance, David has had many achievements. His influence on his kitchen team secured three AA Rosettes for Ellenborough Park's Beaufort Dining Room. As Captain of the Welsh Culinary Team he won Silver and Bronze at the 2012 Culinary Olympics and is proud to have cooked for the Royal Family and Prime Minister on several occasions.

David champions local quality food producers and suppliers, and his menus currently use ingredients sourced from 23 Gloucestershire businesses. This dedication has led to further awards; David was crowned 'Gloucestershire's Best Chef' and The Beaufort Dining Room as 'Best Restaurant' in 2013.

Furthermore, the modest yet exceptional chef has raised thousands of pounds for children's charities such as Ty Hafan, the hospice in South Wales.

Fillet of Old Spot Pork Rolled In Cep Powder

with sage and onion bon bon, puy lentil savoy cabbage, crackling, cider apple puree

INGREDIENTS

For the Pork Fillet
2 x large old spot Pork tenderloins (trimmed and then cut into half)
100g Cep powder

For The Sage And Onion Bon Bon
200g Maris piper potatoes (cooked then mashed)
½ Onion (small diced and cooked in butter)
5g Sage (chopped cooked with the onion)
Salt and pepper
1 whole Egg
20ml Milk
30g Flour
100g Panko bread crumbs

For The Savoy Cabbage And Puy Lentil
1/4 Savoy cabbage (shredded and cooked in salt water until soft, refresh in ice cold water)
20g Puy lentils (washed and cooked in chicken stock until just cooked)
20g of Small diced carrot, swede, leek and shallot (blanched in salt water)

For The Cider Apple Puree And Balls
1 Granny smith apple (peeled)
200ml Apple juice
1 small bit of Cinnamon
For the crackling
1 large Pork skin with very little fat

METHOD

For the Pork Fillet

Trim all the fat and sinew off the fillet

Roll it in the cep powder

Then tightly roll in cling film and tie the ends

Cook in water bath @ 62° for 30 mins, remove from water bath and chill

For The Sage And Onion Bon Bon

Mix the potato, sage and onion together, season and roll into 50g balls

Flour egg wash and bread crumb the ball and set to one side ready to fry.

For The Savoy Cabbage And Puy Lentil

Add all the above ingredients together in a small pan with a small amount of butter, season.

For The Cider Apple Puree And Balls

Using a melon baller take 8 nice balls of apple, add them to apple juice and cinnamon, bring to the boil, when starting to boil turn off. Remove the apples from the juice and chill.

Add the trimmings of apple to the juice, remove the cinnamon and then cook until the juice is almost gone, place the cooked apple trimmings to a blender and blitz until smooth.

Place into a squeeze bottle ready for plating

For the crackling

Steam the skin for 1 hour 30mins, remove from the steamer and scrape any fat off that is left, season and roll up length ways, roll in cling film and freeze

Remove from the freezer and slice on a meat slicer, place the sliced skin onto a baking tray with grease proof paper, lay another sheet over the top and place another baking tray on top.

Cook @ 180° for around 22 minutes or until it starts to puff up and crisp.

For service

Remove the pork from the cling film, season and then pan fry and get good colour all-round, add butter and foam the butter over the pork

Heat up the cabbage mix, fry off the bon bon

Add 3 cooked chanternay carrots, apple balls, puree, cabbage and then add the pork crackling and bon bon.

Serve with a little pork jus .

The dish is now ready to be plated and serves 4 people

PORTHMINSTER
BEACH CAFE

BIOGRAPHY

Ryan Venning started his career in Durban South Africa where he attended the International Hotel School where he trained for 2 1/2 years. During this time he was awarded the principle award for student of the year and cooked for Nelson Mandela.

He moved on to work at a Gastro Pub called The Stokers Arms in Durban and then he met current work mate Mick Smith and moved to the UK.

In 2003 he started in Cornwall as the Head Chef of Porthmeor Beach Café then moved onto Porthminster Beach Café where he worked 3 years as a CDP in 2007 he was promoted to Head Chef at Porthgwidden Beach Café where he worked for 4 years.

In 2011 he became Head Chef at the Red Herring Restaurant at Bedruthan Steps Hotel where he worked for a year and managed to get in the Good Food Guide with a cooking score of 4 in the first year of opening.

In 2012 Ryan Venning came back to Porthminster Beach Café as Head Chef where he is still established and is at the forefront of The Cornish cooking scene. He uses big flavours with modern twists and is also inspired by the lightness of Asian ingredients.

Summer Vegetable Risotto

INGREDIENTS

Risotto

1 small Onion brunoise

1 stalk of Celery brunoise

½ a bulb of Fennel brunoise

100 ml of Dry vermouth or dry nolly prat

1 liter of simmering Chicken stock

1 kg of Canaroli (preferred to aborio)

While the risotto is resting gather the following

2 Courgettes diced

½ cup of Broad beans

¼ cup of fresh Oregano, basil and mint chopped

t.s Chives

2nd stage

½ a Lemon juiced

1 shot of Nolly

½ tbspn Parmesan

2 Basil leaves

1 heaped kitchen spoon of Rice approx 80g

½ a tbspn of Mascarpone / butter

METHOD

Risotto

Sweat brunoise until soft in flat based pot with a covered surface of olive oil. When no steam is left rising from brunoise add rice toss don't stir: toss until rice is coated and to hot to touch (DON'T COLOUR) add vermouth and evaporate it. Then cover rice with hot stock keep covered until 1 litre of stock as evaporated (DO NOT STIR) do not stir during this process as encourages to much starch out of the rice when cooking has not truly began it also damages the exterior of the rice with this process you want the rice to be close to raw it is just a speeding up technique. When all liquid is evaporated spread evenly on a tray and cool quickly.

While the risotto is resting gather the following
2 Courgettes diced
½ cup of Broad beans
¼ cup of Fresh oregano, basil and mint chopped
t.s Chives

Add all of this to the

2nd stage
½ a Lemon juiced
1 shot of Nolly
½ tbspn Parmesan
2 Basil leaves
1 heaped kitchen spoon of Rice approx 80g
½ a tbspn of Mascarpone / butter

Place rice in cover with hot stock and cook for 6 minutes stirring and adding hot liquid all the time rest at 6-7 minutes and return to the heat after 2 minutes stirring rapidly take
off the heat and add marscarpone limoncello touch of ripped basil leaves then stir in parmesan grated serve immediately rice should be at 2 small dots.

THE SHORE RESTAURANT

BIOGRAPHY

The Shore Restaurant is a small seafood restaurant in Penzance. Bruce Rennie, the chef and owner, uses the knowledge he has gained from experience working in some of the country's top kitchens to offer interesting seasonal dishes using the best of the produce from the fish market in nearby Newlyn and throughout the county.

After working at The Balmoral Hotel in Edinburgh and then on to a head chef position with Gary Rhodes, Bruce moved to Ireland in 2002 as senior chef at the Michelin starred Shanks in Bangor for the late Robbie Millar and then moved back to Edinburgh heading the kitchen at Martin Wishart's Michelin starred restaurant until 2008 when he moved to Cornwall with his wife. Since running the kitchen at The Gurnard's Head pub for nearly 5 years and as head chef for Rick Stein, Bruce and Anita decided to take the plunge and open The Shore Restaurant in June 2015.

Monkfish, Nitsuke, Flower Sprouts, Daikon

INGREDIENTS

6 portions Monkfish fillet, 160g each

3 Nori seaweed sheets

salt

Cling film

6 portions of Flower sprouts (or kale or samphire), blanched in salted water

100g Daikon (white radish or mooli), thinly sliced

120g Japapnese wheat noodles (or Ramen if you prefer)

120g Shimeji mushrooms, base trimmed

Nitsuke broth

500g Water

10g Kombu seaweed

10g Bonito flakes

50ml Soy sauce

50ml Sake

50ml Mirin

METHOD

Begin by soaking the kombu in the cold water for 30 minutes and then cut it into 1 inch strips.

Next place the kombu and water into a pan and slowly bring it to the boil.

Allow it to boil for no more than 3 seconds and remove the seaweed.

Return the pan to the heat and add the bonito flakes.

Bring it back to the boil and then remove the pan from the heat.

Allow it to sit for 2 minutes before removing straining the liquid through a fine sieve lined with muslin cloth.

Bring the sake to the boil in a separate pan and then add it to the strained liquid along with the mirin and soy. Set it aside until required.

To serve

Bring a pan of water to the boil and then turn it down to a very gentle simmer.

Season the monkfish portions with salt and wrap each in a piece of nori seaweed cut to the size required to wrap all the way round.

Roll each portion in cling film leaving no air gaps and tie the ends to seal it.

Cook the monkfish portions in the barely simmering water for 8-12 minutes depending on the thickness.

Allow the monkfish to rest while you assemble the dish.

Blanche the noodles for 1 minute and divide equally between 6 bowls.

Add the warm flower sprouts and daikon to the bowls.

Warm the nitsuke stock with the mushrooms until they soften slightly and divide this between the bowls.

Slice each monkfish portion into 3 and arrange in the bowls.

BLAGDON MANOR

BIOGRAPHY

Chef Stephen Morey

My philosophy on food is simple. I am grounded in the classics and I cook with the seasons. Hearty, flavoursome dishes are served with elegance and finesse and it is the way we live our lives. We are proud of every plate that leaves the kitchen and we work tirelessly to create an environment in which our guests can switch off and relax.

We believe in delivering the highest standards and we are passionate about our work. I cook from the heart & use ingredients that excite me.

I'm passionate about local, independent produce. I tend to favour small producers who put love and devotion into their ingredients. My passions aren't a fad or some sort of fashion statement. It amazes me when people jump aboard the 'Buy Local' bandwagon, as though they're leading a revolution. I've always bought local. I've always followed the seasons.

I was born and raised in Paignton and went to South Devon Technical College. I always enjoyed cooking as a kid. I cooked when I was still at primary school, then in secondary school I loved home economics. I also loved art. I enjoyed drawing and painting. That creative streak serves me well when I presented food in my restaurant.

Today, Blagdon Manor is firmly on the map. We have remarkably loyal guests, who appreciate the relaxed ambience and contemporary cuisine. We've created a venue that has all of the high standards but without any of the stuffiness or formality.

Breast of Guinea Fowl
beer battered corned beef, truffled cabbage, almond croquette potatoes and beetroot

INGREDIENTS

4 breasts of Guinea fowl

198g Corned beef

100g Tempura flour

small bottle Light beer

300g Savoy cabbage

1 tspn Truffle peelings

500g Potatoes

75g Butter

100g Ground almonds

100g Breadcrumbs

500g Beetroot – keep some for garnish

1000ml Beef stock

Garnish

Pan fried seasonal vegetables and beetroot

METHOD

For croquettes potatoes
Cook potatoes in boiling salted water. Drain when cooked and dry potatoes. Mash and mix in butter. When cool enough – roll into walnuts sized balls. Pass through seasoned flour and then eggwash and finally through a mix of the ground almonds and breadcrumbs. Fry croquettes at the same time as the fritters.

Beetroot sauce
Cook beetroot in boiling salted water when tender leave to cool in water. Reduce the beef stock by half and put into liquidiser with peeled beetroot. Pass through a fine sieve.

Cabbage
Pick the leaves off the stalks and pick into small pieces. Cook in boiling salted water. When cooked place into iced cold water to refresh. Warm the cabbage in a little butter with some truffle peelings just as you are about to serve.

For corned beef fritters
Dice the corned beef into bit size chunks. Mix the tempura flour very lightly with the beer. Toss corned beef into batter and deep fry at 180°c at the last minute. If you can't get tempura flour you can use self-raising flour.

For guinea fowl
Seal the breast all over and cook in oven for 5-6 minutes then leave to rest. Assemble as in photograph.

TIMBRELL'S YARD

BIOGRAPHY

Ricky Ford was born in Bath. A West Country boy born and bred, he began cooking at the age of 15 as a commis chef at his local pub. He worked his way up through the world of fine dining, honing his skills at Gary Rhodes and then as head chef at The Museum Inn, Farnham.

Ricky joined Timbrell's Yard in Bradford on Avon, as their head chef, on its opening in March 2015. Since then, he has built up a loyal following and a fantastic network of local growers and suppliers. Ricky specialises in creating simple, fresh local food from the very best West County produce.

Pan Roasted Wild Sea Trout
with English peas, bacon fregula, grilled baby gem, rocket pesto

INGREDIENTS

4 portions of Wild trout, about 160g-180g each

2 Baby gem lettuce, halved

250g Fregula

150g Dry cured bacon cut in to lardons

150g fresh English peas

4 tbsp Crème fraiche

1 Lemon

25g English butter

Rapeseed oil

Salt & pepper

For the rocket pesto

1 small Garlic clove

pinch of Sea salt

25g Pine nuts, very lightly toasted

50g Wild rocket

25g Parmesan, finely grated

juice of ½ Lemon

125ml Extra-virgin olive oil

METHOD

For the pesto

Put the garlic and salt into a small food processor and pulse. Add the pine nuts and pulse until roughly chopped (be careful not to over-process). Add the rocket and pulse so it is well mixed but retains texture. Turn into a bowl and stir through the Parmesan and lemon juice. Add olive oil and mix well to form a juicy paste, seasoning to taste as you go.

Add the fregula to a pan of boiling salted water and cook for 8-10minutes. Refresh and put to one side.

In a frying pan, cook the bacon lardons in 1 tbsp rapeseed oil until crispy. Add the peas, fregula and a splash of water and combine.

Place the baby gem lettuce under a medium to high grill and cook until slightly charred and tender. This will only take five minutes at most.

Add 2 tbsp of rapeseed oil to a frying pan and add the wild trout, skin side down. Cook on a medium heat until the skin becomes crispy (it will be almost cooked by this point) and then turn the fish over and add the butter and a big squeeze of lemon juice. Take pan off the hob and let the residual heat finish cooking the fish.

Add crème fraiche and a squeeze of lemon to the fregula.

Divide between four plates and serve.

LE CHAMPIGNON SAUVAGE

BIOGRAPHY

David Everitt-Matthias has been the co-owner and head chef of two Michelin starred LeChampignon Sauvage in Cheltenham since 1987, a joint venture he shares with his wife Helen.

In the 29 years that Le Champignon Sauvage has been opened, David and Helen have never missed a service. If the restaurant is open, David will always be in the kitchen, whilst Helen runs front of house. Le Champignon Sauvage has been a two Michelin starred restaurant since 2000.

David is the author of three highly regarded recipe books: Essence: Recipes from Le Champignon Sauvage in 2006 and Dessert Recipes from Le Champignon Sauvage in 2009, the latter earned runner-up for Best Cookbook in the World from the Gourmand Book Awards. His third, Beyond Essence: New Recipes from Le Champignon Sauvage was launched in spring 2013.

No stranger to awards, some of the accolades David and the restaurant has received include 2015 ninth place in the Good Food Guide Top 10 UK restaurants, 2014 Good Food Guide Chef of the Year, 2013 Observer Food Monthly 'Outstanding Contribution' award, 2007 Catey Chef of the Year, 2006 BMW Square Meal Restaurant of the Year, as well as retaining two Michelin stars since 2000.

Fillet of Cornish Sea Bass
with wild mushroom tea, good king henry

INGREDIENTS

Sea Bass:

8 pieces of Sea bass fillet (middle section, if possible), 100–120g each

Grapeseed oil, for brushing

a little Lemon juice

Mushroom Tea:

50g Olive oil

500g Onions, finely sliced

50g dried Ceps (porcini)

1.5kg brown Chicken stock

500g Dashi

Parsley Oil:

75g Rapeseed oil

30g Flat-leaf parsley leaves

juice of 1/4 Lemon

The Tapioca:

250g Mushroom tea

40g Tapioca

Wilted Sea Aster:

50g Unsalted butter

50g Water

200g Sea aster leaves

To Serve

Maldon salt

Good King Henry leaves

METHOD

Mushroom Tea

Heat the olive oil in a large saucepan, add the onions and stir well, then cover with a lid. Cook, stirring occasionally, for about 5 minutes, until the onions have collapsed and become translucent. Remove the lid and cook until the onions are a lovely deep golden-brown colour, stirring well. Add the ceps followed by the stock. Bring to the boil, then simmer for 50 minutes, skimming as necessary. Carefully strain through muslin into another pan. Add the dashi, bring to the boil and simmer gently for 5–10 minutes so the flavours can develop. Remove from the heat. The tea should be extremely well flavoured by now; if it is a bit watery, place back on the heat and slowly reduce, without boiling. If it is too reduced add a little water. Leave to cool, then set aside.

Sea Bass

Lay a sheet of cling film on the work surface and cut out a piece just large enough to wrap a portion of sea bass. Brush oil and lemon juice over a square in the centre of the piece of cling film and season. Place the sea bass portion on this, skin side down, and wrap the fish tightly. Repeat to wrap the remaining pieces of fish. Keep in the fridge until needed. Remove about 30 minutes before steaming.

Parsley Oil

Place all the ingredients in a blender and pulse to blend: the oil should have flecks of parsley, but not become a purée. Season and set aside.

Tapioca

Pour 250g of the mushroom tea into a small saucepan and bring to the boil, then rain in the tapioca, stirring. Simmer gently until the tapioca is cooked, about 30 minutes. All the liquid should have been soaked up by the tapioca; if not, drain off the excess. Season and keep warm.

Steaming The Sea Bass

Place a steamer on the stove to heat up. Put the fish parcels in the steamer and steam for 5–6 minutes: timing depends on the thickness of the fish – you want it just cooked (check by inserting a fine skewer, withdrawing it and touching it to your lips; it should feel warm). Remove from the steamer, place on a tray and keep warm. When needed, carefully remove from the cling film.

Wilted Sea Aster

Place a large sauteuse on the heat, add the butter and water, and bring to the boil. Add the sea aster leaves and cook for 1 minute, until just wilted. Season. Drain and keep warm. Place a little tapioca in the centre of each

Serving

Reheat the mushroom tea without boiling. bowl. Arrange the wilted sea aster on top in a little pile and set the fish on this. Spoon a little of the parsley oil over the fish and sprinkle with Maldon salt. Arrange the Good King Henry leaves on top. Ladle over the tea or serve it in a little teapot, as described in the introduction.

BURLEY MANOR

BIOGRAPHY

Trained under Peter Griffiths MBE at the Manor Hotel Meriden.

Ian is a winner of many international salon culinaire competitions and experienced judge, Rioja Chef of the Year and more recently Dorset and Hampshire Chef of the Year.

Ian is a Chef de Cuisine Member of the British Culinary Federation.

He also was asked to organise and cook for Her Majesty the Queen and the Duke of Edinburgh at Gloucester Cathederal in 2003

Ian moved to Dorset 10 years ago and had great success while involved with the gastro pub the Coventry Arms in Wimborne winning AA rosettes and Dorset Dinning Pub of the Year. Ian also achieved a 2 rating from the Good Food Guide while working as Head Chef at the 2 AA Rosette Print Room in Bournemouth.

Ian became Head Chef at the Kings Arms Hotel (Harbour Hotels Group) Christchurch in May 2012 and has transformed the property into a very profitable and successful business, being number 1 on trip advisor and achieving the only Michelin Bib Gourmand Award in Dorset for 2013/14 and Retaining the Bib for 2014/2015. Also added to the Good Hotel Guide for 2014 and the Telegraph top 500 Restaurants 2013/14 and Table top diners choice award 2014.

Ian has vast amounts of experience in public demonstrations showing at the Christchurch, Highcliffe, Bournemouth and Wimborne Food festivals and has been compere for the Feast of Dorset.

Ian is also featured in the 'Dorset on a plate' charity recipe book.

Ian is now Head Chef at the 4* Burley Manor restaurant & rooms, cooking Mediterranean style dishes using the finest local produce.

Mediterranean Beef Daube

INGREDIENTS

1, Shin of Beef

2pnts Beef stock

1 glass, Red wine

Salt and pepper

Provençale Sauce

500g, chopped Tomatoes

1 large Onion, finely dice

2 cloves Garlic, crushed

1 Carrot, finely diced

1 stick, Celery

2, rashers of thick cut Streaky bacon cut into lardons

16, Olives, sliced

1 bunch Parsley, chopped

Dumplings

140g soft, cold Butter, diced

250g Self-raising flour

1 bunch of Basil, chopped

METHOD

To begin,

Place the shin of beef into a roasting tray, add the Beef stock, cover with foil and slow braise at gas mark 3/140oc for 4 hours.

When the beef is 'falling apart', remove from the stock.

Pour the stock into a sauce pan, add the Red wine and reduce until a sauce consistency. Reserve

With 2 forks, flake the Beef, place onto a sheet of cling film and roll into a large sausage style shape. Place in a fridge to firm up.

To make the Provençale sauce,

In a heavy bottom pan, sauté the lardons of bacon, onion, garlic, carrot and celery. Add the chopped tomatoes, season with salt and pepper, bring to the boil and simmer until the vegetables are cooked.

Finally add the olives and parsley.

To make the dumplings, mix the butter, S/R flour and basil into a bowl and mix, add a splash of water to create a dough like consistency and roll into golf ball sized spheres.

To put the dish together,

Cut the Beef into 4 good portions and place into an oven proof dish, cover with the Provençale sauce, place the dumpling around and finally add the reduced stock.

Bake in the oven at gas mark 5 170oc for 20 mins until the beef is above 75oc and the dumplings and cooked, soft and light.

Serve with some buttered greens.

THE PAVILLION

BIOGRAPHY

Originally from the English Lake District, Tony has made Guernsey his island home of 25 years. Tony is driven by the diverse array of fresh seasonal produce that is available within the island and surrounding waters, believing that quality produce is best cooked simply with little fuss. Many of the producers and growers are known personally and you will often see them either in his kitchen or dining at the Pavilion.

A keen advocate of Guernsey produce, and was awarded 'Guernsey Ambassador of the Year' for showcasing Guernsey Food. Having previously received the 'Outstanding Achievement Award', Tony is now the present Chairman of 'Taste Guernsey' a collective group funded by Culture & Leisure working to promote and stages food and drink events within Guernsey.

Tony recently had his first cook book published which has received rave reviews not to mention Winner in the 'Gourmand World Cook Book Awards 2012', Winner of best cook book, 'London Book Festival 2012' and an Honourable mention at the

'2012 New York Book Festival'.

Fig & Almond Tart
with guernsey honey & lavendar cream

INGREDIENTS

Sweet Pastry:

120g Strong flour

90g Eggs

10g Yeast

15g Water

60g Guernsey butter
(unsalted & melted)

60g chopped Apple

2 level teaspoons of
Caster sugar

Syrup:

120g Caster sugar

150ml Water

80ml Calvados

pinch Cinnamon

½ Orange

METHOD

Prepare a dough with sieved Strong Flour, Water and Lightly Beaten and sieved Eggs, this dough should be beat well until smooth and elastic (ideally at a temperature of approx. 80°F / 27°C.

Allow the dough to rest for approx 30 minutes in a warm place. Keep the dough covered to prevent a skin or crust forming.

When the dough has proved up beat in gradually the melted butter to create a batter style dough, finally add the chopped Apple at this stage.

Grease individual moulds and dust each with a little flour, tap out any excess flour.

Divide the batter / dough equally filling the dariole dishes approx. 1/3 full.
Allow to prove fully before baking at 450°F / 230°C for 20 – 25 minutes.

Remove from moulds while still warm and set aside on a cooling rack.

When cool saturate each Baba by dipping into the warmed Syrup.

Glaze each Baba with Apricot Glaze and serve with some homemade Nutmeg Ice Cream.

PONY AND TRAP

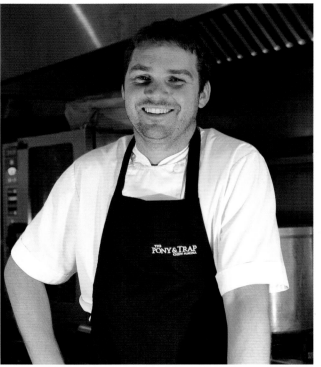

BIOGRAPHY

The brother and sister duo have earned a reputation for quality with Josh managing the kitchen, and Holly, front of house. A testament to great food and a welcoming atmosphere, The Pony & Trap has held a Michelin Star since 2011 and was ranked 2nd in the Publican Morning Advertiser's Top 50 UK Gastropubs in 2015. The pub champions a "field to fork" ethos serving food sourced as locally as possible from suppliers around the Chew Valley and the South West

English Egg Custard Tart

INGREDIENTS

For the Pastry

200g Plain flour
100g cold Butter (diced)
50g Caster sugar
1 Vanilla pod
1 Egg and 1 yolk (beaten)
Butter & flour for greasing
1 Egg (beaten) for glazing

For The Custard Filling

500ml Double cream
100g Sugar
8 Eggs
1 Vanilla pod

Rhubarb Garnish

2 sticks of forced Yorkshire rhubarb
200ml Water
100ml Sugar

Mini Meringues

4 Egg whites
55g Caster sugar
55g Icing sugar

Granola

1tsp Vegetable oil
60ml Maple syrup
1tbsp Honey
½ tsp Vanilla essence
300g Rolled oats

Rhubarb Sorbet

2kg fresh Rhubarb (washed and chopped)
500g Caster sugar
60g Liquid glucose
200g Water
½ tsp Vitamin C powder
Sorbet stabilizer

METHOD

Sieve the flour into the bowl of an electric stand mixer fitted with the paddle attachment. Add the butter and turn on to a low speed until the mixture resembles bread crumbs. Split the vanilla pods and scrape out the seeds into the bowl. Mix in the sugar and add the eggs. As soon as the pastry comes together into a smooth mass, remove it from the machine, clingfilm and allow to rest in fridge for 1 hour. Preheat the oven to 180C. Grease the inside of a 20cm flan ring with butter and sprinkle with flour. Grease and flour a flat baking tray and sit the flan ring on top. Roll the pastry out on a floured work surface to about 3mm thick, carefully drape over the flan ring and push the pastry into the edges for a neat finish. Allow some pastry to overhang the edge of the ring. Put the tart case in the freezer for 10 minutes. Line the case with baking paper and beans or rice and bake for 15 minutes. Remove the case from the oven, carefully remove the paper containing the beans – they will be very hot – and use a fork to prick small holes all over the base of the case. Return it to the oven and bake until cooked through and golden brown (about 5-10 minutes). Remove from the oven, brush all over with the egg and set aside. Turn the oven down to 120C.

In a large bowl, whisk together the eggs and sugar until pale. Put the cream in a saucepan, split the vanilla pod and add the seeds. Bring to the boil and pour immediately over the eggs and sugar, whisking all the time until mixed. Place the tart case in the oven, fill with the custard and generously grate the fresh nutmeg over. Bake for 35 minutes and have a look at the tart. It may need more time. You will know it's ready when the filling is wobbly without being runny. Set aside to cool. Use a small serrated knife to carefully trim the excess pastry from the edge of the flan ring. Gently remove the ring and cut the tart with a hot knife into the desired amount of portions.

Rhubarb Garnish

First, make a sugar stock by boiling the sugar and water. Allow cooling.
Cut the rhubarb sticks into 5cm batons. Thinly slice into fine strips, using a mandolin if you have one. Put these in the cooled sugar stock to macerate for 2 hours. When ready to use, carefully drain the rhubarb strips on a kitchen towel.

Mini Meringues

Place the egg whites in a stand-mixer and whisk on full gradually adding half the sugar. Whisk until the eggs whites are firm and smooth. Then fold in the other half of the sugar. Put the meringue in a piping bag fit with a small round nozzle.
On a baking sheet lined with kitchen paper, pipe out spiked dots of the meringue – each about the size of a 5p coin.
Place in the oven (make sure the fan is not on if it has one) and allow to gently set overnight. If possible, leave the oven door ajar – this will allow the meringues to dry our evenly without colouring. Once cooled, store in an airtight container until needed.

Granola

Preheat the oven to 160°C. Mix the oil, maple syrup, honey and vanilla in a large bowl. Mix in the oats and a pinch of salt. Spread the mix evenly on a large baking sheet and cook for 20-30 minutes until golden – make sure to check and stir the mix every 5-7 minutes. Allow to cool and store in an airtight container.

Rhubarb Sorbet

In a glass bowl, mix the sugar and rhubarb together, cover with cling film and allow to macerate overnight in the refrigerator. The next day, strain the liquid through a fine sieve and keep both the pulp and the rhubarb syrup.
Note: Before the next stage, carefully read the instructions of the stabilizer you have bought. If it requires heating, make sure to heat it with a small amount of rhubarb syrup – otherwise the sorbet may lose its bright, fresh colour.
Put the rhubarb pulp, glucose, water and vitamin C in a saucepan and simmer gently until soft. Remove from the heat and when cool, mix in the rhubarb syrup. Blend in a food processor until very smooth. Churn in an ice-cream churner and freeze for at least 8 hours.

THE BATH PRIORY

BIOGRAPHY

Executive Chef, Sam Moody, offers a memorable culinary journey with a focus on fresh local produce, flavour and balance to create exciting, modern British dishes epitomising the best seasonal dining. Complemented by an exemplary wine cellar and exceptional insight from our Head Sommelier we ensure every detail of your dining experience is perfectly paired.

Sam continues to hold a Michelin star for The Bath Priory, adding it to other awards won during his time at The Bath Priory, notably an Acorn Award in 2011 and in 2013, the Hotel Catey award for Chef of the Year.

Sam's food is simple, with a huge focus on fresh produce, flavour and balance. He loves developing young chefs and works closely with Bath City College helping to inspire the next generation of chefs.

Sam declares that restaurants and food are his life and that he loves eating out. And then of course, there's always the fishing...

Bitter Chocolate Ginger Snap

INGREDIENTS

Earl grey tea ice cream
Chocolate and tea ganache
Ginger snap biscuit
5x dots Ginger butterscotch
5x Iced tea jelly
Earl grey tea ice cream
(crumb ginger bread as glue)

Tea Ganache,
14 portions
400g milk
50g earl grey
300g jivara (40%) chocolate
350g 811, (54%) callebaut
50g butter

Ginger snap Biscuit.
135g butter
315g sugar
90g Gold syrup
180g plain flour
12g ground ginger
2 tsp bicarb

Ginger butterscotch
100g caster sugar
25g water
50g glucose
250g double cream
40g fresh ginger, chopped small
Juice of ½ a lime

Tea jelly
250g water
50g Earl grey tea
50g stock syrup (50/50water/ sugar)
20g ginger, micro plane
8g gelatine, soaked

Earl Grey ice cream
500g FF Milk
25g Loose leaf EGTea
100gCream
25gr Milk powder
100g egg yolks
100gr Sugar

METHOD

Bring to a simmer, cover with cling film, infuse 15minutes, pass

Bring milk up to a simmer, remove heat, add chocolate, whisk. Place whole mix into robot coupe, make emulsion. 2-3minute or until silky smooth

Line 21/ 29cm tray with silicon paper, pour in ganache, set 24hr, cut into 14 rectangles, 3/11cm it should be 1cm deep. Frozen grated Guanaja chocolate (70%) to coat the ganache before serving

Ginger snap Biscuit.

Cream butter and sugar together until white light and fluffy,
Add the golden syrup, add the dry ingredient, beat well.
Rest, roll into sheets between backing paper, cut into 3/11cm rectangles,
Place on silpat mat, rest,
Bake at 160c 8 minute, trim with a serrated knife to sharped edges

Ginger butterscotch

Bring the cream to the boil with the ginger, infuse
Place sugar water and glucose into a large pan, cook to a dark caramel,
CARFULLY add the creamto the sugar,
Strain, add lime juice, cool
Keeps very well

Tea jelly
250g water
Soak gelatine and set aside, bring all other ingredients to a simmer, cling film and infuse, 10 minutes
Weight 300g of liquid, dissolve gelatine into the warm liquid
Set, 3hrs, then cut into small cubes

Earl Grey ice cream

Bring the milk, milk powder and tea to the boil and leave to infuse for 15 minutes.
Beat egg and sugar, Cook anglaise to 83c, pass, rapid cool, churn.

SAUNTON SANDS HOTEL

BIOGRAPHY

Dez Turland
Group Development Chef Brend Hotels/Saunton Sands

Dez started in London with jobs at the Law Courts and a Private Hospital on Baker Street, followed by 2 years at Ritz Hotel. This was followed by spells at the Michelin rated Terrace Restaurant at the NEC, Birmingham before helping to open The Alverton Manor, a country house hotel in Truro, Cornwall. In 1990, he became Head Chef at The Greenbank Hotel, Falmouth which quickly gained recognition and was awarded its first AA Rosette.

The next role saw him taking over at The Royal Duchy Hotel, Falmouth quickly helping achieve their 4 Star status as well as being awarded 2 AA Rosettes. Keen to progress Dez then took on the role of Group Development Chef for Brend Hotels in charge of 11 hotels before moving to North Devon to oversee all kitchen operations at Saunton Sands Hotel.

A keen competition competitor Dez has been BCF Chef of the Year finalist 2010 2012 2014 and semi finalist in CGOC National Chef of the Year 2010 2011 2012 2013 as well as various other competitions.

Main objective is to make sure Saunton Sands & Brend Hotels become a nationally recognised name, where chefs will receive first class training, using the finest ingredients possible, whilst always wherever possible supporting the South West and it's superb producers & products.

Salted Caramel & Hazelnut Tart

INGREDIENTS

Sweet Pastry

450g Plain flour

175g Icing sugar

75g Ground hazelnuts

4g Salt

250g Unsalted butter

100g Eggs

Salted Hazelnut Caramel Filling

250g Caster sugar

100ml Frangelico

1l Double cream

10g Salt

100g Muscovado sugar

300g Egg yolk

Banana & Condensed Milk Ice Cream

200g Condensed milk

200g Banana puree

400ml F/F Milk

100ml Double cream

6 Egg yolks

75g Caster sugar

75g Horlicks

METHOD

For the Pastry

Beat sugar & butter until soft add eggs slowly, then carefully fold in flour, salt & ground hazelnuts, wrap in cling film and allow to rest.

Line 8″ flan ring with pastry, then cling film and fill with baking beans. Cook for 20 minutes at 175°c then remove cling film and beans and brush with egg yolk, place back in the oven for 5 minutes.

For the Filling

Place caster sugar in a pan over a high heat. As soon as the caramel achieves a rich hazelnut colour, add the Frangelico.

Pour in cream and whisk, then add the salt, allow to cool.

Beat the muscovado sugar & egg yolks in a bowl, then add the caramel cream and whisk to combine.

Reduce the heat to 110°C and bake for 40 minutes.

Banana & Condensed Milk Ice Cream

Boil condensed milk for 5 hours in the tin.

Place condensed milk, milk and cream in a pan and bring to the boil. Whisk the sugar, yolks and milk powder until smooth.

Add cream mix to egg yolks, pour back into the pan and cook to 75°c.

Pass through a fine sieve, set aside to cool add the banana puree then churn in an ice cream maker.

ORMER RESTAURANT

BIOGRAPHY

Michelin starred chef Shaun Rankin is a renowned published chef with TV accolades and a passion for the fresh produce of the Channel Islands where he resides.

Shaun has spent the majority of his career in Jersey, Channel Islands. He spent eight years at prestigious Relais & Chateaux Hotel Longueville Manor, followed by the establishment's sister restaurant Sumas. He then opened Bohemia restaurant as head chef in 2003 and gained his first Michelin star in 2005.

In 2009 Shaun represented the southwest in the fourth series of BBC Two's Great British Menu. His winning dish was Treacle Tart with Jersey clotted cream and raspberry ripple coulis. Since appearing on national TV he has also made many further appearances on popular cookery show Saturday Kitchen.

Shaun left his post at Bohemia in January 2013 after nine years at the helm to focus on his own venture. In May 2013 he opened the highly-anticipated 'Ormer' restaurant bringing a sophisticated restaurant, bars and private dining venue to the centre of St Helier, Jersey. The restaurant is commended in the Good Food Guide 2014 and received its first Michelin star in September 2014. In January 2014 Ormer was additionally accredited with 3 AA rosettes later on in the year the business was named 'Best Newcomer' at the coveted Food and Travel Magazine Awards 2014.

In December 2013 Shaun opened his own delicatessen 'Don Street Deli' adjacent to the acclaimed restaurant Ormer. The Deli offers

luxury retail products sourced from all over Europe and fresh artisan food offerings.

In December 2014 Shaun was selected to manage the food and beverage offering of elite members club 12 Hay Hill in London Mayfair. The new breed of club is due to open in Spring 2015 and will provide the international business sector with a luxurious environment for social and business purposes. The establishment will include a high-end brasserie, deli style dining in the basement bar and a light menu for al-fresco dining on the spectacular terrace overlooking Berkeley Square.

Chocolate Popcorn Brownie
recipe taken from the ormer restaurant by Shaun Rankin menu

INGREDIENTS

(LAYER 1) Brownie Base

2 Eggs

175g Caster sugar

240g Park chocolate

150g Unsalted butter

1 Vanilla pod

20g of Cocoa powder

60g of Plain flour

2 tsp Baking powder

100g Roughly chopped dark chocolate

50g Sweet popcorn

(LAYER 2) Caramel

400g of Toffee

50ml of Double cream

(LAYER 3) Middle

300g Dark chocolate

4 Egg yolks

125g Sugar

90g Water

300g Double cream

100g Milk

(LAYER 4) Glaze

8g Bronze leaf gelatine

140g Whipping cream

35g Water

210g Sugar

70g Cocoa powder

METHOD

Tin
30cm x 25cm x 6cm deep tin lined with greaseproof paper.

(LAYER 1) Brownie Base

Whisk eggs and sugar together until light and fluffy.
Melt the butter, dark chocolate and vanilla seeds together.
Then mix into the egg mixture.
Sieve in the cocoa powder, plain flour and baking powder and fold into the mixture.
Mix in chopped chocolate and popcorn.
Place in lined cake tin and bake at 180 degrees C. for 18 minutes.
Leave to cool in tin.

(LAYER 2) Caramel

Slowly melt the toffee in a pan with the cream then pour over cooked base.

(LAYER 3) Middle

Boil water and sugar to 116 degrees C. using a thermometer.
Whisk the yolks in a mixer, when the mixture has doubled in size pour in the hot sugar mixture.
Melt the chocolate in a pan then fold into the egg mixture.
Whisk the cream and milk to soft peaks then fold into the rest of the mixture.
Pour over the base of the caramel then leave to set in the fridge.

(LAYER 4) Glaze

Soften the gelatine in cold water in a sauce pan.
Boil the other ingredients then stir in the gelatine.
Leave to cool to room temperature then pour over the brownie.
Leave to set in the fridge or at least 3 hours.

The last of a dying breed

Johnny Pusztai – Butchery.

Johnny Pusztai, Nottingham's famous butcher, was born into a family with a great respect and love for food, his father moved here from Hungary in 1956. Coming from a country where every day it was a struggle just to get a loaf of bread, Mr Pusztai senior was astounded by the abundance of fresh locally sourced produce. Back then there wasn't supermarkets filled from top to bottom with produce shipped from everywhere but the local farmers, everything was local, fresh and was sold by someone who was passionate about their trade. The family enjoyed going to a local butchers and finding out where the meats came from, learning about who grew their fresh vegetables and what coast the local fishmonger had fished that week. Although they now had access to all this produce the family still to this day maintains the ethos of not wasting anything.

At the tender age of 12 Johnny begged George Beedham and Bill Robinson (of JT Beedhams) for a job. He was rejected time and time again, but he persevered, eventually taking the place as the Butchers delivery boy. He was desperate to pursue this butchery career so even though his bike was far too big for him and his hours were long and tiring he didn't give up. This is something he believes is the ground work for any career and his apprentices often show the same amount of commitment as he did. Even now some of his regulars remember that young boy on the too big bike doing the very best he could and loving every minute of it.

Eventually Johnny made it into the shop, but still he had to show his dedication, at the beginning his career he spent all his time cleaning, making teas, in fact he did just about anything but touch any of the meat in the shop. The JT Beedhams company moto is 'don't just do it right, do it to the best of your ability.' A moto Johnny still lives by to this day. This training clearly hasn't gone to waste as even to this day if the shop is busy Johnny will make the tea and clean the toilets, as will his apprentices for at least the first 6 months of their time in the shop.

At 14, he was finally able to test his Butchery skills, he began by making his first ever sausages, something he still considers to be his favorite part of the job today. Although at the time JT Beedhams only supplied one sausage 'Beedhams old Original', which is still a best seller. This sparked Johnny's creativity within the trade and the shop now stocks almost 50 different unusual and experimental flavours of sausage, many of which have won awards.

Because sausage making is how Johnny started out, this is where his apprentices begin to, many come up with new flavours and all of them are tried and tested. Many don't work but to Johnny this is an important part of the shops tradition and apprentice initiation.

At 16 Johnny became the official apprentice at JT Beedhams, a dream come true for him. He learnt everything he knows from butchery duo George Beedham and Bill Robinson with over 100 years' experience between them he couldn't have asked for better mentors. He is now passing on what he learnt to a new generation of butchers, something that can only happen if they continue to receive custom and stay in business. There used to be 4 butchers in Sherwood, JT Beedhams is the last one. This is the case in towns all over the UK, 20 years ago there were around 30,000 butchers now we are down to just 6,000, it's a traditional British trade is being lost.

The facts about Butchers are; you know that the meat will be of a finest quality as the business depends on it, the animals that the meat comes from will have led a very happy life and that life will have been ended humanely, and most importantly the sausages, burgers and other produce you buy will be exactly what it says on the tin, so to speak.

If you are still unsure you can go to any local butchers and ask them about their products, where it comes from and how it was made, they will be able to answer all these questions and more. If you have no other option but the supermarket then there are a number of things you should look out for, if the packet contains water or blood, leave it behind the animal has not been hung properly and so you will be paying for bad meat and lots of water weight. Also if the meat appears to have small red flecks like freckles it most likely means that the animal it came from was distressed during or just before its slaughter, unhappy animal makes for bad meat.

One of the biggest struggles of butchers today is to use all the produce they rear and slaughter, there is an old saying among butchers 'Every part of a pig can be used except for the squeal' but today unfortunately it is so hard to persuade the general population to eat brains on toast, or to boil up pigs feet and make homemade stock, or the 1950's favorite, tripe, which has fallen far out of favour. These have slowly become less appetizing as food has become more processed and less natural. In fact it has got to the point now where sausages are so processed they no longer taste of meat, sausages from a butchers will taste like their contents, rich pork and onion or luxurious beef and tomato.

To Johnny the most important part of butchery is the legacy left behind, at his shows he always get the children and young people in the audience involved. To him they are the most important people there, they want to learn about food and where it comes from. 'I do tell the children at my show that the meat they are making into burgers is an animal, I do tell them they are slaughtered, they need to know that information.' Through his "Burger Challenges" Johnny not only discusses the meat process he also goes through the seasonings and how they enhance the flavour, he also talks about the history behind burgers. He is truly honest about the meat and it's lifecycle as it is so important to capture children with a passion for food to keep the future of food trades alive.

The main argument the general population makes against Butchers is the price, the price of meat from a butchers may be a few pennies more, but as Johnny often shows at his kitchen demos, one good chicken can feed two for 5 days. Chicken breasts from a good chicken can easily make 2 meals, a spicy homemade curry or crunchy goujons. 2 wings and two legs can be added to a rich slow cooked stew until they are tender and fall off the bone. Then you have 2 thighs which again could be used for curry or stew or stir fry and lastly the flavourful carcass which can be used to make a delicious warming soups or stocks. That's 5 meals from one bird and not a single part of the precious meat is wasted.

South East

Starter
Main
Dessert

TERRE À TERRE

BIOGRAPHY

Over twenty years ago, long before vegetarianism became fashionable Amanda Powley and Philip Taylor, The pioneering business partners of Terre à Terre embarked upon a venture that would change the face of British gastronomy. Terre à Terre restaurant was founded as a 28 seat café and quickly evolved into a 110 cover culinary destination restaurant breaking the mould and confounding preconceived ideas about vegetarian food.

Matty Bowling joined the team after years of working oversees and then in London. Within a couple of years he worked his way up to Head Chef. A firm believer that there are no limits to what the humble vegetable, root, fungi, seed, herb, flower, fruit and nut can deliver, inspired by all around him and his journey from New Zealand to the UK he leads a large team of chefs to produce a menu that celebrates all things Brighton beautiful.

Terre à Terre is all about indulgence rather than abstinence. It has been feeding loyal customers and international visitors for more than 20 years. Diners enjoy a culinary experience like no other, with intense flavours, sublime textures and a mixture of ingredients that few have the imagination or would dare to compose. Put simply, Terre à Terre serves a symphony of harmonic flavours.

Bangkok Broken Balls

INGREDIENTS

Pistachio puree
300g Pistachios
90g Vegetable oil
15g Olive oil
120g Water
50g Lemon juice
Sea salt to season

Thai Red Curry Paste
3 tbsp Lemon grass (sliced)
3 tbsp Galangal (diced)
3 tbsp Lime rind (zest)
4 tbsp Red shallot (diced)
4 Garlic cloves
2 Peppercorns
0.5 tbsp grated Nutmeg
3 Cloves
3 Long dry red chillies
3 tsp Coriander seeds
2 tsp Cumin seeds
1 Star anise
500 mls Coconut milk
4 Kaffir leaves

Rice balls
100g Basmati rice
100g Sushi rice
100g Thai red curry paste
70g grated Coconut
10g fresh diced Chilli
20g fresh Coriander

Lemon oil
70 mls Extra virgin olive oil
30 mls Lemon Oil

To Build
8 tbls Pickled lotus root
fine diced (available at
Asian supermarkets or
substitute with any Asian
pickle)
8 tbls Sundried tomato fine
diced
8 tbls Pomelo diced
8 tbls Firm tofu diced
40g Peanuts
8 Large crisp washed Baby
gem leaves

METHOD

Pistachio puree
Puree pistachio and vegetable oil in a blender until smooth.

Transfer to a large bowl. Add olive oil, water, Lemon Juice and season.

Thai Red Curry Paste
Make Red Curry Paste by blending all ingredients other than coconut milk and kaffir leaves until smooth, heat a small amount of oil in heavy based sauce pan and cook out the paste for 15 minutes.

Add coconut milk and kaffir lime leaves and simmer for 20 minutes. Once cooked take off heat and leave to cool. The mixture will not thicken when cooking but will thicken slightly when cooled (You can freeze remaining curry paste)

Rice balls
Bring the rice and 1ltr of water to boil, immediately turn down the heat to low and cover with a lid.

Leave for 12 minutes or till rice becomes soft and all the liquid has been absorbed.

Once cool combine with the remaining ingredients and season with salt and pepper. Roll to 50 gram balls.

Lemon oil
Mix lemon and extra virgin olive oil together. This will make a little more than needed but is great to add a teaspoon to any dish.

To Build
Heat 2 cups of vegetable oil to 180 degrees

Place four 50 gram balls of the rice mix in the hot oil (careful it may spit),Place each serving once browned (about 3 minutes) on an oil absorbent cloth.

Overlap two baby gem leaves per serving to make a taco shape.

Brush a thick layer of pistachio puree onto the leaves. Then neatly at the top half of the leaf place baby spinach and green shiso leaf.

Place 2 tablespoons of pickled lotus, Tomato, Pomelo, Firm Tofu and 1tsp salted peanuts on each of the baby gem leaf.

Tear each of the 15 gram cooked rice ball over the baby gem leaf. Repeat with remaining 3 rice balls over the remaining 3 baby gem tacos.

Spoon the lemon oil mix throughout each taco, season with salt. Finish with micro coriander and micro Thai basil.

THE WHITE HART

BIOGRAPHY

The White Hart – named a "foodies paradise" by the Oxford Times and winner of the coveted Restaurant of the Year Award at the Oxfordshire Restaurant Awards, is a favourite with locals and foodies from far and wide. Set in the picturesque village of Fyfield, The White Hart is the ultimate country pub, offering one of the finest dining experiences in the county. Housed in a stunning 15th century chantry, customers can choose to eat under the soaring eaves of the great hall, up high in the minstrel's gallery or in the cosy bar by the fire.

This is self-taught chef Mark Chandler's eleventh year at the White Hart, where he has thrived, cooking up imaginative dishes and winning a long list of well deserved awards and accolades. Since buying the White Hart and being unexpectedly propelled into the kitchen, cooking has become a real professional passion for this creative all-rounder, who holds two rosettes for culinary excellence and boasts of royal visits from Prince Harry and former American President Carter (along with all 35 of his armed bodyguards!). Mark's style reflects modern British cooking, incorporating produce from the restaurant's large kitchen garden, local woods and rivers and produce swapped with the villagers!

Rabbit, Pistachio and Apricot Terrine
with pickles

INGREDIENTS

2 farmed Rabbits

50ml Port

50ml Brandy

Mirepoix (1 medium onion, 1 carrot, 1 leek, 2 sticks of celery, all roughly chopped)

1L good Chicken stock

100g dried Apricots

Tsp Caster sugar

50ml Marsala

½ bunch Tarragon

150g Green pistachios, toasted

French mustard

Olive oil

Garnish

Crusty bread

Pickles (capers, cornichons, baby silver skin onions, caper berries)

METHOD

Remove the kidneys, liver and heart from the rabbits (or ask your butcher!). Marinate in the port and brandy and refrigerate.

To make the rabbit "bacon", remove the rabbit bellies and place on a plastic tray. Salt generously and refrigerate for 4 hours, or overnight.

Place the remaining rabbit carcasses in a snug-fitting casserole dish with the mirepoix and just cover with the chicken stock. Cover and cook at 150C for 2-3 hours, until tender. Remove the rabbits and allow to cool slightly before picking the meat from the carcasses, taking care to remove ALL the bones. Pass the remaining stock in the casserole dish through a fine-mesh sieve or muslin, into a clean pan. Bring to the boil and reduce until you have about 200ml, skimming frequently. Reserve.

Place the apricots in a bowl, add a good pinch of sugar, the Marsala and just cover with boiling water.

Rinse the rabbit bacon of salt and pat dry. Heat a frying pan over a high heat, then fry the bacon in a little olive oil until golden on both sides. Reserve until cool, then finely slice.

Remove the kidneys, liver and heart from the marinade, pat dry, then fry briefly until pink (use the frying pan from the rabbit bacon). Take care not to overcook.

Slice the kidneys and hearts in halves, and the livers in 2-3 pieces (depending on size). Add to the rabbit meat along with the sliced rabbit bacon, drained apricots, 50g pistachios, tarragon and the reduced stock. Season. Place 2 layers of cling film lengthways and place the rabbit mix in the centre. Roll the mix in the cling film to form a sausage about 10cm in diameter and tie both ends. Refrigerate for 4-6 hours, or overnight, until set.

Blitz the remaining 100g of pistachios in a food processor, to form a crumb.

Once set, remove the terrine from the cling film and brush all over with French mustard and roll in the pistachio crumb.

To serve, slice the terrine and serve with pickles and crusty bread.

64 DEGREES

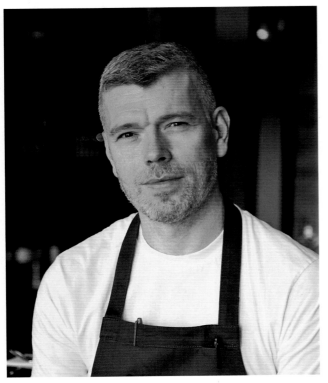

BIOGRAPHY

Chef owner Michael Bremner began his career at the Pittodrie House Hotel in Aberdeenshire, Scotland. Once qualified he spent three years working in London to gain pastry experience working in kitchens at The Orrery and Quo Vadis.

He then spent a few years travelling and working in different countries, including Australia and Canada. On his return to the UK in 2007 Michael became Head Chef at Due South restaurant in Brighton before undertaking his first business venture, 64 Degrees, which opened in October 2013 and has attained countless positive reviews both locally and nationally.

At 64 Degrees the 22 seater, open kitchen restaurant has the philosophy that the food rules; the kitchen is the heart of the restaurant, the chefs are the lifeblood and centre of all the action.

Since opening nearly three years ago 64 Degrees has been voted in the top 100 of the National Restaurant Awards three years in a row, obtained a Bib Gourmand from the Michelin Guide as well as being voted Best Restaurant in both the Brighton and Hove Food and Drink Awards and The Brighton Top 20 Awards. Michael also won Best Chef at the Brighton Top 20 Awards.

The team aim to build on the progress they have made since opening and are continually pushing to improve the standards they set under Michael and his Head Chef, Sam Lambert.

#Prephardcatereasy

Kohlrabi Rounds
goats cheese mousse, watercress puree, walnut crumb

INGREDIENTS

Kohlrabi Rounds

1 x Kohlrabi

50g Table salt

Goats' Cheese Mousse:

225g Golden Cross goats' cheese (room temp)

100ml Double cream

Watercress Puree:

2 x Bunch Watercress (outer shoots – save inner shoots for plating)

1 x Medium Onion

100g Spinach

Table Salt

100ml Double cream

Walnut Crumb

50g Walnuts

Walnut oil to dress

METHOD

Kohlrabi Rounds:

Peel kohlrabi, slice to 2mm rounds on mandolin (watch your fingers – use the palm of your hand with fingers pointing up).

Lay out rounds individually on lipped tray and salt liberally. Leave for one hour or until kohlrabi is soft to the touch.

Rinse the rounds thoroughly to wash off the salt, pat dry and then set aside until plating.

Goats' Cheese Mousse:

Put all ingredients in food processor and blend until you have a thick and smooth mousse.

Transfer to bowl and leave in fridge until needed.

Remove from fridge 10 minutes before plating.

Watercress Puree:

Pick watercress leaves from the thick stems.

Rinse in cold salted water to remove any dirt before blanching in boiling water for 30 seconds and refresh in cold water.

Pat dry and leave to one side.

Repeat this process for the spinach.

Dice the onion and sweat off on a low heat so as not to add colour. Make sure these are still hot when blending.

Heat the cream (but not to the boil) before adding to blend.

Add all ingredients bar the cream into food processor and begin to blend. Add the cream slowly while mixing until a silky smooth, thick consistency is reached (you may not need all the cream).

Cool the mix quickly by putting in a bowl and submerging in an ice bath.

Walnut Crumb:

Put all the walnuts on a baking tray and bake at 200°C for 5 minutes or until dark brown.

Remove from oven and leave to cool before giving them a rough chop.

To Plate:

On a clean work surface lay out kohlrabi rounds (six per person). Add a teaspoon of the goats' cheese mousse to the centre of each round and fold over to make a half-moon crescent before placing them on a large dinner plate in a scattered formation.

Dress the parcels with walnut oil before dotting each with the watercress puree.

Add the walnut crumb with a spoon in the spaces between the rounds.

Garnish with the inner buds of the watercress.

THE AMPHORA SUITE

BIOGRAPHY

A Master Chef of Great Britain, Paul is an award winning chef whose titles include Essex Chef of the Year as well as Essex Restaurant of the Year amongst many others. He is inspired by England's 'natural larder' as, he says, it offers quite probably the most varied range of ingredients available to a discerning cook.

Paul is dedicated to bringing you healthy, local ingredients and refined cooking – with passion, good humour and a painstaking attention to detail. He's interested in the Best of British – and by that he means no European twist, no fusion; no global menu. He simply wants you to enjoy good local food at its very best.

Using a range of modern cooking techniques, Paul has produced some of the finest and most interesting dishes in Essex – this combination of new methods, love and dedication means that banqueting at The Amphora Suite is an exciting and essential art of the guest's experience.

Specialising in bespoke weddings and events, The Amphora Suite is a venue of choice for the discerning clients of North Essex. Set in the grounds of a leading 18 hole golf club it caters to its clients' needs, from small breakfast clubs for the networking business people of Colchester to luxurious weddings and events seating up to 150 people. The focus of attention is always the guest.

Compressed Melon
tomato bread, jamon with tahoon cress

INGREDIENTS

For the Tomato Consommé

1.5kg dark red, over-ripe Tomatoes, coarsely chopped

5 Celery sticks, chopped

1 large Shallots, finely chopped

1 Garlic clove, thinly sliced

pinch Salt

For the Tomato Seed Jelly

1000g Tomato consommé

10g Agar agar

Smoked maldon salt

Konbu dashi powder

Cider vinegar

Tomato seed fillets from 5 tomatoes

METHOD

For the Tomato Consommé

For the consommé, put all the ingredients in a blender. Purée, then pour into a very fine muslin sieve placed over a bowl. Leave to strain overnight in the fridge.

For the Tomato Seed Jelly

Blend the agar with the tomato consommé and bring to the boil. Simmer for 3 minutes, then pour into a shallow tray and refrigerate. When the consommé has solidified, cut into small pieces and blend, ideally in a bar blender for at least 5 minutes to ensure it is completely smooth. Season with Smoked Maldon Salt, Konbu Dashi powder (umami) and Aspalls Cider vinegar to taste. Remember that you will need to blend again to ensure thorough seasoning dispersal. Pass the tomato jelly through a sieve to remove any lumps.

Carefully remove the 4 tomato seed fillets from the tomatoes with a small spoon taking care not to damage them. Add enough of the jelly to the seed to suspend the seed in the jelly.

For the Tomato Snow

Freeze the remainder of the tomato jelly in a shallow tray. When frozen, break up with a fork as for a granita.

Compressed Melon

Trim the watermelon of all rind and cut into pieces approximately 2cm x 3cm x 6cm. Place melon, with rind off in a vacuum packing bag with some soft thyme leaves wrapped in cling film. Vacuum on high for as long as your machine will allow, and refrigerate overnight. If you don't have a vacuum packing machine, then you can still use the straight forward melon. It just won't have quite the same texture or flavour notes.
To serve, cut into triangles and season with Maldon Salt.

Tomato Bread Shards

Slice a loaf of sundried tomato bread as thinly as possible, a slicing machine is best. Place the slices on to a tray with greaseproof paper, and dry the bread slices in a low oven until crisp. Break into shards to serve.

Jamon Iberico Slices

Ensure the slices of ham are at room temperature.

Tahoon Cress to serve

Arrange the seasoned melon on the serving plate, resting the tomato bread shards in between. Dot the jelly around, and arrange the room temperature Jamon Iberico on the plate. Finish up with the tomato snow, and garnish with Tahoon cress.

WHATLEY MANOR HOTEL & SPA

BIOGRAPHY

Martin Burge began his career at the Royal Crescent Hotel in Bath with Michael Croft, who was Head Chef at the time. His first taste of a Michelin star establishment was at Pied à Terre under the watchful eye of Richard Neat and the proprietor, David Moore. The opportunity to work with Raymond Blanc at 'Le Manoir aux Quat' Saisons' beckoned and Martin worked his way up to the position of Sous Chef. Martin then met John Burton Race whilst working at 'Le Manoir aux Quat Saisons' and he went to work with Burton-Race at L'Ortolan as Senior Sous Chef where he was soon promoted to Head Chef at the age of 27. Burton Race decided to move his restaurant to 'The Landmark Hotel', Marylebone, London. They successfully retained the accolades and achieved two Michelin stars in just one year. In 2003 Martin left London for the opening of Whatley Manor in Wiltshire. Here he oversees both the fine dining restaurant – The Dining Room and the brasserie style restaurant, 'Le Mazot'. Martin has achieved numerous accolades, attaining his first Michelin star in January 2005. In September 2008 the AA awarded 'The Dining Room' four AA rosettes and in January 2009 Michelin awarded Burge a second star for his acclaimed cuisine. In August 2010 The Good Food Guide recognises The Dining Room in the top 20 restaurants in the UK.

Roasted Langoustine Tails
with caramelised bacon and soy reduction

INGREDIENTS

Soy glaze and reduction
250ml Ketchup Manis
6g Lemongrass
6g peeled Ginger
1.5g Garlic
1 Red chilli

Cauliflower puree
250g Cauliflower "finely chopped"
65g Whipping cream
25g Butter
0.5g White pepper
1.25g Salt

Langoustine Thai foam
1.250 Langoustine stock
15g Lemongrass
10g Ginger
2g Chilli
125g Milk
7g Stock syrup
Lemon to taste
Salt / pepper

Garnish for the dish
6 Baby onions
30g Butter
100g Cauliflower
5g Olive oil
Salt and pepper
10g Sesame seeds

METHOD

Set up a deep pan of boiling water and a bowl of iced water ready to cook your langoustines. Prepare the langoustines by tearing the tails from the heads and removing the entrails by twisting the bottom part of the tail.

Plunge the tails into boiling water for 30 seconds and then into ice water to cool down quickly. Peel the shells carefully away from the tails but leave the end part for presentation.
Set aside in the fridge on kitchen paper ready to cook later

Soy glaze and reduction
Chop the lemon grass, peeled ginger, red chilli and garlic into fine pieces. Mix the Ketchup Manis and all the finely chopped ingredients together and place into a small pan.
Place the pan on a low heat and warm it to around 50 degrees and then set aside to infuse for one hour.
Pass through a fine sieve and store in the fridge in a plastic squeezey bottle ready to use. This can be made well in advance and stored in the fridge before using it.

Cauliflower puree
Place the finely chopped cauliflower into a steamer and cook on a high heat until soft in texture. Depending on how fine you cut the cauliflower this should be a quick process to retain flavour and nutritional value.
Place the cooked cauliflower into the liquidizer with the cream, butter and seasoning and blend until very smooth.
Pass through a fine sieve and cool it down quickly over a bowl of ice before storing in the fridge until needed.

Langoustine Thai foam
Set up the food processor and blend the lemon grass, ginger and chilli to form a Thai paste and then divide this into two equal parts.
Place the langoustine stock into a pan with half the Thai paste and reduce over a moderate heat by 50 percent. Strain the reduced stock through a fine sieve into a smaller pan and add the second part of the paste and reduce by a further 50 percent. You should now have around 300ml of stock remaining. Strain through a fine

sieve once again then add the milk, stock syrup, seasoning and lemon to taste and set aside to cool and then store in the fridge ready to use later.

Garnish for the dish
Peel and cut the baby onions into halves and cook gently in foaming butter with salt and pepper until golden brown and soft in texture. Slice the cauliflower very thinly with a mandolin or a very sharp knife and season with a little salt, pepper and olive oil.

Toast the sesame seeds under the grill until a light golden brown in colour.

To serve
Caramelise the bacon under the grill until golden brown. Brush with the soy glaze until the bacon becomes sticky and a glaze is formed. Gently heat up the cauliflower puree in a small pan and keep warm.

Take a frying pan on the stove and preheat in preparation to cook the langoustines. Heat up the Cauliflower Puree in a small pan and keep warm.

Heat up the Langoustine Thai foam in a small pan at around 60 degrees.

Season the langoustines with salt and pepper. Take the preheated hot frying pan fry the langoustines in the olive oil until golden brown on one side and then flip the tails over to the other side. Pull the pan off the heat and allow the residual heat from the pan to cook the tails through. Note this whole cooking process should be done quickly to prevent the langoustines over cooking.

Assemble the dish in the following sequence
Soy reduction stripe
Cauliflower puree
Sesame seed
Onions
Bacon
Langoustine tails
Cauliflower slices
Langoustine Thai foam

117

ASHDOWN PARK HOTEL

BIOGRAPHY

Ashdown Park Hotel & Country Club is a luxurious Country House Hotel set within 186 acres of stunning gardens and parkland at the heart of the Ashdown Forest in East Sussex. It offers a magnificent combination of elegance, style, award-winning dining and outstanding business and leisure facilities.

Andrew Wilson has been Executive Chef at the exclusive Ashdown Park Hotel & Country Club since 2011. He has worked in some of the country's most prestigious kitchens including Michelin starred 'The Capital Hotel' in London's Knightsbridge, where he was Executive Sous Chef to world-renowned Chef, Eric Chavot.

He then went on to become Head Chef to Steven Drake of 'Drakes Restaurant' in Ripley. Andrew has been involved with the Roux Scholarship, and was a finalist in 2007. He is also heavily involved with National Chef of the Year, and is a member of the Master Chefs of Great Britain as well as the Chaine des Rotisseurs worldwide.

Beef Wellington

INGREDIENTS

1kg 38 Day aged beef fillet centre cut (trimmed of all sinew and fat, ask your butcher to do this for you)

3 x Chicken breasts (skinless and boneless)

4 x Large field mushrooms

thyme

2 x Cloves garlic

100g x Butter

½ Bunch chervil (chopped)

500g x Double cream

150g x Plain flour

180g x Milk

2 x Whole eggs (one for egg wash and one for pancake batter)

A good quality all butter puff pastry

Salt and pepper

METHOD

The Beef Fillet

Season the beef with salt and pepper and leave to one side. In a heavy-bottom pan place a drizzle of olive oil and a small amount of unsalted butter. When the pan is hot, seal the beef fillet on all sides until it's golden then leave to rest and go cold.

The Mushrooms

Place the mushrooms in a tray with the butter, garlic and thyme and a touch of olive oil. Cover with kitchen foil and bake at 160°C for 15 minutes then leave to go cold. When the mushrooms have cooled down, dice them evenly into 3mm pieces, place them into kitchen towel and squeeze off any excess liquid. Leave to one side.

The Chicken Mousse

Cut the chicken into small, even pieces and place into a kitchen blender. Blitz until the chicken is a nice, smooth consistency then slowly add the cream, small amounts at a time. The mousse should be nice and creamy. Add your cold, diced mushrooms and the chopped chervil. Leave in the fridge until you are ready to assemble the wellington

The Pancakes

Place the milk, plain flour, whole egg and a touch of salt and pepper into a bowl and whisk together until a smooth batter is made. Place a non-stick 10 inch pan on the stove with a small amount of olive oil then ladle in some of the pancake batter making sure they are as thin as possible, the first one might stick, but be positive, the rest won't! You will need around 2-3 pancakes, then leave them to go cold.

ASSEMBLING THE BEEF WELLINGTON

Set your oven at 180°C. Make sure you have a tray lined with greaseproof paper ready to go.
Roll out your puff pastry 30cm (L) x 20cm (W). Place two of your pancakes on top of the pastry, slightly overlapping, making sure you trim the pancakes if required.

Place some of the chicken mousse down the centre of the pancakes, spread the mousse out to the width of the beef, about 3mm in depth, then place the beef fillet on top of the mousse. Cover the rest of the beef with the remainder of the mousse making sure it's even and well-covered.

Lift the pancakes and cover the mousse with them. Egg wash the puff pastry and wrap the beef in the pastry carefully. Egg wash the whole wellington with a touch of salt on the top and bake for 30-35 minutes.

To ensure it's cooked to perfection, probe the wellington in the centre after 30 minutes, it should be around 32°C, this will be cooked medium rare.

When cooked, remove from the oven and make a hole with a knife at each end to release the steam and leave to rest for 10 minutes, then slice and serve.

OCKENDEN MANOR

BIOGRAPHY

Stephen was born and lives in Sussex. Stephen joined to Historic Sussex Hotels in 1998 , first to The Spread Eagle and then to Ockenden Manor. Today, the Restaurant at Ockenden Manor is one of only three restaurants to hold a Michelin Star in West Sussex. It is the perfect setting for Stephen's menu that cleverly mixes innovation and tradition beautifully echoing Ockenden Manor. He continues to serve some of the finest food in southern England incorporating the freshest, locally sourced ingredients.

Home Smoked Duck Breast
waldorf salad, sauté foie gras

INGREDIENTS

For the duck

25g Rock salt

8 Juniper berries

2 tbspn Black peppercorns

1 springs Rosemary

2 tbspn Coriander seeds

2 Bay leaves

100g Rock salt

100g Demerara sugar

Confit Tomatoes

4 Baby plum tomatoes

20ml Extra virgin olive oil

3 sprigs Chopped thyme

½ Clove garlic, finely sliced

Salt

Apple Puree

2 Granny smith apples

50g Sugar

10ml Water

French Dressing

15g Dijon mustard

10g Wholegrain mustard

60ml Sherry vinegar

150ml Olive pomace oil

Cold water

Salt

Sugar

To finish

Celery leaves

Lambs lettuce

Apple batons

Celery batons

Chopped walnuts

50g Foie gras

METHOD

For the duck

Combine the spices and the rock salt and blend together in a thermomix until a fine dust, around three minutes. Then mix with the remaining rock salt and Demerara sugar. Line a container with the marinade and place on top your duck breast. Cover the top of the duck in the remaining marinade and place in the fridge; cling filmed, for 48 hours. Wash the marinade off and rinse the duck in running water for ten minutes to remove the salt. Place on a dry towel and pat off any moisture. Wrap the breast in muslin, tying at the top and bottom and place in the fridge for four days to air dry. Transfer to a smoker for six hours. The duck is now ready and can be sliced as thinly as possible with a sharp knife.

Confit Tomatoes

Take your baby plum tomatoes and score the top and bottom with a cross. Place into rapidly boiling water for five seconds and immediately transfer into a bowl of ice water. The skins should burst, allowing you to peel them easily. Once peeled, slice in half. Spread a thin layer of extra virgin olive oil onto a baking tray and cover with a few pinches of salt. Place the halved tomatoes on top and cover with more oil, salt, the chopped thyme and garlic. Place in the oven at 160 and cook for 4 minutes or until they start to feel soft to touch. Transfer to a smoker for 25 minutes before using.

Apple Puree

Peel and core the apples and dice roughly to ½ cm dice. Combine the sugar and water in a saucepan and place on a medium heat to bring to a smoky caramel. Add your apples and cook until broken and completely soft. Transfer to a blender and blend until smooth. Place in a container and cover with cling film until cool. Ensure it is cold before using.

Pickled Apple

Peel and core the apples and dice roughly to 1cm dice. Combine the sugar and water in a saucepan and place on a medium heat to bring to a smoky caramel. Add your apples and toss in the caramel until the edges start to soften. Add the white wine vinegar and toss into the apples. Take off the heat and allow to cool. Place onto a cloth to remove excess moisture before using.

French Dressing

Combine the mustards and vinegar in a bowl with a whisk. Slowly pour in the oil, always whisking until it is all used. Let down with a splash of cold water if the dressing is too thick. Season with salt and sugar to taste.

To finish

Combine the above ingredients with some of the French dressing to coat.

Sauté the foie gras in a hot pan for one minute either side until a golden crust is formed and the middle begins to soften. Season generously with salt.

BRAYE BEACH HOTEL

BIOGRAPHY

Head Chefs Stephen Scott and Glenn Smith of the Braye Beach Hotel have the perfect combination of skills and knowledge. Glenn has many years' experience working in a variety of award winning restaurants around Europe learning different styles and techniques. Stephen worked for the majority of his career at Galton Blackiston's Michelin star Morston Hall learning from the likes of Richard Bainbridge. Their careers have brought them to the Channel Islands on the beautiful island of Alderney.

They focus on what the island has to offer, from the sea to the beaches and fields. Picking home grown seasonal produce, meeting the local farmer and fishermen, foraging for wild foods and using their experience and passion to bring it all together on the plate.

Butter Poached Lobster
lobster tortellini, seaweed tartare, lobster sauce, confit potato, saute samphire and heirloom tomatoes

INGREDIENTS

Serves 2

Pasta

250g `00` Flour

10g Salt

1 Whole egg

6 Egg yolks

Olive oil

Lobster

500g Fresh (local) lobster

Pasta Filling

Lobster knuckles

1 tbsp Herbs

1 tsp Lemon

1 tbsp Mascarpone

Seasoning

Lobster Sauce

200ml White wine

600ml Quality fish stock

1 Lobster shell

1 Shallot, diced

30g Mushrooms, sliced

1 Clove garlic, crushed

1 tbsp Tomato paste

30ml Brandy

100ml Cream

30g Butter

Seasoning

Seaweed Tartare

20g Local seaweed

20g Capers

10g Shallot, diced

1 tbsp Olive oil

GARNISH

6 Large Jersey royals

300g Clarified butter

100g Picked samphire

100g Heirloom tomatoes

METHOD

Pasta
Sift flour and salt into food processor
Add eggs and pulse to form a crumb
Gradually add oil whilst kneading to form firm dough
Cling film and refrigerate for at least 2 hours

Lobster
Place lobster into a pan of seasoned boiling water, cover and cook for 4 minutes on high heat
Plunge into iced water
Once cooled, cut lobster in half lengthways, crack claws and knuckles, remove all meat
Set aside the meat and crush the shell of the lobster

Sauce
In a hot pan, add the white wine and reduce by half
Into the wine, add fish stock and the lobster shells, simmer for 20 minutes
In a separate pan, sweat the shallot, mushrooms and garlic
Add the tomato paste and brandy, cook out for several minutes
Strain the lobster stock into the shallot pan and discard the shells
Reduce by a quarter, add the cream and blend, finish by whisking in butter

Pasta Filling
Chop the lobster knuckles, add herbs, lemon juice, mascarpone and season

Making The Tortellini (or other desired shape)
Roll pasta dough gradually in a pasta machine going from widest setting to the penultimate setting
Cut circles using a medium sized ring
Place a small amount of lobster mix into the centre, egg wash the edges and fold in half ensuring no air is trapped inside
Egg wash the corners and bring together in the centre

Confit Potatoes
Peel and shape the potatoes
Heat clarified butter in a pan and add potatoes
Cook gently until soft, remove potatoes and reserve the butter

Seaweed Tartare
Roughly chop the seaweed and capers, add shallot and mix with olive oil

METHOD

Cook pasta for 3 minutes in boiling water
Warm the clarified butter and poach the lobster claw and tail
In a hot pan, add oil and sauté the samphire, potatoes and heirloom tomatoes
Warm the lobster sauce
Present using the tartare as a base to rest the lobster meat
Place the tortellini around the plate and lace the sauce within the gaps
Scatter the tomatoes, samphire and potatoes around the dish
Enjoy

GBI SEAFOOD RESTAURANT AT THE GRAND BRIGHTON

BIOGRAPHY

Alan White has been a chef for 30 years. He started his career at the Forest of Arden Country Club in the Midlands when he was still training at catering college and is now Executive Chef at 2 AA Rosette Seafood Restaurant GB1, at The Grand Brighton, where he has worked for over 11 years. Alan has worked in hotels and restaurants throughout his career, including the Midland Manchester, Selsdon Park, London and St. Pierre Park in Guernsey. He also worked at Castle Kitchens, a catering operation that offers aviation customers extraordinary restaurant style cuisine – that has been redesigned for the cabin at 40,000 feet. He also implemented a production kitchen whilst with the company, cooking 3,000 portions twice a week for Waitrose and also designed 21 dietary specific and special meals for Qantas Airlines.

GB1 opened in 2013 and quickly established itself as one of Brighton's most sought after culinary hotspots serving the freshest and finest of seafood sourced locally.

Provenance of ingredients is of particular importance to Alan and he holds a fantastic relationship with the local fish suppliers, where over 80% of the seafood served in GB1 is sourced from.

GB1's philosophy is quality with simplicity. Alan and his brigade of passionate and inventive chefs add a contemporary touch to classic British cuisine and seafood favourites. Standout menu items include the striking lobster burger and the king prawn pan-roasted fruit de mer platter, while seasonal additions include wonderful twists on retro classics such as the Neapolitan ice cream with pistachio crumb dessert. The seasonally changing menu also boasts meats from the grill such as the delectable Aberdeen Black rib-eye steak, classic Sussex favourites and vegetarian dishes.

Fusing a unique culinary vision with The Grand's tradition and new-age style, GB1 brings a dynamic energy to an iconic hotel and offers a variety of culinary experiences to suit any occasion.

Local Plaice & Shellfish
with Andre's puff pastry and beurre blanc

INGREDIENTS

75gm Belgian Puff Pastry
Specialists Maître André

1 Egg yolk

Salt and pepper

100gm Plaice filleted

1 Lobster claw

4 Mussels

3 Asparagus spears

1 Bulb fennel

50gm Squid

Lime segments

Peashoot tendrils

2 Clams

50ml White wine

Butter

Tomato concasse

METHOD

Cut 2 x 1cm strips of puff pastry and wrap around a greaseproof paper lined metal ring, glaze with the egg yolk, season with sea salt and cracked black pepper, bake until golden and fully cooked.

Prepare the plaice fillet and cut into two evenly sized pieces.

Prepare the squid and ensure it is clean cut into pieces and score with a sharp knife ensuring to not cut all the way through.

Poach the lobster claw in boiling water for 6 minutes. Remove from the shell ensuring to keep the meat intact.

Slice the fennel and blanch, finish in a hot pan with fresh butter to colour.

Peel and trim the asparagus and blanch in hot salted water and refresh.

Cross the tomatoes and blanch in boiling water for 10 seconds then place into cold water.

Remove from the water and skin, deseed and cut into small even dices.

Place the mussels and clams into a hot pan add the white wine and cover, steam until open. Remove the mussels and clams from the wine and bring the wine to the boil, whisk in cold diced butter to make a butter sauce.

Heat a pan with a little olive oil and pan fry the plaice fillet, squid and scallops, season well. Ensure not to over cook, needing just one minute on each side, then remove from the heat finishing with butter and a squeeze of fresh lime.

Warm back the mussels, clams, lobster claw, asparagus and diced tomatoes on the stove, heating gently without boiling.

Plate as per the photo, drizzling over the white wine sauce to finish.

PARK HOUSE HOTEL

BIOGRAPHY

Callum Keir is the Executive Chef at Park House. Born in Scotland, Callum started his career twenty years ago in Perthshire and embraces the ethos of traditionally reared and produced foods. He is classically trained and has worked in Paris and with the British Michelin-starred chef Martin Blunos. Callum was previously Head Chef at Verzon House Hotel in Herefordshire.

Artichoke Tart

INGREDIENTS

ARTICHOKE PUREE:

400g Jerusalem
artichokes, peeled
Water to cover
75g Butter
50g Milk
Lemon juice to taste
Salt & pepper

SHORT PASTRY:

225g Plain flour
100g Butter
pinch of Salt
30/50ml cold Water

FOR PARSLEY PUREE:

200g of Parsley
100 ml of Water
50 ml of Olive oil
Salt to taste

SCALLOPS:

8 large Scallops sliced
20 ml Olive oil
Salt, Lemon to season

TRUFFLE:

20 slices of Winter truffle

METHOD

ARTICHOKE:

Sweat artichoke in saucepan with butter, cover with water and milk, cook until tender, reserve a couple for slicing. Blend in a food processor, season to taste.

SHORT PASTRY:

Combine ingredients together until firm, chill, roll and line tarts. Blind bake until pale golden.

PARSLEY PUREE:

Cook parsley leaves in boiling water until soft, refresh in ice water, strain, blitz parsley in blender with olive oil until smooth, pass through a fine sieve, season.

SEARED SCALLOPS:

Heat a heavy-based pan, then add oil. Season scallops, sizzle for 1-2 minutes, flip and remove.

Re-season with lemon juice.

APPLEGARTH FARM RESTAURANT

BIOGRAPHY

In 1976 John and Stephanie Benson purchased a piece of land in Grayshott to start growing a range of soft fruits and vegetables. Selling via a barrow at the entrance and a van to Covent Garden Market, John steadily built up a pick your own business which thrived throughout the 1980's.

The farm has seen a number of iterations since it's humble origins but in the last ten years has built into a strong and vibrant restaurant & country deli. Serving an exceptional range of freshly cooked seasonal foods for both eating in the restaurant and taking home Applegarth is thriving.

William Benson, managing partner of the business has been spearheading this development.

"We are still true to our roots today, growing a range of seasonal fruit and veg ,to provide the freshest ingredients for the kitchen.. We work closely with local growers, from little allotment holders to larger local farms . Infact our exceptional Rhubarb crème brulee on the menu today is using spears grown in a back garden not half a mile from Applegarth.

 The next phase in Applegarths development is substantial. Planning permission was granted early this year for a £4m development which will see a market garden, growing school, cookery school, food hall small artisan food producer centre and new restaurant serving up the best of British seasonal foods.

"Applegarth has allowed me to develop a new and exciting relationship with food. Growing, harvesting and then cooking food on site is amazing. Through a labour of love I have developed dishes that complement the surroundings and utilise what nature (and the poly tunnel) can give me".

Roasted Corn Fed Chicken Breast
with almond and lemon thyme stuffing, almond puree,
rogate asparagus, egg yolk, home grown pea shoots

INGREDIENTS

4 x Corn fed chicken breasts

1 x bunch of Rogate asparagus

250g fresh Peas

250ml Chicken stock

50ml Dry sherry

250g dried Marrowfat peas

Egg Yolk

4 x Eggs

Waterbath

Sea salt

Almond And Lemon Thyme Stuffing

1 x 400g Sourdough loaf

100g toasted skin on Almonds

1 x bunch Lemon thyme

1 x Onion (chopped)

1 x Egg

150ml Chicken stock

25ml Sherry vinegar

Sea salt and pepper

Almond Puree

75g blanched Almonds

150ml Whole milk

2 x cloves of Garlic

25g Sourdough breadcrumbs

Sherry vinegar to taste

Arbequina olive oil to taste

Sea salt

METHOD

Start by growing the pea shoots. Cover the marrowfat peas in water and leave to soak overnight. Drain the peas and lay them in a shallow tray, cover with a small amount of soil and put them on a sunny windowsill, or outside in the summer. Water every day for about 10 days and you should be ready to harvest!

Now it is time to cook! Preheat the water bath to 65C and place the whole eggs inside for 55min. When the eggs are ready, crack them open and remove the white (which should be like jelly). Push the yolks through a fine sieve into a piping bag, seasoning on the way. Remove the air and tie the bag, put aside until ready to plate.

To make the stuffing, blitz the bread into chunky crumbs (reserving 25g for the puree), and the almonds into similar sized rough chunks. Sweat the onions in a little olive oil until translucent. Pick the thyme leaves (reserving the stalks for the chicken sauce). Mix all the ingredients together, season and press into a non stick 30cm baking tray. Bake at 180C for 40min.

To make the puree, simmer the almonds in the milk for 20min. Add the garlic and bread, transfer to a blender and blend until silky smooth, season with the sherry vinegar, olive oil and salt (I like mine quite sharp, rich and salty). Keep warm until ready to plate

Oil and season the skin of the chicken, sear on a medium high heat for 3min in an ovenproof pan. Scatter over the lemon thyme stalks and transfer to the oven for approx 12min.

Meanwhile, pod the peas and trim the asparagus, plunge into ice water for two minutes, immediately blanch in salted boiling water for 1min, then refresh in the iced water again for another 2min, drain.

When the chicken is cooked allow to rest for 5min on a rack, put the pan back on the heat and deglaze with the sherry, add the chicken stock and reduce by 1/2 . strain into a jug ready to serve.

To plate up, turn out the stuffing and portion, reheat the peas and asparagus in the boiling water then season and drizzle with olive oil, add a few dollops of the almond puree, then dot around the egg yolk. Carve the chicken breast in two, season the inside. Run to the windowsill, pick a handful of pea shoots and scatter around the plate. Pour over some of the sauce and dig in!

ROOT CANDI

CLOSED

BIOGRAPHY

Reuben Waller is as much an innovator as he is a chef. After spending decades as the head chef of fine French restaurants, Reuben felt a burning desire to try something different and explore new cuisines.

In 2015, he was instrumental in the founding of Rootcandi in Brighton where he rapidly deployed his years of experience to forge his way to the forefront of plant-based dining. With classically trained chefs absorbed in the use of animal ingredients, Reuben felt this created myopia about the vast opportunities available in plant-based foods. A limitless world of textures, flavours, and methods of cooking were just waiting to be discovered and understood in new ways, and Rootcandi is his vehicle for doing that.

Reuben recognises that food isn't just about tastes and flavours. It encompasses culture and speaks of meaning and values. To this end, Rootcandi and its food strives for a more sustainable dining experience. It speaks a clear environmental message: we all need to eat more plants.

Reuben's vision for Rootcandi is still in its relative infancy, with many exciting plans for the future as he navigates the untapped world of plant-based eating. For now, this recipe provides a small taste of what's to come.

Marinated Glazed Tofu
with beetroot mooli & wasabi cream

INGREDIENTS

Marinade:

2 tsp Coriander seeds

2 Fresh chopped red Chillis

2 Lemongrass stems

4 Garlic cloves

50 ml Rice wine vinegar

125ml Tamari

3 tsp Grated Ginger

25g Coriander

Tofu:

350g Firm Tofu

4tsp Agave syrup

10ml Sesame oil

Beetroot & Mooli:

25g Chopped Coriander

2 Beetroots - washed, peeled & grated

1 Mooli - finely grated

2 tsp Thai basil

3 tsp Wasabi paste

4 tsp Soya cream

To serve:

50g Steamed Samphire

fresh edible flower head

pinch micro-Coriander

METHOD

Marinade:

Place ingredients in pan and gently simmer for around 20 mins, do not boil. Leave to infuse at room temperature until cool.

When cool, pass marinate through fine sieve and set aside.

Tofu:

Press tofu with with an even weight (no more than 2kg) otherwise the Tofu may split.

Slice Tofu into 8 equal pieces.

Pour marinate onto Tofu.

Leave in fridge for minimum 8 hours but preferably 24 hours.

Beet/mooli:

Mix in bowl:

Bind Beetroot & Mooli then add Wasabi, ensuring each strand is coated. Ensure no lumps of Wasabi otherwise this will be too overpowering!

Gently fold in Soya cream. Finally, add the coriander, Thai Basil and then season to taste.

Cooking:

Heat sesame oil in non-stick pan.

Take Tofu out of the marinade and place in pan.

Pour over the agave syrup, gently turning the tofu until golden brown on each side.

Put to one side in warm place.

Gently poach or steam the samphire for 2 minutes.

To serve:

Plating:

Place Beetroot and Mooli mix in circular mould on plate.

PASS AT THE SOUTH LODGE

BIOGRAPHY

Head Chef of The Pass Restaurant, West Sussex, Ian Swainson has a long and successful career in the industry. Having joined The Pass in April 2016, Ian previously held 3 AA Rosettes and a Michelin Star for three years as Head Chef of The Samling in Cumbria. Previous roles also include l'ortolan in Reading, Seaham Hall in County Durham, Le Becasse in Ludlow and Chewton Glen in Hampshire.

Influenced by surrealist art in particular, Ian's food is intended to look relatively simple yet pack huge flavour. The aim of the menus available in The Pass is to introduce guests to new tastes and a new experience as the restaurant is set in the heart of the kitchen.

The Pass Restaurant is located within the five-star South Lodge Hotel part of the Exclusive Hotels and Venues family. Taking the 'Chef's Table' concept and exquisitely developing it, diners within the 28 cover award-winning restaurant are closely involved in the kitchen drama as they make their selection from the tasting menus on offer.

Monkfish And Prawn Bisque

INGREDIENTS

Monkfish fillet
Squid ink
Salt
Sauce
Baby leeks
Trompettes
Duxelle
Pasta sheet

Bisque

2kg Prawn carcase, crushed
½ bulb Garlic
200g Tomato puree
4l Double cream
1 bunch Tarragon
1 Lemon (juiced)
50ml pernod

Duxulle

300g Chestnut mushrooms (diced 2mm)
20g Lemon grass, chopped finely
20g Root ginger, chopped finely
5g Garlic, pureed
10ml Pomace oil

Pasta sheets

530g OO' Pasta flour
265g fine Semolina
200g Egg yolks
150g whole Eggs

METHOD

Monkfish

Rub fish with squid ink and season with Maldon salt, add to a hot frying pan with a dash of oil, lightly colour with oil, add 2 nuggets of butter baste and finish in the oven for approximately 5 minutes, and rest before serving.

Bisque

Roast the carcass of the langoustines and then add to a saucepan with the tomato puree and the garlic, cook with colour, once the mix becomes quite dry add the cream and bring to a simmer. Cook for a further 10 minutes and add the tarragon, leave to infuse for 30 minutes off the heat.

Blend in the thermo, then pass, first though a conical sieve, then a chinoise and finally through muslin, add the lemon juice and pernod and season to taste

Duxulle

Take the oil add to a medium hot pan, then everything except the mushrooms, sweat for about 3 minutes, then add the mushrooms, cook down until everything is soft, then season.

Pasta sheets

Blend the pasta flour and semolina on speed 3, before adding the egg yolks, then add the whole eggs slowly until it all comes together.

If needed add more egg working on 1 egg and 3 yolks, add little by little.

Mould into a square container , vacuum tight and reserve for 24 hours.

Roll out until it hits the thinnest setting and repeat once more, cook in salted boiling water for 1 minute, cool in iced water, then cut out on the largest ring cutter.

To finish put the duxelle on to the bottom of the plate, then the pasta, sauce over the bisque, next place in a line the trompettes lightly fried in butter, baby leeks cooked in the emulsion pan, put over the top. Cut the monkfish and lie 1 side black up, 1 down.

DRAKES OF BRIGHTON

BIOGRAPHY

Andy Vitez

Andy is not new to Drakes...he has been with us for over 5 years under the direction of and standing in for ex-Head Chef Andrew MacKenzie during this period. We congratulate Andy in his well deserved promotion from Senior Sous Chef to that of Head Chef at Drakes.

Andy was born and raised in Hungary and realised from a young age that he had a penchant for cooking. His Chef's Training took him on Exchange Programmes in both Italy and Sweden where he benefitted from the experience of the different European cooking styles and practices. This resulted in further development of his skills, knowledge and attaining full qualification.

He arrived in the UK ten years ago, initially settling in Yorkshire where he was employed as Chef de Partie at Raven Hall Hotel before making his way south to the warmer climes of the Sussex. Being in Brighton offered more opportunity to show his undeniable talent in the kitchen and Andy was quickly employed as Senior Chef de Partie at Hotel du Vin but soon came to work at Drakes. Within months, he was promoted to Sous Chef and now has earned his rightful place as Head Chefs at The Restaurant at Drakes.

Lemon Ash Crusted Brill
with jersey potatoes, sea vegetables, clams and lemon caper butter

INGREDIENTS

500g skinned Brill fillets

400g Clams

4 Lemons

200g Sea vegetables (monk's beard, samphire or sea kale)

200g Unsalted butter

50g White wine

200g Jersey royal potatoes

50g Lilliput capers

Sea salt

Olive oil

Pepper

squeeze of Honey

METHOD

Lemon Ash
Wash and cut the lemons in half and juice them. Keep the juice for seasoning and for the sauce. Roast the lemon skins in oven heated to 200°c until completely blackened and powder them in a food processor.

Lemon Caper Butter
Melt 150g of the butter in a pan. Mix the honey with half of the lemon juice and stir the melted butter slowly into the lemon honey mixture. Add the capers.

Vegetable Garnish
Wash and boil the jersey potatoes in salty water until they are cooked through but still firm. Strain and cut them in half, seasoning with salt and pepper. Boil the clams in the white wine until they open fully.

Brill Fillets
Fry one side of the brill fillets in some olive oil for about two minutes (until golden). Flip them over, adding the remaining butter and a squeeze of lemon juice. Cook the fillets through in the foaming butter. Remove and place on a tray. Sweat the sea vegetables in the same pan with remaining lemon butter sauce and add seasoning to taste.

To Finish
Place potatoes in the centre of the plate and surround with the sea vegetables along with the clams. Place the brill fillets on top, sprinkling with the lemon ash to an even covering over the surface. Drizzle the lemon caper sauce around it.

THE WEST HOUSE
RESTAURANT

BIOGRAPHY

Graham Garrett has had a bright and colourful career, first as a successful rock musician, and then defecting to the kitchen to work for the likes of Nico Ladenis and Richard Corrigan, as head chef of multiple restaurants. He has cooked for the government and royalty, at 10 Downing Street, and at a private dinner for the Her Majesty the Queen.

The Garrett's bought The West House Restaurant in Kent in 2002 to create their own private dining room, and to allow Graham to pursue his own vision. Graham's food has gained the restaurant multiple awards – they've held a Michelin star since 2004, are featured in Harden's list of top restaurants in the UK, and hold 3 AA Rosettes. Graham has been awarded Best Chef in Kent in the Kent Life Awards.

On television Graham has featured on Great British Menu and Ramsay's Best Restaurant. The West House also featured in the 2014 book '1001 Restaurants to Experience Before You Die' (Cassell), and Graham has recently been the subject of the 2015 book Sex & Drugs & Sausage Rolls (Face), which is an autobiographical cookbook, with recipes inspired by his transformation from stadium-filling rock star to groundbreaking chef.

Escabeche of Sea Bass

INGREDIENTS

juice of 1 Orange, and zest of 1/2 an Orange

30ml Spanish moscatel vinegar

60ml Dry white wine

5g Fennel seeds

5g Coriander seeds

5g Pink peppercorns

1 Star anise

1 Bay leaf

1 sprig of Thyme

100ml Extra virgin olive oil

Sea salt flakes

1 bulb of Fennel, sliced

1 Banana shallot, peeled and sliced

1 large Carrot, peeled and sliced

4 fillets of Sea bass

METHOD

This is good for home cooks as it isn't labour-intensive on the night. It's important not to boil the oil, or you will lose its flavour. You can vary the fish, and also the marinade, the vinegars, the oil and the vegetables.

To make the marinade, put all the ingredients (except the oil and salt) into a non-reactive pan and bring to the boil. Add the sliced vegetables and bring back to the boil then remove from the heat.

Season the fish on both sides then fry skin side down in a little vegetable oil. When the fish is about two-thirds cooked, turn the fillets over and continue to cook for 10 seconds before removing to a dish just big enough to hold the fish in one layer. Whisk the olive oil into the marinade and add salt to taste. Pour the warm dressing and vegetables over the fish and leave to cool. This is great eaten at room temperature but will keep in the fridge for a few days and can be gently warmed under the grill.

To serve, place each fillet with the vegetables divided evenly between them. Whisk the remaining marinade to emulsify it a little, and then spoon over the fish and sprinkle with a few crunchy salt flakes.

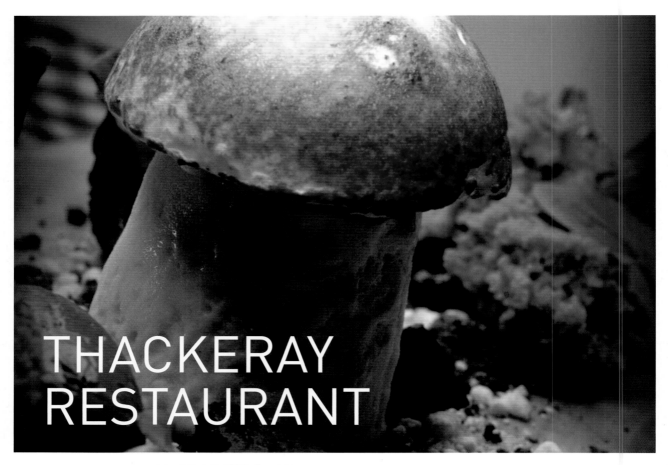

THACKERAY RESTAURANT

BIOGRAPHY

Shane Hughes is the Head Chef at Thackerays in Tunbridge Wells working alongside Pastry Chef Carl Ormesher Having trained under some of the UK's most skilled chefs, John Burton Race, Martin Burge at Whatley Manor and Michel Bourdin at the Connaught to name a few Shane developed his style of Modern French Cooking at Ynyshir Hall In Wales Where he was awarded a Michelin Star and A rising Star In Relais and Chateaux among other accolades. He is passionate and driven and prides himself on still being a stove based chef.

Thackeray's Black Forest

INGREDIENTS

70% Chocolate cremeux, cherry fluid gel

Kirsch parfait

Aero chocolate pieces

Pulled chocolate 'Bark'

Marshmallow dome with cherry sorbet insert

White chocolate snow

Dark chocolate Streusel

Wild sorrel

Bitter lime genoise sponge

Amarena cherries

Bitter lime sugar

Red vein sorrel

Blue borage flowers

METHOD

Using a tea spoon, make a small rocher of the chocolate cremeux in the top right hand corner of the board. Using a small pallette knife, swipe downwards diagonally. Make another rocher sitting at the end of the swipe. Randomly sprinkle the chocolate streusel, white chocolate snow and bitter lime sugar in the centre of the board, covering the swipe. This is to resemble a 'Forest Floor'. Place two pieces of the pulled chocolate bark on top of the cremeux rochers. Inside, tear 2 large pieces of wild sorrel sponge inside of the bark. Place 4 dots of cherry gel and 4 amarena cherries around the 2 sections of the dessert.

TO FINISH

Garnish with blue borage flowers, red vein sorrel cress. Place the kirsch parfait in the middle and the marshmallow dome sitting on top. Lick a blowtorch around to colour the mushroom.

THE LECONFIELD

BIOGRAPHY

Paul has trained with some of the best chefs in Britain including Gary Rhodes, Andrew Pern and Richard Corrigan , and has years of Michelin-star cooking behind him, achieving and holding a coveted star and 3 AA Rosettes for five years at Rhodes W1 Restaurant .

Cooking gently nostalgic British dishes with a modern twist, his career has already spanned top London restaurants, taking him a long way from his Scarborough roots.

Appearing on the 2014 series of 'Great British Menu', Paul proudly represented his region of the North East, achieving a perfect 10/10 for the main course by veteran judge Phil Howard, before narrowly losing out to Colin Mcgurran in the regional finals,

Recently Paul has left London and heading up the Kitchen at The Leconfield Restaurant in Sussex where the restaurant is going from strength to strength.

Compressed and Raw Local Strawberries , Douglas Fir and Basil

INGREDIENTS

Strawberry Consommé

1kg Strawberries

50g of Sugar

Strawberry meringues

1/2 tsp Hy-foamer

1/2 tsp Xanthan gum

25g of Icing sugar

12g of Egg white powder

10g of freeze-dried Strawberries

Compressed Strawberries

10 Strawberries

Douglas Fir Panna Cotta

125ml of Milk

125ml of Double cream

25g of Douglas fir pine needles

75g of Sugar

250ml of Buttermilk

2 Gelatine leaves, softened in cold water

Strawberry foam

500g of Strawberry purée

150ml of Stock syrup

2 Gelatine leaves, softened in cold water

To plate

50g of Pistachio nuts, finely chopped

8 Strawberries, sliced

Basil cress

METHOD

First make the strawberry consommé.

Place the strawberries and sugar into a large bowl and cover with clingfilm. Place the bowl over a pan of simmering water and leave for 1 hour, until all the juice has been extracted from the strawberries. Pass the strawberry mix through a muslin cloth, being sure to strain as much juice as possible

Next make the strawberry meringues.

Put the Hy-foamer, xanthan gum, icing sugar and egg powder into a stand mixer along with 125g of the strawberry consommé and whisk until it forms a thick foam. Spread the meringue mix thinly onto a silpat mat, sprinkle with the freeze dried strawberries and dry in a low oven until crisp

For the compressed strawberries

cut them in half and transfer to a vacuum bag with 100ml of the consommé. Seal and leave to compress for 1 hour

For the panna cotta.

Bring the milk, cream and douglas fir to the boil, then remove from the heat and leave to cool. Once the mixture has cooled, strain into a bowl and set to one side. Heat the sugar and gelatine leaves with a little of the strained cream until dissolved, then remove from the heat and mix with the buttermilk and remaining cream. Pass through a fine sieve and leave to set in a tray with a depth of 3cm

To make the strawberry foam

warm the stock syrup and dissolve the gelatine in it. Lightly warm the strawberry purée and mix it thoroughly with the stock syrup. Leave the strawberry mixture to chill, then transfer to a gas canister and charge with 2 charges

To serve

arrange both compressed and fresh strawberries around the plate along with small scoops of the panna cotta. Place shards of meringue in between and pipe on the strawberry foam. Sprinkle over the pistachio nuts, garnish with the basil cress and pour over the remaining strawberry consommé

ALEXANDER HOUSE HOTEL

BIOGRAPHY

Chef Darrel Wilde brings more than 14 years' experience to his role, having worked with three highly regarded Michelin Star chefs Raymond Blanc, John Burton Race and Gary Rhodes. Chef Darrel formed part of the successful team who assisted Gary Rhodes when he secured a win on series 2 of Hell's Kitchen UK.

A number of influences have shaped Darrel Wilde's culinary career including a 12 year journey with one of his culinary hero's, Gary Rhodes. Darrel started his career at Gary Rhodes's flagship restaurant City Rhodes 1* Michelin 3AA Rosettes in 2000, he then went onto Rhodes in the Square 1* Michelin 3AA Rosettes. Further to this Darrel was also in the opening team of Rhodes 24 in London City where he contributed 2 years helping the restaurant achieve 1* Michelin and 3AA Rosettes and his most recent 7 years with Rhodes restaurants where Darrel worked on numerous projects including Head Chef at Rhodes West One Brasserie and Bar and the opening of the Arcadian Rhodes, on board the Arcadian P&O Cruise Liner.

Blackcurrant Bavarois
with blackcurrant jelly

INGREDIENTS

Frangipane base
250g softened Butter
185g ground Almonds
5 whole Eggs
240g Sugar
60g plain Flour

Blackcurrent custard
900g Milk
12 Egg yolks
240g Sugar
1tbsp Vanilla essence
600ml Blackcurrant puree
12 leaves gelatine bronze leaf (bloomed)
225ml Double cream
225ml Whipping cream

Blackcurrent jelly
6.5 leaves Gelatine
350ml Blackcurrant puree
250ml stock Syrup

Meringues
250g Egg whites
250g Caster sugar
250g Icing sugar

Anis cream
1l Whipping cream
500ml Double cream
11/2 tblsp ground Star anis

Crystallised pictachios
200g Caster sugar
150ml Water
200g Toasted pistachios

Blackberry sorbet
1kg Blackberry puree
880ml stock Syrup
320ml Water
juice of ½ a Lemon.

METHOD

Frangipane base

Cream the butter and sugar until light and fluffy.

Add in the eggs, one at a time.

Fold in the flour and ground almonds.

Spread onto a lined tray 5mm thick

Bake at 180°c for 5-7 minutes until a light golden brown.

Blackcurrent custard

Bring the milk and vanilla essence up to boil.

Meanwhile whisk the together the egg yolks and sugar to a thick pale cream.

Whisk the hot milk onto the egg yolks and return the custard to a gentle heat to thicken, stirring continuously, pass and set aside to cool.

Gently heat the blackcurrant puree and add the pre-soaked gelatine leaves, stirring until dissolved.

Pour into the custard mix and stir well. Set aside and leave to cool, skimming where necessary, allowing the mix to cool and slowly thicken and set.

Whip the creams together to a soft /firm peak and slowly introduce to the custard mix, folding in until fully mixed.

Pour slowly into the prepared rings, so as not to create too many air bubbles, leaving about 3-4 mm from the top.

Leave to cool and set on an even surface in the fridge.

Once set slowly pour the cooled jelly on top and once again return to the fridge to set.

Blackcurrent jelly

Blackberry, Anise and Pistachio nut Fool/Mess Components

Meringues

Whisk the egg whites until aerated; gradually add the caster sugar then the icing sugar.

Whisk until the mixture is smooth and no longer grainy.

For fresh meringue fill a piping bag and chill in the fridge.

For the dried meringue pipe small meringues and dry at 60°c for 12-18 hours

Anis cream

Mix all the ingredients and whip to a soft peak.

Crystallised pictachios

Heat the sugar and water to 130°c.

Add the pistachios and whisk quickly.

When crystallised transfer to a lined tray to cool.

Blackberry sorbet

Mix all ingredients together pass well and churn.

THE CAT INN

BIOGRAPHY

Head Chef Alex Jacquemin born in Cuckfield West Sussex.
Cooking has always been in the family history, with my Great
Grandad winning the first ever national Chef of the year award.
The trend followed from there on with my grandad following his
footsteps becoming a chef. My father missed the trend and became
a mechanic. For me I never envisioned myself ever being a chef but
was always handy in the kitchen as a kid, well I like to think
so anyway.

So my journey started at 15 working in our local Hotel as a kitchen
porter, within a few months I knew the kitchen was my place, I loved
the buzz, fast pace and the pressure. So I approached the Head Chef
and asked him if he would take me on as an apprentice. He strongly
advised me against it because of the unsociable hours and hard work
of the trade. He said only if you are 110 % sure because it isn't a job
for the lighthearted, I took the gamble and here I am 13 years on.

Now I'm working as the Head Chef at The Cat Inn where I've been
for the past 19 months. I love working here and truly feel at home.

Set Rice Pudding Brûlée
with balsamic strawberries and strawberry sorbet

INGREDIENTS

Rice Pudding
75g Pudding rice
350g Milk
150g Double cream
50g Caster sugar
1.5 Bronze leaf gelatine
1 Vanilla pod

Pastry Cream
100g Whole milk
75g Double cream
20g Egg yolk
5g Corn flour
40g Caster sugar

Strawberry Gel
250g Strawberry puree
50g Stock syrup
3g Agar agar

Strawberry Sorbet
200g Strawberry puree
200g Stock syrup

Nut Crumb
70g Unsalted butter
70g Light brown sugar
70g Caster sugar
70g ground Almonds
30g chopped Hazelnuts
30g chopped Almonds
70g Strong Flour
pinch of Maldon salt

Balsamic Strawberries
English strawberries
Balsamic vinegar
Caster sugar

METHOD

Rice Pudding

Before you start, soak the gelatine in cold water

Stir in the rice, milk, sugar, de seeded Vanilla Pod and 75g cream into a pan and bring to the boil. Simmer for 20 minutes or until the pudding rice is cooked. Now add the soaked gelatine and cool to below 30^{OC} before going onto the next step.

Pastry Cream

In a pan, mix together the cream and milk and bring to the boil. In a separate bowl whisk the egg yolks, sugar and corn flour. Pour a small amount of the cream and milk mix over the egg mix to combine then add the remaining. Return to the heat and cook out for a few more minutes or until you bring to the boil. Now leave to cool.

Mix rice pudding mix and pastry cream

Whisk the remaining 75g of cream and fold into the mix

Pour into pastry ring moulds

Set in the fridge for 4 hours.

Strawberry Gel

Whisk all the ingredients together, place in a pan and bring to the boil. Once the mixture has boiled, leave for 30 seconds; this will activate the agar. Remove from the heat, pour into a tray and place in the fridge to set. Once the mixture is set place in a food processor and blitz, scrapping occasionally to remove any trapped bits on the sides, place in a bottle and it is ready to use.

Strawberry Sorbet

Whisk the two together then place into the ice cream machine to churn. Once the mixture has churned and set place into a container and leave covered in the freezer until needed.

Nut Crumb

Combine all the above ingredients until it forms a crumb. Place on a baking tray and bake at 180 for approximately 20-25 minuets or until golden brown. Once cooled, place into the food processor and blitz to a crumb.

Balsamic Strawberries

Firstly cut the Strawberries into quarters then lightly dust with caster sugar and a splash of Balsamic Vinegar mix together.

WOODLAND PARK HOTEL

BIOGRAPHY

Recently arrived at Woodlands Park Hotel, Andrew Mackenzie is keen to make his mark and showcase his creative flair for simple, strong flavours with a firm French influence. Culinary talent runs in Andrew's family, with both his uncles being chefs. Andrew trained under Alan Hill at the renowned Gleneagles Hotel in Scotland before working under Paul Rhodes at Chez Nico in London. Andrew chooses his suppliers for their passion about their produce, and he loves the great seasonal vegetables and salads in the South East, as well as the fantastic meat, and the fresh fish from the south coast. Autumn is his preferred season in the culinary calendar because of the game that is available, with partridge being a particular favourite. Andrew enjoys the challenge of every section of the kitchen and says that to be a good chef you need to be Patient, hard-working and thick-skinned, and to keep your knives sharp.

Raspberry And White Chocolate Trifle

INGREDIENTS

Genoise Sponge

20g Unsalted butter

3 large Eggs

95g Caster sugar

95g Plain flour

a pinch of Salt

Raspberry Jelly

500g frozen Raspberries

100g Caster sugar

juice of 1 Lemon

100ml Water

White Chocolate Custard

50g White chocolate

200ml Whipping cream

6 Egg yolks

50g Sugar

Whipped Cream

200ml Whipping cream

25g Sugar

METHOD

Genoise Sponge

Melt the butter

Whisk the eggs, sugar and salt until very light and very fluffy

Fold in the four very carefully trying not to knock all the air out of the mixture

Spread out on to baking a baking mat on a heavy baking tray

Cook at 150°c till it just starts to colour

Remove from the oven and cool

Cut into discs that will fit into the bottom of the whiskey glasses and freeze with silicone paper between each disc

Raspberry Jelly

Put all ingredients apart from the gelatine into a heat resistant bowl and cover with cling film

Place over a gently simmering Bain Marie for about 30 minutes

Remove from the heat and pass through a muslin cloth, trying not to squeeze as you want the jelly as clear as possible

Add the gelatine and cool till about 20°c

White Chocolate Custard

Heat the cream in a heavy bottomed pan when it reaches about 80oc remove from the heat and stir in the white chocolate

In a separate bowl mix the egg yolks and sugar, whisk over a Bain Marie until ribbon stage

Whisk the chocolate and cream mixture into the sabayon and cook out over the stove till thick and creamy. Remove from the heat and pass through a fine sieve put some baking parchment on top and cool down

Whipped Cream

Put cream, vanilla and sugar into a bowl and whip till a firm hold

Put into a piping bag with a large star nozzle

To Finish

Place a slice of genoise sponge in the bottom of the whiskey glass then pour on a little jelly and set in the fridge till set (at this point only just cove the sponge)

Remove from the fridge cut 12 of the strasberrys in half and put on top of the set jelly and then fill about 1/3 full with the reaming jelly and set in the fridge

When the jelly has set pour in the white chocolate custard till the glass is 2/3 full and allow to set in the fridge

Sprinkle on a little popping candy (optional)   then pipe on the sweetened whipped cream and garnish with the chopped nuts the remaining strasberrys and mint tips then serve

Wales

Starter
Main
Dessert

THE WALNUT TREE

BIOGRAPHY

Shaun Hill

A famous inn and restaurant since the early 60's, The Walnut Tree sits two miles east of Abergavenny. It offers proper dining and drinking in an informal setting. There are around 20 tables simply laid. The restaurant seats up to 70 diners and we open from Tuesday to Saturday, lunchtime and evening.

The food is an eclectic mix, based on Shaun Hill's personal taste, paired with sound cooking techniques; rather than a particular country's cuisine. A unifying feature is the core of excellent ingredients.

"Shaun Hill is one of Britain's most enduringly successful chefs. He began his career in 1966, working for Robert Carrier in his Islington restaurant. He went on to work in some of London's most prestigious addresses including The Capital Hotel in Knightsbridge with Brian Turner and Blakes in South Kensington.

He won a Michelin star for Gidleigh Park in Devon where he was a key player in the Modern British food movement of the late 80's that fused local, seasonal produce with global influences.

Red Mullet
with ginger garlic and tomato

INGREDIENTS

4 x 12gr of Red mullet
fillet per person

little Olive oil and butter
for cooking – also
naturally salt, pepper and
a few drops of lemon juice

8 plum or beef Tomatoes
(skinned and deseeded)

1 tbsp Vegetable oil

50g Shallots (peeled and
finely chopped)

50g fresh Ginger (peeled
and finely chopped)

4 Garlic cloves (peeled
then crushed)

1 small Chilli (chopped)

1 tbsp Tomato passata

2 tbsp White wine or stock

50g Unsalted butter

1 tbsp chopped fresh
Coriander

1 tbsp chopped Parsley

½ Lemon

METHOD

Cut the tomato into small dice

Warm the oil then cook the shallot, garlic. Ginger and chilli so that they are cooked but not coloured

Add a tablespoon tomato passata – single strength tomato puree rather than the concentrate then 2 tablespoons stock or white wine

Finally add the fresh tomato, herbs and the butter. Stir until thickened then adjust the seasonings

Fry the fish then place on a bed of warm sauce

MORGANS HOTEL

BIOGRAPHY

Christopher Law is the Head Chef of Morgan's Hotel, a luxurious boutique hotel located in the centre of Swansea. His love for good quality food and fine dining is evident in the modern classic dishes he delivers, with creativity and flair.

The seasonal menu is centred round using an abundance of fresh and Welsh local produce which the Gower area has to offer.

Supporting Christopher is Senior Sous Chef, Peter Ruggles and Junior Sous Chef, Josh Elliott.

Peter demonstrates a dedication and passion in producing high quality, creative and innovative dishes.

Josh is a bright and talented young Chef who loves the freedom of expression that cooking gives him, and the buzz of a busy working kitchen.

This creative team were featured in the Michelin Guide for 2015.

Confit Duck Leg
frisee salad, pancetta crisp

INGREDIENTS

6 cumin seeds,

12 Coriander seeds,

3 Juniper berries,

50g flaky Sea salt

6 Duck legs,

1 small bunch of Thyme,

1 bunch of Rosemary

1 unpeeled Garlic glove,

1 whole Garlic bulb halved

500g Duck fat or enough to submerge the duck legs

6 baby Carrots,

6 Asparagus spears,

3 whole Radish,

1 whole head Frisee lettuce torn into pieces

6 sliced Pancetta,

2 Bay leaves,

1 tsp Black peppercorns

METHOD

The day before cooking, put cumin, coriander seeds in a dry pan toast until slightly coloured and aromatic. Remove to board and crush, add juniper and salt. Rub the mixture over duck scatter with fresh herbs and sliced garlic and chill for 24 hours, turning 2 or 3 times as they marinate.

Next day heat oven 150c/130c fan /gas 2 wipe duck with kitchen paper and pat dry, but don't wash off the marinade.

Put the duck in cast-iron casserole and cover with duck fat. Add bay leaves and peppercorns, cook for 2 ½ hrs. To store, cover them with fat and refrigerate.

To cook, remove confit duck legs from their fat. Heat up an ovenproof pan and add the duck legs, skin-side down, cook for 4 mins. Turn the legs and transfer the pan to the oven, cook for 30 mins until crisp.

Add asparagus and baby carrots to a pan of salted boiling water and cook for 4 mins.

Arrange pancetta slices on a baking sheet, cook for 8 – 10 mins at 180c / gas 6.

Use asparagus ends for a puree to decorate the dish.

CORRAN RESORT

BIOGRAPHY

Executive Head Chef Cyril Royer brings his extensive food experience from training and travelling around the continents to develop his passion, flair and fresh approach to modern food.

That experience now resides at The Corran Resort & Spa and allows Cyril to work with Carmarthenshire produce and local suppliers so he is able to develop the modern cuisine here at the resort using techniques, flavours and textures rarely seen in West Wales.

"My ethos is simple, fresh produce is key, balanced flavours, keeping it simple and rustic whilst embracing the visual reaction of the guest when they enjoy the food and the ambience of the venue."

Scallops
lava bread – cockles and samphire.

INGREDIENTS

1 Scallop

40g Samphire

4 live Mussels

4 live Cockles

20g Larva bread

1 shot Pernot

1 Shallot

40kg Leeks

Viognier (dry white wine)

Vanilla sea salt

White pepper pinch

50g Butter

60g Parmesan

Beetroot powder

Lemon oil

Edible flowers

METHOD

Put half of the butter, diced shallot and finely sliced leek in a saucepan with the mussels and cockles, cook with the Viognier until the mussels and cockles are open.

Remove from the heat and de shell.

Add the lava bread, Pernot and return to the stove to cook the alcohol outl.

Add the samphire and pepper.

Grate the parmesan, place in the oven on grease proof paper and cook at 180 c for 10 minutes, remove and allow to cool down.

In a frying pan add the left over butter and pan fry the scallop 2.5min each side and rest for 2 min.

Plate in the shell and dress with the vanilla sea salt, wild garlic steams and flowers.

CHATEAU RHIANFA

BIOGRAPHY

Chateau Rhianfa is a romantic French styled Chateau in the heart of Snowdonia, carved into the Isle of Anglesey by the Lord of Bodelwyddan over 160 years ago the Welsh heritage is just as strong today as it was when it was built for Lady Sarah Hay Williams in 1849. In Wales there is a staple tradition of living off the land, stretching back as far as the ancient Celts. Food has historically been simple wholesome fare – low cost dishes made with just a few simple, quality ingredients. Head Chef Paul Wenbourne and his team have crafted their menu carefully to entwine both Welsh influence and French cuisine which is presented in our award winning restaurant Le Dragon Rouge.

Pressed Ham Hock & Cider Terrine Spiced Cauliflower Piccalilli

INGREDIENTS

Stock:

2 Green ham hocks

1 Smoked ham hock

500ml Cider

1litre Water

2 chopped Carrots

2 chopped Celery

1 chopped Onion

6 Thyme sprigs

3 Star anise

tsp White peppercorns

Terrine:

80g chopped Poached apricots

3tbsp Flat parsley (chiffonade)

3tbsp chopped Capers

3tbsp diced Pickles

1tbsp Pommery mustard

2tbsp chopped Pistachio nuts

Piccalilli:

200g Cauliflower florets

50g diced Red pepper

50g diced Courgette

50g Green beans

1 clove Garlic (grated)

80g Course rock salt

80ml Cider vinegar

2tbsp Sugar

1tsp each of Mustard powder & turmeric

50g diced Onions

200ml Orange juice

3tbsp Corn flour

Salt & Pepper

METHOD

Put the ham hocks in the pan and cover with cider & water, add chopped vegetables. Simmer for 2/3 hours then leave to cool

Pick ham hocks, and set aside.

Reduce left over stock by 2/3rds and cool

Add stock to picked ham then add the pink peppercorns, chopped apricots, parsley, capers, pickles, pistachios & mustard, season to taste

Press into lined terrine mould and leave overnight to set

Put the vegetables into a non-metallic bowl. Sprinkle the salt over the top, toss together, cover and leave in a cool place for 12 hours.

The next day put the vinegar & orange juice into a large saucepan or preserving pan, add the spices and bring to the boil.

Drain the vegetables and rinse well under running water for 3-5 minutes. Add to the simmering vinegar & orange juice, cook over a low heat for 20-25 minutes or until the vegetables are tender. Add the sugar and continue to simmer for a further 1-2 minutes.

Mix 2 tbsp. of corn flour with a little water and blend into the hot vegetables. Bring back to the boil and cook for a further minute, the mixture should be glossy and thick. Add the remaining corn flour in the same way if necessary.

Remove the piccalilli from the heat and leave to cool for 15 minutes and serve with Ham terrine

MACHINE HOUSE

BIOGRAPHY

Head chef/Owner Kevin Lynn has worked previously along-side Raymond Blanc and David Cavalier before becoming executive chef at the Belle Époque where he gained two AA Rosettes and was entered into the Michelin guide. After this wonderful achievement Kevin decided to take his passion up another level and open The Machine House in his name where he can now show off all his past experiences and grace Rossett with his wonderful food.

At the machine house we use locally sourced ingredients to reflect on Wales' profusion of produce, because we do this our menu will change with the seasons meaning we will only serve meat, fish and game which is in season and has been locally sourced. For example our seafood comes from Anglesey day boat, our cheeses come from welsh farms along with our rare bread meats which are most importantly Free Range and the flour we use for out breads comes from the local Walk Mill Water Mill, using wheat from the surrounding fields of Cheshire.

Salt Marsh Lamb Rump, Samphire, Quail Eggs, Cockles

INGREDIENTS

Brown Chicken Stock

500g Chicken wings

1x Carrot

2x cloves of Garlic

1x white Onion

¼ bunch of Thyme

5ml Vegetable oil

Salt Marsh Lamb Rump:

14g Samphire

2x Quail eggs

2x Baby leeks

20g Fresh Cockles (frozen cockle meat can always be used but fresh is the preferred option)

25ml White wine

20ml White wine vinegar

METHOD

For the brown chicken stock chop each chicken wing into three or four pieces. Chop the vegetables fairly rough and keep them all separately.

Heat a large roasting tray In a preheated oven at 200oc/400of/ gas 6. Carefully pour half the oil into the tray and return to the oven for 5 minutes so that the oil gets extremely hot.

Put the chicken wings into the oil, spreading them evenly in the tin. Cook the wings until they are golden brown all over, occasionally turning them with a wooden spoon.

Meanwhile, in a hot heavy casserole heat the remaining oil, add the butter and wait until it starts to foam (take care not to let it burn). Add the chopped carrots and garlic and caramelize evenly. Then add the chopped onion and thyme and caramelize for a further 5-10 minutes. Once all the vegetables are golden brown drain the butter and oil away and return the vegetables to the pan.

Drain the oil away from the roasted chicken wing (use a colander for this) and add the wings to vegetables.

Cover with white chicken stock. Adding the salt. Bring to the boil and skim any excess fat from the top. Simmer for at least six hours, skimming occasionally.

Pass the stock through a fine sieve and reduce to the consistency you require.

Salt Marsh Lamb Rump:

You will need a vac pack machine and water bath for this recipe!

Remove any sinew and fats from lamb trim into a nice square shape.

Gently rub with vegetable oil and season with Anglesey sea salt.

Place trimmed lamb rump into vac pack and seal on 90%.

Once sealed place into a pre-set water bath at 5 7°c for 3 hours.

If using fresh cockles wash them in running water for three hours minimum to remove any excess grit or sand.

Place heavy bottomed medium pan on a high heat add white wine add the cockles and cover with a lid steam for 5-8 minutes. Remove from the heat when the shells are open, drain the liquid. Place the cockles in a flat tray leaving them to cool.

Once cool remove cockle meat from shells and discard shells.

In a separate small pan bring to the boil 250ml of water and 25ml of white wine vinegar place in the quail eggs and boil for 2 minutes 2 seconds. Remove and submerge into an ice bath and allow to cool down.

Once quail eggs are fully cold peel the shell from the eggs and discard the shell.

Trim the baby leeks and remove outer leaves Gently pick any woody stems from samphire if any.

Boil 150ml of slightly seasoned water add baby leeks and cook for 1 minute remove and place into ice bath immediately. Once cool remove and pat dry with a towel.

Remove the lamb from the bag and pat the lamb dry. Place a small frying pan on a medium to high heat place the lamb into the pan skin down for one minute turn over for another minute then turn back onto skin and add 5g of butter and baste it keep basting the lamb with butter once the lamb has a nice golden brown colour remove from heat and leave to rest for 5-8 minutes.

Whilst lamb is resting cut the quails eggs in half width ways and slightly season with Anglesey sea salt.

Reheat the baby leeks and samphire add cockles then remove from the heat after 2 minutes.

To plate slice the lamb in half-length ways open up and place on to the plate pink side facing upwards place samphire cockles and leeks on top of lamb arrange quails eggs as pictured. Finish with a spoonful of chicken stock.

THE GOWER HOTEL

BIOGRAPHY

Chris Keenan started his career in the West End of London, cooking in some of the city's most prestigious restaurants before returning to Wales, where he won multiple awards with his own restaurant, Keenan's.

He went on to gain praise and recognition at several other well-known Swansea restaurants, including Morgan's Hotel, which won multiple awards and accolades with him in the kitchen.

He has also put his name to a range of cooking sauces and made numerous appearances on Carlton Food Network, Granada Breeze, and BBC 2W. His work as a consultant chef has seen him creating beautiful dishes for major UK supermarkets.

"Having a kitchen this good at the Gower means there are no limitations in terms of what I can do here. I'm enjoying the freedom, and it's great to work for owners who are real foodies."

Roast Rump of Welsh Lamb, Leek & Potato Gratin, Baby Carrots & Leeks,
with an orange, cracked pepper and blueberry jus

INGREDIENTS

Lamb

2 x 8 oz Rumps of welsh lamb

Cracked black pepper halen mon sea salt

Jus

zest from 2 Oranges

2tsp Redcurrant jelly

200ml Red wine jus stock

10 Blueberries

1oz chilled Butter

Seasoning as above

Garnish Vegetables

4 baby Carrots

4 baby Leeks

small piece of Butter

Dauphinoise Potatoes

600 ml Double cream

1 Garlic clove

3 large King edward or maris piper potatoes

1 x leek

METHOD

Lamb

Heat a heavy pan until very hot with a little oil in it. Season the lamb rumps well and sear on both sides.

Pop in a pre-heated oven at 180 C (this will already have the dauphinoise potatoes in it) for approximately 20 minutes. The lamb should be well seared on the outside but juicy and pink in the middle.

Jus

You can roast lamb bones and root vegetables and make your own stock or you can buy one of the excellent fresh stocks available at most good supermarkets. Add to the stock the orange zest, redcurrant jelly and reduce to a thick consistency. Check for seasoning.

A couple of minutes before you are about to plate up, add the blueberries and cook until they pop. Add the butter to give the jus a gloss.

Garnish Vegetables

Whilst your lamb is cooking and your stock reducing, place your carrots and leeks in a small open pan with a little water and a drop of butter. Simmer uncovered for a couple of minutes until tender but not soft.

Dauphinoise Potatoes

Peel the garlic and cut in half, rub all sides of a flat oven proof dish with the garlic, you are looking for the slightest hint of garlic. Pour the cream into a large saucepan and bring to a simmer. Slice the potatoes very finely, about 3-4mm, add them to the cream and simmer for 3 mins until just tender. Gently stir to separate the potato and stop it sinking and catching on the bottom of the pan.

Wash and finely dice the leeks.

Remove half the potatoes with a slotted spoon and place in a wide shallow ovenproof dish so that they are about 2cm in depth. Top with the diced leeks then add the remaining potatoes. Pour over the cream slowly making sure that it seeps through the layers and leave a little moisture on the surface, then bake for 30 mins until the potatoes are soft and browned.
Tip: if you want the potatoes to have a neat shape, make in advance. Line your dish with parchment leaving an overlap so you can use to lift the potato out of the dish. Cook and let cool overnight in the fridge and then you can lift out of the dish and cut neat pieces and re-heat with the lamb.

Or just spoon the unctuous soft potato onto the plate!

THE BUILD

Add the chilled butter to the jus to get a glossy consistency. Rest the lamb for a couple of minutes before slicing through but retain the rump shape. Place the rump on the plate, with the dauphinoise, carrots and baby leeks, spoon over the glossy jus... and enjoy!

161

WOLFSCASTLE COUNTRY HOTEL

BIOGRAPHY

Wolfscastle Country Hotel is located in the small village of Wolfscastle, only 8 miles from the stunning Pembrokeshire coastline and mystical Preseli Mountains. Under the ownership of Andrew Stirling for the past 38 years, a deserved reputation for excellent food and amiable hospitality is long established.

"Growing up in the wine and catering business, good food was something I grew up with. My parents owned The Hat and Feather in Knutsford, which in 1966, was voted by the Good Food Guide as one of the best 20 restaurants in Britain."

Recent additions to the hotel, such as the contemporary Brasserie, give the team of experienced chefs ample opportunity to develop the menu of traditional as well as upscale dishes using the best of Pembrokeshire produce. Recently awarded Two AA Rosettes, Wolfscastle is continuing to build upon the success of the past.

Slow Cooked Welsh Pork Belly
hand-dived scallop, pork rillette, brandy jus, apple fluid gel

INGREDIENTS

Pork Belly
1 Pork Belly

Brine For Pork
150g Demerara sugar
200g Table salt
1 tbsp Black peppercorns
2 Bay leaves
Sprig of thyme
6 Sage leaves

Pork Rillettes
1 kg Pork belly
½ kg Pork fat
13g Table salt
14g Muscovado sugar
3 Bay leaves
14 Juniper berries
15 Black peppercorns
5 Whole cloves
1/4 Bottle white wine
5 Garlic cloves
2 Sprigs of thyme
25g Duck fat

Brandy Jus
1 kg Pork trimmings
½kg Chicken wings
4 Celery sticks, diced
4 Carrots, diced
10 Thyme springs
2 Bay leaves
2 Star anise
80ml Brandy
2 Litres water

Apple Fluid Gel
600g Apple juice
6g Sugar
2g Agar agar
Pinch salt

METHOD

Pork Belly

Place boneless pork belly in tray and cover with brine. Cover and place in fridge for 12 hours.
Rinse off the brine, leave to dry, then vacuum pack airtight
Place in sous vide for 36hr at 64 degrees C
Remove from water bath, press flat between two trays, leave to cool
Remove skin, leaving a layer of fat, keep skin for puffed pork rind
Cut into portions
Colour in pan, skin side down. Heat through in oven.

Puffed Pork Rind
Remove all fat from the pork skin
Portion into 1 inch squares
Place in dehydrator at 52 degrees C until crisp
Place in 200 degree C fryer until they puff up

Scallop
Oil and season scallop
Place in hot pan
Turn after 1 minute
Finish with lemon & butter

Pork Rillettes
Skin 1 kg pork belly, dice into 2 inch cubes, place in a deep pan
Dice ½ kg pork back fat and add to pork belly
Add in 13g table salt, 14g light muscovado sugar and 3 bay leaves
Grind 14 juniper berries, 15 black peppercorns, 5 whole cloves, add evenly to pan
Cover and leave to cure overnight
The next day, preheat oven to 140 degrees C, add 1/4 bottle of white wine to the pan
Place 5 garlic cloves and the picked leaves of 2 sprigs of thyme into grinder, pulse until fine
Add evenly to pan of pork
Add 25g of duck fat to pan and place in oven for 3 ½ hours
Remove from the oven and allow to cool
Strain the liquid and reserve
Remove the bay leaves from the meat
Place three ladles of the meat and one of the liquid into a food processor, pulse until you have a coarse

paste, place into another deep container
Continue mixing the meat until all meat is blended

Add in small handfuls of ground cloves and white pepper
Season
The mix should be very highly seasoned
Roll into small balls
Coat in flour, egg, then breadcrumbs
Deep fry

Caramelised Balsamic Onions
Finely slice 6 large onions
Add knob of butter to saucepan
Cook onions on low to medium until onions begin to caramelise
Add two tbsp. of small capers and 50 ml good quality balsamic vinegar
Continue cooking until onions are caramelised

Brandy Jus
Roast chicken and pork at 200 Degrees C until brown
Roast carrot, onion and celery in a separate tray
Transfer meat and veg into sauce pan and add remaining ingredients (excluding brandy)
Reduce by two thirds
Pass through fine sieve and stir in brandy

Apple Fluid Gel
Add sugar to good quality apple juice
Reduce to 300g
Bring to simmer, then remove from heat
Add agar agar, leave to set then blitz in food processor

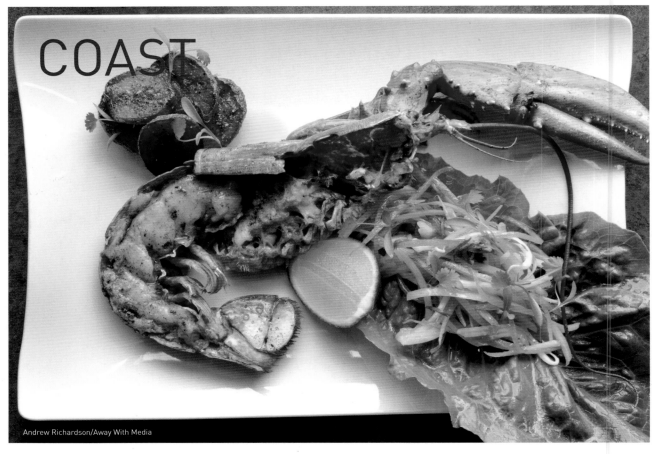

COAST

Andrew Richardson/Away With Media

BIOGRAPHY

Chef Will Holland earned a Michelin star before the age of 30, was named in The Good Food Guide's list of their predicted "ten most influential chefs of the next decade" and was awarded an Acorn Award as one of the industry's highest achievers under the age of 30. Will has appeared on national television programmes including numerous appearances as guest chef on James Martin's Saturday Kitchen, beating the Hairy Bikers on their "Food Tour of Britain" and was the central region champion on BBC's Great British Menu. He has featured in many publications such as The Telegraph, BBC Olive Magazine and GQ Magazine.

In 2014 Will opened Coast Restaurant, Saundersfoot as Head Chef. Coast is a stunning brand new purpose built restaurant situated on the shoreline of Coppet Hall beach, Pembrokeshire. At Coast, Will heads up his team and uses his years of experience in some of the UK's best hotels and restaurants to create dishes using the best produce available.

Caldey Island Lobster

grilled with vanilla, black pepper and charcoal salt butter, papaya and coriander salad, spicy potatoes

INGREDIENTS

Vanilla and Black Pepper Butter

250g Unsalted butter

1 Vanilla pod

15 twists Black pepper

3g Charcoal salt

Hot and Sour Passion Fruit Dressing

1 Lime

100g Passion fruit pulp (approximately 5)

20ml Thai fish sauce

5g Mint leaves

5g Red chilli

5g Green chilli

5g Demerara sugar

Piri Piri Potato Wedges

12 large Par boiled new potatoes

10g Piri piri seasoning

30ml Olive oil

30g Butter

Papaya and Coriander Salad

2 Carrots

2 Green papayas

1 Onion

Coriander leaf

60g Beansprouts

Preparing and Cooking the Lobsters

2 x 900g Live lobsters

Other Ingredients and Finishing the Dish

2 Limes

1 Romaine lettuce

40 sprigs Coriander cress

METHOD

Soften the butter. Place in a mixing bowl. Split the vanilla pod lengthways and scrape out the seeds. Add the seeds to the bowl with the pepper and salt. Mix well.

Remove the zest from the lime with a fine grater. Squeeze the lime and measure 15ml juice. Place the zest and juice in a mixing bowl with the remaining ingredients. Leave to macerate for 24 hours before passing through a fine sieve and reserving the juice. Store in the refrigerator until required.

Cut the new potatoes in half lengthways and place them in a small roasting tray with the piri piri, oil and butter. Roast in a preheated oven at 190°C for 20 – 30 minutes or until golden.

Peel the carrots and papayas and julienne them as thinly as possible using a Japanese mandolin. Peel the onion and slice it thinly. Finely chop the coriander. Mix the beansprouts and the prepared carrot, papaya, onion and coriander. Store in the refrigerator until required.

Bring a pan of water to the boil. Blanch the lobsters in the boiling water for 4 minutes before removing and plunging into iced water. Remove from the iced water and split each lobster in half lengthways. Wash the lobsters under running cold water to remove the contents of the head. Place the 4 cleaned lobster halves in a roasting tray. Spoon the vanilla butter over the lobsters generously and place under a preheated grill on a medium heat for 10 minutes basting regularly.

Cut the limes in half. Break the romaine into individual leaves. To serve, place a half grilled lobster, a lime wedge and 6 potato wedges on each plate. Place a lettuce leaf on each plate. In a mixing bowl combine the papaya and coriander salad and the hot and sour dressing. Divide between the plates by placing on top of the lettuce leaf. Add 10 sprigs of coriander cress to finish each plate.

THE GATE AT LLANFRECHFA

BIOGRAPHY

The Gate has operated in its current format as a "Country Pub with Premium Dining" for two years under the vision and direction of Julie and James Dawson. In that time - from a standing start, it has acquired an unquestionable reputation throughout Gwent for outstanding food and premium, service.

The Gate was recognised as "Torfaen's Most Recommended Restaurant" in 2013 and Head Chef, Johnathan Fryer was voted Chef of the Year 2013" by readers of the South Wales Voice Magazine. The kitchen team, led by Jonathan and his right hand man, Rob Sands (a head chef in his own right) have developed a unique style for The Gate with menus incorporating Welsh, British and European cuisine styles. Ingredients are locally sourced where possible with the help of our trusted suppliers, Castello Howell Foods and their Celtic Pride butchery brand. Fish is also much in evidence at The Gate – supplied by renowned Cardiff fishmongers E.Ashton (Fishmongers) Ltd. Blending the right ingredients with the Gate's passion for food and service, there can only be one outcome. Great Food and Drink.

Sauteed Cod fillet

with smoked haddock sausage on butternut squash & spinach risotto with crispy pancetta & parmesan crisp

INGREDIENTS

The Cod
4 norwegian Cod steaks
1 tbsp Flour
Salt & pepper

Smoked Haddock Sausage
500g Smoked haddock
1 tbsp Horseradish sauce
1 Egg white
300ml Double cream
Salt & pepper
Cling film for prep

Risotto
300g Risotto rice
1 Butternut squash peeled seeded & diced. (Set the seeds aside for an optional garnish)
a bunch of Spinach (finely diced)
1 medium sized Onion (finely diced)
56g Butter
1 Fish stock cube (to make a pint of fish stock)
2 cloves of Garlic (crushed)

The Coulis
2 Red peppers
2 Yellow peppers
1 tsp Sugar
4 tbsp Olive oil

Garnish
4 finely sliced Pancetta strips/slices
100g block of fresh Parmesan cheese (finely grated)
Micro herbs (Optional)
Pomegranate & butternut squash seeds (Optional)

METHOD

Smoked Haddock Sausage

Place the haddock in a blender with salt and pepper, blend in the egg and add in the cream slowly. Add horseradish and mix for a further 30 seconds and then chill for 5 mins. Place the chilled filling onto cling film and roll out into 3 inch (75mm) sausages (Make 4). Wrap in cling film, tie the ends and poach in boiling water for 5 mins. Drain, cool and store in the fridge until ready for serving.

Risotto

Gently fry the butternut squash, diced onion, garlic and rice in the butter for 2-3 mins being careful not to colour the ingredients. Add fish stock a little at a time and simmer gently until the rice is "al dente" (firm to taste). Add the spinach until it wilts and remove the mix from the heat. Continue to fold the spinach into the mix until it is well distributed. Add salt and pepper to season.

Coulis

Roast and then skin the yellow peppers. Place the skinned pepper in a blender with sugar, oil and seasoning. Blitz to a puree and then push the coulis through a fine sieve and keep warm. Repeat this process with the red pepper.

Sautéed Cod

Lightly dust the cod with seasoned flour. Place the cod (skin side down) in a hot pan to which you have already added a little oil. Fry for 4-5 mins. Turn over and cook for a further 2-3 mins.

Garnish (Suggested)

Place the four pancetta strips on grease proof paper and bake at 180°C until crispy. Grate the parmesan onto grease proof paper in 4 circular heaps. Bake at 180°C until melted and golden. Leave to cool and crisp.

Presentation

Pour the red and yellow coulis onto one end of a long plate. Cut the sausage diagonally and stand in the coulis. Place risotto and stand the parmesan crisp and crispy pancetta up in the risotto. Position the cod in the centre of the plate and garnish (optional) with micro herbs and pomegranate and butternut squash seeds. Present the dish as shown.

BISTRO PREGO

Closed

BIOGRAPHY

Steve Robbins left catering college at the tender age of 16, heading for the bright lights of London to chef. From a boyhood helping his Grandfather growing Vegetables on their allotment and preparing them back at home with his Mum and Grandmother, he was naturally drawn towards cooking with local, seasonal foods, and only too happy to get back to the land of his fathers, aged 24 as head chef and manager at Bistro Prego of Monmouth in the Welsh borders. Here, he makes the most of the diverse regional produce, preparing it with his signature Mediterranean style. With his menu's roots planted firmly in the Welsh soil, the harvest from local allotments and friends gardens finds its way into the aromatic dishes served at Prego, which under Steve's direction has been awarded its second AA Rosette in as many years, establishing a reputation as a destination for the food-savvy. In the rare times when he is not to be found pan-in-hand amongst the sizzling buzz of the busy restaurant, he turns off his phone and escapes for some very, very quiet fishing, where he can dream-up more mouth-watering dishes in peace.

Roast Partridge
with cavolo nero, braised lentils and harissa jus

INGREDIENTS

4 Partridges

500gms Cavolo nero

small clove Garlic, chopped

1 tbsp Olive oil

knob of Butter

Lentils

300gms Umbrian lentils

1 Carrot, diced small

1 stick Celery, diced small

1 Shallot, diced small

4 tbsp Olive oil

500ml Vegetable stock

2 cloves Garlic, chopped

200g chopped Tomatoes

Harissa

6 dried Red chillies

1 cloves Garlic, minced

¼ teaspoon Salt

2 tablespoons Olive oil

½ teaspoon ground Coriander

1/2 teaspoon ground Caraway seeds

½ teaspoon Cumin seeds

½ pint Beef jus

METHOD

For the Partridge Gas mark 4/180°C

Seal the partridges in a hot frying pan all around with a little olive oil then add a knob of butter and put in the oven and cook on each side (three sides in total, left leg, right leg and head) for 5 minutes, (15 minutes altogether) once cooked take out and rest the bird (the partridge should be cooked medium rare).

For the Harissa

Soak the dried chillies in hot water for 15 minutes. Drain.

In a food processor blend the chilli, garlic, salt, and olive oil, add remaining spices and blend to form a smooth paste.

Add to the meat jus and warm, you can add as little or as much harissa as you like.

For the lentils

Wash the lentils in plenty of cold water, there is no need to soak the lentils.

Sweat the carrots, onion, celery & garlic until soft.

Add the lentils and cook for 2 minutes, add the chopped tomatoes, salt and pepper and some of the water.

Bring to the boil and then simmer for around 20 minutes until the lentils are soft, you may have to add more water as you simmer the lentils, you want to end with a thick soup consistency.

For the cavolo nero

Strip the cavolo nero from the stalk and boil in salted water for 6 minutes and fry in a little olive oil and garlic.

To serve, put the cavolo nero on the plate, top with the braised lentils and sit the partridge on top and serve with the harissa jus.

MOKSH

BIOGRAPHY

Born in Mumbai, Stephen Gomes is the fourth generation in his family to become a Chef. Taking inspiration from his heritage, experience and gastronomic travels, he is renowned for his pioneering and unique interpretation of Indian recipes. Stephen is recognised as being among the first chefs to experiment with natural food science in his dishes. A true Gastro-physicist at heart, his passion for innovation and using local Welsh produce transforms itself in the sensational and unique tastes, textures and presentation of his dishes.

As the very first Indian Chef in Wales to receive an AA Rosette and to be named Ethnic Chef of the Year at the Craft Guild of Chef's awards in 2015, being recognised for his contributions within the Industry is certainly not a new concept. His highly acclaimed restaurant Moksh is multi-award winning, and has recently been identified as "a very progressive restaurant that is always breaking boundaries and representing on a national scale". The restaurant has a very distinctive concept where dishes combine authentic Indian flavours with contemporary presentation, to provide diners with a culinary experience that will not easily be forgotten.

Lucknowi Welsh Lamb Cutlets

INGREDIENTS

5 to 6 x french trimmed Welsh lamb cutlets

1 teaspoon Chilli paste

10ml Lemon juice

3 teaspoons Yoghurt

1 teaspoon Garam masala

1 teaspoon Coriander powder

½ teaspoon Cinnamon powder

½ teaspoon crushed Black peppercorns

30g Ginger garlic paste

Salt - as per taste.

10ml Vegetable oil (for frying)

For the spicy mashed potatoes

2 large Potatoes, peeled and quartered (preferably Maris piper)

½ teaspoon Salt

4 tablespoons Milk

60g Butter (cubed)

½ teaspoon Turmeric

½ teaspoon red chilli powder

5g fresh chopped Coriander leaves

Salt and ground black pepper

For the mint and coriander chutney

½ cup fresh chopped Mint leaves

½ cup fresh chopped Coriander leaves

1 Green chilli (if possible remove all the seeds)

½ inch Ginger

1 tablespoon Lemon juice

A pinch of Salt

METHOD

Marinate the Welsh lamb cutlets with all the ingredients for an hour. Heat the sous vide bath to 130°F around 55°C for medium rare or 140°F/60°C for medium. Vacuum seal the lamb cutlets, and drop them into the sous vide bath for 2 hours. Once the 2 hours have elapsed, open the bag and pat dry each of the lamb cutlets. Heat the oil in a large pan and fry each cutlet for about 20 seconds each side. Serve hot on spicy mashed potatoes with mint and coriander chutney.

Alternatively, place the cutlets in an oven set to 200°C/gas mark 6 for 15 to 20 minutes depending on how you like the meat cooked. You could also pan-fry the cutlets 5 minutes each side.

Meanwhile for the spicy mashed potatoes, boil the potatoes for about 20 minutes until soft but not breaking up. Drain the potatoes. Place the butter in the pan, add the turmeric and stir continuously for 30 seconds. Add the chilli powder. Add the potatoes and mash using either a potato masher or a fork. Add the milk and whip the mashed potatoes lightly with a wooden spoon. Add the fresh coriander leaves and give it a good whip. Season with salt and pepper to your taste.

To accompany the dish, grind all of the ingredients for the mint and coriander chutney in a blender to a smooth paste. Use a little water. Mix salt in with the chutney.

Enjoy Lucknowi Welsh lamb cutlets with a naan.

FFRESH BAR AND RESTAURANT

BIOGRAPHY

Housed in Wales Millennium Centre – an iconic arts and culture venue situated in the heart of Cardiff Bay – ffresh Bar & Restaurant, described by The Guardian as 'a lovely place offering cracking value', creates stunning dishes using the best Welsh produce.

New to the team at ffresh is head chef Marc Corfield, bringing with him over six years' experience at The Walnut Tree Inn, one of Wales' most celebrated Michelin starred restaurants. In consultation with former mentor Shaun Hill, Marc and his team have developed menus that bring seasonal Welsh produce into the spotlight.

Typical dishes include; twice baked gorwydd soufflé, lamb cawl, perl las tart with roasted chicory and walnut salad, smoked haddock boudin with lentil and coriander sauce, venison with goats cheese gnocchi, Muscat crème caramel and warm chocolate mousse with pistachio ice cream.

Lamb Cawl

INGREDIENTS

1.5kg Lamb shoulder

Salt and pepper

2l Lamb stock

150g Carrots (peeled, left whole)

250g Carrots (diced)

100g Onion (peeled and halved)

100g Celery (washed whole sticks)

200g Celery (peeled and cut into 1cm cubes)

Swede (peeled and cut into 1cm cubes)

150g Leeks washed (cut into 1cm slices)

100g Pearl barley (rinsed under cold water)

400g Potato (cut into 1cm chunks)

50g Parsley (finely chopped)

2 Bay leaves

2 sprigs Thyme

3 sprigs Rosemary

50g Garlic/1 bulb

METHOD

Preheat oven to 140°C/130°C (fan)/275F/Gas mark 1.

Place shoulder in a large pan or roasting tray and season with salt and pepper.

Cover with the stock, adding more water if required and bring to the boil on top of the stove. Skim any impurities from the top using a ladle and discard.

Add the whole carrots, onions, bay leaves, thyme and celery sticks to the pan and bring back up to the boil. Skim any impurities from the surface with a ladle. Cover the tray/pan with foil ensuring a good seal and transfer quickly to the centre of a preheated oven.

Braise in the oven for one hour. Remove from oven and remove foil. Sprinkle the pearl barley into the mixture, bring the mixture back up to the boil on the stove, replace the foil and return to the oven for 1 1/2 hours.

Remove from the oven and ensure the lamb is cooked through and tender. Remove the lamb from the liquid and set aside. Discard the vegetables from the liquid and pour the liquid through a sieve into a pan reserving the pearl barley for later.

Bring the liquid to the boil, add the potato and swede and bring back up to the boil. Boil for 3 mins, then add the carrot to the pan before bring the mixture back up to the boil. After 3 mins add the leek and the celery to the pan. Boil for another 3 mins or until cooked through.

Add the sieved off pearl barley back to the pan and stir.

Cut the lamb into 2 – 3cm cubes and add the lamb to the pan stirring well. Season to taste.

Serve with crusty bread.

√ THE WHITEBROOK 28/06/17

BIOGRAPHY

The Whitebrook is a Michelin star restaurant with eight rooms, set in the blissfully peaceful Wye Valley. In 2013 Worcestershire born Chef Chris Harrod and his wife Kirsty followed their ultimate dream of owning their own restaurant, and within 11 months The Whitebrook was awarded a Michelin star. Every dish served from breakfast through to dinner boasts locally sourced ingredients, many of which are foraged within a short distance from the restaurant.

Prior to The Whitebrook, Chris opened Colette's as as head chef at The Grove Hertfordshire, he spent almost four years working for Raymond Blanc at Le Manoir aux Quat'Saisons, and began his steady rise in the kitchen as sous chef to Alan Murchison at L'Ortolan in Shinfield, Berkshire, for 18 months.

It was Raymond Blanc and his time at Le Manoir aux Quat'Saisons that influenced Chris profoundly:

'What I thought about food changed completely when I got there. Everything is about quality and the freshness of the produce. As a chef it's all about questioning and tasting, and that's really stayed with me'.

Cornish Plaice
heritage carrots, buttermilk, estuary findings

INGREDIENTS

Plaice
4 x 130g Plaice fillet
40g Salt
400g Water

Heritage Carrots
20 x Heritage carrots, cleaned
500g Plain flour
250g Sea salt
250g Water

Buttermilk emulsion
25g Milk
25g Double cream
200g Buttermilk
Xanthan gum
Lecithin powder
Salt
Lemon juice

Buttermilk powder
200g Buttermilk
50g Butter

Estuary findings
200g Water
100g Unsalted butter
12g Salt
Sea spinach, picked and cleaned
Sea blight, picked and cleaned
Sea aster, picked and cleaned
Rock samphire, picked and cleaned

METHOD

Plaice fillets: Make a brine by mixing the salt and water until dissolved. Submerge the plaice fillets and leave for 4 minutes. Remove and dry on absorbent cloth.

Salt baked carrots: Place the flour and salt in a bowl and gradually incorporate the water until you have smooth dough; you may not need all of the water. Roll out the dough and completely encase the carrots, making sure there are no gaps. Bake at 190C for 20 minutes. Allow to cool before cracking open the salt dough and remove the baked carrots. Reserve.

Buttermilk emulsion: Bring the milk and cream to the boil, remove from the heat and add the buttermilk, Xanthan gum and lecithin. Blitz with a hand blender until all incorporated and frothy. Season lightly with salt and lift with lemon juice as required.

Buttermilk powder: Put the buttermilk and butter in a saucepan and bring to a simmer. Allow to split and continue cooking out until you have a golden sand texture. Strain before spreading onto a tray with absorbent cloth and allow to dry overnight.

Make an emulsion for cooking the estuary herbs by bringing the water, butter and salt to the boil, emulsify with a hand blender. Reserve until required.

To Finish/Serve:

Gently warm the salt baked carrots through the oven. Meanwhile heat non stick frying pan until very hot. Add the fish and cook over a medium-high heat for 2-3 minutes, then carefully turn over and cook for 1-2 minutes longer. The fish should be golden but only just cooked through. Remove from the pan, lift with lemon juice and keep warm. Bring the emulsion for the estuary vegetable to the boil and cook the sea aster and rock samphire together for 1 minute, add the sea blight and sea spinach for 10 seconds then drain the vegetables immediately, you want to keep them crisp and vibrant. Warm the buttermilk emulsion and froth with a hand blender, spoon a bed of sauce onto each plate. Arrange the carrots around before adding the plaice fillet in the centre. Sprinkle the top of the plaice with the caramelised buttermilk powder. Finish the plate with the estuary herbs.

✓TYDDYN LLAN 27|07|12

BIOGRAPHY

Bryan was brought up in the mining valleys of Wales in a village called Crumlin. As soon as his O levels were finished, Bryan was heading for the restaurant trade.

So to the Crown at Whitebrook, run by French lady, Sonia Blech and her husband Neville. Which at the time was the first and only Michelin starred restaurant in Wales, a great starting block.

Sonia taught the basics, how to respect food which gave him his passion and love for the business.

After 3 years he headed to Swansea where Colin Pressdee at the Drangway taught him everything there is to know about fish.

After winning the William Heptinstall award in 1980 he travelled through France working and eating at the young age of 21.

Four years later he was asked to head up a kitchen in London, which within 3 months, the restaurant was rated 13/20 in the good food guide, two years later he was head hunted to take over the stoves at Hilaire after Simon Hopkinson left for Bibendum, it was here where he found his direction and style of food that he still serves today.

After 14 years at Hiliare, 11 of them as the chef/owner together with his wife Susan, they sold up. Took a year off to travel the world and finally returned to Wales. This time in the North of the country at an elegant Georgian house called Tyddyn Llan.

During the 14 years Bryan and Susan have been at Tyddyn Llan, they have been highly rated in most of the food guides, collect Welsh restaurant of the year 3 times in the good food guide and being awarded a Michelin star in 2010, which they still hold today.

Bryans cooks with sophisticated simplicity that embraces the best and most carefully sourced produce with consistent excellence.

Roast Wild Bass
with laverbread butter sauce

INGREDIENTS

4 150g pieces of Wild bass, skin on and all pin bones removed

4 finely chopped Shallots

1 tablespoon of White wine vinegar

1 175 dry White wine, Muscadet if possible

250g Unsalted butter

Salt and a pinch of cayenne pepper

juice of half a Lemon

2 tablespoon of Laverbread

2 tablespoon of Double cream

300g raw picked Spinach

50g extra Butter

METHOD

Put the white wine, vinegar and shallots into a saucepan and slowly reduce to a syrup.

On a light heat slowly add the butter a little at a time until it forms a slightly thick sauce, season with salt and cayenne pepper, add the juice of the half lemon.

Strain the sauce into a clean saucepan, in a separate saucepan add two tablespoons of Laverbread with 2 tablespoons of cream, bring to the boil and add half the beurre blanc.

Season the fish and coat lightly with olive oil place onto a hot griddle skin side down, until the skin is crisp, place onto an oiled tray and bake in a hot oven 200c for five minutes.

While the fish is cooking, in a large pan melt the extra butter and cook the spinach until wilted.

Serve the bass on a bed of spinach and pour the lavabread sauce around one side and the remaining beurre blanc around the other side.

GROVE OF NARBERTH

BIOGRAPHY

Born and raised in Kent, Allister has spent all his professional career working in Michelin starred restaurants, as a trainee chef at Read's Restaurant in Faversham working his way through the sections, followed by eight years working alongside the acclaimed Michael Caines of two Michelin starred Gidleigh Park.

Allister moved to Devon at just nineteen. He was blown away by Michael's food, and the discipline in the kitchen was just what Allister needed to progress his career. After three years of working his way up and through the sections Michael gave Allister the opportunity to be his Sous chef at The Bath Priory alongside Sam Moody. They were a great team and the restaurant was awarded a Michelin star in 2012.

Allister moved back to Gidleigh in 2013 as Head chef where he spent three years successfully retaining 2 Michelin stars and reclaiming 5 rosettes, and in 2015 Allister was awarded an Acorn Award.

As of January 2016 Allister is Executive chef of the Grove of Narberth, Pembrokeshire, where he and a close knit team of chefs strive to produce quality food using the freshest of ingredients.

Poached Sea Bass
shitake & soy puree, bok choi salad, lemongrass foam

INGREDIENTS

Sea Bass

600g fillet of line caught Sea bass

Table salt

Shitake and soy puree

300g slice Shitake mushrooms

30g Soy sauce

50g Butter

100g Chicken stock

100g Water

Lemongrass foam

50g sliced Shallots

150g sliced Button mushrooms

50g Butter

250g Gewürztraminer wine

250g Fish stock

250g Double cream

7g Lemon thyme

70g Lemongrass chopped small

Lemongrass oil

100g blended Olive oil

20g Lemongrass chopped small

Garnish

16 Bok choi leaves

Toasted sesame oil

toasted Sesame seeds

4 large Shitake mushrooms cut into sixths

20 Shimiji mushrooms

150g Madeira

Lemon balm shoots

8 Lime segments

METHOD

For the Sea Bass

Start by skinning the fillet and removing as much of the brown fat as possible. Now weigh the fillet. Separately weigh the salt using a ratio of 4g for every 100g of fish. Evenly sprinkle the fish with the salt all over, cling film and refrigerate for 3 hours. When ready rinse well under a cold tap, pat dry and portion into 4. Vacuum pack each portion with a little lemon grass oil and a sprig of lemon thyme. When needed drop the fish into a 55C water bath for 8-10 minutes.

For the shitake and soy puree

Melt the butter in a sauce pan and add the mushrooms, cook on a medium heat until slippery in look. Add the soy sauce and reduce by half. Now add the liquids and cook out for 20 minutes. Drain the mushrooms, reserving the liquor, and place into a blender. Add just enough liquor so that it can blend freely until smooth. Pass through a fine sieve and correct seasoning and place into a squeezy bottle.

For the lemon grass foam

Start by melting the butter in a saucepan, add the shallots with the lemongrass and a pinch of salt. Sweat for 10 minutes until they start to soften. Now add the mushrooms and sweat for a further 2 minutes. Pour in the fish stock and reduce by 1\2. In a separate sauce pan reduce the wine by 1\2 also. Once the wine and stock is reduced, add them together followed by the cream and lemon thyme. Simmer for 20 minutes and pass through a fine sieve. Correct seasoning.

Lemon grass oil

Heat the oil and lemongrass together to 80C and blend for 5 minutes. Pass through a muslin cloth and place into a squeezy bottle.

To finish and serve

Place the shitake, shimiji and Madeira in a sauce pan with a small knob of butter and a pinch of salt. Reduce this down until a stick glace and keep warm. Cut the lime segments into 4 and keep warm in a little stock syrup. Now blanch the Bok choi in boiling salted water for 20 seconds until they just start to wilt and drain off into a bowl. Dress the leaves in a little toasted sesame oil and a sprinkling of sesame seeds, and season. Make sure all the elements are hot, if needs be flash the fish under a hot grill for 30 seconds but don't overcook it! Plate the dish as pictured and finish with a few lemon balm shoots and a drizzle of lemon grass oil.

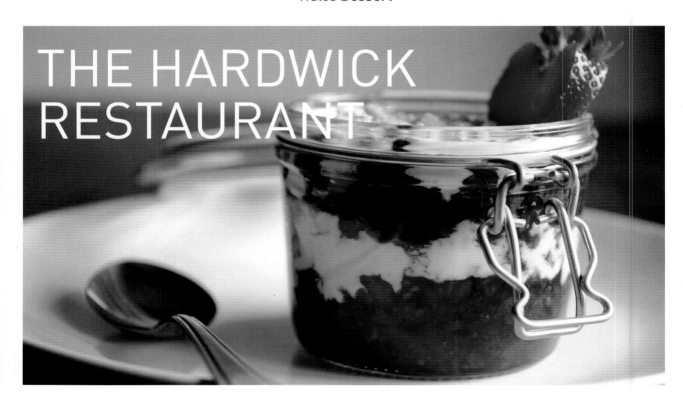

THE HARDWICK RESTAURANT

BIOGRAPHY

Stephen Terry is Chef Patron of The Hardwick in Abergavenny, and has worked with some of the best chefs in the world over a long and successful career.

Stephen was mentored by Marco Pierre White at Harvey's, and then moved to La Gavroche to work under Michel Roux Jr; this introduction to classical French cookery became the foundation to Stephen's own food philosophy. A season at The Breaval Old Mill under Nick Nairn and two years as Head Chef at The Canteen in Chelsea Harbour followed, where Stephen was awarded his first Michelin star at the age of 25. He then worked in the South of France, in Paris with Alain Passard, and then came back to London to open Oliver Peyton's Coast as Head Chef in Mayfair. Many chefs worked under Stephen at this time, including Jason Atherton, Hywell Jones, Mark Sargent and Dan Lepard.

In 2001 Stephen opened The Walnut Tree Inn, which was awarded a Michelin star the following year. Before opening The Hardwick, Stephen took the role of Head Chef at Cecconi's in Mayfair and The Pear Tree Inn in Wiltshire, which was then awarded Best Pub in England by the AA Guide in 2005. Stephen appeared on BBC 2's Great British Menu in 2008, representing Wales and cooking the fish course at the final banquet for the World's top chefs. He appeared again in 2009 and 2012, and was a mentor in 2010. Stephen has appeared regularly on Saturday Kitchen since 2011.

Summer Fruit Pudding

INGREDIENTS

150g Strawberries
(reserve the most
beautiful one in the pack
for garnish!)

150g Raspberries

150g Blueberries

150g Blackberries

150g Red Currants

½ Loaf good quality
(preferably artisanal)
sourdough bread

225g Caster sugar

4 tbsp Crème fraîche

4 suitable Jars for serving
(approximately 200ml)

METHOD

Remove any stalks from the fruit and wash thoroughly in cold water & drain. Place all the fruit in a stainless steel roasting tray combine with the caster sugar and place into the oven at 180°C for 8 – 10 minutes. Remove form the oven, strain the juice from the fruit into a large bowl. Transfer the fruit to a suitable container and allow to cool.

Cut the sourdough bread into approximately 2cm dice and place into the warm cooked fruit juice. Stirring occasionally & allow to soak for 45 minutes.

Strain the bread from the cooked fruit juice using a metal sieve gently pushing on the bread to remove any excess juice.

To serve, in the bottom of each glass jar build a layer of soaked bread then a layer of cooked fruit, layer of bread, finishing with the last layer of fruit.

Finish with a large tablespoon of crème fraiche and a quarter of strawberry.

SIGNATURES

BIOGRAPHY

Jimmy Williams is an award winning chef whose passion for cooking has helped him progress from washing up to having his restaurant named 'best place to eat in Wales'.

As owner and executive chef at Signatures Restaurant in Conwy, Jimmy uses local Welsh ingredients to create dishes inspired by classic French cooking. He credits Michel Roux Snr as his all time food hero. Jimmy initially made a name for himself by putting on award winning performances at international competitions such as the World Culinary Championship, where he won both gold and silver medals. Sixteen years on and several kitchens later, he still exhibits the same drive and determination that marked him apart as a young chef.

Constantly experimenting with dishes, Jimmy lists the hallmarks of a great meal as being 'preparation, quality ingredients' and most importantly of all 'passion – otherwise it gets boring.'

"Study Of Peach" Warm Roasted Peach, Peach Schnapps Pannacotta, Peach Trifle, Peach Melba Ice Ceam.

INGREDIENTS

Peach Schnapps Panna Cotta

80 ML Double cream

80 ML Whipping cream

20 ML Peach Schnapps

20 ML White peach coulis

30g Sugar

1 leaf Gelatine (soaked)

Peach Melba Ice Cream (best done day before)

5 Egg yolks

50g Sugar

1 Vanilla pods (split and scraped)

350ml Double cream

Basket Mix

40g Icing sugar

10g Plain flour

15ml Orange juice

15g melted Butter

Peach Coulis

125g Sugar

250ml Peach puree

Peach Jelly

100ml Peach coullis

1 leaf Gelatine

2 Sponge fingers

Crème Patisserie

2 Egg yolks

10oz Caster sugar

18g Plain flour

130ml Milk

Warm Roasted Peach

2 Peaches

2tbsp Sugar

METHOD

Peach Schnapps Panna Cotta

Put the 80ml whipping cream into a pan with the sugar and bring to scalding point. Whisk in the soaked gelatine until dissolved and strain into a mixing bowl.

Whisk in the remaining ingredients, re strain the mix and pour into Dario moulds. Refrigerate to set.

Peach Melba Ice Cream (best done day before)

Put the egg yolks and the scraped vanilla seeds into the machine mixing bowl and whip until trebled in volume. Put the sugar into a pan with just enough water to create a wet sand texture and take to soft ball.

Once the sugar has reached soft ball, carefully drizzle it onto the rapidly whisking egg yolks and leave to whisk until cold.

Fold in the double cream and churn in an ice cream machine

When churned, place diced cooked peaches and raspberry coullis in between each layer of ice cream, then place in freezer.

Basket Mix

Sift the flour and icing sugar together and put in the small blender.

Turn the blender on and gradually add the orange juice. Once completely combined, gradually add the melted butter.

Allow the mix to blitz for a further minute. Transfer the mixture to a tub and refrigerate for at least 2 hours before using.

Place a small round template on a slip mat and spread mixture thinly. When ready to bake, cook in oven on 160c till golden brown.

When cool, take the circles off gently and place them on top of a Dariole mould.

Finally, gently blowtorch the disc until it slowly forms into a basket.

Peach Coulis

Soft ball sugar, boil puree and add to sugar. Boil until very thick and chill in fridge.

Peach Jelly

Add soaked gelatine to hot coulis

Place diced sponge fingers into bottom of shot glasses. Pour warm liquid into 4 shot glasses just under halfway up and set in the fridge

Crème Patisserie

In a pan, cream the yolks & sugar together well. Then mix in the flour.

Bring milk to boil in another pan, then whisk a little into egg pan.

Add the rest of the liquid and cook over a gentle heat stirring to a smooth cream.

Place into a piping bag and chill in fridge.

Warm Roasted Peach

Half peaches and take out the stones.

Facing up, put on a tray and cover with sugar. Put a little water on the tray and cook on low until soft.

Turn peaches over and cook for one minute before taking out to cool down in the syrup, then cut into quarters.

To Assemble Trifles

Take shot Glasses out of fridge, pipe creme patisserie on top of jelly, then finally top with peach Coulis and half whipped cream.

To Plate

Place trifles, panna cottas, baskets and warm peaches on plates, finally scoop ice cream into baskets.

Garnish:

Raspberries, Baby Mint, Peach Coulis.

THE BULL - BEAUMARIS

BIOGRAPHY

Hefin Roberts joined the 5*, Bull on Anglesey in 2009 but has been cooking as long as he can remember. His first job at the age of 14 as a kitchen porter triggered his ambition to become an award winning Chef. He signed up and joined the Welsh National Culinary Team in 2002 and to date and won a string of medals and awards all over the world. While with the Welsh team Hefin also cooked for HRH Prince Charles and David Cameron. 2009 came along with the opportunity he couldn't miss. Head Chef at the renowned Loft restaurant in the Bull. Here is where he achieved the first ever 3 Rosettes accolade to be announced on the Isle of Anglesey and in the same year achieved Best restaurant in Wales.

Rum Baba
lime & cherry ice cream

INGREDIENTS

Baba

250g Plain flour

pinch of Salt

15g of fresh Yeast

2 free range Eggs, beaten

15g Golden caster sugar

125ml warmed Milk

50g of soft melted Butter

Lime cream

500ml Cream

100g Caster sugar

2 leaves Gelatine

4 Limes

Meringue

Caster sugar

Water

Egg whites

Cherry ice cream

500g pitted Cherries

3 tablespoons of squeezed Lemon juice

1 tablespoon of Balsamic vinegar

200g Sugar

250ml of Milk

500ml Double cream

1 Vanilla pod

250g Caster sugar

5 tbsp Dark rum

250g Caster sugar

5 tbsp Dark rum

METHOD

Baba

To make the baba's, dissolve the fresh yeast in the warmed milk, in a stand up mixer add the flour, salt and sugar, mix with a beater for a few minutes until thoroughly combined. Add the eggs slowly and then the warmed milk with yeast with the mixer still on a slow gear. Once all combined, mix the dough at high speed to give it more body, at least 5 minutes or until it comes away from the sides of the bowl. Add the melted butter again at a slow speed to incorporate all the butter. Scrape all the dough out with a pastry scrapper and place in a large bowl, cover the bowl tightly with Clingfilm and leave the mixture prove and doubled in size. Knock back the dough with your hands and place in a pipping bag. Slightly grease the moulds with oil using a paper towel. Once the moulds are ready pipe the dough 3/4 full, then leave the dough rise again until they are full. Bake at 180c for 15 minutes or until the baba's are all puffed up and are a nice golden brown. Pop out of the moulds and cool down using a cooling rack

Lime cream

To make the lime cream, first soak the gelatine for 5 minutes, then squeeze the gelatine to get rid of any excess water,

Boil the cream and infuse with the lime zest add the sugar, stir in the gelatine and pass the whole mixture through a fine sieve. Now place the cream mixture in the fridge until set. Once set blend mixture with a hand blender, once smooth pour into a pipping bag. Set aside for later use.

Meringue

For the Italian meringue, place the sugar and water in a pan and bring to the boil until the syrup reaches 110c.

At this stage whisk the egg whites in a free standing mixer until you have firm peaks. Continue heating the sugar up until it reaches 121c remove from heat and immediately resume whisking with the machine on its lowest setting then pour the syrup in a steady stream. Continue whisking until the meringue has become tepid. Place the meringue in a pipping bag and spread the mixture evenly and about a pound coin thickness on a rubber mat. Place in a dehydrator until crisp.

Cherry ice cream

Mix the cherries, lemon juice, 100g of the sugar and leave to infuse for an hour.

Drain the cherries but retain the juice, and mash up the rest until you have a pulp.

In another bowl mix the milk and sugar with an electric mixer until the sugar dissolved then stir in the cream, cherry juice, pulp and scrape out the seed from the vanilla pod.

Put the mixture into an ice cream machine and churn until thickened and creamy. Scoop out and freeze.

Rum syrup

For the syrup, put the sugar and rum in a small saucepan with 200ml of water and bring to the boil.

CWELLYN ARMS

BIOGRAPHY

Tom started in the Industry quite young helping his parents on weekends and after school at the Cwellyn Arms, which they have had the last 35 years, before moving away to study and work in the industry around the Cheltenham area.

He returned home some 8-10 years ago to take over the running of the kitchens at the Cwellyn Arms, sticking to their ethos of supporting local suppliers by using local ingredients & run the business alongside his parents, Julie and Graham and sister Zoe.

"We try to offer a friendly place where you can pop in for a drink (we have 9 real ales on tap) or sit down and enjoy good food without the stuffy atmosphere, the menu varies from traditional pub fayre-sometimes with a twist - to our varied restaurant dishes and specials.

Last year we built a new restaurant area to the side of the pub, looking up to mount Snowdon, finished our poly tunnel and garden area (including our onsite smokehouse) and finished extending our kitchens – this extra space along with freshly grown ingredients on site has given our team in the kitchen much more opportunity to experiment with new dishes – it's quite an exciting time!"

Apple With Crumble

INGREDIENTS

Brioche Ice Cream

600ml Milk

400 Double cream

150g Lightly toasted brioche, 2cm cubes

8 Egg yolks

150g Caster sugar

50g Liquid glucose

Spiced Syrup

250g Caster sugar

580ml Water

2 Star anise

1 Cinnamon stick

1 Orange zest

¼ tsp Ground ginger

6 Apples

2 Rhubarb sticks

Crumble

8 oz Flour

8 oz Butter

5 oz Demerara Sugar

2 oz Ground almond

2 oz Hazelnut, lightly crushed

½ Lemon zest

½ Orange zest

Brandy Snaps Baskets

50g Granulated sugar

50g Unsalted butter

50g Golden syrup

50g Plain flour

½ tbsp Lemon juice

½ tbsp Ground ginger

METHOD

For the brioche ice cream, heat the milk and cream gently in a heavy bottomed pan. Do not boil. Remove from the heat and add the brioche, leave to infuse at least 2 hours or overnight. Liquidize the brioche/milk mixture until smooth and bring back up to heat. Meanwhile, whisk the egg yolks, sugar and glucose until pale and creamy. Add half of the hot brioche mixture to the yolks and mix then pour back into the pan. Heat gently whilst stirring constantly until the mixture begins to thicken enough to coat the back of a spoon or reaches 83-84°C. DO NOT BOIL.

Transfer to a plastic container and stir until cooled. This mixture can then be churned in an ice cream machine or even in a freezer if you take care to stir the mixture every 10-20mins.

For the Baskets, melt the butter, sugar and syrup in a pan. Add the flour, ginger and lemon juice and mix. Spoon the mixture onto a lined tray (approximately one level teaspoon each). Bake at 190°C for approximately 10minutes or until golden. Leave to cool flat.

For the crumble, dice the butter and add to a bowl with all the other ingredients. Rub through your fingers until combined. Shape half of the mixture into small discs using a mousse ring or cutter onto a lined tray. Spread the rest of the mixture onto a separate lined tray, in no particular way- this tray will be crumbled and used to stuff your apples. Bake both trays at 190°C for 10-15 minutes or until golden. Leave to cool.

For the apples and rhubarb, combine the sugar, water & spices and orange zest in a pan and simmer for 5 minutes to infuse. Meanwhile cut the rhubarb into batons 1cm x 5cm and blanch until tender, 1 to 3 minutes. Do this in batches and allow to cool.

Peel and core the apple and place in a deep roasting tray. Using the 2nd tray of the crumble mix, sprinkle into the apple core and press firmly. Pour in the spiced syrup. This should come half way up your apples. Place in the oven at 170°C-175°C for 20-30 minutes or until the apples begin to swell and become tender. Don't worry if you spill crumble mix into the tray as this will help to thicken your sauce

Serve the apples immediately while hot and pour in some of the syrup/sauce, place one crumble disc onto each apple then top with your ice cream and a brandy snap disc.

THE BLACK LION INN

BIOGRAPHY

Anglesey born and bred Wayne Roberts is the Head Chef of the Black Lion Inn Llanfaethlu. He started his career working at a Country House Hotel from the age of 17 to become the youngest second chef at 23yrs of age.

Wayne was the first Welsh Chef to be awarded with the Applied Ability Award, Chefs Certificate and in 2015 he was awarded his first AA Rosette Award

As well as being interviewed on local Radio and TV station along with articles in the local press, Wayne has taken part in many cookery demonstrations in local events and festivals.

Wayne is an extremely talented, creative, highly-motivated, skilled and passionate chef with a proven track record of providing exemplary levels of service to a broad range of food establishments.

He uses his wealth of experience and skills at the Black Lion to make it a unique place to come and eat and to have a wonderful experience.

Wayne has an excellent working relationship with everyone that he comes in contact with, his team, local suppliers and producers as well as his customers.

Wayne says " This is the second year that we have been asked to take part in creating a dish for the great British Cookbook and we feel very honoured and privileged to be asked to do so, giving support to two so worthy charities. "

'Bara Brith' Bread & Butter Pudding, Marmalade Crème Anglaise

INGREDIENTS

Bara Brith Bread and Butter pudding

2 x 516g Bara brith loaf
6x slices of White bread
4 tbsp Castor sugar
5 tbsp Demerara sugar
3 Free range egg yolks
350ml Cream
100ml Milk
100g Sultanas
25ml Dark rum
25ml Baileys
40g Marmalade (to glaze)
100g Unsalted butter

Marmalade Crème Anglaise

4 x Free range egg yolks
200g Castor sugar
2tbsp Cornflour
200ml Cream
100ml Milk
100g Fine cut marmalade

METHOD

Soak the sultanas in the Dark rum and baileys for approximately 2 hrs

Set oven to 160°C

Grease loaf tin with baking parchment / grease proof paper

Slice the bara brith 1- 2 cm thick, butter bara brith and white bread on 1 side only

Layer the bara brith & white in the loaf tin, butter side down (alternate each layer)

Sprinkle the demerara and soaked sultanas between each layer, should be 5/6 layers deep

Meanwhile whisk the egg yolks & castor sugar until the sugar is well incorporated and the mix is pale in colour

Heat the milk & cream on a medium heat, simmer but do not boil

Add the milk & cream into the egg yolk mixture whisking all the time

Pour the mixture over the bara brith through a sieve

Bake in the oven @ 160°C for 10 minutes then turn the oven down to 140°c for further 20 minutes

The pudding is ready when slightly set but still has a bit of give (wobble!)

Heat marmalade & glaze the pudding using a pastry brush

Leave the pudding to cool and place in the fridge to set overnight

To complement the pudding, we recommend serving with a marmalade crème anglaise

Heat the milk & cream in a pan to simmering but do not boil

Meanwhile whisk the egg yolk, castor sugar & cornflour in a heatproof bowl until light in colour

Pour the cream in to the egg yolk mixture and whisk

Pour back in to a clean pan through a sift

Add the marmalade

Bring back to simmer point whilst stirring with a wooden spoon

The finished sauce should coat the back of the spoon

To serve

Cut the bread and butter pudding into portions

Bake in the oven for 10 minutes at 180°C

Meanwhile warm the crème anglaise in a pan on the stove

BRITISH
WINES

The popularity of English wine has been growing steadily over the last decade. You can now find plenty of the stuff at leading supermarkets, and restaurants up and down the UK. Last year Gordon Ramsay made headlines for serving English wine at a newly opened venture in Bordeaux, an act unthinkable 10 years ago.

One vineyard at the forefront of this charge is Camel Valley. Tucked inland in balmy Cornwall its story started over 20 years ago with the Lindo family. Bob and his wife Annie began back in the 1980's - but the nature of the wine making meant their first drop didn't reach any lips until 1995. As much as this is a family story, Bob pays homage to the local community too. The Vineyard now sponsors the Cornwall tourism awards – their way of reciprocating the support they received in their fledgling years.

It seems such a relaxed, enjoyable environment to work in and Bob Lindo, admiring his lush green hills bathed in sunlight, says "I think this should take at least half the credit". This simple modesty suits Camel Valley and the Lindo's. The couple originally farmed livestock and little imagined their future success when they turned their hands to vines.

"We've never picked up the phone to sell a bottle of our wine", Bob tells me. It becomes evident during my time at this family-run vineyard that this sums up how things come to pass for the Lindo's. A favourite story of his concerns a visitor whom was so impressed with their tour and tasting that they watered their wedding with the stuff. Who was a guest at that occasion? A buyer from Fortnum and Mason. Had they gone directly to pitch to that most famous of stores they wouldn't have been given time of day. They are also supported by food and drink personalities who are champions of their product. One of Cornwall's most famous sons, Rick Stein, featured them on his Food Heroes in the early days of their popularity. More recently, he has stocked his widening empire of restaurants with Camel Valley wine, as has Nathan Outlaw, whose flagship eatery in Port Isaac is one of the best in the country. It doesn't stop with the great and the good of the culinary world. Camilla, Duchess of Cornwall has visited the vineyard on multiple occasions and recalled seeing it served at a function as far away as Sri Lanka.

Sam, the son of Bob and Annie, grew up on the vineyard and has become ever more involved as years have gone on. He still remembers tending vines from the age of nine, though he didn't appreciate picking grapes whilst his friends were enjoying the Cornish beaches! Despite this, it was always a free choice for the natural heir to the vines. At the end of his university days Sam flirted with ambitions to work in the city but soon realised that others were jealous of the opportunity to work at a vineyard. Shirt and tie were swapped for shorts and he returned to Camel Valley, falling in love with his new lifestyle. He had bought some modernisation to the business, dragging Bob into the 21 st century - he recalls it was some time before a computer was invested in and an ice cream tub was no longer used for change.

With the product travelling all over the world, what is the future of fizz from our fair land? There will be much more to come, says Sam. They have seen the competition in the English wine market grow. Between 2003 and 2013 the total hectares of vineyard in the UK has more than doubled*. Broadly this has been beneficial for the industry, raising knowledge and visibility of England as an excellent producer. Many of the recent entrants to the field have been cashing in and quickly setting up large scale productions. In the same ten years the average size of vineyards has also nearly doubled. What these bigger operations gain in speed to market they lose in refining the product to the excellence of Camel Valley. They also lack the age and family story unique to the Lindo's. That special something is most evident in a wine called Annie's Anniversary. A patch of vines has been pruned solely by Annie for 25 years. As Bob tells it, she refuses to let anyone else help come rain, snow or shine. It is made from Seyval Blanc, not a fashionable grape, and one which other vineyards overlook in favour of more well-known vines. A more distinctive creation would be difficult to find.

Of course, a great back-story counts for nothing if the product isn't also great. Fortunately, Camel Valley deservedly sits amongst the most lauded producers in English wine. Recently their wine was listed for best sparkling in the world - the first time anyone not from Champagne has been nominated. Other plaudits include; best rosé sparkling in the world three times, eleven international gold medals and UK wine maker of the year three times. My favourite quote of the day came from Bob - "We are quite good at PR, but crucially none of it is bollocks. Our view is to do something, and then tell people about it".

The future of Camel? "We aren't looking to get any bigger. The quality of the product is at the peak right now". The team here will happily continue with their modest scale rather than commercialise and grow the business further.

Central

Starter
Main
Dessert

THE PANTRY

BIOGRAPHY

The Pantry is an independant award winning restaurant and deli based in Newmarket with a focus on all day dining. It is headed up by a husband and wife team Vincent and Anne-Marie, who take pride in offering the very best of what Suffolk as to offer.

The Pantry specialises in classic English food, showcasing traditional cuts of meat and preparation methods such as calves liver or pigs head and trotter terrines. Our menu also features French and Italian influences, which fit with the continental deli style of our restaurant with its open kitchen and deli counter.

Breakfast is not to missed at the Pantry, with our weekend brunches being particularly popular. We are also open for lunch, dinner and afternoon tea, our business is alive and buzzing through out the day.

In 2013 the restaurant and deli successfully expanded into the neighbouring premises in order to meet demand for additional seating, allow for a greater range of deli items and create space for a great wine and cocktail bar.

Pan-Fried Calves Liver
with braised lentils, roasted root vegetables and bacon jam

INGREDIENTS

1 kilo of Calves liver

200g Carrot batons

200g Golden beetroot

200g Squash

250g Braised lentils

500ml of Ham stock

100g Bacon jam
(see blog for recipe)

Splash of balsamic
vinegar

15g Butter for frying

6 Bulbs of garlic

1 Bunch thyme

Salt and pepper

METHOD

To prepare the vegetables, baton the carrots and cut the beetroot and squash into cubes.

The beetroot and carrot will cook at the same time so place in a large roasting tray with the thyme and 3 garlic bulbs (unpeeled) roast off for 30 minutes at 180c with seasoning and vegetable oil.

Toss the vegetables and add the squash, roast for another 30 minutes or until tender.

To cook the lentils cover with the stock and remaining garlic, simmer on a medium heat until tender (about 30 minutes).

To cook the liver season with salt and pepper, get a pan hot and add the butter, when foaming add the calves liver, cook for about a minute on each side till golden brown but still pink. Fry in batches rather than overloading the pan.

Once the liver is cooked deglaze the pan with balsamic vinegar and add the bacon jam to warm through.

Finish the dish by draining the lentils, keep a little stock back to finish the dish. Toss through the roasted vegetables and serve in warm bowls with liver on top of the lentils and the bacon jam pan sauce spooned over the top.

THE FOREST AT FECKENHAM

BIOGRAPHY

Chef Tom Robinson joined the award winning CD Pub Co. in 2010 and in 2013 Tom helped launch The Forest at Feckenham in Worcestershire.

Tom thrives on the ethos of the company which believes in using the best quality ingredients with simple cooking techniques to create the finest dining experience in the area.

Beef Brisket Hash
fried duck egg, brown sauce

INGREDIENTS

For the brown sauce
125g Pitted prunes
(chopped)

425ml Malt vinegar

40g Sea salt

.5 teaspoon Cayenne
pepper

1.5 teaspoon Ground
allspice

1 teaspoon Ground ginger

1 teaspoon Ground
nutmeg

2x medium Spanish onions
(chopped)

500g Granny smith apples
(peeled & chopped)

250g Caster sugar

**For the braised beef
brisket (this can be
cooked beforehand)**
500g Beef brisket

1 Carrot peeled & chopped

2 Onions chopped

2 stick Celery

3 cloves Garlic

2 tablespoon Tomato
puree

4 sprigs fresh Thyme

1 sprig Rosemary

150ml Red wine

1 ltr Beef stock

2 tablespoon Worcester
sauce

For the hash
400g Braised beef brisket

500g Potatoes (peeled &
chopped)

50g Unsalted butter

3x Shallots (finely
chopped)

1x Carrot (peeled & finely
chopped)

half a fresh Red chilli
(deseeded & finely
chopped) optional

1 tablespoon Worcester
sauce

10g flat leaf Parsley
(chopped)

10g Chive (chopped)

3g Sea salt

2g ground Black pepper

4x Duck eggs

METHOD

For the brown sauce

Place all ingredients in a heavy bottomed saucepan bring to the boil then
simmer for 2 hours stirring occasionally
Remove and place in a blender and blend until smooth
Check seasoning and leave to cool

For the braised beef brisket

Preheat oven to 170 degrees
In a large casserole pan heat a little oil
Sear the brisket on all sides and remove from the pan
Add the veg to the pan and sweat for 5 mins
Place the beef back in and deglaze with the red wine
Add the rest of the ingredients and bring to the boil, skim off any scum
Place the lid on and put in the oven for 4.5 hours (the brisket is ready when
it can be easily pulled apart with a fork)
Leave to cool in the pan

For the hash

Boil potatoes until tender
Pour into a colander and leave to stand for 5 minutes
Place in a large bowl and mash lightly
Dice up the beef and mix through the potato
Sweat the shallots in half the butter for 2 minutes and add to the potato mix
Add the rest of the ingredients into the hash and mix well
Check the seasoning and form into 6 equal sized cakes & leave to set in the
fridge for 20-30 minutes
Pre heat oven to 180 degrees
Heat a saucepan and melt the remaining butter
Dust the cakes with a little flour and fry the hash on both sides until golden
Place in the oven for 12-15 minutes.
Meanwhile, heat a little oil in a frying pan and fry the eggs until cooked
Place the hash on a plate with the egg on top, serve the brown sauce on the
side.

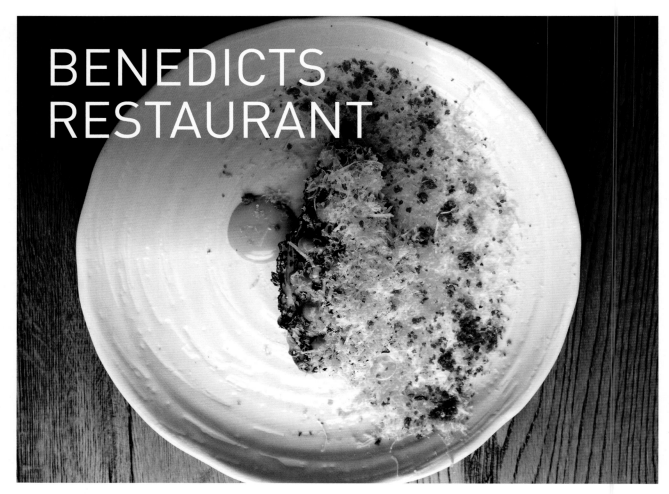

BENEDICTS RESTAURANT

Photo by Rich Brown

BIOGRAPHY

Richard is a Norfolk boy through and through, starting in a pub kitchen in Norwich aged 13, he travelled the world to learn all he could about the industry that has ignited so much passion in him as a young man. He has finally returned to Norwich 20 years later to set down his roots in his own Restaurant in the heart of this beautiful city with his beautiful wife Katja by his side.

Richard's vision was to create "somewhere that we wish we could go to on our day off with only a small menu of perfectly put together dishes using the best possible seasonal produce from local suppliers. A small but perfectly formed neighbourhood restaurant" Richard started out working in his local pub in the kitchen but his potential was soon spotted by Galton Blackiston and he started working at michelin starred Morston Hall aged 16.

From there, Richard contined learning his craft at the three Michelin star Waterside Inn in Bray (still rated in the top 10 best restaurants in the world, even after Richard left) under the prestigious Roux brothers. He worked his way up from commis chef to junior sous chef over 3 years. His classical French training underpinning the contemporary British style of food on the menu at Benedicts.

Caesar Salad

INGREDIENTS

2 whole small Baby gems

Gentlemen Relish Mayo

1 small tub of Gentlemens relish

2 Duck egg yolks

1teaspoon Dijon mustard

1tea spoon Cider vinegar

juice of 1 Lemon

250 millilitre Norfolk rapeseed oil

Lemon Puree

1 whole Lemon (stab with a knife all over)

100 gram Sugar

100 millilitre Water

Garlic Puree

1 bulb of Garlic

pre-heat oven to 180c

Parmesan

50 grams of Parmesan to grate over the whole dish

Bread Crumbs

50 gr Dried bread crumbs

10 gr Salted butter

Cured Egg Yolk

2 fresh Hens Yolks

100gr Table Salt

METHOD

Slice the baby gems in half and wash. Season lightly with salt and using a blowtorch colour the flesh side of the lettuce.

In a bowl place the egg yolks, mustard, vinegar and lemon juice, whisk well then slowly start to add the rapeseed oil a little at a time until you have a thick and rich mayo.Then fold in the gentlemen relish season with salt and cayenne pepper to taste. place in a pipping bag for later.

Place the lemon in a pan of clean water and bring to the boil, repeat this 2 times this is helping to remove bitterness and cook the lemon. Then place the sugar and 100ml of water into a pan and place the lemon in. Bring to the boil and repeat this 3 times. Place all into a blender and blend until smooth. Place into a pipping bag for later.

Place the whole garlic bulb on to a bed of salt, place in the oven and bake for 1hour. Remove the skin from the garlic and blend into a puree and place into a pipping bag.

place the Butter into a frying pan on a high heat. As your Butter starts to foam, add the Bread Crumbs, season with Salt and Pepper and fry until golden brown. Remove from the heat and place onto kitchen towel to drain.

In a small bowl place half the Salt as a base layer, then add your egg yolks and cover completely with the rest of the Salt. Leave this is a cool dark place for 24 hours. Carefully remove the Yolks from the Salt and brush off excess Salt. Then place on a cooling Rack in your oven (if you have a gas Oven, on Pilot Light or on Electric Ovens the lowest setting) and dry out for between 4 to 6 hours, until it resembles a dried Apricot. Place in an airtight container until ready to use. Will keep for up to 2 weeks.

Place the baby gems in the middle of the plate and pipe dots of the garlic, lemon and gentlemen mayo all over the baby gem. Then to finish grate the parmesan and cured egg yolk over the gem and to finish sprinkle the bread crumbs over. Serve. ENJOY !

ARROW MILL

BIOGRAPHY

Arrow Mill Hotel and Restaurant is set in the heart of rural Warwickshire, close to Stratford upon Avon by the Roman market town of Alcester and surrounded by a spectacular secluded riverside setting. Arrow Mill is an independently owned country hotel run by Chef Simon Woodhams and his family. The Woodhams' approach to running the hotel and restaurant is all about flexibility, so if you want something really special for a function, reception orconference you'll find Arrow Mill will adapt to whatever you need. At the heart of the hotel is the kitchen, headed by Chef Simon Woodhams. Simon has over 30 years- experience gaining Arrow Mill an enviable reputation for fine dining. Whatever brings you to Arrow Mill you can be sure of a memorable dining experience. Simon's food is classic and simple, using seasonal produce grown at the mill or from the host of local high quality producers.

Nepalese Masala Partridge Breast alu tikka & chutney

INGREDIENTS

Partridge Breasts

2 Boneless supremes per person
1 tsp heaped Garam masala powder
Finely chopped Garlic clove
1 tsp minced Ginger
Oil
diced Butter

Alu Tiki

200g mashed Potato
Butter for frying
1/2 sliced Shallot
pinch of Chiili flakes/fresh Chilli (optional)
1 tsp chopped Coriander
10g Peas
Curry masala

Tomato & Onion Seed Chutney

3 tbsp Vegetable oil
1 tsp Black onion seeds
2 Bay leaves
3 dried whole Red dried chillies
1 tsp Chilli powder
250g diced Tomato
100g Brown sugar
1 tbsp Sultanas/ raisins
pinch of Salt

Coriander Chutney

100g fresh Coriander
1/2 Lemon juice
4 Garlic cloves
3 Green chillies
3 tbsp Olive oil
1 tsp Salt
1/2 tsp Sugar

METHOD

Partridge Breasts

Put the partridge into a plastic freezer bag with the garlic paste, oil and masala. Marinate for about 2 - 4 hours. Heat the oil and sauté the breasts adding additional butter and baste. These will only take a couple of mins to cook, so don't overcook them and dry them out. Slice each breast diagonally and place on kitchen paper ready to assemble.

Alu Tiki

Sauté and soften the shallots in the butter, add to the other ingredients and mashed potato and mix well. Form uniform sized small potato cakes using a pastry cutter, dust in flour and fry on both sides until golden. Set aside and keep warm.

Tomato & Onion Seed Chutney

Heat the oil and add the dried chillies, bay leaves and onion seeds. When they start to crackle, add the remaining ingredients and cook until most of the liquid has reduced. Will keep in an airtight container for up to two weeks.

Coriander Chutney

Blitz all the ingredients in a blender until it's of spoonable consistency. Top the potato with the partridge and spoon out the chutney. Finish with a spoonful of minted yoghurt, coriander and some crispy shallots. Voila. I spent five years working alongside a Nepalese chef, whose wife cooked this for me when I was invited to their home, having donated the partridge. The different flavours are amazing and yes, they do have partridge in Nepal.

From there it has evolved into what I present every game season. Something a little different when there is an abundance of local game and also works well with pheasant. Be careful not to dry it out.

DORMY HOUSE

BIOGRAPHY

Ryan's career has taken him through a gourmand's fantasy of Michelin-starred and AA-rosetted kitchens across Europe, including stints in Lords of the Manor, Hambleton Hall, Mallory Court and many more, where he worked alongside some of the most admired chefs in the business.

Ryan is a passionate advocate of fresh produce and seasonal ingredients, not least because they take him back to his childhood. "I'd walk down my nan and granddad's huge garden, where they grew everything you could imagine in four huge greenhouses, " he recalls: "My granddad supplied the family with all sorts of fresh fruit and veg, and my nan cooked with me all the time, using produce from that garden. I'd sit in the veg patches with my mum, eating peas straight from the pod."

To this day Ryan gets giddy when the veg delivery arrives in the kitchen – although, these days, he leaves most of the peas for the guests.

Cornish Mackerel
with heritage carrot and soy

INGREDIENTS

1 whole Mackerel

6 Carrots

1 purple, 1 white, 1 yellow
Heritage carrot

10ml Sesame oil

1 Shallot

100ml Pickling vinegar

50ml Soy sauce

Black sesame seeds

Coriander

2 sheets of Feuilles de
brick pastry

METHOD

Juice the carrots until you have 250ml of juice, add 50ml of the pickling vinegar then reduce down until thickened. Season to taste.

Fillet the mackerel (reserve 2cm of the mackerel tail) wash in some salted water, cover and leave to chill in the fridge.

Dice the mackerel tail and mix with a small handful of chopped coriander, half of the sesame oil and 10ml of the soy sauce.

Finely dice the shallot and rinse under warm running water and add to the diced mackerel mix.

Thinly slice the heritage carrots and place into the remaining 50ml of pickling vinegar.

For the cannelloni, brush one side of the pastry sheets with the remaining sesame oil.

Wrap the sheet of pastry oil side down around the round handle of a kitchen utensil.

Bake the pastry cannelloni at 180 degrees for 10 minutes or until golden.

Whilst the cannelloni is in the oven, pan fry the mackerel for 2 or 3 minutes making sure the skin is crispy.

Take the cannelloni out of the oven, brush with sesame oil and roll in the black sesame seeds. Allow to cool.

Fill the cannelloni with the mackerel tartare.

Plate dish as per picture.

KINGHAM PLOUGH

BIOGRAPHY

Emily Watkins' journey as a chef began in the kitchens of Ristorante Beccofino, Florence, Italy. She loved the passion and energy the Italians put into everything, particularly their food, and the importance they gave to the ingredients and their provenance. Following two years of learning everything including, pasta, desserts and the language, she looked for her next challenge.

In 2002 she moved to The Fat Duck in Bray, working for Heston Blumenthal. The experience opened her eyes to the world of cooking. Heston broke all the traditional rules that were passed down from generation to generation and it was here she learnt that to get the best out of ingredients, it was sometimes better to use modern methods of cooking.

Following The Fat Duck, Emily began to develop her own style while working as a private chef in London. Using techniques learnt not only during her time in Italy and at The Fat Duck, but also from across the world where she spent time working in restaurant kitchens for a few weeks at a time.

In 2007 she opened the Kingham Plough in Chipping Norton, Oxfordshire. As head chef, she put everything into her cooking, working tirelessly to produce delicious dishes in her developing style of modern British cuisine.

Emily is delighted that during this time, so many people have come to The Kingham Plough to enjoy the food. Since its opening in 2007, Emily has featured on The Hairy Bikers, Tom Kerridge's Proper Pub Food and in the local, national and international press. In 2014, Emily competed in Great British Menu and won with her fish course. It was a huge honour for Emily to cook for war veterans at St Paul's Cathedral in a banquet commemorating the 70th anniversary of the D-Day landings.

Rabbit Wellington

INGREDIENTS

1 farmed Rabbit
(1.5kg roughly),
or 2 Wild rabbits
Livers, kidneys and heart

20 Green peppercorns

1 tsp Coriander seeds

1/4 tsp Cumin seeds

15g Panko crumbs

1 tsp chopped Tarragon

pinch Parsley

Chiffonade

50g Mushroom and shallot
duxcelle

Wild garlic leaves

Hot suet pastry

METHOD

BUTCHER THE RABBIT

Remove the loins, trim and keep separate.

Take off all of the offal and keep separate.

Take off the legs, bellies, shoulders and any other meat.

Mince all of the meat (except loins) from the limbs and scraps.

Mince the offal – separately.

Finely chop the peppercorns.

Toast the spices and finely grind to a powder in the spice grinder.

Place all of the infgredients for the mix in a bowl and mix well.

Pull out a long piece of cling film.

Spread the mix on the cling film.

Place the loins on top and roll into a tight roulade. Tie tightly and cook to 58°C.

Chill in an ice bath.

Wrap in blanched wild garlic leaves and then wrap in hot suet pastry.

Cut into 4 portions (roughly 4 to 1 roll).

AURORA

BIOGRAPHY

After studying for 3 years at the Colchester institute, I've spent the last 10 years working in some of the best restaurants in the UK and around the world, including America, Australia, New Zealand and Austria. I've moved around a fair bit and learnt a lot along the way. Notoriously our industry can be a tough old game, with long days, unsociable hours and high pressure all being part of the nature of the beast. Fortunately that part for me is heavily outweighed by my love of cooking and the sense of pride and accomplishment that comes with it. Whilst still in college I saw a quote that read ' If you want to see the rainbow, you have to first go through the rain' I found this to be most motivating, nothing is handed to you on a plate but if you set your mind to it and work hard, anything is achievable.

Aurora is a privately owned bar and restaurant in Ipswich's waterfront area. Set on two levels with the restaurant upstairs and the bar downstairs, both can boast panoramic views of the marina thanks to the external walls being primarily glass. Callum and Steve Hewitt are the directors and I have been their Head Chef since we opened the doors in December 2013. Since then we have built a reputation based on top quality food and high standards of service. The style of food we serve could be described as modern British, sourcing as much produce as we can locally where the quality allows.

Stuffed Blythburgh Pork Fillet
crispy trotters, wholegrain mustard mash, pork sauce

METHOD

Stuffed Pork

Place all the brine ingredients in a pan and bring to the boil, allow to cool and store in the fridge.

Trim the tenderloins of any excess fat and sinew (reserving the trimmings for later use in the sauce) cover with the cold brine. Allow to soak in the fridge for 24 hours.

Rinse the pork under cold running water for 5 minutes and pat dry. Slice the pork lengthwise but not all the way through, so you end up with a larger, flatter service.

Sweat down the shallots and garlic until soft with no colour add the mushrooms, once cooked add the washed spinach, season and allow to cool.

Line the centre of each tenderloin with ½ the stuffing mixture, dust with protein glue, roll the pork around the stuffing then roll tightly in cling film. Place the loins into bags and poach at 63°c for 2 hours. In a domestic environment you could omit the protein glue and instead wrap the loin in caul fat, tie it with string and roast in a pan until nicely browned before finishing it in 180°c oven.

Trotters

Brown the trotters off in a hot pan with a little oil until golden brown add the vegetables and the sugar, allow to caramelise slightly before deglazing with the port and red wine.

Reduce the wine down to a glaze whilst basting the trotters. Add the cider, chicken stock and braise slowly for about 8 hours until the meat falls away from the bone.

Remove the trotters from the cooking liqueur, allow to cool slightly before picking the meat from the bones and roughly chopping. Add the shallots and parsley, adjust the seasoning with salt, pepper and vinegar. Spread the mixture onto a tray lined with parchment paper so it's about 5cm thick. Place another tray on top and press overnight with a weight on top. Cut the pressed trotters into strips about 1cm wide and coat in breadcrumbs ready for deep frying at the last minute.

Sauce

Brown the pork trimmings in a pan with a little oil the remaining carrot and the diced shallot. Once the veg is browned add some thyme, rosemary, garlic, peppercorns and bay leaf then deglaze with white wine, reduce by half then add the brown chicken stock and the trotter cooking liqueur. Simmer for two hours, pass through a fine sieve, reduce to the desired consistency and season with salt and pepper.

INGREDIENTS

2 Pork Tenderloins

Brine
1000ml Water
100g Fine Salt
100g Brown Sugar
10g Pink salt
10 Black peppercorns
2 Bay leaves
1 pinch Fennel seeds
5 sprigs Thyme
2 sprigs Rosemary

Sauce
1 litre Brown chicken Stock
Tenderloin trimmings
1 large Carrot (roughly chopped)
2 Banana shallots (roughly chopped)
large glass of White wine
Thyme
Rosemary
Peppercorns
Bay leaves

Pork Loin
200g diced Flat field Mushrooms
1 Banana shallot
1 clove of Garlic
200g Baby spinach

Trotters
2 Pigs trotters
200ml Red wine
100ml Port
75g Brown sugar
500ml Aspalls cider
700ml White chicken stock
1 Carrot
1 Onion
2 Celery sticks
Thyme
Rosemary
Garlic
Peppercorn
Bay leaves
1 Shallot
A good pinch of chopped flat leaf Parsley
splash of Cider Vinegar
Panko breadcrumbs

Mash
5 large Maris piper potatoes
500g Butter
60ml Milk
2tbs Wholegrain mustard

Mash

Wash the potatoes thoroughly, prick the skins and place on a tray of salt. Bake in the oven at 170°c for around an hour, cut the potatoes in half, scoop out the cooked flesh and pass through a ricer.

Place the mash back in a pan and gently warm it, add the butter in 4 stages allowing the majority of the butter to melt before adding the next batch, add the milk and adjust the seasoning with salt pepper and the wholegrain mustard.

Finishing

Take the tenderloin from the water bath, remove any cling film, pat dry with a J cloth and sear in a hot pan with butter and rosemary, until golden brown. Carve at the last minute, deep fry the trotter element and carve off the ends. Serve with the mash and some seasonal vegetables.

THE BEECHES
BAR AND GRILL

BIOGRAPHY

Matt is a 26-year- old Englishman, born and bred in Solihull. He was inspired to cook at a young age and started his first job as a commis chef at 16, then spent his early twenties working in kitchens overseas and back here in the UK, developing his own style before joining the Beeches Restaurant as Head Chef in 2012. Says Matt: "What we try to do is to produce original, beautifully crafted food with a big emphasis on textures and a great depth of flavours, to create an overall sense of balance. Food that tastes real and wholesome, which showcases the ingredients that have been carefully selected from the field to fork, that hopefully makes you think about where it came from."

Since the Beeches opened in 2007 sourcing the best fresh produce has been at the top of their agenda, with everything from the chutneys to the puddings made from scratch using seasonal, local ingredients, including everything the chefs grow in our own kitchen garden wherever possible.

The Beeches is a fine example of the sum of its parts being greater than the whole. Our team has experience that far surpasses their individual job requirements and such passion that the end result is an experience of food, wine and service that is simply, spot on.

Maple Smoked Pork Belly
apple mash, rhubarb and black pudding

INGREDIENTS

1kg boneless Pork belly skin off

200ml Maple syrup

200ml Cider

100ml Liquid smoke

1 Onion

2 Carrots

2 sticks of Celery

Mash

4/6 Desiree potatoes

200ml Double cream

150g Butter

Maldon Salt & white pepper

Apple puree

4/6 Braeburn apples

100g Caster Sugar

50ml Cider

pinch of Cinnamon

Garnishes

200g good quality Black pudding

melted Butter

200g Rhubarb in 3cm batons

Red Wine

stock from Pork belly

Micro Cress

METHOD

Wash the carrots and celery, cut them into large 2 inch pieces and place these into the base of your roasting tray. Peel and cut the onions into large wedges and add to the tray. Put the seasoned pork belly on top of the vegetables, then mix the maple syrup, cider and liquid smoke together and pour over the pork. Cover with tin foil then roast at 160°C for 2 hours. Remove the pork from the oven and test to see if it pulls apart easily. If not put it back in the oven until the pork is ready then remove from the oven. Take the meat from the tray and place onto a board, cover with the tin foil and allow to rest.

Put the tray of roasted vegetables onto your stove top on a low to medium heat and add in 1/3 of a bottle of red wine to deglaze the pan, then reduce by half to thicken, taste and pass sauce through a fine sieve into a small pan Thinly slice the the black pudding and brush with melted butter, place in the oven with the pork on 160°C keep checking until crispy.

Meanwhile peel the apples, quarter and remove the cores, place in a pan with the cider, sugar and cinnamon. Boil on high for 10 minutes, stirring occasionally. Pour the contents of the pan into a blender and blitz until a smooth puree.

Quarter the potatoes and just halve the smaller ones, place in a large pan and cover with cold salted water. Place over a high heat and bring to the boil, then simmer for 15 to 20 minutes until tender. Drain the potatoes and allow them to steam dry, then return to the same pan with the warmed cream, butter, a pinch of Maldon salt and white pepper. Mash until smooth, add 4 tbsps of the apple puree mix then leave covered until needed.

When ready to plate add the rhubarb batons to the sauce, cook for 2-3 minutes on a low heat until just cooked with a slight bite. Keep the sauce for pouring over the roasted belly. Place apple puree onto plate, then pork belly, then pipe on the mash potato. Garnish with the black pudding and rhubarb using the stock as the sauce. Finish with some home grown micro cress.

RESTAURANT ALIMENTUM

BIOGRAPHY

Mark Poynton is one of the UK's leading chefs and is Chef Patron of the award-winning

Alimentum restaurant in Cambridge. Within a year of arriving at Alimentum and taking the head chef position, the restaurant gained three AA rosettes. Two of Mark's regular customers were so impressed with his cooking that they invested in the business and he took over Alimentum in 2010, becoming Chef-Patron.

In 2011 and 2012 the restaurant was named one of the 'Top 100 UK Restaurants' in the National

Restaurant Awards and in October 2012 was awarded its first Michelin star in the 2013 guide.

Mark was shortlisted for The Craft Guild of Chefs 'Restaurant Chef of the Year' award 2013.

In July 2014, Alimentum was voted number 10 in Square Meal Lifestyle's Top 50 restaurants outside London.

Roasted Halibut
with cauliflower, endive salad and caviar sauce

INGREDIENTS

4 x 150g pieces of Halibut
(skinned and boned)

Roasted Cauliflower Puree

500g finely sliced
Cauliflower

100g Buerre noisette

100ml Water

Pickled Cauliflower

40 small florets of
Cauliflower

100ml White wine vinegar

100g Sugar

200ml Water

Caviar Sauce

750ml reduced Chicken
stock

250ml White fish stock

1 Halibut bone (roasted)

1 Shallot (sliced)

1 clove of Garlic (sliced)

Caviar to finish

Confit Onion

2 Red onions (peeled)

2 White onions (peeled)

1 head of Garlic

5 Bay leaves

300ml Rapeseed oil

METHOD

Sweat the cauliflower in the buerre noisette until lightly roasted, add the water and continue to cook until emulsified blend pass and check for seasoning.

Pickled Cauliflower

Bring pickling liquor to the boil and chill.

Vac pac the florets with enough liquor to cover on full pressure.

Caviar Sauce

Sweat the shallot and garlic in a little rapeseed oil, add the fish stock and reduce by ¾ add the chicken stock and bring to the boil, skim and ad the fish bone and simmer for 10 minutes.

Pass through a chinios and muslin cloth.

Add caviar to finish

Confit Onion

Wrap all the ingredients in tin foil and cook en papielot for 40 minutes at 180°c,

When cooked reserve all liquid and let onions cool, ¼ the onions and char one side straight on to the solid top.

To serve panfry the halibut skin side down in a hot pan when the fish is golden brown and a small knob of butter and place in the oven at 190°c for 2-3 minutes until the inside of the fish is opaque.

Swipe the cauliflower puree on the plate add 10 pieces of pickled cauliflower and 14 of each confit onion and dress with a salad of chicory dressed in the onion cooking juices, add 6 pieces of raw sliced cauliflower place the fish next to the salad and sauce over the fish and salad.

WATERS RESTAURANT

BIOGRAPHY

Andy Waters.

Over the past thirty years he has run the kitchens of several Michelin-starred restaurants and built a highly respected reputation for refined modern British cooking. At his new eponymously named restaurant at Resorts World, Andy now has a new venue to showcase his tremendous talent. Situated in the heart of Birmingham's National Exhibition Centre (NEC), Resorts World is a large shopping and casino complex made up of eighteen bars and restaurants, fifty shops, a cinema, casino, spa and luxury hotel.

Waters Restaurant is on the first floor of the complex and has a cosy, comfortable yet modern interior design. Soft leather booths line the dining room wall, while the restaurant's bright lobby and cocktail area is characterized by deep, yellow sofas and exposed light fittings. When designing the restaurant, Andy was determined that restaurant goers felt relaxed and at home while enjoying his food – whether you are out celebrating a one-off special event or simply want a quick lunch after a morning's shopping – all are welcome at Waters Restaurant. This is also enforced by the friendly front of house staff, managed by Andy's wife Beverly.

Salmon
with shellfish and leeks en papillote

INGREDIENTS

100g Butter

4 x 125g of Salmon fillet

2 Baby leeks

4 Mussels

4 Clams

2 x 100g Seabass fillet (cut in half)

4 Scallops (out of shell)

4 King prawns

50ml White wine

50ml Olive oil

fresh chopped Chervil

Sea salt & ground pepper

To plate:

Squeeze of Lemon juice

Sprinkle of chopped Chervil

METHOD

Pre-heat oven to 180°C

Smear 4 large pieces of grease proof baking paper with butter

Place 1 salmon fillet in center of each piece with 1 half of a baby leek on top. Add seabass, scallops, king prawns, clams, and mussels. Sprinkle with white wine, olive oil, season well and add chervil.

Draw up the edges of the paper and seal the parcels. Place the parcels on a baking sheet and cook for 10-15 minutes

Carefully unwrap the parcels so that you do not lose the juices. Place on a plate, garnish with a sprinkle of chervil and a squeeze of lemon juice and serve.

✓ SIMPSONS 21/10/17

BIOGRAPHY

Simpson's chef director, Luke Tipping didn't set out to become a chef. In fact he

actively avoided the career, having been put off by the lack of time that his chef father could spend with his family during his childhood years.

All that changed following a placement arranged by his father where he discovered his passion for cooking. He subsequently enrolled at Halesowen Catering College to

supplement his placement and he hasn't looked back since.

More than two decades on and Luke is one of the most accomplished chefs in the UK. He formed a potent partnership with legendary chef and restaurateur Andreas Antona back in 2000 - while working at the once famed Plough and Harrow restaurant in Birmingham - and the pair have since established Simpsons as one of the region's best.

Luke describes his style as 'very natural, very seasonal and free flowing', which belies the creativity and thoughtfulness that goes into his cooking. He may not be one to self-promote, but his success at Simpsons, where he has held a Michelin star for 15 years, truly speaks for itself.

He is also a professor of culinary arts, having received a professorship from University College Birmingham.

Scallop
cauliflower, seaweed and avruga

INGREDIENTS

For the scallops

4 XL Scallops

1 tbsp Rapeseed oil

1 lime

For the sauce

100ml White wine vinegar

2 tsp Water

200g Butter, diced and chilled

60g Shallots, finely chopped

50ml Double cream

4 tbsp of dried Seaweed

1 head of Cauliflower

1 head of Romanesque

Garnish

1 large floret of Cauliflower

5g of picked Sea purslane

5g of picked Sea fennel

4 cups of Dill

1 cup of Grapeseed oil

METHOD

Remove the scallops from their shells and discard the attached skirt and roe, then rinse in cold water and gently pat dry. Reserve for service.

Combine the vinegar, shallots and water in a small saucepan, reduce the liquid by two thirds, add the cream.

Reduce by one third, whisk in the butter, a little at a time, the sauce must not boil.

Season with salt and pepper

Rehydrate the seaweed in boiling water, put aside and allow to cool to room temperature.

With a sharp knife, remove all the florets off the cauliflower and the romanesque; the florets need to be about 2mm in diameter (similar size to a small grain of risotto rice)

Blanch the florets in boiling salted water for 1 minute

Refresh in ice water and reserve for service

Using a mandolin, slice the cauliflower thinly. Reserve in iced water

Place all ingredients in a blender, blend for three minutes.

Place in pan and bring to the boil, once boiled pour into an empty container that is over ice.

Once cold pass through muslin cloth and reserve for service

Place a frying pan over a medium-high heat and add the oil to heat through. Add the scallops to the pan and sear for 1–2 minutes until golden on the bottom.

Whilst the scallops are cooking, heat up the sauce.

Once warm, add the cauliflower, Romanesque and seaweed; heat through.

Once hot, add 2 tbsp of avruga caviar, season with lemon juice, salt and pepper.

Place the 2 tbsp of the cauliflower mixture in the bottom of the bowl.

Place the scallop on top of the cauliflowers, sporadically place the raw cauliflower slices and sea herbs.

Drizzle with the dill oil.

THE FUZZY DUCK

BIOGRAPHY

The Fuzzy Duck, is situated near Stratford upon Avon in the quaint hamlet of Armscote, on the South Warwickshire-North Cotswold border. At the cosy and fashionably attired inn, created by the owners of Baylis & Harding, you will find great local ales and a carefully selected wine list. The food cooked by head chef, Ben Tynan and his team, is 'Contemporary Cotswold'. Ben believes in working closely with the best local suppliers, using only the highest quality fresh, local produce treated with care, to please guests with seasonal and decadent dishes.

Roast Rump of Lighthorne Lamb & Pulled Breast Shepard's Pie
roast cauliflower & caramelised cauliflower purée, wild garlic & black olives

INGREDIENTS

2x 250g Lamb rumps

1x boneless Lamb breast

1kg good peeled & evenly diced Mashing potatoes (maris piper/3cm dice)

1x large Cauliflower

1x Onion

1x large Carrot

1x head Celery

1 x small bunch Asparagus

1x good sprig fresh Rosemary

1x good pinch fresh Thyme

1x bulb Garlic

100g x Pitted black olives

1 litre x good quality Chicken stock

1 litre x Red wine

Olive oil/butter/sea salt/pepper/brown sugar

METHOD

Trim excess fat from lamb breast, seal off in a hot pan with a sprig of rosemary & thyme, 1/2 an onion, peeled & halved carrot, few sticks of peeled celery and a couple cloves garlic. Once browned, deglaze pan with a good splash of red wine, cover with stock and tin foil, oven cook at 150 degrees for approx 5 hours/ until fully tender. Allow to cool. Once cooled, retrieve onion, carrot and celery from stock, and finely dice. Strain stock through fine sieve and skim fat with a ladle. In a saucepan, reduce 500ml red wine, with a spring of rosemary & thyme and a clove of garlic by half, add cooking stock and reduce to 1/3 or coats back of a spoon consistency. Strain through fine sieve. (This will be used to sauce lamb at the end and to make the Shepherd's pie filling.)

Carefully pull the lamb breast into strips, combine with diced vegetables from cooking liquor, add some reduced stock to bind, season. (Remember to keep some stock for saucing later.) Put into individual serving dishes, gently press down evenly, and allow to cool. Put potatoes on to boil gently in lightly salted water, strain once tender and mash down with a good knob of butter, check seasoning. Allow to cool slightly and top the lamb breast pies ready for oven later. Glaze the top with butter and sea salt for a nice finish.

Take cauliflower, remove outer leaves, trim base of cauliflower core neatly. Take four good slices from middle part of cauliflower, so you get four 'cross section slices' approx 2-3cm thick. set aside until later. Roughly chop remaining cauliflower, sauté with a tablespoon brown sugar and small knob of butter, just cover in saucepan with milk and gently simmer until soft, strain off some excess liquid but keep to adjust consistency, puree in blender, season, keep warm for serving.

Take lamb rumps and season, seal in a hot pan with splash of oil and butter, brown evenly all around with a sprig of rosemary, put onto roasting tray and cook in oven at 180degrees, approx 15 mins for pink-medium. Allow to rest for 5-10 mins. In same frying pan, seal off slices of cauliflower, give a nice colour and turn, finish through oven with a knob of butter for 10 mins with lamb rumps, leave slightly al-dente.

Warm pies trough oven for approx 15-20 min's un-till piping hot. To assemble dish, use cauliflower puree as a base for slices of lamb and roast cauliflower, use 1/2 a rump per person. Warm olives through remaining sauce from liquor, wilt wild garlic leaves in a pan with a little oil and butter, carefully arrange on plate over lamb rump and sauce over the top with black olives. Garnish with a couple of spears of English asparagus just gently blanched in boiling water for 30 seconds. Serve pies on the side.

THE FAT FOX INN

BIOGRAPHY

Mark started out at the Old Bridge Hotel in Huntingdon learning his trade under head chef Chris Tabbit and owner John Hoskins MW. Moving to London to work at the Bibendum where his love for the classics, the history behind them truly developed under Matthew Harris. Moving onto the Oak W12, The bird in hand, Queens arms E17 and White Horse Hascombe and Now working at the Fat Fox Inn Watlington in south Oxfordshire mark has taken a strong liking to the Mediterranean and describes his style is Anglo French modern British with a true emphasis on using as locally sourced food as possible but not forgetting the world is his oyster.

Roasted Lamb
with herb gnocchi, mousserons, garlic greens and aged balsamic

INGREDIENTS

Gnocchi

300g Baked potato (skinned & passed through a potato ricer)

1 small Egg yolk

75g 00 Flour

pinch chopped Tarragon & parsley

pinch of grated Parmesan cheese

Salt & pepper to taste

Salsa verde

1 clove Garlic (peeled)

1 small handful Capers

1 small handful Pickled gherkins

4 Anchovy fillets

2 handfuls Flat leaf parsley

1 handful Mint

1 tbsp Dijon mustard

2 tbsp Red wine vinegar

8 tablespoons Extra virgin rapeseed oil

Sea salt and ground black pepper

Roasted Lamb

180g Lamb rump (trimmed)

handful washed Mousserons

handful washed Garlic greens

tbsp blanched Peas

tbsp Rapeseed oil + extra for cooking

table aged Balsamic vinegar

tbsp reduced Lamb stock

Salt + pepper to taste

METHOD

Gnocchi

Mix all together and roll out into sausage shape, cut into 5. Put into boiling water and remove into ice water as soon as they float and pat dry.

Salsa verde

Blitz all together in a food processor

Roasted Lamb

Preheat oven 180°c. Season lamb put in a hot cast iron pan skin side down with rapeseed oil.
When there's a little colour on the skin put in the oven for 10 mins (the more basting you do the better).
Pre-heat a non-stick pan when lamp comes out the oven add oil then put gnocchi in pan turn when golden add mushrooms and wild garlic cook till gnocchi is hot, add blanched peas and remove from heat plate gnocchi around the plate garlic greens in the middle, slice lamb and place on top of the garlic greens, scatter peas and mushrooms, mix rapeseed oil, balsamic and lamb stock and drizzle over and serve with salsa verde.

THE FEATHERS

BIOGRAPHY

Stuart Forman has been head chef at the Feathers Hotel for over 6 years having previously worked at Bovey Castle for 3 years and Selsdon Park Hotel for 7 years, before moving to Ludlow

Stuart says moving to Ludlow was a good move because of the amazing amount of local produce available and the high number of Fine Dining Restaurants that were available in the area.

The food that Stuart and his team produce is modern British cuisine and whenever possible he will include local produce in his menus. The menus are changed seasonally to reflect this.

Stonebass
crushed jersey royals, cauliflower & vanilla puree,
red pepper sauce.

INGREDIENTS

Stonebass

4 x 150-160g Stonebass
fillets
20ml Vegetable oil
50g Butter
juice of 1/4 Lemon

Cauliflower Puree

1 x medium sized
Cauliflower
1 x Vanilla Pod
225ml Semi skimmed milk
200ml Double cream
1 x Bay leaf

Red Pepper Puree

2 x Red peppers
1 x Garlic clove, finely
chopped
1 x small Shallot, diced
20ml Olive oil

**Crushed Jersey Royal
Potatoes**

460g Jersey royal potatoes
45ml Olive oil
3g chopped Chervil
3g chopped Parsley
3g chopped Chives
Salt & pepper

**Baby Leeks, Baby Gem
Lettuce and Chorizo**

4 x Baby leeks
2 x Baby gem lettuce
Olive oil
Salt & pepper
30g Chorizo

METHOD

Stonebass

Score the skin side of the Stonebass fillet and then place into a hot pan, skin side down, with a little oil, until coloured and crispy. Put the 50g of butter into the pan to melt and nappé over the fish for approximately 2 minutes, Squeeze the lemon juice over the fish and then place into the oven at 175 degrees for 5 minutes until cooked.

Cauliflower Puree

Put the cauliflower florets into a saucepan along with the split and de-seeded vanilla pod, the milk, cream and bay leaf. Cook on a medium heat until the cauliflower is soft. Put the ingredients into a Thermomix or food processor, with a little of the cooking liquid and process until the required thickness. Pass through a sieve and season to taste.

Red Pepper Puree

Drizzle the peppers with olive oil and wrap in foil then roast the whole pepper in a oven at 180 degrees until soft, approximately 30 minutes. When cooked remove from foil and peel off the skin. Heat some oil in a pan and then add the shallot and garlic. Sweat off for about 2 minutes until soft. Add the de-seeded and chopped pepper and cook for about 5 minutes on a low heat. Remove from heat and blitz, pass through a sieve and season to taste.

Crushed Jersey Royal Potatoes

Wash and scrub the Jersey Royal potatoes and cook in salted boiling water until tender. Drain and put into a bowl along with olive oil and chopped herbs. Using a fork crush the potatoes a little and mix together, season to taste. Press the potato mixture into a mould and turn out onto greaseproof paper. When ready to serve heat through in the oven at 175 degrees.

Baby Leeks, Baby Gem Lettuce and Chorizo

Wash and blanch the baby leeks in salted boiling water until cooked, drain and drizzle with melted butter.

Cut the baby gem lettuces in half and remove the bottom root, drizzle with olive oil, season to taste and chargrill until cooked.

Dice a good quality chorizo into cubes and dry fry the cubes until cooked.

CONGHAM HALL

BIOGRAPHY

Nick Claxton-Webb joined the team at Congham Hall Hotel in December 2012, having previously worked at The Salthouse Harbour and The Ickworth Hotel. As Head Chef one of the first things he embarked upon was to nurture the relationship between the gardeners and the kitchen to ensure we utilised the renowned Herb Garden, plentiful apple orchards and the beautiful produce from the kitchen garden. Today the garden supplies the restaurant tables with an abundance of seasonal vegetables and salads.

Pan Roasted Fillet of Rainbow Trout
with sweet potato, garden greens, pickled congham beetroot and carrots

INGREDIENTS

6 Rainbow trout fillets

4 Sweet potatoes

200mls White wine vinegar

5 White peppercorns

peelings from 1 Orange

10mls Liquid Honey

50mls Pernod

200mls Beetroot juice

½ tsp Soya lecithin

25g Capers

1 squeeze of Lemon juice

150g Spinach, picked and washed

150g Pak choi, picked and washed

300g Sprouting broccoli, blanched

1 large Carrot, long peelings

2 Baby beetroot, peeled, in very thin slices

METHOD

Gently warm the vinegar, white peppercorns, orange peel and honey. Place the beetroot and carrots into separate zip-lock bags and cover with the hot vinegar solution. Allow to cool and expel the air from the bags and seal. Allow to pickle for at least 1 hour.

Pre heat the oven to 180. Bake the sweet potatoes whole for 1 hour or until well softened. Half the potatoes and scoop out the flesh, blend until very smooth and season to taste.

Sauté the Pak Choi, spinach and broccoli together with a knob of butter, add the capers, season.

Gently warm the beetroot juice, Pernod and lecithin. Add a squeeze of lemon and season to taste.

Season the fish and place into a hot heavy bottomed pan and cook for 2-3 minutes on a medium heat. Add a knob of butter and a squeeze of lemon juice. Carefully turn the fish over, remove from the heat and continue to cook with the residual heat for a further 1-2 minutes.

Arrange the green vegetables neatly in the centre of the plate with the sweet potato puree. Arrange the fish on top of the greens. Agitate the sauce with a stick blender and spoon over the fish.

HENRY TUDOR HOUSE

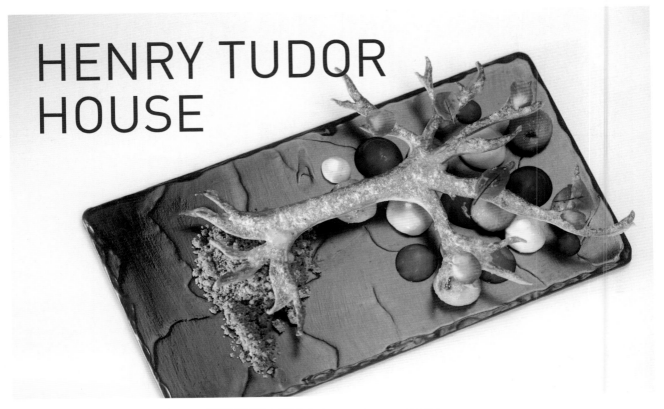

BIOGRAPHY

Nick Claxton-Webb joined the team at Congham Hall Hotel in December 2012, having previously worked at The Salthouse Harbour and The Ickworth Hotel. As Head Chef one of the first things he embarked upon was to nurture the relationship between the gardeners and the kitchen to ensure we utilised the renowned Herb Garden, plentiful apple orchards and the beautiful produce from the kitchen garden. Today the garden supplies the restaurant tables with an abundance of seasonal vegetables and salads.

Autum Apples

INGREDIENTS

Crumble

45g Butter

45g Brown sugar

45g Flour

45g Ground almonds

Crème Patisserie

500ml Milk

100g Caster sugar

60g Cornflour

2 Eggs

2 Yolks

1 Vanilla pod seeded

Sweet Pastry

250g Butter

250g Sugar

625g sifted Flour

75g Cream

2 Eggs

Apple Pie Puree

500ml Apple juice

8g Agar agar

2 tbsp Apple pie compound

Caramelised Apples

Braeburn apple spheres

100g Brown sugar

50g Butter

METHOD

Crumble

Place the flour, almonds and sugar in a large bowl and mix well.

Take a few cubes of butter at a time, rub into the flour mixture until the mixture resembles breadcrumbs.

Place on a baking tray and bake until golden, breaking the mixture up as its cooking

Crème Patisserie

Whisk together, sugar, flour, seeds, yolks and eggs.

Bring milk to a boil and pour over egg mix.

Place in a pan and cook out the mix until its thick, stirring continuously.

Sweet Pastry

Cream together butter and sugar, add the sifted flour then add the eggs and cream being careful not too overwork the dough, leave to rest for half an hour before rolling out to approx. 3mm, using the tip of a knife cut out the desired 'tree trunk'.

Bake at 180°C for 12 mins.

Dust with cinnamon sugar.

Apple Pie Puree

Put all ingredients into a pan, bring to the boil for 20 seconds.

Put mixture into the fridge until set.

When set, blitz the mixture with a hand blender until a smooth puree.

Caramelised Apples

Using a melon baller, cut out spheres from the apple.

Make a caramel using the sugar and butter.

Toss the apples in the caramel until coated, allow to cool.

RESTAURANT 56 @ SUDBURY HOUSE

BIOGRAPHY

Nestling on the edge of the picturesque Cotswolds between Oxford and Swindon in the market town of Faringdon. Sudbury House Hotel and their two restaurants, Magnolia Brasserie and Restaurant 56 received two awards in 2015, just months after a complete refurbishment.

Sudbury House and Magnolia Brasserie were presented with the new AA Four Star Silver Award for the whole 'guest and diner' experience.

The talented team at Restaurant 56 received 3 AA Rosettes in October 2015 for their contemporary British food using classic combinations.

Executive Head Chef Andrew Scott joined Restaurant 56 in January 2014 from The Curlew in East Sussex and with his team, he quickly established a restaurant with a reputation for excellence. Talented Sous Chef Nick Bennett, recently a finalist in a professional TV cookery competition, specialises in patisserie work. Together the team of chefs create a dining experience to ensure their customers are constantly excited by the food they are served and wines selected by Sergio Martinez Rios Restaurant Manager.

Since May 2013 the property has been transformed through sensitive refurbishment, creating a luxurious 49 bedroom hotel with the fine dining Restaurant 56 at its cornerstone located in the 'Old House'. Now restored and decorated with a classic style, infusing modern design with carefully selected antiques, artworks, luxurious fabrics and soft furnishings, both the hotel and restaurant facilities offer guests and diners alike a truly enhanced visitor experience.

Raspberry Pavlova
with mascarpone ice cream

INGREDIENTS

Mascarpone Ice Cream
564g Skimmed milk
167g Sugar
70g Yolks
200g Mascarpone
Vanilla pod

Raspberry soufflé base
2kg Raspberry puree
(Reduced by half to 1kg net)
250ml Sater
500g Sugar
75ml Raspberry liquor
125g Corn flour

French Meringue
160g Whites
170g Icing sugar
Lemon juice

Soufflé Meringue
150g Egg white
75g Caster sugar
Lemon juice

Equipment/ Garnish
Ramekins
Soft butter
Caster sugar
freeze dried Raspberries
fresh Raspberries

METHOD

French Meringue for dehydrating (6 hours in advance)
Whisk whites to soft peak with 2 drops of lemon juice. Slowly add sugar. Pipe small peaks onto trays and dry out in a low oven or dehydrator for 6 hours.

Ice Cream
Whisk sugar and yolks. Boil vanilla and milk. Pour onto yolk mix. Whisk in the mascarpone. Strain then freeze in a paco beaker. Traditional vanilla ice cream will go equally as well homemade or shop bought if you don't own a paco jet

Soufflé
Cook the sugar to 121°c, add to reduced puree. Mix corn flour, raspberry liquor and water to a paste. Add cornflour mix and cook out until mixture boils simmer for 2 minutes then allow to cool.

Compiling the dessert
Make soufflé meringue 5 minutes prior to cooking whisk whites to soft peak with 2 drops of lemon juice. Slowly add sugar and whisk till stiff peaks. Put 3 Tbsp of the raspberry soufflé mix in a bowl and fold in enough meringue to taste, place the mixture into butter lined and sugared ramekins. Smooth the top and run your thumb around the edge, bake soufflé for 6-8 mins at 170°c (depending on ramekin size).
Serve with a rocher or ball of ice cream sat on meringue and freeze dried raspberry pieces. Garnish with fresh raspberries and more meringue.

The soufflé base keeps well in the fridge for up to 10 days and obviously so does the ice cream...So to put a number on how many this will serve depends on how big you like your soufflé! But I will say it makes 12 at least.

LYGON ARMS

BIOGRAPHY

The Great Hall, The Lygon Arms hotel, Broadway, The Cotswolds

Head Chef Ales Maurer and his skilful, passionate team of chefs drive exceptional high standards of food, by using old and new techniques, appreciating fresh flavours and most importantly the use of seasonal and local produce. Now imagine a hotel nestled in the Cotswolds, 'an area of outstanding natural beauty' with stunning views where roaring log fires hint at its roots dating from the 15th Century. Picture a Great Hall with its vaulted ceiling and traditional wooden panelling built in the 17th Century, a hotel that has been coloured by the characters of history. This is a perfect combination to meet the needs of the modern day guest.

Lygon Garden Poached Pear, Jelly, Whiskey Panna Cotta, Granita And Ginger Oatcake

INGREDIENTS

Whisky granita
500ml Water
75ml Whisky
50g Sugar

Poached pears
1 litre Water
500g Sugar
Vanilla pod
Cinnamon stick,
Star anise,
Clove,
Slice of ginger

Pear puree
10 Pears

Pear jelly
285ml Pear puree
142ml Water
142m Pear stock from
poaching, passed through a
fine sieve
3 leaves Bronze gelatine

Whisky panna cotta
300ml Whipping cream
300ml Milk
150ml of your favourite
Whisky
3 leaves Bronze gelatine
100g Sugar

Ginger oatcakes
150g Porridge oats
Pinch of salt
70g Light brown soft sugar
100g Wholemeal flour
1 tsp Baking powder
1 tsp ground Ginger
60 ml cold Milk
100g cold diced Butter
70g Stem ginger

METHOD

Whisky granita
Combine and boil water and sugar for three minutes then cool.
Once cooled add the whisky. Transfer to a shallow container and freeze for two hours until partially frozen.
Use a fork to break up the semi frozen granita, stirring the crystallised flakes around the edges into the liquid centre and return to the freezer.
Repeat this two to three times during freezing until granita is completely frozen and a granular texture.

Poached pears
Poach, peeled pears whole until tender, remove from the liquid and cool.
Cut into desired shape
Keep the remaining stock.

Pear puree
Peel, core and quarter pears. Cut each quarter into three smaller pieces. Gently cook in a saucepan with four tablespoons of water, covered until soft, stir occasionally.
Cool slightly then blend with food processor until smooth

Pear jelly
Bloom gelatine in cold water until soft. Mix water and stock and heat, dissolve in the gelatine. Cool slightly, add pear puree. Set in desired mould

Whisky panna cotta
Bloom gelatine in cold water until soft. Boil together, milk, cream and sugar and dissolve in gelatine. Cool to room temperature. Add whisky, do not add to hot liquid, otherwise you'll lose the all-important whisky taste. Pass through a fine sieve. Set in desired mould

Ginger oatcakes
Set oven to 170°C
Blend oats in a food processor until they are finer in texture, about thirty seconds. Add the remaining ingredients part from the milk and process until mix resembles crumbs
Put the mix in a bowl and add the milk and form into a dough, do not over mix.
Dust the surface with oats and make a cylinder shape out of the dough
Make sure desired shape is evenly covered with oats
Chill until firm. Slice 2cm thick
Line a baking tray with parchment and cook for 10-12 minutes, should be golden in colour.
Cool

Assemble dessert to your liking.

233

16/5/06

THE NEPTUNE   06/05/16

Bruce Bovington at photisulize.com

BIOGRAPHY

The Neptune Restaurant with Rooms is set in a charming 18th century former coaching inn, refurbished to provide an intimate restaurant and comfortable accommodation; warm and friendly but with a generous portion of outstanding quality.

The fine dining restaurant serves modern British food, excellently cooked and served in a relaxed ambience by husband and wife team Kevin and Jacki Mangeolles.

A stone's throw from the beach at Old Hunstanton, the Neptune with it's 3 double rooms and 2 superior double rooms is ideally placed both as a gourmet bolthole and for exploring the attractions of the North Norfolk coast.

In August 2007 Kevin and Jacki Mangeolles relocated to Norfolk to open The Neptune Restaurant with Rooms. The restaurant has been awarded 3 AA rosettes and has retained a Michelin star since 2009.

The restaurant has an emphasis on fresh, local produce served in relaxed surroundings with attentive, friendly service.

White Chocolate Mousse & Hot Strawberry Sauce

INGREDIENTS

White Chocolate Spheres
400g White chocolate

White Chocolate Mousse
200g White chocolate

3 Egg yolks

150ml Milk

1 ½ leaves of Gelatine (soaked in cold water)

200g Whipped cream

6tsp Strawberry jam

Strawberry Sauce + Garnish
6 punnets of Strawberries

6tsp Crackle crystals

100g Sugar

METHOD

White Chocolate Spheres

Melt 300g white chocolate, add 100g white chocolate and mix the paint onto 12 ½ sphere moulds and leave to set then take out of the mould and keep in a cool place until ready to assemble.

White Chocolate Mousse

Boil the milk and whisk the egg yolks pour the milk onto the yolks and whish put back into the pan and place on a low heat stirring all the time cook until the mixture coats the back of a spoon or 85oc add the soaked gelatine and pour onto the chocolate allow to cool and fold in the whipped cream place into 12 mini ½ shaped spheres and set in the fridge when set turn out of the mould and stick them together with the jam leave in the fridge until ready to serve.

Strawberry Sauce + Garnish

Cut the tops off and cut in ½ 30 strawberries try and pick similar size strawberries for the garnish. Put the trimmings and the rest of the strawberries in a pan with the sugar and a little water cook on a low heat and strain through a sieve and keep hot.

Assemble

Place 10 of the strawberries cut in ½ in a circle put 1 of the white chocolate sphere in the middle and put the mousse inside put a tsp of the crackle crystals on the mousse, place the top sphere on and take to the table and pour the hot strawberry sauce over the sphere to start melting the chocolate.

ST GILES HOUSE HOTEL

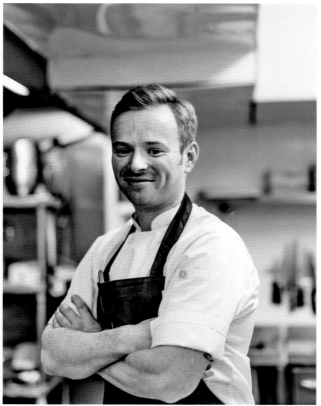

BIOGRAPHY

Ellery was brought up in an exciting food household with his parents being obsessed with organic gardening and owing a large whole food store so he naturally grew with a great passion for food. Upon leaving school he attended the Academy of Culinary Arts in Bournemouth and really started feeling his way in the world of food.

After a few years of working in some of the England's finest country hotels he moved to Australia and New Zealand for 3 years and caught the foraging and wild food bug that has progressed into a more serious side of hunting and fishing.

Upon returning to his home town of Norwich he took the head chefs position at St Giles House Hotel and has pushed standards and delighted customers ever since.

Cinnamon Yogurt, Apple and Maple

INGREDIENTS

Set Yogurt
500ml Greek yogurt
75ml Maple syrup
2tsp Cinnamon (ground)
2 Gelatine leaves
½ Lemon (juiced)

Ice Cream Base
300ml Milk
300ml Double cream
100g Custard sugar
4 Egg yolks
1 Vanilla pod
50g Toasted oats
100g small diced Cox apple

Apple Puree
2 Cox apples
2 medium Bramley apples
25g Unsalted butter
pinch of Custard sugar

METHOD

Set Yogurt

Warm maple syrup and cinnamon in a small pan to around 80 degrees Celsius and remove from the heat. Dissolve the gelatine leaves in this mixture. Whisk the yogurt and lemon juice together, and then add the maple mixture. Place on a tray or in a mould and refrigerate for at least 4 hours.

Ice Cream Base

Cut the vanilla pod length ways and scrape seeds into the milk and cream. Place on heat and bring to simmer. Once simmering for 1-2 mins remove from the heat and set to one side. Whisk the yolks with the sugar in a large bowl and slowly pour in the hot cream mixture. Once mixed well, press trough a fine sieve and cool. When cool churn in an ice cream machine and towards the end when it is thickening and the oats and apple. Freeze until needed.

Apple Puree

Peal all the apples and dice small. Place in a pan with the butter and look and a low heat slowly with a lid until apples are soft and fluffy. Remove from the pan and blend until smooth. Add sugar to taste. Place in a plastic sauce bottle until needed.

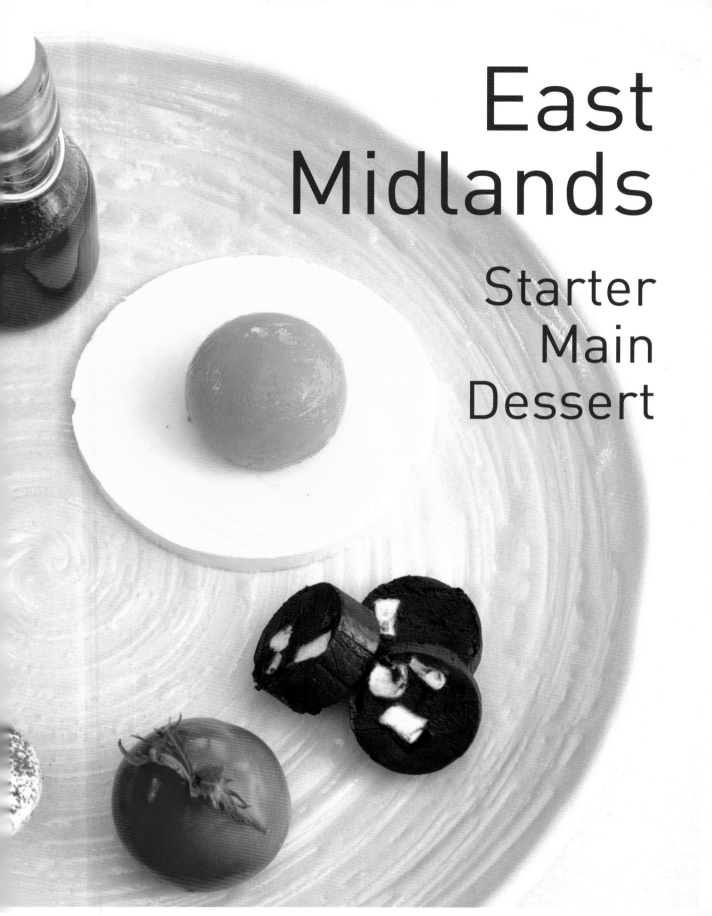

East
Midlands

Starter
Main
Dessert

MEMSAAB

BIOGRAPHY

MemSaab Restaurant is Nottingham's premier Fine Dining Indian Restaurant. The 200 seater restaurant with it's contemporary design and furnishing has been established since 2002. Owner, Amita Sawhney's passion for perfection in terms of cuisine, hospitality and ambience has been rewarded by the recognition of many food bodies and food critics. Here, the myth of 'Curry and Lager' has been dispelled and Indian food is truly 'Fine dining'.

Amongst the traditional dishes that can be seen on the Menu, can be seen Steamed Monkfish, Tandoori Ostrich, Venison Infused Kebab and Pan Fried Seabass! In March 2015, the supreme accolade was given by the AA - Two Rosettes for Culinary Excellence! This is the first time such recognition has been given to an Indian Restaurant in the East Midlands. MemSaab has been named the British Curry Awards 2014 Best Restaurant in the Midlands -nicknamed a 'Curry Oscar' by The Prime Minister, David Cameron! This is the first time in the Awards' history, that it has been bestowed upon a restaurant in Nottingham.

The Observer Food Monthly Awards has named MemSaab as Best Restaurant Runner Up 2001, 2014, 2013 and 2014, alongside Nottingham's only Michelin Star Chef, Sat Bains - great company to be with!

Jhinga Hara Masala
with masala risotto

INGREDIENTS

12 King prawns

Marinade

10 gms Ginger garlic paste

1 tsp Lemon juice

1 tsp Cooking oil

100g Hara masala paste

20g Yoghurt

Salt to taste

½ tsp Garam masala (add more to taste)

2 tbs Coriander powder

50g Mint sauce

100g Hara masala paste

5 Bunches fresh corriander

2 Bunches fresh mint

250g Green chillies

250ml Olive oil

Masala Risotto

100g Risotto rice

10g Chopped onions

½ tsp Turmeric powder

20g Mascarpone cheese

100ml Seafood stock

10g Paneer (Indian cottage cheese)

1 tbs Butter

1 tsp Garam masala

1 tsp chopped garlic

White wine

¼ Fresh red pepper

Salt to taste

METHOD

Marinade

Chop the Fresh Coriander, Fresh Mint and Green Chillies for the Hara Masala. Add the Olive Oil and blend / liquidise into a paste.

Turn the Hara Masala Paste into a large bowl and add the remaining ingredients of the marinade. Stir well.

Masala Risotto

Lightly sauté the onions and garlic in the butter. Add the risotto rice and continue to sauté for another 10 minutes on a medium heat. Stir in the white wine and seafood stock and cook until the risotto becomes al dente. Stir in the turmeric powder, garam masala, grated paneer, mascarpone and salt (to taste). Then add and stir in the butter.

Grill the pepper so it's 'chargrilled' and bake in the oven.

Serve the risotto using a mould. Cut the pepper into four and place on the rice as a garnish.

Gently stir the raw prawns in the marinate. Cover and leave in the fridge for 8 to 24 hours. Preheat grill to a high heat. Place the prawns on the sigri (flat charcoal barbeque) and heat for approximately 6 minutes, turning over half way through. Remove from the heat and serve immediately on the masala risotto. Garnish with fresh herbs. Enjoy!

LA ROCK RESTAURANT

BIOGRAPHY

Chef Nick Gillespie launched La Rock Restaurant in 2011, with his years of experience within the kitchen, bringing his passion for food and service to Sandiacre on the outskirts of Nottingham.

His ethos is to source ingredients that can be found locally and the best of what the British Isles has to offer, with twists of flavours and textures to create his modern British food with classical around the world influences.

"It's all about the balance between flavours and textures where I create visually stunning and flavour inspired dishes with my passionate and dedicated team"

Argyll Sea Trout
with rock samphire, mango and tomato salsa & iced bloody mary gazpacho

INGREDIENTS

Sea Trout
4 x 4oz Argyll sea trout

Salsa
100g Sea asparagus / rock samphire

100g Cherry vine tomatoes

1 x Mango

1 Spanish onion
(finely diced)

Good quality olive oil

Fresh thyme
(just the leaves)

Seasoning (to taste)

Bloody Mary Gazpacho
100ml Tomato juice

60ml Vodka

4ml of Worcester sauce

2 Dashes of tobasco

4ml Lemon juice

I Celery stick

Seasoning to taste

Pea Puree
Garden peas

Seasoning

Hot water

METHOD

Salsa
Peel and fine dice the mango
Wash and pick the samphire to remove any woodiness from the stems
Quarter the cherry tomatoes
Gently combine the mango, onion, tomatoes and thyme with olive oil and season
Allow to marinade for 1 hour in a fridge

Gazpacho
In a food blender, place all of the ingredients for the Gazpacho and blend until smooth.
Pass and correct the seasoning
Place the liquid in a container and freeze.
Check the gazpacho every hour and rough up with a fork until fully frozen and loose.

Sea Trout
Prepare your sea trout by firstly descaling the fish using the back of a knife and rubbing in the opposite direction to the flow of scales
Wash the trout to remove any loose scales from the fish.
Next job is to remove each of the fillets from the fish and remove the pin bones with fish pliers.
Cut the fillets into identically sized portions (approximately 4oz each)
Place in the fridge ready for use.

Pea Puree
Heat some garden peas and place into a food processor.
Add a little of the hot water and blend vigorously until smooth and paste like.
Pass through a fine sieve.
Season to taste and refrigerate.
(take care not to use too much hot water as this will make the puree to wet)

Before you start, place the iced gazpacho into small glasses, leave in the freezer ready for use. Do not do this too far in advance as the glasses will gain a frost if left in the freezer too long.
When ready, place a frying pan on the stove with a little clarified butter or olive oil and season, allow to get hot.
Place the sea trout portions skin side down and allow the skin to crisp up, remove from the pan and place on a baking tray skin side up, ensure the tray is greased slightly and seasoned to stop the trout from sticking to the tray.
Place the sea trout in an oven at around 180°c and cook for around 3 to four minutes, keep checking until the trout is cuisson / just cooked.
Place a spoon of puree onto your plate and using a spatula, twist your wrist quickly moving around the plate to create the swirl of the puree.
While your trout is cooking in the oven and almost ready, drain the salsa and fry quickly in a hot pan for around 20 to 30 seconds,, check the seasoning and place the ingredients onto your plates.
Lift the sea trout from the baking tray and place onto the salsa.
Garnish with some fresh herbs such as micro coriander and red mustard frills.
Remove your iced gazpachos in their glasses and place to onto the plate next to your trout.
Enjoy.

THE DEVONSHIRE ARMS AT BEELEY

BIOGRAPHY

Alan's career has gone from strength to strength, after gaining a professional catering qualification from High Peak College, Buxton, and Alan has worked in some of the finest eateries in the country. From his first appointment as Sauce Chef in Baslow Hall's Fishers restaurant, to the celebrated Michelin Starred Juniper Restaurant in Altrincham, Cheshire. In 2002, Alan moved back to his roots in Derbyshire to help set-up Rems Café Bar Restaurant.

In 2003, Alan returned to fine cuisine, taking the job as Head Chef for the Michelin Starred Box Tree in Ilkley. In late 2003, Alan was head-hunted, to assist in set up and running of a new venture as Head Chef at The Old Tramshed Bar and Restaurant in Yorkshire. Finally in 2006 Alan joined Devonshire Hotels and Restaurants, where he is Chef Patron for both The Devonshire Arms at Beeley and The Devonshire Arms at Pilsley. Here he celebrates the abundance of good quality local produce, much of which comes from the Chatsworth Estate - this is reflected in the quality of the food served at The Devonshire Arms.

Crab Mayonnaise
with mashed avocado

INGREDIENTS

Mashed Avocado

3 ripe Avocados

½ Lime, juice only

Salt to taste

4 mild Chillies, finely chopped

Crab Mayonnaise with Balsamic Reduction

I whole Crab (cooked for 14 mins in simmering water) or 1 x 500g packet from Fishmonger

I jar Hellman's Mayonnaise

4 Banana shallots, diced

4 heads Red chicory

4 heads White chicory

½ pt Balsamic vinegar

2 oz Brown sugar

1 Lemon zest and juice

bunch of Chives, finely chopped

METHOD

Mashed Avocado

In a pestle and mortar, pound the chillies to a fine paste. Add a little water and lime juice to make a looser mixture. Mash in the avocados. Season to taste.

Crab Mayonnaise with Balsamic Reduction

The white crabmeat is to be found in three places: the claws, which give generously, the legs and the cavities within the body, while the brown meat (which is sometimes almost wet and at other times quite dry) mainly lines the upper shell. Remove the claw and three legs beside it on either side by breaking them off where they are attached to the body. Smash all three joints of the claws using the end of the rolling pin on a board. As crabs get larger the shells of their claws can get really quite tough, so you may need to be pretty forceful. Picking off the broken shell, extract the crabmeat. Now crack the joints of the legs using a nutcracker and carefully pick out the meat inside. You need to have a crab pick or skewer here to extract every last bit. Insert a sharp knife between the upper shell and the body at the opposite end to the tail and lever the body section loose. Lift it free of the shell and pull it off. There will be a little brown meat clinging to the underside. Spoon this out, then cut the body in half. You may find some more brown meat inside. Using a skewer pick out the white meat from the row of cavities in each half. Now scrape out the brown meat lining the upper shell with a teaspoon. Pick the crabmeat over for any stray splinters.

Method

Put diced shallots, herbs, lemon juice and white crab meat in a bowl and just enough mayonnaise so that the mixture is fairly stiff but not too runny mix thoroughly put to one side. Slice a tiny portion off the bottom of the chicory head so the leaves fall of it naturally, put to one side. Reduce the balsamic vinegar with the brown sugar until liquid slightly thickens and sweetens (not too far as it will taste burnt) leave to cool.

Assembly

For this you will need a 3 inch pastry cutter

Put the cutter on the centre of a plate and fill half full with avocado mash then top up with the white crab mix take the chicory leaves and carefully insert down the side between the cutter and the filling in alternate colours until they meet. Carefully remove cutter and drizzle the balsamic reduction around the edge of the plate.

THE SMOKE PIT

BIOGRAPHY

With almost 40 years of varying catering experience between them brothers James & Matthew Ingram decided it was time to open their own restaurant. Growing up in Northamptonshire it seemed only right that they should open the restaurant in the town. With a real passion for barbecue and smoking after trips to the United States it was obvious which direction they should go. The site of the restaurant is a 19th century bakery on a back street in the Northampton town centre; the industrial feel of the building was perfect for their vision. Partnering with their brother-in-law James Miller, the trio opened The Smoke Pit in January 2015.

While the menu has a heavy American influence it is important to the brothers to use as many local suppliers and producers as possible, including craft beer, fruit and vegetables even the uniforms are made in the town. The cheese in the recipe "Northampton Blue" is produced in the county. The dish selected for this book is a different take on the classic "Buffalo Chicken" home smoked chicken thighs with hot sauce, blue cheese and pickled sweetcorn is a favourite from the menu.

Smoked Chilli Chicken
with pickled corn & blue cheese

INGREDIENTS

Hot Sauce
10 Serrano chillies, stemmed & sliced
4 Cloves of garlic sliced
1 small thinly sliced Onion
1/2 tsp Salt
1 tsp Vegetable oil
100ml Water
140ml Cider vinegar
1 tbsp Light brown sugar

Blue Cheese Dressing
100g Northamptonshire blue
60g Sour cream

Smoked Chicken Thighs
8 Skin on boneless chicken thighs
60g Salt
50g Light brown sugar
10g ground Fennel seeds
10g ground Black pepper
10g ground Sage
10g ground Oregano
10g Smoked paprika
10g Chilli powder
20ml Olive oil

Pickled Sweetcorn
200g Sweetcorn kernels
200ml Cider vinegar
3 tbsp Caster sugar
½ tbsp Mustard seeds
¼ tbsp Salt
¼ tbsp cracked Black pepper
75g diced Shallots
2 Cloves garlic finely chopped
1 Serrano chilli finely diced
½ tbsp Olive oil

METHOD

In a pan sweat the chillies, garlic & onions in the vegetable oil for 4-5 minutes, Add the water and cook over a low heat until almost all of the liquid has evaporated. Remove from the heat and add the sugar and vinegar and puree using a hand blender until smooth. Strain the mixture through a fine mesh sieve and then transfer to a sterilized jar or bottle refrigerate and let age at least 2 weeks before using.

In a food processer puree the cheese and sour cream until smooth, transfer to a bowl and refrigerate until needed.

Mix together the salt, sugar, fennel, black pepper, sage, oregano, paprika and chilli powder. Rub the chicken with the olive oil and then rub the dry mix all over. Using a pre lit kettle BBQ to smoke the chicken, push the hot coals to one side and lay the thighs on the rack on the opposite side to the coals. Add chunks of cherry wood to the hot coals at the same time you put the thighs on the rack. The ideal internal temperature of the BBQ should be around 110-125°c you can use the vents to regulate the temperature. Smoke the chicken thighs for around 1 – 1½ hours and rotate them to ensure they cook evenly. Use a temperature probe to check for an internal temperature of 73°c

In a pan sweat off the chilli and shallots with the olive oil without adding colour, then add all the other ingredients and bring to a gentle simmer for 2 minutes, the mix can then be left to cool. Once cooled put in an airtight container and refrigerate.

When plating the dish we garnish with charred corn and a few micro herbs, but these are optional the dish works great without them too.

FOX AND GOOSE INN

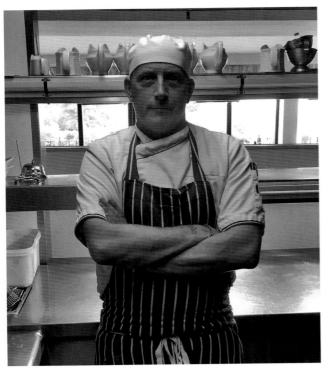

BIOGRAPHY

The Fox and Goose is sat on Pudding Pie Hill and offers Panoramic View of Chesterfield and beyond. The food offered is pretty special. Chef Craig Spall is taking the venue to another level with his culinary delights. Craig who is 41 and originates from Grimsby North East Lincolnshire is passionate about the food he serves. Craig has followed in his father's footsteps as his father has been his greatest inspiration. His father was a cook on the trawlers in his home town. Craig started his career from the roots of the kitchen. Craig's first job was working as a pot wash in an Italian restaurant and then moving to be a Commis. Before Craig joined the team at the Fox and Goose he was the Head Chef of a Boutique Hotel. Craig's 27 year career has taken him to France and London and he has cooked for the rich and famous. When Craig is dining out his favourite dish would be Confit Duck Leg with French style cassoulet and French classics. When Craig isn't working and preparing food he spends his time visiting food markets and sampling the food that's on offer.

Razor Clam Tartar

INGREDIENTS

16 fresh Razor clams
12 Radishes (Pickled) -
see Pickling Liquor
2 ripe Tomatoes for
concasse
1 punnet of Samphine
1 Banana shallot (diced
finely)
zest of 1 Lime
slice of half a Lime
pinch of Sugar
1 Cucumber (deseeded
and diced finely)
1tbsp chopped Dill
Seasoning to taste

Pickling Liquor:
2 Star anise
10 White peppercorns
2 Bay leaves
1 Cinnamon stick (whole)
1 Banana shallot (split
lengthways)
100g Caster sugar
500ml White wine vinegar

Gremolata:
1 bunch Fresh leaf parsley
zest of Lemon and juice
2 Garlic cloves
handful of Breadcrumbs
Seasoning to taste

METHOD

Take the Razor Clams and place in a pan, steam for 2 minutes until open and set aside

Place the radishes and samphire into warmed pickling liquor and set aside for 15 minutes until soft to the touch. Take clams and trim on the V shaped end below the join and discard keeping the rest. Cut clams into 2 or 3mm pieces. Place clams into a bowl with shallots, zest and juice of the lime to infuse for 2 minutes.

Stir the clam mix thoroughly. Dice tomato for the concasse add to clam mix along with cucumber, radish and samphire. Place enough of the clam mix back into the shell and top with gremolata

ALDO ZILLI

BIOGRAPHY

Aldo Zilli is an award-winning celebrity chef and restaurateur who specialises in Italian, vegetarian and seafood cuisine.

He was the founder and chef-patron of some of London's most exciting and innovative restaurants, Signor Zilli, Zilli Green, Zilli Café and Zilli Bar. His Italian seafood restaurant, Zilli Fish, was a Soho institution and had been open for over 15 years until March 2012 when Aldo decided to hang up the chef's whites and embark on other ventures.

Aldo is currently executive consultant chef to San Carlo Group, providing advice and expertise alongside devising new seasonal menus for their numerous restaurants, particularly Cicchetti in Manchester, London's Piccadilly, and Covent Garden.

Aldo has written 10 books including two autobiographies, Being Zilli and My Italian Country Childhood, as well as various cookery books. 'Fresh & Green: over 100 new exciting vegetarian recipes' was featured in the Telegraph's Top Ten Cookery Books 2012. He has also written for many publications including The Sun, and currently writes a weekly column for the Daily Express Saturday magazine and presents a weekly show on Soho Radio.

Great food and Aldo's exuberant personality means he appears regularly on television and radio both as presenter and chef.

Aldo has been a strong supporter of a number of charities

Risotto Filled Baby Squash With Truffle

INGREDIENTS

4 small squash /
pumpkins OR 2 slightly
bigger (to share
between 2)

400-500g Arborio rice

1ltr Veg stock

1 Shallot

50ml White wine

20ml Truffle oil

100g Butter

150g grated Parmesan

20g shaved fresh Truffle

50ml Olive oil

4-5 cloves of Garlic

METHOD

Roast the baby squash (with the top cut off) with a little oil and garlic on a baking tray for 30-45 minutes at 180 degrees.

When cooked scoop out the middle and remove the seeds, with the remaining squash meat, blend into a cream adding seasoning and oil to taste.

Make a classic white risotto with the shallot, white wine and vegetable stock. When the risotto is nearly cooked, add in the blended squash and truffle oil. Stir in the parmesan and butter and serve back into the hollowed out squash.

Finish with shaved truffle on top.

GEORGE'S GREAT BRITISH KITCHEN

BIOGRAPHY

George's Great British Kitchen – Nottingham, first opened in December 2014, and has since become one of the most popular restaurants in the City. Being awarded 'Best New Venue' at the Nottinghamshire Food & Drink awards 2015 and Restaurant & Bar Design award for Best restaurant in a 'heritage building' 2014/15.

George's food offering is all about taking modern British dishes and adding a unique twist to every single one, making their food offering as unique as they are! They've created an environment that wows you when you enter and really celebrates Britishness in a fun environment.

The dishes on offer are the brain child of Duncan Poyser, development chef at George's Great British Kitchen. Duncan, an award winning chef has years of experience within the restaurant industry with a background training in Michelin starred restaurants, has many a claim to fame including cooking for the royal family, catering private events for film, music and premier sports stars and creating dishes for well-known high street food retailers.

Duncan has taken his inspiration for his stacked fish burger from trips to Louisiana where cornmeal is widely used to dust fish and seafood for frying, adding a nutty tasting thin and crispy coating before being added to a po boy sandwich topped with 'fixins' such as pickles, slaws and sauces. Ours is given Britishness using cod cooked in a traditional range with our own pickles and Great British Maris Piper Chips!

Duncan's Stacked Fish Burger
With Campfire Slaw

INGREDIENTS

4 Cod fillets

4 Brioche or posh burger buns as some supermarkets call them

BBQ rub

Chipotle mayo

Chilli and coriander batter

200g Polenta in a large bowl

A bag of Mixed salad leaves

1 Beef tomato cut into four slices

Homemade chips or sweet potato fries

Rub;

2tbsp of Salt

1tbsp Demerara sugar

1tbsp Smoked paprika

1tsp Garlic powder

1tsp Onion powder

1tsp Cayenne pepper

1tsp fresh ground Black pepper

Chilli and Coriander Batter;

200g Self-raising flour

350g Cold water

1tsp Salt

1tbs Malt vinegar

2tbs roughly chopped Coriander

1tsp Chilli flakes

METHOD

Mix all the ingredients for the rub together well, this will make more than you need. Store in a glass jar or air tight container.

Cut the fish fillets in half and season well on both sides with the rub, place on a plate and refrigerate for 30 minutes to marinate.

In a bowl combine the water and flour and mix well until lump free.

Add the coriander, chilli flakes and salt, mix well and place in the fridge for 30 minutes to rest or until needed.

Get Ready!

Turn your fryer on to its highest setting.

On the left hand side of your fryer place your bowl of polenta then next to that your batter, now's the time to whisk in that all important remaining 1tbs of malt vinegar.

To the left of the batter place your pieces of cod, pat dry any excess moisture with kitchen paper.

To the right of the fryer place a tray lined with kitchen paper to drain the cooked fish.

Next drain four good pinches of pickles and place on a plate side by side in a line, put the rest in a serving dish for the table. Put four good tablespoons of campfire slaw next to each pile of pickles, put the rest into a serving dish.

Now take a piece of fish and dip in the batter, drain and toss through the polenta, continue with the remaining pieces then place into the fryer. You may have to fry them in 2 batches depending on the size of your fryer. If so keep the first batch warm while you fry the second. Fry each batch for a total time of 4 minutes 30 seconds each, remove and drain on kitchen paper.

While the fish is frying cut your brioche buns in half and toast lightly then spread with some of the remaining chipotle mayonnaise, top the bases with some salad leaves followed by a slice of tomato.

Construction;

With the fish all now fried and drained, place a piece of fish on each tomato slice.

Top the fish with a pile of slaw.

Top the slaw with another piece of fish.

Top this piece with the pickles, take care the burgers are now stacking up!

Top each with the remaining burger half securing each one with a cocktail stick as you go.

Serve as quickly as possible with homemade chips seasoned with some of the bbq rub and chipotle mayo.

253

LILU

GREAT
OOD & DRINK
FESTIVALS

BIOGRAPHY

Lilu is fulfilling a dream to bring the best of British and Indian cuisine to the culturally diverse city of Leicester. Pratik Master (Managing Director) and Chef Amardeep Singh Anand have really created a market place that didn't exist. Lilu is an Indian Fine Dining restaurant with a British-Indian fusion menu where you will find such culinary delights as Ostrich, Seabass and Venison.

'When the restaurant was first envisaged we realised that we had to be different from our contemporaries.'

The restaurant is fast becoming a local hot spot for foodies looking for an altogether different take on Indian cuisine and with an Award winning Chef like Amardeep, they are really achieving something special. Amardeep won the coveted Asian Chef of the Year title in 2012, that year he also won the award for innovation in food.

Cooking is Amardeep's life, he uses only the very finest ingredients creating a blend of subtle flavour combinations that really tantalize the tastebuds. He also received the Asian Chef of the Year Healthy Heart Award in 2010 due his his minimal use of oils and fats whilst cooking.

To Amardeep, presentation is as important as the taste. As he says 'First, you eat with your eyes'. Some dishes look so good that you won't want to eat them, we are sure you will though!

With Pratiks passion for food and Amardeeps skill and expertise in executing flavour combinations – they really have a recipe for success.

Hiran Ki Kadhi
(venison fillet on a bed of vine tomato, shallots and potato ragout, carrot vichy served with a tempered yoghurt sauce.

INGREDIENTS

Venison fillet: 140gm
Salt & pepper- ½ tsp each
Rapeseed oil- 1 tsp
freshly squeezed Lemon-
¼ Lemon

Ragout
Shallots: 1 small
Vine tomatoes: 1 small
Potatoes: 1 medium boiled
Salt - to taste
Butter: 20 gms
fresh Ginger : 1 tsp
chopped
Cumin seeds: 1 tsp
Red chilli powder: ½ tsp
fresh Coriander: 2 tsp
chopped
Tomato puree: 1tbsp
Rapeseed oil: 1 tsp

Sauce
Yoghurt: 75 gms
Gramflour: 2tbsp
Coriander powder: 1tsp
Cumin powder:1 tsp
Turmeric powder: 1tsp
Red chilli powder: 1tsp
Garam masala: 2tsp
Salt : to taste
Water: 100ml
Cumin seeds: ½ tsp
Ginger-Garlic paste: 2 tsp
Dried fenugreek leaves:
1 tsp

METHOD

Marinate the venison with oil, lemon juice and seasoning and set aside for 3-4 hours in the fridge.

Dice the shallots, tomatoes and potatoes into one inch cubes

Heat oil in a non-stick pan and add ginger and cumin, when it crackles add shallots and saute till pink and translucent.

Add salt, chilli powder and tomatoes and cook further for 5 mins and then add the potatoes and

Simmer for further 2 mins, add tomato puree and cook till all the ingredients combine together and finish with fresh chopped coriander

For the sauce, mix together the first 8 ingredients with a whisk and keep aside

Heat oil in a heavy bottomed pan and add cumin seeds and ginger garlic paste, cook till it splutters

Now add the Spiced yoghurt mixture into the pan and mix vigorously, add water if desired as the sauce starts to thicken.

Once a medium sauce consistency is obtained then simmer it for further 10 mins and finish it off by adding the dried fenugreek leaves.

Heat the grill/pan and cook the meat as desired, rest the steak for couple of mins (after cooking and serve it with the ragout, sauce and buttered vichy carrots

Tip: served best medium-rare accompanied by a Green pea rice or Red Leicester naan (available at Lilu Restaurant)

Remember we are limited to 2 pages, recipes may need to be changed if too large

HORSLEY LODGE

BIOGRAPHY

I have been cooking since the age of 16 but it wasn't until I finished university and took a job with my twin brother that I truly fell in love with food and found my passion. My brother spent 5 years teaching me all he knew and we still work together today at Horsley Lodge where we have transformed the food into a blend of seasonal and local dishes, with a contrast of textures.

Our focus is not overcomplicating things, tried and tested cooking methods with good quality produce is what matters.

In my spare time, I enjoy golf, walking with my dog and DIY.

BBQ Lamb Rump
with lambcetta, rainbow chard, sweetcorn, ricotta, smoked potato

INGREDIENTS

4 x 6oz Lamb rump

300ml Rapeseed oil

4 medium Coals

2 cooked Sweetcorn

5 medium Potatoes

200ml Milk

50ml Double cream

Salt

2 litres of Whole milk

1.5 tsp Citric acid

chopped Chives

250g Unsalted butter

Lamb stock

2 Lamb bellies

150g Sea salt

50g Fennel seeds

20g Peppercorns

1 Cinnamon stick

4 Cloves

1 Sat anise

200g Rainbow Chard leaves/stalks

chopped Parsley

Burnt onion powder (burn sliced red onion in oven until black and dry, blitz)

METHOD

BBQ Lamb

Diamond the fat on rumps, sear in medium heat until fat is rendered.

Make a coal oil by burning coal and dropping into rapeseed oil and infusing for 3 hours, pass through kitchen cloth

Sous vide lamb with coal oil in bag, at 60 degree for 1 hour and then into ice water

(can skip the sous vide process and cook through in the oven if required)

Sweetcorn

Chargrill / bbq 2 cooked sweetcorn until nicely coloured. Take off kernels and reserve 1/4 , add the rest into a saucepan with ½ peeled potato, 200ml of milk and 50 double cream.

Simmer for 30 mins and then blend, pass and season

Ricotta (from whole milk)

Add 1.5 tsp of salt to 2 litres of whole milk

Heat to 70°c

Add 1.5 tsp of citric acid, diluted in 1tbsp of water.

Wait for the curds to start forming on the top and bring them into the centre with a slotted spoon, bring milk to 90°c and carry on gathering the curds.

Take off the heat and allow to sit for 15 mins then ladle the curds onto some kitchen paper to drain, sit for 2 hours then refrigerate. Mix with a little coal oil, chopped chives and extra seasoning if needed.

Potato fondant

Cut rounds out of potato with a cutter and square off the ends.

Add 200g of butter to a heavy based pan and a 1 tbsp of water.

Press the potato fondants into the butter and season generously

Heat until butter foams and then turn the potatoes once coloured.

Add lamb stock to cover the potatoes and cook through either on hob or in the oven at a low heat

Take out of butter and smoke under a cloche for 2 minutes (can skip this step)

Lambcetta

Cure two lamb bellies until 50g fennel seeds, 150g sea salt, 20g peppercorns, 1 cinnamon stick 4 cloves and a star anise (ground up) for 5 days

Then wash off and braise at 70° for 20 hours

Drain off and press in the fridge overnight

(can use pancetta if you don't want to make this)

To serve

Add lamb to medium heat pan skin side down in a little oil, put potato fondant in same pan and put in oven at 190° for 5 minutes

Meantime, heat 1 tbsp of oil and add diced lambcetta until crispy

Add knob of butter then the sweetcorn and rainbow chard leaves until wilted

Season and add chopped parsley

Remove lamb from oven and add butter to baste, add rainbow chard stalks and carry on basting until cooked. Rest lamb for 5 mins before serving, dress in coal oil and sprinkle onion powder on

Construct the plate using the chard and sweetcorn mix, the reheated sweetcorn puree, ricotta, fondant potato and sliced lamb rump

Dress with coal oil and crispy lambcetta crisps

THE CASTLE INN

BIOGRAPHY

Enthusiastic and passionate young head chef, Alex Shatford, took a degree in Culinary Arts Management at University College Birmingham. Having graduated, he moved on to work in both Michelin and Rosette kitchens. Alex took his first head chef position in the newly refurbished and extended Castle Inn, Castle Donington which prides itself on fine ales and quality food. His menu was an immediate success, bringing a new style of dining to the area.

Alex's cooking is inspired by modern, mediterranean influences with a passion for the Spanish style of cooking and flavours which has developed over many years whilst holidaying with family living in Mojácar.

The dishes themselves use the finest local produce where ever possible and there is a strong focus on creating simple, uncomplicated food that people can enjoy: "The greatest dishes are always simple".

Alex's aim over the coming year is to build on the already excellent reputation of his kitchen & team with the opening of The Castle's function venue 'The Rose Room' to bring fine dining and a more intimate atmosphere to both local residents as well as the wider community.

Roast Pheasant Breast

with truffle, wholegrain mustard and confit leg bon bon.
Served with apricot puree, sous vide salsify, broad beans,
celeriac puree, potato straw and a game jus.

INGREDIENTS

1 whole Pheasant (plucked and prepped)

32g dried Apricots

30ml Dry white vino verde

1/2 tablespoon Sherry vinegar

1/2 whole Celeriac

100ml Water

300ml whole Milk

20ml Honey

20ml White wine

1 Maris piper potato

2 Salsify

1 Lemon

500ml Olive oil

10ml reduced Chicken stock

6 sprigs of Thyme

200ml Game stock

200ml Red wine

3 Juniper berries

4 cloves Garlic

20 popped Broad beans

10g wholegrain Mustard

2ml Truffle oil

1/4 Gelatine leaf (soaked in cold water)

10g Chives (finely chopped)

50g Panko breadcrumbs

1 Egg (whisked)

30g Plain flour

METHOD

Roast pheasant

Season with salt and pepper, add olive oil to a frying-pan and colour off both breasts for 30 seconds before adding thyme and roasting at 180°C for 16 minutes. Then baste in foaming butter for 1-2 minutes and allow to rest for 6-8 minutes. Calve the breast cleanly off the carcass.

Bon Bon

Remove the legs from the pheasant and trim down appropriately, season and cover with olive oil, add 2 garlic cloves and sprigs of thyme and place into the oven at 90°C and cook for approx. 2 hours or until falling of the bone. Once cooked, pick down ensuring no bones and mix with wholegrain mustard, truffle oil, chives and the gelatine leaves removed from the water. Combine the gelatine with 20ml game jus (simmering) until dissolved.

Mould into a ball and place in fridge for 30 mins or until firm, then panna in the panko breadcrumbs rolling it in 1) flour 2) egg 3) panko breadcrumbs, and set aside until required. Cook at 180°C in a fryer for 2-3 mins or until golden brown.

Apricot puree

Combine the apricots and vino verde in a saucepan and bring to the boil over a medium heat. Cook until it reduces by half then add the vinegar. Blend until smooth and press through a fine-mesh sieve then set aside until required.

Sous vide salsify

Peel the salsify and place in lemon water. When ready to use dice into 5cm pieces and place into a vac pac pouch with the thyme sprigs, olive oil and reduced chicken stock. Season lightly and seal. Place in a sous vide bath at 80°C for 40 minutes or until tender. Once cooked, keep the salsify in the pouch and instantly refresh in iced water. Set aside until required and once needed remove from pouch and toss in foaming butter.

Broad beans

Place the broad beans into a gentle simmering butter emulsion for a few minutes and then remove.

Celeriac puree

Remove the skin and dice into 3cm cubes, roast for 20 minutes with honey, white wine and thyme and then remove and place in 100ml water and 300ml milk and gently simmer until soft. Blend until smooth and finish with seasoning and a 10g block of butter, and set aside until required.

Potato straw

Put the potato onto a Japanese spiraliser (use the finest blades) and spin the potato. Place the potato straw in a fryer at 170°C for a few minutes until crisp and golden, then remove and lightly season with sea salt.

Game jus

Put the juniper berries, thyme and garlic cloves in the pan with the game jus and red wine and reduce together by half and make sure it has a good sheen. Once reduced, leave to infuse for an hour, strain and set aside until required.

MASA RESTRAUNT

BIOGRAPHY

Matthew Gabbitas Head Chef - Masa Restaurant & Wine Bar

Masa is a converted Wesleyan Chapel in The Heart of Derby's City Centre Owned by Didar & Paula Dalkic. Matt has been at the helm of Masa's kitchen since 2014. With a ethos of the best seasonal and local produce cooked well, using modern cooking techniques and contemporary presentation Masa's reputation has excelled leading to them winning Derby's Restaurant of the Year in 2015. Masa are also listed in the 2016 Good Food Guide and AA Guide.

Inspired by British produce and influenced by Classical French Flavours, Matt offers a great variety of Flavours and Skills across his Ala carte and Tasting Menu's.

Trio of Rose Veal
parma ham, onion seed, wild garlic

INGREDIENTS

Rose veal fillet – 200g

Veal throat sweetbread 200g

Meat glue

Plain flour

Rose veal shin - 320g

Veal stock – 1litre

Red wine – 350ml

Garlic Puree

1 bulb of peeled Garlic

Chicken stock – 500ml

Double cream – 500ml

Butter – 100g

Onion Seed Crumble

Pork rind 100g

Black onion seeds 35g

Sea salt

Garnish

Grelot onion - 4

peeled Asparagus - 8

Parma ham – 4 slices halved

Morel mushroom - 12

METHOD

Season the veal shin. Place in Tray covered with the veal stock & Red Wine, Foil, then Braise for 4 Hours at 130c till Soft. Once soft remove from the braising liquor, Remove bone, then any white fat from around the outside. Pick down meat and roll into a sausage shape in Clingfilm, once set cut into portions

Soak the Sweetbreads in Milk Over night, pat dry then blanch in boiling water for 60 seconds. Drop straight into cold water, once cool, peel off any white fat, place in a bowl and add in meat glue and seasoning, roll in Clingfilm tightly to create a boudin. Place in water bath at 63c for 1 hour, chill immediately in ice water, once chilled portion into similar size as the shin

Trim any white fat and sinew off the outside of fillet, then roll in clingfilm again to hold the fillets shape. Chill immediately then portion once required.

For the Crumble

cook the pork rind until it resembles crackling then blitz in a food processor with the black onion seeds until it resembles 'crumble'

Garlic Puree

Colour garlic in a pan with butter, add stock, reduce by half, add cream reduce by half again, blitz in food processor emulsifying cold butter into the puree until smooth

Wash and Trim Morel Mushrooms ensuring all dirt is removed, Peel Asparagus and Grelot Onion. Blanch the Grelot Onion in boiling water, then add to a hot pan with butter, add the morels and asparagus to the same pan once cooked removed from the heat.

Portion the Veal Fillet and Vacuum Pack. Drop Veal Fillet into water bath at 55c for 40 minutes, remove from vacuum pouch and allow to rest, reheat the veal shin through a warm oven. Flour the sweetbread. Seal the Veal fillet in a hot pan with the floured sweetbread until golden

Place the meet in a straight line in the middle of the plate, arranging the grelot onion, asparagus and morels neatly. Garnish with the Garlic Puree, thinly sliced Parma ham, wild garlic leaves and the black onion seed crumble.

THREE HORSESHOES

BIOGRAPHY

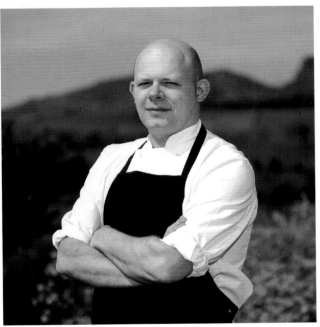

Executive Chef Gary Woolliscroft began his career at the Three Horseshoes Country Inn & Spa aged 15. Following a period in the U.S Gary joined The Alderley Edge Hotel where he quickly progressed to Sous Chef and supported the acquisition of a highly sought after 3rd AA Rosette. Whilst here Gary also co-wrote 'Sous Vide, the Art of Precision Cooking' which demonstrates modern cooking techniques, aimed at the amateur cook. Gary re-joined the Three Horseshoes early 2015 to establish The Stables Restaurant and maintain the 2 AA rosettes already awarded to the former Brasserie. Gary has created a new menu utilising his extensive experience of balancing textures and flavours, using modern cooking techniques and the very best local produce. The Lamb in this dish is sourced from the Roaches.

Hot Pot of Roaches Lamb
pickled red cabbage, hay smoked loin & parsnip

INGREDIENTS

serves 1 person

Lamb Neck Braise:

1 Lamb neck fillet 500g

1 litre good quality Lamb stock

50g Carrots diced

50g Onion sliced

5 Rosemary leaves

Hot Pot Potato:

1 large Maris piper potato

200ml Lamb braise liquid

1/3 braised piece of Lamb neck fillet

Parsnip Puree:

500g Parsnips

200ml Milk

Pickled Red Cabbage:

500g Red cabbage, thinly sliced

1 Star anise

200ml Red wine

100ml Malt vinegar

80ml White wine vinegar

80ml Balsamic vinegar

2 Bay leaves

5 Cloves

½ tsp Black peppercorns

½ tsp Pink peppercorns

½ Cinnamon stick

150g Sugar

20g Sea salt

Hay Smoked Lamb Loin:

200g Lamb cannon

1 handful of Hay

Beetroot:

1 large Beetroot

To Serve:

1 Baby carrot

1 Parsnip

½ Spring cabbage leaf

200ml Lamb sauce

METHOD

24hrs in Advance:

Season the lamb neck fillet liberally with salt, colour on all sides in a hot pan with oil. Add the sliced onions, diced carrots and rosemary leaves to the same pan and colour until golden brown. Place everything in an ovenproof dish, cover with the lamb stock and wrap tightly with foil to create a sealed lid. Braise for 6 hours at 95oc. After this time check the lamb is soft all the way through and leave in its braising juices to mature in flavour.

Season the sliced red cabbage with the salt, and leave to steep for 60mins.

In a pan, add the remaining ingredients and bring to the boil, pass off and discard the aromatics. Then add the washed red cabbage to the pickling liquor and reserve in an airtight container for 24 hours in the fridge.

On the day:

Pre heat the oven to 160oc

Peel and thinly slice the potato. Shred 1/3rd of the lamb neck and layer alternately with the potato, seasoning as you go. Pour enough of the braising liquid over to cover the top layer of potato and place a piece of grease proof paper on top. Wrap tightly with foil and bake in the oven at 160oc for 35 minutes. Check the potato with a knife, if the knife goes through with no resistance it's ready. Place the grease proof paper back on top and press with a weight in the fridge for an hour to firm up.

Peel the parsnips and cut up the same size so they cook evenly. Place in a pan with the milk and cook slowly until soft. Pour the parsnips and milk into a blender, blend until smooth and season to taste.

To cook the beetroot place it in a small pan with enough water to cover and cook until tender. Portion into a barrel shape

In a deep tray add the hay; place the lamb cannon on a wire rack on top of the hay. Set alight the hay and cover with a lid, allowing the lamb to smoke (5mins)

Place the remaining 2/3 of lamb neck in a steel serving pot with the carrots and onions from the original braise. Add enough braising liquid to cover the meat but leaving a 2cm gap at the top for the potato. Cut out a circle the same size as the steel pot from the hotpot potato. Place on top of the meat and reheat in the oven to create a mini lamb hot pot. Meanwhile reduce down the remaining braised liquid to a sauce consistency to coat the back of a spoon.

Cook the lamb cannon in a hot pan with oil (medium rare – 8-10mins), add 20g of butter and allow to foam. Baste the lamb cannon with foaming butter for 2 minutes, season and rest for 4mins.

Blanch the baby carrot, 1/2 the parsnip cut into 2 pieces until tender. Add the carrot and parsnip pieces to the same pan as the lamb, to add some colour. Cook the cabbage leaf just before ready to serve in boiling water and season.

Very thinly slice (using a vegetable peeler) the remaining parsnip and deep fry until golden brown on 160oc, season.

To serve:

Place the hot pot potato pan on the plate, spoon on the parsnip puree and spread in a diagonal direction. Slice the lamb cannon in two and plate pink side up at opposite ends. Place the baby carrot, parsnip pieces, parsnip crisp, cabbage leaf and beetroot to your liking. Garnish with several pieces of pickled red cabbage, and sauce over and around the dish.

JEWS HOUSE

BIOGRAPHY

Gavin Aitkenhead

Gavin started work at a gastro style pub at 17, learning the basic skills. He then moved on to the renowned 2** Winteringham fields, working his way up to head chef under the watchful eye of Germain Schwab.

His ambition of running his own kitchen took him to York for 10 months, until the opportunity of opening his own place back in Lincoln was too good to miss.

With its 10 year anniversary coming up, Gavin has found his own style, basically cooking what he likes to eat, from his travels bringing a mix of fusion and classic dishes together.

Pork Belly Miso, Melon Sorbet, King Prawns

INGREDIENTS

1kg Pork belly

1 litre of Duck fat or vegetable oil (other cooking

method - 48hr in Sous Vide if possible)

200g coarse Sea salt

3 cloves of Garlic

handful of fresh Thyme and Rosemary

8 large raw Tiger prawns

small bunch of Coriander

200g Miso paste

50g Sake (Japanese rice wine)

50g Mirin

150g Brown sugar

250ml Melon juice (cantaloupe if possible)

125g stock Syrup (equal quantities of sugar and water)

General stuff ;
Maldon salt, Veg oil, Butter

METHOD

Mix together the Sea Salt, Thyme and Rosemary. Put a layer of salt mix on a tray, place Pork Belly on top and put rest of salt mix over the Pork. Refrigerate for 8 hrs then wash off salt and pat dry with a cloth. Place Pork in a deep tray, cover with the Duck fat. Place in oven at 140c/ gas mark 2 for 2 1/2 hrs or until tender. Take Pork out of fat and place on a tray, cover with grease proof paper, place another tray on top and weigh down with soup cans or some form of weight. Place in the fridge to set so it's easier to cut into portions later.

For the miso glaze

Place the paste, sugar, Mirin and Saké in a bowl and place over a pan of water and simmer for 1 hr. Stir from time to time and make sure the pan doesn't boil dry. When it's a nice thick past take off heat and let cool.

Melon sorbet

Boil up the water and sugar to make stock syrup, measure 125g and mix with 250g of Melon juice, churn in an ice cream machine, place in freezer until required.

Serving

Portion Pork Belly, brush over the Miso glaze, don't worry if it falls over the sides.
Place on a tray and heat in oven for 10 minutes on mark 5/ 180c or until a nice caramelisation has been achieved.

Pan fry the Prawns in hot oil for 30 seconds on each side, take the Prawns out of the pan and keep warm. Place Pork Belly on a plate, position the prawns, scoop a ball of Melon sorbet on to plate and place a few coriander leaves over the dish, and serve, Enjoy!

THE PHEASANT AT KEYSTON

BIOGRAPHY

Simon Cadge is Chef Patron. Simon has been in the catering trade since he was 16. He started his career at The Swan Hotel in Lavenham then moved to the Old Bridge at Huntingdon, before running his own gastro pub, The Crown at Broughton and then taking over The Pheasant at Keyston. His food is simple, lead by the seasons and full of flavour.

Monkfish Ossobucco
with saffron risotto, cavolo nero and gremolata

INGREDIENTS

4 baby Monkfish tails (200 gram each)

1 tea spoon Tomato puree

100 gram Alborio rice

4 Banana shallots

1 head of Fennel

2 Bay leaves

2 Celery sticks

1 Carrot

½ bottle White wine

3 gloves Garlic

100 grams Parmesan

1 head Cavolo nero

2 Lemons

½ bunch Flat leaf parsley

2 pints of Fish stock

Olive oil of good quality

Saffron,

Fennel seeds

Chilli flakes

METHOD

Marinade monkfish tails in olive oil, lemon zest and ground fennel seeds

Remove leaves of cavolo nero and blanch for 6 min. Remove onto a tray, season and add olive oil

Fry chopped shallots, garlic, alborizo rice in olive oil without adding any colour.

Add saffron, white wine and half the fish stock. Slowly keep stirring till just cooked

Fry diced vegetables, garlic, fennel seeds, chili flakes, bay leaves. Then add other half of fish stock and simmer for 30 minutes.

Char-grill monkfish till just cooked

Make gremolata from olive oil, grated garlic, lemon zest, juice, segments and flat parsley.

Add monkfish to the vegetables last minute. Then put risotto, cavolo nero, monkfish into a bowl. Finish with gremolata and parmesan

Credited to- Moment magazine

DOG IN A DOUBLIET

BIOGRAPHY

John McGinn

After appearing on BBCs Masterchef, John has followed his dream and has worked his way to the top. He now owns the Dog in a Doublet just outside of Peterborough and enjoys serving food that is from his garden, his farm, a neighbours or just the best the world has to offer. His policy of unpretentious well prepared food has earned him regional Pub of the Year and he has had numerous appearances on BBC Breakfast. John has always enjoyed traveling, with over 30 countries visited, it shows in the Dog in a Doublets cuisine where his take on fish and chips sits happily alongside curry goat, rice and peas. "I've been all over and I can happily say that British cuisine is the most accepting and diverse in the world... and I'm glad to represent it."

Devilled Lambs kidneys and porcini mushrooms on brioche with pea salad

INGREDIENTS

8-12 Lambs kidneys
(depending on size)

500g fresh Porcini
mushrooms (or any
mushrooms will do)

Butter brioche
(sliced 1inch thick)

1tsp Veg oil

200ml Double cream

Handful of Flat leaf parsley
(chopped)

Devilled butter

40g Butter at room
temperature

1tsp Caster sugar

1tsp English mustard powder

1tsp Cayenne pepper

1tsp Paprika

1tsp ground Coriander

2tbls Red wine vinegar

1tsp ground Black pepper

2tsp Sea salt

Pea salad

Handful each of Pea shoots,
sugar snap peas, fresh peas

a few fresh Garden mint
leaves

Salad Dressing

1tsp Wholegrain mustard

1tsp Cider vinegar

3tsp extra Virgin rapeseed oil

1 slither of Garlic

Salt and pepper

METHOD

Devilled butter

Combine all ingredients thoroughly. Set aside.

Salad dressing

Combine all ingredients in a jar and shake well. Set aside

Devilled kidneys and mushrooms

Trim the kidneys to remove the sinew. Cut the mushrooms to half kidney size. Heat a large frying pan until very hot. Add the veg oil, then the mushrooms and then the kidneys. Move around the pan to colour then ad a good knob of the devilled butter (the rest will keep for a week or two in the fridge). You don't want to burn the butter so move it around quickly and have a little water to hand to pour in to stop it burning (the water will soon evaporate). When the kidneys are just cooked add the cream and remove from the heat. The kidneys will continue cooking while you prepare the rest of the dish so if you like those rare remove from sauce and set aside. Taste the sauce and adjust... it may want more devilled butter, cream or salt to your liking.

To finish

Toast the brioche (beware it burns very easily!). Place the brioche on the plate and top with the kidneys, mushrooms and sauce. Toss the salad in the dressing (minus the garlic slither) and serve with the kidneys. Finish with the parsley

The twist

This dish is also great with just one kidney per person as a starter or some boiled new potatoes to make it a bigger main... a Dog in a Doublet, John has even served it with a soft fried Peahen egg from the garden and some grated pecorino.

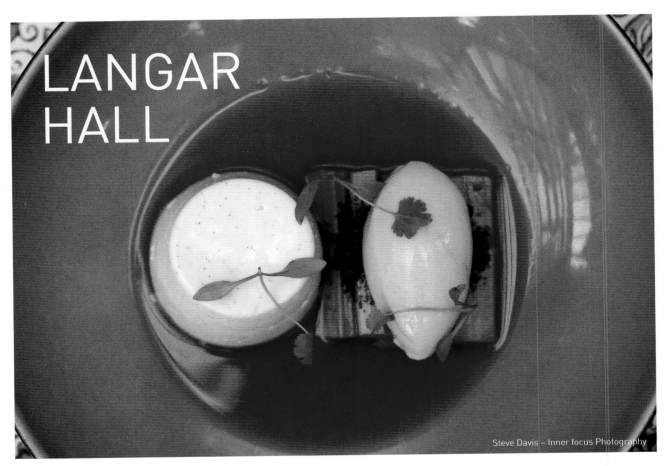

LANGAR HALL

Steve Davis – Inner focus Photography

BIOGRAPHY

Set in the Vale of Belvoir, Langar Hall is a charming small hotel near Nottingham offers a haven of tranquillity, away from the stress of city life. Langar Hall is a genuine country house which has gently evolved into a hotel and restaurant without losing the air of a family home. It enjoys the reputation for exceptional hospitality, friendly and efficient service, comfortable bedrooms, good food and an interesting wine list.

There's a conservatory restaurant and a more formal dining room, serving an upscale modern European menu plus afternoon tea.

The recipe has been dedicated to the late Imogen Skirving who will be truly missed

Rhubarb Panna Cotta

INGREDIENTS

Panna cotta
600ml Milk
600ml Cream
2 Canilla pods
6 Gelatine leaves
150g Sugar

**Rhubarb & ginger
beer sorbet**
1 inch peeled grated Ginger
600g Rhubarb
600g Water
450g Sugar
4 teaspoon Honey
360ml Ginger beer
1 Canilla pod
Juice & zest of Lemon

Poached rhubarb
400g Raspberry jam
400g Water
100g Sugar
10 sticks Rhubarb

To garnish
Coriander shoots
Rhubarb cooking syrup
Crumbled ginger bread

METHOD

Panna cotta

Heat milk, cream, sugar & vanilla   together until sugar dissolves. Soak gelatine in cold water until bloomed. Remove from water & add to warm cream mixture. Stir to dissolve pour into moulds and leave to set in fridge

Rhubarb & ginger beer sorbet

Put all ingredients in a pan and cook until rhubarb is soft. Blend in a liquidiser. Leave to cool then churn in ice cream machine

Poached rhubarb

Combine jam, sugar & water in a pan and heat until sugar is dissolved, pass through sieve to remove raspberry pips. Cut rhubarb into 2 inch pieces and place in a baking tray. Pour over the raspberry syrup and cover with foil. Bake at 160c until tender 12-15 mins. Leave to cool in syrup.

LAUNAY'S RESTAURANT & BAR

BIOGRAPHY

Alain is celebrating his 30th year in catering, starting as an apprentice on the south coast of Brittany and shortly after, broadening his horizons moving to the UK, working in the south and the Channel Islands.

Alain and Alison took the plunge back in 2004 investing everything into a little restaurant in the heart of Sherwood Forest and so began the long process of transforming the rather tired restaurant into the contemporary fine dining establishment they are very proud of today.

Keeping the menu seasonal (some ingredients coming from the kitchen garden) and inventive, Alain is always looking for and working on new ideas in the way the food is served, bringing a serious element to the fun part of the dining experience. Launay's breakfast dessert represents exactly that!

Launays Breakfast

METHOD

Egg White
Soak gelatine in cold water.
Heat rest of ingredients in a pan, add softened gelatine, mix thoroughly. Pour into rings on a flat surface to set

Egg Yolk
Blend all ingredients in a food processor, pour into ½ sphere molds and freeze.

When it's time to use the yolks, remove from mold, place in algin bath, making sure its well coated and defrosted

Assembly Of Egg
Remove white from ring,(sprinkle a little sugar in the centre to avoid yolk slipping off)
Using a slotted spoon, remove yolk from algin bath, place in container of cold water then carefully remove, placing on top of white.

Bacon
Cream butter & sugar, add egg whites, flour, essence – cream until smooth.
Divide mix into 2 – add colouring to one half of mixture.
Pipe onto silicon mat (alternative stripes close together – about 4 inches long)
Bake 180 10-15 mins until golden brown
Remove whilst hot, place on wire rack to crinkle

Black Pudding
Melt butter & chocolate over bain marie, sieve dry ingredients together, add to melted chocolate along with egg yolks.
Whisk egg whites to soft peak
Whip cream
Fold whites, marshmallows & cream into chocolate mixture
Pipe mixture onto clingfilm and roll into a sausage shape – chill then cut into slices, removing clingflim when required.

Mushrooms
Whisk whites to soft peak
Mix cornflour & sugar – add to whites, whisking until firm peaks. Pipe onto greaseproof paper into small mounds, dust these "mushroom tops" with cocoa powder and short sticks. Bake at lowest temperature until dried.

Chocolate Buttercream
Cream all ingredients together to form glossy soft buttercream

Assembly
Use chocolate buttercream to sandwich mushroom tops & stalks together

Ketchup / Tomato
Boil all ingredients together, then pass through sieve to remove seeds. Use some of this mixture as ketchup – pour into small bottle.
Rest of mixture is to coat the tomato .

INGREDIENTS

Egg White
100ml Coconut milk
50ml Double cream
1 leaf Gelatine
10g Sugar

60g Cocoa powder
2 Seperated eggs
75 ml Cream
5 Marshmallows, diced

Egg Yolk
100ml Mango puree
0.5g Xanthum gum
2g Gluco

Mushrooms
2 Egg whites
100g Caster sugar
1tspn Cornflour
Cocoa powder to dust

Algin Bath
250ml Water
1.25g Algin

Chocolate Buttercream
75g Salted butter
50g Icing sugar
25g Cocoa powder
Few drops vanilla essence

Bacon
Few drops red food colouring
30g Butter
50g Sugar
1 Large egg white
35g Plain flour
Vanilla essence

Ketchup
250g Raspberries
50g Sugar
Juice of ½ lemon

Tomato
125ml Double cream
125ml Cream cheese
1 leaf Gelatine
40ml Passion fruit juice

Black Pudding
100g Dark chocolate
120g Butter
70g Icing sugar

Tomato
Soak gelatine in cold water, heat up passion fruit juice, dissolve gelatine in juice, mix well & cool.
Mix cream & cream cheese together, add passion fruit juice. Pour into sphere molds, freeze.

Using rest of raspberry coulis (200ml), add 50ml water, 2.5g gellan – boil together and whilst warm, dip the frozen spheres 2-3 times for a good red coating, place to one side to set.

AMALFI WHITE

BIOGRAPHY

Derbyshire Chef Matthew Clayton is the driving force behind the glamorous start up restaurant and wedding venue, Amalfi White. A true Derbyshire talent, Matthew grew up and trained in the Peak District and has built his career in some of the region's finest establishments having had ten years of AA Rosette and Michelin experience. A meticulous and inventive chef he uses the best local ingredients and cooks with passion to create modern British food with contemporary cosmopolitan flair.

Matthew cooked for the Queen in 2011 and is now guiding the talented young team at Amalfi White to push a new concept in fine dining. "We are taking classic cooking techniques and using striking new flavour combinations with a vibrancy and youth not seen before in this region. New technology and methods are also giving us an opportunity to be more creative and have a bit more fun here at Amalfi White. Think of it as 'Urban Fine Dining' – we are a bit more rock and roll"

White Chocolate Cheesecake
with apple textures, caramelized bananas,
cinnamon crumb and banana ice cream

METHOD

White chocolate cheesecake
Heat sugar in a pan with a drop of cold water, boil until all the sugar
is dissolved
Pour over the egg yolks and whisk until pale
Soak gelatin in cold water, warm the 12ml of cream and dissolve
gelatin
Once dissolved add to the eggs and sugar and whisk until cool
Pour mix over mascarpone and fold together
Melt the chocolate and add to mixture one third at a time, folding in
gently along with the whipped cream
Transfer into a piping bag and chill for a minimum of 1 hour

Cinnamon crumb
Rub butter, flour, sugar and salt together to a sandy texture
Add granola and maple syrup combine
Spread the mixture onto a baking tray and bake for 10 minutes at
180°C until golden brown
Remove from the oven and allow to cool, blitz into a fine crumb in a
food processor, adding cinnamon and all spice to taste
Spread the crumb on a silicone mat and bake for 5 -8 minutes at
180°C until crunchy

Banana ice cream
Whisk together egg yolks and sugar and set aside
Bring to the milk and double cream to the boil and pour over egg
mixture, whisk to combine
Roast 2 bananas at 160°C for 15 minutes until soft, then set aside
Blend the other 3 bananas until smooth and add to mixture
Heat the mix in a thick based sauce pan to 86°C, stir continuously in
a figure of eight
Blitz the roasted bananas and add to the mixture
Pass through a sieve and churn for 40 minutes
Remove from the machine and place in the freezer in a sealed
container, leave to freeze for a minimum of 2-3 hours

Caramelised bananas
Slice bananas into slices, top with sugar and glaze by using a blow
torch or placing under a grill until caramelised

Apple and Vanilla puree
Peel and dice the apples into small cubes and place in a metal bowl
Scrape out the vanilla pod centre, add sugar and cling film well
Cook over a bain marie until apples are soft to touch
Blitz in food processor until smooth and then refrigerate

INGREDIENTS

**White chocolate
cheesecake**
55g Caster sugar
12 ml Double cream
1 leaf Gelatin
3 Egg yolks
150g soft Mascarpone
125g White chocolate
chips (55% Fat content)
160ml Double cream -
whipped lightly

Cinnamon crumb
65g Butter
55g Plain flour
55g Sugar
55g plain Granola
35g Maple syrup
pinch Salt
ground Cinnamon
ground All spice

Caramelised bananas
1 Banana
20g Demerara sugar

Banana ice cream
Makes 1 litre Ice cream
7 Egg yolks
125g Caster sugar
5 Bananas
250ml whole Milk
250ml Double cream
Ice cream maker

Apple and vanilla puree
4 Granny smith apples
1 Vanilla pod
75g Icing sugar

Banana paper
250g pre-prepared
Banana puree
85g caster sugar
1.5g Pectin
1g Crytex

Banana paper
Bring sugar, puree and pectin to the boil
Remove from the heat and stir in the crytex
Sieve and spread evenly onto a silcone mat, dry at 80°C for 3 hours
Store in a sealed container

To serve
Pipe the cheesecake onto cling film and roll into a cylinder shape,
tie the ends and freeze for two hours
Remove and wrap the cheesecake log in the banana paper
Garnish with apple and vanilla puree, caramelized bananas and
banana ice cream

FISCHERS
BASLOW HALL

15|01|10

BIOGRAPHY

Rupert Rowley graduated from Sheffield Catering College in 1995. He secured a placement to Raymond Blanc's 'Manoir au Quat' Saison in Oxford, where he created such a good impression that Raymond asked Rupert to stay on and he was there until 1997.

His next strategic career move took him to work for the infamous John Burton Race at the 2 Michelin starred L'Ortolan restaurant in Reading.

In 2001 he decided to brave the kitchens of Gordon Ramsay at his flagship 3 Michelin starred Chelsea restaurant where he stayed for a year before coming to Fischer's at Baslow Hall in 2002. In 2003 he was appointed Head Chef.

Rupert has continued to develop dishes and maintain the Michelin star at Fischer's in Baslow, Derbyshire over the years. Rupert cooks with the seasons and incorporates an abundant source of home-grown produce from the Kitchen Garden at Baslow Hall into dishes. Over 90% of the produce used is British; he relies on local suppliers for Derbyshire Beef, Venison and Lamb, as well as Rapeseed Oil from Ashford-in-the-Water and honey from The Sheffield Honey Company.

Rupert co-owns and has established the two red rosette restaurant, Rowley's at the Prince of Wales Village Pub in Baslow, Derbyshire. He has helped to create a relaxed and informal atmosphere serving exciting local food with menus that change with the season.

Banana and Toffee Crunch Soufflé

INGREDIENTS

Banana Soufflé Sauce

1kg Banana Purée

200g Caster sugar

175ml Crème de banana

150ml Double cream

100ml Milk

Banana and Toffee Crunch Soufflé Base

2kg Banana puree

60g Cornflour

300g Crème de banana

350g Sugar

100g Water

100g Sugar

Pecan Praline

200g Fondant

200g Glucose

50g Pecan

15g Cocoa powder

Digestive Biscuits

Broken up Werther's originals

Soufflé

120g Egg whites

60g Sugar

METHOD

Banana Soufflé Sauce

200g of Caster Sugar caramelised, once caramelised add the 1kg of Banana Puree & Double cream.

Once cooled add the Crème de Banana so you don't cook out any of the alcohol.

Add 100ml of Milk or until the desired consistency is reached.

Banana and Toffee Crunch Soufflé Base

Reduce the banana puree to 1kg.

Boil the sugar and water to 121c.

Take the 100g of sugar to a caramel.

Mix the crème de banana and cornflour.

Mix all into the puree and cook until thick.

Pecan Praline

Boil the sugars to 150c.

Warm the pecans in the oven.

When it reaches 150c add the cocoa and pour over the nuts.

Leave to cool.

Digestive Biscuits

Fold some of the broken up sweets through the mix once you have folded in the egg white.

Soufflé

Whisk the egg whites.

Slowly add the sugar until stiff peak then gently fold into 160g of the soufflé base.

Line the soufflé moulds with the pecan praline (keeping a little to one side). Blitz 5 digestive biscuits to a fine powder, mix with the remaining pecan praline and sprinkle of top of the soufflé before cooking.

Once cooked, serve the soufflé with the Banana soufflé sauce and dark chocolate sorbet.

THE BLACK BULL

BIOGRAPHY

Craig Hadden & Lewis Kuciers head the talented, young kitchen team at The Black Bull Blidworth. Sited in the very centre of Nottinghamshire, The Black Bull has been serving food and drink since the seventeenth century but we are confident that the dining experience delivered by Lewis and Craig surpasses anything previous centuries have provided or aspired to.

They seek out and use the highest quality, seasonal ingredients from local producers to develop dishes which combine flavours and textures that allow the quality of the produce and their skill to shine through. To ensure confidence in their supply chain Lewis & Craig work closely with free range and organic sole suppliers with in the small village as well as more recognised Nottinghamshire producers including award winning butcher Johnny Pusztai.

Both chefs trained for three years at Vision, West Nottinghamshire College and achieved Level 3 NVQ in Professional Cookery whilst gaining practical experience working part time at The Black Bull. Their academic studies complete, the pair went separate ways for a time, gaining Michelin star experience with a series of stages at acclaimed restaurants and gastro pubs across the country.

In late summer of 2015 Hadden & Kuciers joined forces again at The Black Bull. Developing new creative forms of classic dishes, constantly adjusting the menu to get the very best from locally sourced produce and reflect the relentless development of their work. As The Black Bull heads into her 4th century of business, interest in the old coaching house has never been greater, due to imaginative finely prepared menus of Hadden & Kuciers.

Chocolate Aero, Mint, Popcorn

INGREDIENTS

Shortbread

350g Butter

150g Caster sugar

450g Plain flour

Caramel

400g Butter

2 tins Condensed milk

4 tbsp Golden syrup

pinch Salt

Aero

450g Dark chocolate

180ml Olive oil

Mint choc chip ice cream

250ml Milk

250ml Double cream

6 Egg yolks

90g Sugar

2 tbsp Glucose syrup

bag of Mint (picked no stalk)

Chocolate chips

Mint gel

Mint (picked no stalk)

100ml Water

50g Sugar

Ultratex

Green food colouring

Popcorn

30g Popcorn kernels

120g Caster sugar

20g Butter

20g Maple syrup

METHOD

Shortbread

Cream butter and sugar together until light and fluffy.

Add flour until it comes to dough.

Split shortbread in to half and push into two, 30cm trays.

Cook at 160 C for 16 minutes.

Leave to cool once cooked.

Caramel

Put the butter, condensed milk and golden syrup into a pan and melt.

Once melted continually whisk until the mixture turns a deep golden colour.

Once golden brown pour over the shortbread and leave to set in the fridge for 6 hours.

When set portion each tray into 10 pieces.

Aero

Melt the chocolate in a bowl over a ban marie.

Once melted whisk in the olive oil.

Place the chocolate mixture into an isi gun with two gas chargers and shake for 20 seconds.

Spray the chocolate mixture into a cling film lined rectangular tub.

Place the tub into the vacuum pack machine and aerate until doubled in size.

Remove from machine and place a tight fitting lid on the tub and put in the fridge for 40 minutes till set.

Once set cut in to 5 the same length and width as the caramel shortbread and half the height so you get ten out of each tub.

When portioned place on top of the caramel shortbread and that is the aero bar finished.

Mint choc chip ice cream

Warm the milk and cream together in a pan.

Whisk the egg yolks and sugar together until pale in a bowl.

Pour the warm milk & cream mixture over the egg yolks and whisk, this creates the anglaise.

Add the glucose syrup into the anglaise and cook out in a pan until 63 C and slightly thicker.

Cool in the fridge.

Blanch the mint leaves in boiling water and refresh in ice cold water.

Blitz the mint into the cold mixture using the thermomix.

Stir the chocolate chips through the anglaise.

Place the finished anglaise into the ice cream machine and churn until the ice cream is set, place into tub in the freezer until needed.

Mint gel

Warm water and sugar in a pan and leave to cool.

Blanch mint leaves in boiling water and refresh in cold water.

Place in to the thermomix and blitz with water and sugar mixture.

Blitz for one minute on high speed.

Pass through muslim cloth to remove and small bits of mint so its smooth and clear.

Add food colouring till desired colour.

Add ultratrex whilst whisking to thicken the mint mixture.

Popcorn

Warm a deep pan with oil on the stove.

When smoking hot add the popcorn kernels in and place a lid on, cook until you stop hearing the popcorn pop.

Once all the popcorn is ready sit aside until needed.

Melt sugar until a caramel forms.

Whisk in the butter and maple syrup.

Add the popcorn in and coat all of it, pour on to baking parchment and leave to set and cool.

Break into chunks and leave aside for when you plate the dish.

To plate

Start with the mint gel in a circle on the bottom of the plate.

Place the aero on the left hand side.

Put 5 dots of mint gel on top of the aero, and place to bits of popcorn on either end.

Scoop the mint ice cream and put next to the aero bar.

North-
North East

Starter
Main
Dessert

RIVER BEAT

BIOGRAPHY

Nestled on the south bank of the River Tyne, in the old River Police Station, River Beat brings together the flavours of Asian and Spanish food.

Head chef and owner Andrew Drape creates a relaxed dining experience where people can shrug off the shackles of the three-course meal and the pre-conceptions that tapas is only from Spain. Andrew is revolutionising dining with his infectious blend of European indulgence and authentic Asian tastes mixed with great beats and entertainment.

With more than 20 years experience Andrew's culinary style draws inspiration from his love of Asian cuisine along with his skills and knowledge of flavours to create menus that mesmerise any patron.

He's gone back to the roots of how Thai is eaten. Eating is the most social aspect of Thai life and people love sharing food. This tradition is the basis of his menu giving customers the opportunity to share a variety of tastes, salty, spicy, sour & sweet, and enjoy them together!

Offering amazing views over Newcastle's historic quayside, River Beat is a place where customers are as comfortable dining alone as they are with friends and family and they can order what they want, when they want and in whatever order.

Prawn & Crayfish Roll

INGREDIENTS

Prawn and crayfish roll

125g Crayfish

125 kg King prawns

1/2 Egg

A pinch of Five spice

A pinch of Salt

1/2 tsp Soy sauce

1/2 tsp Oyster sauce

Rice flour to thicken

A pinch of Garlic

1/4 tsp Sesame oil

1 packet of Filo pastry

Hot piquant Thai dressing

2 Birds eye chillies

2 Spring onions

2 tbsp Coriander

2 tbsp Lemon grass

1 tsp Palm sugar

2-3 tbsp Fish sauce

4 tbsp Lime juice

METHOD

Prawn and crayfish roll

Pulse the crayfish and prawn together, not too finely

Add all other ingredients and mix well together

Separate your pastry until you have 6 sheets

Leaving a gap at the top and side of your sheet, add a spoonful of your mixture to the top of your sheet and form into a sausage shape

Fold the edges in and gently roll to the end

Continue until you have 6

Steam for 8/10 mins until firm and then deep-fry until golden

Season to taste and dress with coriander stem and piquant dip to serve

Hot piquant Thai dressing

Place all the ingredients in a food processor or for a more rustic look chop everything down finely and leave to marinade for at least 2 hours for the flavours to release.

SILVERSMITHS

BIOGRAPHY

Silversmiths is a multi award-winning restaurant in Sheffield. Independently owned and operated. The Head Chef is Lee Mangles who has worked at the restaurant for over 5 years.

He has over 20 experiences working in top hotels and restaurants in Sheffield and has brought an ethos of selecting the best Yorkshire produce, supporting regional farmers and bringing Silversmiths a true field to plate experience.

The restaurant is based in an historic cutlery works in the City and Silversmiths aim to present a true Yorkshire dining experience that is founded on history and embraces fresh innovative sourcing and presentation of food.

Everything that comes out of Lee Mangles kitchen has been prepared, preserved, pickled, roasted, baked, mixed and handmade by his team. He knows exactly the provenance of all of their food and the stories behind it.

Rabbit Spring Roll
with a spiced tomato chutney

INGREDIENTS

Rabbit Spring Roll

1 Whole rabbit – ask butcher to prepare & skin

6 Sheets of spring roll pastry

½ tsp of Coriander powder

½ tsp of Cumin powder

1 Egg

Small bunch of coriander

Mixed leaf (garnish)

Spiced Tomato Chutney

5 Large tomatoes

2 Chillies

100 ml of White wine vinegar

50g Caster sugar

50g Mixed dried fruit

Mixed leaf for garnish

METHOD

Rabbit

Place the rabbit in an oven proof dish half filled with cold water.

Cover with foil and slow cook on 100 degrees for 10 hours till tender

Remove from the oven, remove the rabbit from the liquid, and allow to cool slightly

Carefully pick all meat from the bones

Place all the meat in a separate dish and add some of liquid to moisten

Add the spices, herbs and seasoning then mix well

Allow to chill properly by covering and refrigerating for 1 hour

Spoon the meat onto pastry, form a cylinder with meat roll in the pastry

Roll tightly and use the egg wash to seal the pastry

Shallow fry until golden and crisp (can be oven cooked)

Chutney

While the meat is chilling make the chutney

Roughly chop all tomatoes and chillies

Put the vinegar sugar, fruit, tomatoes and chillies into a pan – bring to the boil, turn down to a simmer and cook for 25-30 minutes

Allow to cool to room temp

To Serve

Cut the spring roll at angle, place on top of the mixed leaf, place chutney on the side

Serve With – a dark and hoppy local ale or a light red wine such as a Pinot Noir

DUKE OF WELLINGTON

BIOGRAPHY

The Duke of Wellington Inn is nestled in the Tyne valleys village of Newton just off the A69 near Corbridge, within easy access to Newcastle, Hadrian's Wall Country, Hexham, and Northumberland's National Park.

Lunches and dinners are served seven days a week in the bar and dining room. The food provides traditional British comfort eating to an exceptional standard and makes use of local, seasonal ingredients. A comprehensive range of beers and ales compliments an extensive wine list.

Tempura King Prawn
with fennel, scampi and mussel popcorn

INGREDIENTS

4 King prawns (Peeled and
Deveined)
8 Scampi (Peeled and
Deveined)

20 Mussels (Cooked and
Shells Discarded)

2 Fennel bulbs

50ml Pernod

1 Orange

10g Thyme

3 cloves of Garlic

!00ml Vegetable stock

100ml + 3tbsp of Rapeseed oil

2 Apples

1 Honey

1 tbsp Grain mustard

½ tsp Salt

150ml Lemon juice

150ml Water

150ml Sugar

4.5g Agar agar

50g Mayonnaise

50g Cornflour

75g Plain flour

5g Baking powder

Soda water

Panko breadcrumbs

Milk

1 Egg

150g Self raising flour

75g Polenta

50g Rice flour

METHOD

Mandolin both the fennel bulbs thinly, placing one in a container with ice and water place in vac-pac machine a few times till it goes transparent.

Place the other fennel bulb in a metal container with the zest and juice of the orange, add the vegetable stock,thyme,2 cloves of garlic, pernod and the 100ml of rapeseed oil and cook in the oven at 180 degrees for approx 18 minutes then blast chill.

Peel the apples and slice into 1/2cm pieces and using an apple corer make some discs of apple then place in a vac pac bag with the honey, grain mustard, salt and remaining rapeseed oil and vac, leave for at least 2 hours.

Bring the lemon juice, water and sugar to the boil add the agar agar and blast chill. Once cooled and set thermomix until smooth.

Place the cooked mussel meat in a container with enough milk to cover. Mix the Self Raising Flour, Polenta and Rice flour together and coat the mussels.

Pane the Scampi tails using Flour Eggwash and Panko breadcrumbs.

Crush The garlic and add to the mayonnaise and season.

Mix the cornflour, plain flour and baking powder and add enough soda water to make a batter that should just coat your finger.

TO ASSEMBLE

Place king prawn into batter and deep fry with the mussels and scampi, Pipe garlic mayo on plate and then roasted fennel, pipe lemon gel on and dot compressed apple on place king prawn on the fennel and place scampi and mussel popcorn around and finish with the transparent fennel.

CAFE ROYAL

BIOGRAPHY

From a very early age food was a huge part of my upbringing, as a young boy I was inspired by my grandmother who was an exceptional cook, we spent hours in the kitchen together. I was both fascinated and intrigued with the process of cooking and seeing the final product on a plate.

I am proud to hold the position of head chef at Café Royal in Newcastle, it's a very unique and stylish café bistro in the historic heart of the city with beautiful Georgian architecture, it's also home our Café Royal bakery where we produce our very own range of speciality breads, cakes and desserts. I am eager to create exquisite seasonally inspired dishes, something a little different with extra touches, full of great flavours, textures and bursting with colour, it's so important to prepare both visually appealing and exceptional tasting dishes for our customers.

Elements of Gazpacho
with peppered soft cheese

INGREDIENTS

Peppered Cheese
50g Soft cheese
2 Black peppercorns
(crushed)
1 Lemon (juiced)

**Compressed Cucumber,
Red Onion And Peppers**
1 Cucumber (peeled)
1 Green pepper
1 Red pepper
1 Baby red onion
1 Lemon (juiced)

Gazpacho Sauce
1 Cucumber
3 Tomatoes
1 Garlic clove
handful of Parsley
1 Red pepper
1 Onion
2 Tsp tomato puree
1 Tsp sugar
2 Tsp red wine vinegar
Seasoning

Vinegar Olive Oil Powder
25g Maltodextirin
25g Olive oil
20g Breadcrumbs
10ml Vinegar

Tomato Sheet
25g Sosa elastic
400g Tomato juice
100g Stock syrup

Cucumber Gel
1 Cucumber
2 tsp sugar
1 tsp salt
75g water
20g Msk ultratex

METHOD

Peppered Cheese
Beat together slowly until soft enough to work with.

Compressed Cucumber, Red Onion And Peppers
Portion cucumber, red onion and peppers to required size and place into a sealable bag with the lemon juice. Seal on a vac machine and leave until needed, the longer the better.

Gazpacho Sauce
Blend all ingredients together and taste for seasoning. Pass through a fine chinois.

Vinegar Olive Oil Powder
Pour the vinegar over the breadcrumbs and bake until dry and golden. Blend until powder form.

In a bowl add the maltodexterin and the powdered crumbs, gradually add the oil rubbing between fingers until all mixed.

Tomato Sheet
In a pan add all ingredients and whisk in elastic, bring to the boil and pour out onto a flat tray.
Portion once cool.

Cucumber Gel
Blend the cucumber with the water. Add the sugar then pass through a fine chinois. Add salt to taste.
In a bowl gradually whisk the ultratex into the cucumber mix until thick enough to form a ball.

Re-blend to get a smooth a shiny gel then disperse into bottle.

Assemble The Plate
Place the tomato sheet on the base. Add the gazpacho gel to a glass and serve on the far side of plate.
Arrange vegetables on top of the tomato sheet. Pipe on the cream cheese and garnish.

Micro basil, red basil, nasturtium and blue borage flower used to garnish the plate.

289

STAITH HOUSE

BIOGRAPHY

When it comes to self-sufficiency and utilising the best local produce, The award winning Staith House on North Shields' Fish Quay is at the top of its game. As Gastropub Chef of the year 2016 at The Top 50 Gastropub awards John Calton's unwavering passion for excellent food, and dedication to quality have put The Staith House on the culinary map. Game, fish and meat are responsibly sourced locally and only the finest produce gets through the kitchen doors. The Staith House is named as one of the top 10 establishments for Fish cookery in the 2016 Seafish Awards, as well as a prestigious Catey nomination in the Newcomer category.

The Staith house is named as one of the top 5 establishments for Fish cookery in the 2016 Seafish awards 'Seafood restaurant of the year', and was awarded a prestigious Catey award for Newcomer of the year 2016.

Raw & Smoked Mackerel
with salt baked clams and oyster vinaigrette

INGREDIENTS

1 Mackerel filleted and pin boned

1 Mackerel lightly salted and hot smoked

8 Oysters opened with juices passed off and reserved

8 Langoustines blanched for 1 minute refreshed and peeled

12 Palourde clams plus sea salt to sit them on

32 Cockles (8 each) plus a glass of dry white wine , 1 shallot finely sliced , 2 cloves of garlic to steam (Juices reserved)

1 tbsp. pickled Wild garlic buds (use extra fine capers if not available)

8 spears of Wye valley asparagus, peeled left raw & cut into 1cm pieces dressed with a squeeze of lemon

1 Cucumber

1 Gelatine leaf soaked in cold water

1 handful of Samphire

2 Lemons

200ml good quality extra Virgin olive oil

100g Crème fraiche

30g Chives finely sliced

A few sprigs of Chervil

METHOD

Peel the cucumber, slice a few ribbons for garnish on a very sharp mandolin then liquidize the remaining cucumber. Pass the cucumber juice off through a sieve, you need about 200ml of liquid plus 50 ml reserved for the vinaigrette. Take 50 ml and warm on a stove, remove from heat add the pre-soaked gelatine, whisk to dissolve, pass onto the cold juice whisk again then evenly divide the liquid onto four plates, place in the fridge to set. It should be of a slightly set consistency not too firm.

Sweat the shallots and garlic with a touch of olive oil over a gentle heat , add the cockles & white wine cover with a tight fitting lid , steam for 2 – 3 minutes till they open , pass the reserved liquor through a sieve , set aside to cool , pick the meat from the shells set aside.

Arrange the clams on the sea salt in oven proof serving dishes then bake 3 – 4 minutes at 200 degrees till they open, serve at the table in the same dish.

Skin and finely dice the raw mackerel fillets, season with a pinch of sea salt and a squeeze of lemon, set aside.

Flake the smoked mackerel checking for pin bones, bind with the crème fraiche and chives, season with a twist of freshly ground black pepper. Set aside.

Now make the vinaigrette by adding equal amounts (50ml) of lemon juice, cockle stock, oyster juice, cucumber juice and extra virgin olive oil.

Now it's time to assemble. Remove the plates from the fridge and start by scattering the chopped asparagus and wild garlic buds all over. Now divide the smoked mackerel crème fraiche, raw mackerel, langoustines, oysters and cockles evenly between the plates. Now add the cucumber ribbons and a few pieces of samphire before whisking the vinaigrette together and dowsing all of the components evenly. The dressing should split out making it look even more attractive. Finally grate a little lemon zest over the top before garnishing with the beautifully fresh aniseed rich chervil.

Tuck into the salt baked clams, pour yourself a chilled glass of Albarino or Muscadet and enjoy the delicious flavours, textures and scents of the sea.

MAGPIE CAFE

BIOGRAPHY

Whitby Born and Bred Paul Gildroy has been in the restaurant trade for many years, he developed a love of good food while visiting relatives in France. Training at Scarborough Technical College before gaining experience in The Lake District. When Paul returned to his Home town he also returned to The Magpie where he had worked Weekends and Holidays as a Schoolboy.

Since assuming the role of Head Chef in the mid-nineties Paul has devised hundreds of recipes but has never lost sight of the fact that the Freshest of Fish and Seafood ingredients that we have available on our doorstep should be the Star of the show and not overpowered by other ingredients.

Paul is a regular at the Local Whitby and Scarborough fish markets where he buys fish and shellfish for both the Restaurant and The Magpies Whitby Catch fishmongers and has developed good working relationships with many of the fishermen.

The fish and seafood used can be purchased at the fishmongers 1 Pier Road – 100 yards from The Magpie or online at www.thewhitbycatch.co.uk

Lemon Sole and Whitby Crab
with hollandaise sauce

INGREDIENTS

4 fillets Lemon sole (skinned and boned)

300g Whitby crab (use equal brown and white meat)

2 Spring onions (finely chopped)

6 crushed Peppercorns

1 tablespoon of White wine vinegar

2 Egg yolks

200g clarified Butter

Salt and Pepper

METHOD

For the Clarified Butter
To make the 200g of clarified butter put around 300g unsalted butter in a heavy saucepan over low heat. Melt gently. Skim off all the froth from the surface. You will then see a clear yellow layer on top of a milky layer.

Carefully pour the clear fat into a bowl or jug, leaving the milky residue in the pan. Discard the milky residue or add it to mashed potato.

For the Lemon Sole
Take one fillet of sole at a time and place into a freezer bag. Use the side of a knife to flatten the fish so that it is of an even thickness. Very lightly season the skinned side, combine the crab meat with the spring onions and divide the mixture between the 4 fillets. Spread evenly over each fillet. Starting from the tail end roll each fillet up (you can stick a cocktail stick into each fillet to help keep the shape). Place the fish and crab rolls onto a baking sheet and lightly butter, place into a pre-heated oven (220°C, gas 8) for about 8 minutes. The fish should feel firm if lightly pressed.

For the Hollandaise
Heat the White Wine Vinegar and Crushed Peppercorns in a pan and reduce by a third, remove from the heat and add 1 tablespoon of water, cool slightly. Whisk the egg yolks over a Bain Marie (water bath) to a sabayon (this is to cook the egg, it should be the consistency of thick cream). Remove from the heat and cool slightly, gradually whisk in the warm clarified butter, do this slowly as if you add too much butter at once the sauce may split. If the sauce does split don't worry, just whisk in a little warm water. Once all the butter has been added taste and season with salt.
Serve the Lemon Sole on crushed potatoes and spoon over the hollandaise sauce. Finish with lemon wedges and fresh herbs.

CHADWICKS INN

BIOGRAPHY

Chadwicks Inn is an award-winning restaurant in the small village of Maltby in Teesside, on the edge of the North Yorkshire Moors. Following new ownership six years ago, the 19th century public house underwent a major refurbishment, and very quickly achieved an outstanding reputation for food in the area. Head Chef, Steven Lawford, is at the helm of the kitchen, where he and his team pride themselves on using the best of fresh, local and seasonal produce to create their modern, British menu. Steven, born and raised in Leeds, West Yorkshire, started his career working in small local restaurants before landing a job in one of Yorkshire's finest Michelin-starred restaurants. Over the next few years, he found himself working under some of the regions' best chefs in various different restaurants. He soon worked his way up to Head Chef status, running kitchens in the North East's best 5 Red Star hotel, where he was allowed to develop his own style of cooking, before moving to Chadwicks Inn, where he and his team cook, what he likes to think, is the 'best' of pub food.

Lamb Saddle & Shoulder
wild garlic, broccoli & mint

INGREDIENTS

Lamb
500g x Lamb saddle
(butchered)

750g Lamb shoulder
(boneless)

All our meat is sourced
through local butcher,
Country Valley.

Vegetables
1 x Carrot

1 x Onion

1 x Bulb garlic

1 x Sprig rosemary

1 x Bay leaf

10 x Peppercorns

Lamb Sauce
1L x Dark chicken stock

1 x Onion

250ml x Red wine

1 x Sprig rosemary

Mint Jelly
200ml x White wine vinegar

200g x Castor sugar

250m x Water

1 x Bunch mint

Agar agar

Garnish
8 x Maris piper potatoes

150ml x Double cream

100g x Butter

250g Tenderstem broccoli

1 x Head broccoli

300g x Wild garlic (picked from
local woodland areas – only
available during Spring)

Pane
3 x Eggs

200g x Breadcrumbs

100g x Plain flour

METHOD

Lamb
Pan roast the lamb shoulder until golden brown then transfer
to a casserole dish. In the same pan, brown mire poix then add
to lamb. Cover with warm water and cook for 10-12 hours @
95°C. Once cooked, pick down the lamb and roll in cling film
to form a cylindrical shape and chill. Save lamb braising liquid
for sauce. Once chilled, slice lamb shoulder into 4 portions and
pané. First dust with flour, then roll in beaten eggs and finally
in breadcrumbs.

Sauce
Slice onion into pan, add red wine and rosemary. Reduce to a
glaze then add chicken stock and lamb braising liquid. Reduce
to consistency.

Mint Jelly
Place all ingredients in a pan and simmer for 10 minutes.
Strain off and weigh liquid. Add 1% of final weight of liquid of
agar agar and bring to boil. Set in fridge.

Garnish

Creamed Potato
Bake potatoes until centre is soft then scoop out into pan. Add
cream and butter and cook out. Pass through a fine sieve.

Broccoli & Wild Garlic Purée
Slice the head of broccoli and place in a pan of boiling salted
water until soft. Add 100g of wild garlic leaves. Strain off all
water and blitz in a food processor. Pass through a fine sieve.

To Finish
Pan fry lamb saddle until core temperature is 45°C and
rest. Deep fry lamb shoulder until bread crumbs are golden
brown. Dice mint jelly and blanch tenderstem broccoli. Sauté
remaining wild garlic leaves in butter. Season all components
to taste. Assemble dish, finish with sauce and enjoy!

LANGLEY CASTLE

BIOGRAPHY

North East born Daniel Grigg has returned to his roots to begin his next challenge as the Executive Chef at Langley Castle hotel and restaurants. His career started in Northumberland, after which he moved over to the Lake District where he trained under many talented and influential chefs such as Michelin starred Nigel Mendham of the Samling Windermere. Daniel became a Head Chef at the age of 25 and has been credited by the AA on more than one occasion with the achievement of three AA rosettes for the deliverance of excellence in food standards. 'I'm delighted to have become a part of the team here at Langley. After many years in the Lake District I have developed an immense passion for good, fresh, honest local produce. What better a place than Northumberland with its valleys packed with natural produce such as mushrooms, berries, nuts and herbs. The excitement of being able to hand pick my own produce from the local area is second to none. My team and I are deeply excited to be in such a stunning setting and are looking forward to a great future for Langley Castle.'

Wild Sea Trout
crispy grapes ~ langoustines ~ verjus

INGREDIENTS

Fish
80g piece of Wild sea trout
(centre cut, skin on),
2x live langoustines

Bean Cassoulet
30g of fresh Cannellini beans

100ml Fish stock

50ml Double cream

15g diced Shallot

1 clove Garlic

5g Thyme

5g Parsley

Crispy Grapes
2x Muscat grapes

100g Isomalt

10g Fennel seed

10g Seseame seed

10g Wasabi powder

10g Pistachio

Verjus Syrup
200ml Dark verjus,

45g Honey

100g Beetroot

20g Elderflower

Garnish
4x large Girolle mushrooms

10g Sea fennel

2x Rainbow chard seedlings

METHOD

Vacuum pack the sea trout and cook in a water bath for 8 minutes at 48˚c.

Take the head off the langoustine, blanch in heavily salted boiling water (10 seconds) and refresh into iced water to cool.

Cook the cannellini beans in the fish stock with thyme. Once cooked, take the beans from the fish stock and peel the outer skin off (keep the fish stock). Sweat down the shallot and garlic, add the peeled beans, add the fish stock and reduce by half, finish with cream and parsley (season with salt and lemon juice to required taste).

Toast the sesame, fennel seed, wasabi and pistachio and lightly crush together in a pestle and mortar to create a powdered aromat, Melt down the isomalt in a sauce pan taking it to 150˚c, place your grapes on cocktail stick and dip into the isomalt, then roll them in the powder.

Combine the verjus, elderflower and honey, grate in the raw beetroot and simmer for 30 minutes, pass through muslin cloth.

To plate the dish
Take out the trout from the water bath and blow torch until charred.

Pan fry the girrolles and langoustines in oil, finishing with foaming butter.

Pick and wash the sea fennel and rainbow chard seedings.

Bring together all of the ingredients and plate accordingly as shown in the photos.

HOUSE OF TIDES

✓ 14/1/20

BIOGRAPHY

Danny Parker is head chef at House of Tides in Newcastle. The 26-year-old originally from Stockton, featured on our TV screens in 2014 when he made it to the final four of MasterChef: The Professionals but away from the limelight this talented chef works alongside Great British Menu winner and owner of House of Tides, Kenny Atkinson. The restaurant has won a host of awards, including, 3AA Rosettes, 1 Michelin Star, Cateys Newcomer of the Year and AA Restaurant of the year for the U.K. Danny fell into cooking like many others, but after becoming a kitchen porter age 14 he hasn't looked back since. He is a strong believer of keeping food and flavours simple, natural, and of course as seasonal as possible, respecting the produce, and understanding it, when it comes to putting it on the plate, it should just flow and come together naturally. Don't force anything.

Norfolk Quail
celeriac, raisin, hazelnut

INGREDIENTS

For the Quail

2 x oven ready Norfolk quail (200g approx)

1 litre x Chicken stock

½ clove of Garlic

2 x sprig Thyme

knob of Butter (soft)

Table salt

For The Puree

250g x Raisins

enough Water to cover

Salt

For The Remoulade

1 x Celeriac

1 x Granny smith apple

2TBSP x Pommery grain Mustard

4TBSP x Hellman's mayonnaise

20g x Flat leaf Parsley julienne

juice of 1 Lemon

Table salt

For the vinaigrette

2 TBSP x Le Blanc hazelnut oil

4TBSP x Champagne vinegar

2TBSP x chopped Parsley

2TBSP x chopped Chives

2TBSP x minced Shallots

For the Pickled Sultanas

50g x Golden sultana

200g x White balsamic vinegar

To Finish

50g x toasted Hazelnuts

Hazelnut oil

Coriander cress

Maldon salt

METHOD

For the Quail

Bring quail to room temperature

Remove legs and remove bottom bone

Remove Wishbone

Trim Wing tips

Bring Stock to just below boiling

Add the legs to the stock and simmer for around 30-40 minutes until tender

Place quail in stock and poach for 5 minutes

Brush with butter and blow torch till golden

Leave the quail in a warm place to rest for at least 5 minutes

Remove the breasts from the crown and season with Maldon sea salt

Blow torch the legs again for a little bitterness

For The Puree

In a sauce pan, cover the raisins with water and bring to the boil

Turn down to a simmer and place a lid on top

Cook until very soft and tender

Pass and reserve liquid

Blend raisins in thermo mix for 3 minutes

Add a little of the reserved raisin liquor if needed.

Correct the seasoning if needed, place in a squeezy bottle and keep warm

For The Remoulade

Peel the celeriac

Slice thinly on the mandolin

Juliene the slices of celeriac

Sprinkle over a little salt and some lemon juice.

Peel the apple, slice thinly on the mandolin and julienne the same as the celeriac

Weigh out the remaining ingredients

Squeeze excess juice off the celeriac, mix together with the rest of the ingredients, adjust seasoning if needed using lemon juice and salt.

For the vinaigrette

Whisk ingredients together

Keep at room temperature

For the Pickled Sultanas:

Boil the vinegar rapidly in a sauce pan

Pour over the sultanas and leave as long as possible before using.

Serve warm not hot

To Finish

Plate the dish up in a tasteful way, spread it out a little so as not to cramp the plate.

24/11/1☆

THE STAR INN

BIOGRAPHY

Andrew Perm's name is synonymous with that of his pub, The Star Inn at Harome, acquired in 1996 and consistently appearing on a host of awards lists for its hospitality and Andrew's cooking ever since, including a Michelin star held for 13 years. The loyal following for Andrew's highly seasonal and instinctively 'local' food has placed this picturesque North Yorkshire Moors village pub, with its boutique 9-bedroomed hotel, firmly on the destination location map and it is a particular favourite of industry professionals who consistently vote The Star Inn one of the top restaurants north of London.

Autumn 2013 saw the opening of 'The Star Inn The City' in York, a Brasserie-style all-day dining concept offering food from breakfast to lunches, afternoon teas to full-blown dinners on the banks of the River Ouse. The food and beverage offering is a showcase for Yorkshire produce set in the amazing surroundings of the Museum Gardens.

This summer, Andrew will be opening another, smaller place in the shadows of York Minster, called Mr P's Curious Tavern and serving small plates from further afield with ales, wines and spirits to match.

Roast Grouse
with ampleforth abbey apple purée, mulled brambles and sloe gin juices

INGREDIENTS

4 young Grouse, oven ready

Seasoning

4 slices of Pancetta

3 cooking Apples

100g Sugar

100ml Mulled wine

100g Brambles

50ml Sloe gin

100ml Veal stock

Seasoning

METHOD

Preheat the oven to 180°C/Gas Mark 4.

Place the grouse on an oven tray, season, then take the pancetta and cover over the bird's breasts, to keep them moist, and roast for about 16 to 18 minutes. Then remove from the oven and leave to rest.

To make the apple purée, first peel and core the apples, then cut each apple into quarters. Place the apples into a small saucepan adding a little water and the sugar, then bring to boil and cook until very soft. Purée in the food processor until smooth.

Bring the mulled wine to the boil, then place the brambles in a small dish and cover with the wine, leaving to cool and take on the flavours of the wine.

For the sauce, heat the veal stock and reduce by half. At this point, add the sloe gin, which will add a rich and fruity flavour to the sauce.

To serve, take the breasts and legs off the birds and keep warm, spoon the apple purée on to the plate and place two breasts and legs on each plate, spoon the mulled brambles around the plate and finish with the sloe gin sauce, adding the pancetta to garnish on top.

THE FAT ABBOT

BIOGRAPHY

Leslie Leak was born in the town of Beverley in the East Riding of Yorkshire in 1979.

When Leslie was 18 he went to Hull catering college and was also an apprentice at Willerby Manor Hotel, he completed his NVQ level 2 and 3 with distinction.

In 2000 he moved on to the five star four rosette and one Michelin star le Gavroche in London Mayfair and then to the two Michelin star Winteringham Fields.

Then Leslie took on his first Head Chef role at the young age of 24 at the No 1 restaurant, where he gained two rosettes.

Leslie went to work in the two rosettes Tickton Grange Hotel for the next two years Leslie worked in Australia learning new techniques and working in some of the best Restaurant Hotels.

In 2009 Leslie worked for Hogarth Hotel group as Head Chef. Working at Cave Castle and then Monk Fryston Hotel.

After that he went to work at the award winning Light Dragon Gastro Pub.

Leslie joined the Parsonage Hotel and opened the fat Abbot Gastro pub as the Head Chef.

Duo of Escrick Lamb
Served with mini lamb hotpot, cawood heritage carrots, braised red cabbage, lamb cutlets and minted cranberry jus

INGREDIENTS

Hot Pot

1 x Onion

1 x Carrot

600g diced leg of Lamb

1 sprig of Thyme

1 x bulb of Garlic

1 glass of Red wine

New potatoes

Red cabbage

1 x small Red cabbage

2 Red onions

1 x glass of Red wine

1 x stick of Cinnamon

1 tbsp of Nutmeg

150g of Demerara sugar

50g Raisins

3 large spoons Red currant jelly

Carrots

1 x each heritage Carrot

1 x carton of fresh Orange juice

1 x Thyme

2 x Star anise

Rack of lamb

1 x 4 bone rack of Lamb

Sauce

250 ml Chicken stock

250ml Beef or lamb stock

One glass Red wine

2 tbsp Cranberry sauce

2 sprig of chopped Mint

METHOD

Hot Pot

Dice the carrot and onion, seal off the diced lamb in a casserole dish, once browned add in the diced carrot and onion, then add the sprig of thyme and bulb of garlic in whole, add one glass of red wine, reduce down and cover with chicken stock, cover and leave to simmer for 2 to 2 ½ hours, once the meat is tender you might need to thicken the liquid with some corn flour or gravy mix.

Then part boil the new potatoes for 6 to 8 minutes, cool down in water, once cooled slice into rings. Then put the hot pot mix into a small ramekin and place the new potatoes on top of the ramekin in a circular fashion, brush with butter and bake in the oven until potatoes are golden brown.

Red cabbage

Finely slice the cabbage and onions, sweat down in a pan for 6 minutes, then add the red wine cinnamon, nutmeg, sugar, and raisins, red currant jelly, then slow cook for 30 minutes until tender and sticky.

Carrots

Peel a selection of heritage carrots. Then cut into batons, then place in a pan and cover with fresh orange juice add 2 sprigs of thyme and 2 star anise, slow cook until the carrots are tender.

Rack of lamb

Pan fry the rack of lamb on all sides until golden brown, then roast in the oven for 8 to 10 minutes.

Then leave to rest for a further 4 minutes and slice the cutlets and serve.

Sauce

Mix the chicken stock with the lamb or beef stock one glass of red wine and reduce down by two thirds or until it becomes sauce consistency, then add the cranberry sauce and chopped mint, bring together and serve.

THE BLACK SWAN

BIOGRAPHY

Alan's style of cooking and professional experience complements The Black Swan's 3AA rosette restaurant, having achieved this same standard of excellence at Wynyard Hall and Gilpin Lodge. His other accolades include Michelin's Bib gourmand at several establishments, Small North East Hotel of the Year (La Route Guide) and being voted 'Top Coastal Restaurant' in The Times and The Observer two years running at Sidney's.

Alan's individual style is essentially classical modern British with simplicity being the key, using a discerning choice of only a few sensational ingredients with bold flavour combinations. Alan also has a passion for quality, local produce along with a detailed knowledge of farming methods and artisan producers

Langoustine, Watermelon, Ponzu, Pork Crackling

INGREDIENTS

Langoustine

Langoustine (steamed for 4 minutes)

Raw Langoustine

Pickled Water Melon

300g x diced Watermelon rind (2mm)

300g x Sugar

300g x Rice wine vinegar

300g x Water

Watermelon Compression

1 x Watermelon

Carrot Sponge

420ml x whole Egg

60ml x Egg yolk

60g x Self raising Flour

80g x Demerera sugar

5g x Baking powder

10g x 5 Spice

15g x Mixed spice

80g x Suet

80g x Golden syrup

200g x raw diced Carrot

Coriander Gel

2 x large bunch of Coriander

5g x Salt

20g x Basic syrup

10 g x Ultratex

Carrot Gel

2 x litre Carrot juice

Ultratex

Salt

Ponzu Dressing

10tbsp x Soy sauce

10 tbsp x Ponzu juice

5tsp x grated Ginger

10 tbsp x Chicken Stock

10 tbsp x Extra virgin olive oil

METHOD

Remove intestine from all langos

Cook half for 4 mins in the steamer, remove, cool, shell and store in the fridge

Shell the remaining and keep in the fridge

For the pickled rind, combine the diced rind, sugar vinegar and water, bring to the boil and simmer until tender (around 10 mins) remove from the heat and cool in the pickle, store in the fridge till needed

For the compression of melon, cut the melon into large rectangles, vac pac on full, remove and cut into the correct size (large dice) as previously shown. Store in the fridge

For the carrot sponge, combine all ingredients in a thermo, blitz on full for 2 minutes, pass, place in ISI gun and charge 3 times with Co2 and use as for microwave sponge

For the coriander gel Blanch coriander in boiling salted water for 2 minutes and refresh in iced water, Blend the basil with 500g of iced water, Pass, return to the blender on low and add the syrup, salt and ultatex

For the carrot gel, reduce 2 litres down to 500ml, season well with salt, thicken with ultratex and store in a squeezy bottle

For the ponzu dressing, mix all ingredients, boil and remove immediately

78/12

✓

THE WOODMAN INN

07/08/12

BIOGRAPHY

Lawrence Yates

After working in Michelin-starred establishments for over a decade, including two stints at Daniel Clifford's two-star Midsummer House in Cambridge, The Vineyard at Stockcross, Whatley Manor hotel, The Connaught hotel and Held the star at The Box Tree in Ilkley for Two years is know managing director and executive chef of Leslie Country Inns which includes The woodman Inn in Thunderbridge.

John Dory
Fennel Salad, Orange reduction

INGREDIENTS

John Dory

1 large John Dory (filleted and skinned)

50g Unsalted butter

1tbsp Lemon juice

pinch of Salt

Fennel Salad

1 head of Fennel

pinch of Fennel pollen

1 Orange

Orange Reduction

500ml Orange juice

100ml Extra virgin olive oil

Pasta recipe

500kg Pasta flour

20g Water

4 whole Eggs

2 Yolks

20g Olive oil

100g handed picked Crab

5g freshly chopped Ginger

METHOD

John Dory

Carefully place the John Dory fillet into a pre heated pan with a little oil

Colour one side until golden brown then turn over and add the butter

Place in the oven for approx. 2minutes until cooked

When removed from the oven add the lemon juice and season with a pinch of salt

Fennel Salad

Thinly slice the fennel using a Japanese mandolin (watch your fingers) add this to a bowl of iced water for 5 minutes, this will give you fennel a crunchy texture.

Segment the orange, removing any excess white areas on each segment

Drain the fennel on to kitchen paper until dry and then place into a bowl add your orange segments, extra virgin olive oil, fennel pollen and a pinch of salt then mix

Orange Reduction

Place the orange juice in a saucepan and bring to the boil

Simmer the orange juice, reduced it to approx. 200ml

Whisk in the extra virgin olive oil whilst warm

Pasta recipe

Place the flour on to a flat work surface and all the other ingredients, mix well until it forms a dough

Knead the dough for 3 minutes, this should make it be firm to touch

Leave to rest for 1 hour, the roll out your pasta almost as thin as you can go

Cut 3in circle and place 16 grams of picked crab and ginger into the centre

Fold the circle in half and using you thumb and finger to ensure the is no air

Then hold the two corners and join them together this may need a little bit of water to make them stick.

Cook for 3 minutes in boiling, seasoned water then drain & serve

MIDDLETONS HOTEL

BIOGRAPHY

New for February 2016, The Sawmill is nestled in the secluded courtyard garden of Middleton's Hotel in the heart of York City walls. Independently owned and steeped in history the eclectic mix of 18th Century Grade 2 listed buildings offer a unique place to dine having been lovely restored by the Clark family.

At The Sawmill you will find a gastro delight with provenance. Working closely with local Yorkshire suppliers the new Head Chef Peter Toth is able to source the best in seasonal produce, creating a quintessentially British menu that keeps pace with modern trends, whilst still offering a taste of Yorkshire classics.

Hungarian born Peter is no stranger to the hotel being part of the brigade 2012 and after four years of honing his culinary skills in 2 AA rosette establishments Peter is proud to be back, heading up his own team and putting The Sawmill on the Yorkshire map.

Pork Fillet
with mashed potato savoy cabbage, sautéed radishes and cider jus

INGREDIENTS

2 whole Pork tenderloin, trimmed

2 slice of Bacon

4 waxy Potatoes such as King Edward

50g Butter

2 leaves of Savoy cabbage

5 pieces of Breakfast radishes cut half lenghtwise

100ml Cider vinegar

100g Sugar

500 ml Apple cider

Salt and pepper to taste

METHOD

Peel the potatoes and place them in to cold water and bring it to boil. Meantime pour 100 ml cider vinegar in a sauce pan and add the g sugar ias well. Bring it to boil and leave it to simmer until it reduced bay half then add the cider and leave to simmer until it reduced by 1/10 th.

When the potato cooked, drained it amd mashed it with potato masher. Add some butter and leave it on the side to cool slightly.

Fry the bacon off and place in the oven at 180 C until cooked and leave on side to cool and dry . When it is dried place them into a blender and blitz to become powdery. Add to the mash and mix them well.

Heat the oil in a frying pan and sear the whole fillet all side seasoned and put it in the oven for 8 minutes .

Meanwhile put some water on the stove to boil. When it is bubbling add the cabbage leaves and blanche about 3 minutes before it is start to loosing colour. Filled them with mash potato and roll them up Place on the plates.

Take the fillets out from the oven, cut it half and add to the plate. Finally heat a small amount of butter in a pan and sautee the radishes and add to your dish.

Finally warm up the cider glaze and pour on the top on the fillets.

RUDDING PARK

BIOGRAPHY

Award winning Rudding Park Hotel is considered to be one of the best places to eat in Yorkshire.

The Chefs serve modern British food taking inspiration from local producers, products and suppliers within a 75 mile radius. Over 100 different herbs, salads, edible flowers and fruits are grown in the Rudding Park Kitchen Garden allowing the chefs to create dishes packed full of flavour using quality heritage varieties that are usually hard to find.

Guests can dine at Clocktower Restaurant with its striking pink glass chandelier, or the bright and airy conservatory alongside the 400 year-old olive tree. The a la carte features dishes including whitby crab with sweetcorn puree, potato salad and yorkshire chorizo; pork fillet, wild boar toertellini, black pudding, caramelised apple puree, sage, cider jus and holme farm venison cutlet with king oyster mushrooms, crushed salad blue potatoes, kitchen garden chard and spinach veloute. A large south-facing terrace is perfect for alfresco dining and the perfect spot to take Afternoon Tea.

Rudding Park Kitchen Garden is at its best during the summer and guests can experience a tour followed by afternoon tea in the Breeze House, located within Kitchen Garden. The Breeze House is also available for private events whether a drinks reception, lunch or dinner. Horto Pop Up restaurant is also available and offers a tasting menu, where guests are encouraged to resist the temptation to look at the menu and discover the dishes and taste sensations throughout the evening.

Pork Fillet, Wild Boar Tortellini
wild black pudding, caramelised apple puree, sage, cider jus

INGREDIENTS

For the pork
Pork fillet 180g

Serrano ham 1 slice

Boudin noir 100g

Kale 25g

Sage 4g

Apple juice 200ml

Veal/beef stock 200ml

braised Wild boar shoulder

For the pasta
225g Flour

2 Eggs

3 Egg yolks

splash of Olive oil

pinch of Table salt

METHOD

First make your pasta, placing all your pasta ingredients into a food processor. Blitz until all the ingredients come together, roll in Clingfilm and leave to rest for an hour in the fridge. Next roll your pork fillet in your slice of serrano ham, vac pack and place in a water bath at 60° for 20mins, then roast with your boudin noir in the over for another five mins.

Roll out your pasta and fill with your braised wild boar and place in to boiling salted water for about five mins. Put the apple juice and beef stock in a pan and reduce by three quarters. When all this is done assemble the dish.

JAMES MARTIN

11/1/15

Photograph by Peter Cassidy

BIOGRAPHY

Since making his TV debut in 1996 James Martin has rarely been off our screens. Currently presenter of BBC1's highly successful, Saturday Kitchen, he was a regular on Ready Steady Cook, and has hosted many other series from Operation Hospital Food to Home Comfort. In 2006 he was a semi-finalist on Strictly Come Dancing. He is the author of 15 best-selling and award-winning cookbooks including Desserts, Slow Cooking and Fast Cooking, also published by Quadrille. When not pursuing his love of food, James spends his time driving his collection of vintage cars.

Chocolate Ganache
with blackberries and blackberry sorbet

INGREDIENTS

Ganache
280g Dark chocolate (70% cocoa solids), roughly chopped

100ml Rapeseed oil

50g Butter

225ml Double cream

For the Blackberries

100g Blackberries, plus 24 blackberries for garnish

50ml Water

50g Caster sugar

To Serve
75ml Double cream, whipped to soft peaks

1 Small handful violet flowers

1 quantity Blackberry Sorbet

Raspberry or Blackberry Sorbet
500g raspberries or blackberries

200ml stock syrup (see above)

50ml glucose

1 tsp lemon juice

200ml water

METHOD

For The Ganache
Melt the chocolate in a heatproof bowl over a pan of simmering (not boiling) water. The bowl should not touch the water. Remove from the heat and cool slightly before beating in the rapeseed oil.

Heat the butter and cream until boiling then remove from the heat and cool to just above room temperature. Whisk into the chocolate mixture. Place eight 7cm x 3cm oval rings or moulds on a baking sheet and pour in the chocolate mixture. Chill for 1–2 hours until set.

Cut the 24 blackberries in half, then set them aside. Place the water and sugar in a saucepan and heat until the sugar has dissolved. Add the remaining blackberries to the pan then pour into a blender and blitz to a purée. Pass through a fine sieve into a bowl and chill until ready to serve.

Take the ganaches out of the fridge 30 minutes before serving and remove the rings. To help do this cleanly, warm each ring very quickly with a blow torch, or dip a cloth into hot water and run it around the ring. Turn one chocolate ganache out onto each serving plate, positioning it slightly off centre.

Spoon dots of purée around the ganache then place 6 blackberry halves onto each plate. Finish with small dots of whipped cream and a few violet flowers and petals. Place a spoonful of Blackberry Sorbet on top of the ganache.

Raspberry or Blackberry Sorbet
Purée the raspberries or blackberries, then pass through a fine sieve. You should have about 400ml purée.

Combine the purée with all the other ingredients, then transfer to the ice cream machine and churn as normal. Once set, transfer the sorbet to a sealable container and freeze until needed.

Sweet by James Martin, published by Quadrille

THE
ALNWICK
GARDEN

BIOGRAPHY

Head of The Alnwick Garden Treehouse Restaurant, Gary Pickles. Hailing from Michelin Star restaurants such as Per Se Restaurant, New York (3 Michelin Stars and 5 Zagat Stars) and the Box Tree, Ilkley (1 Michelin Star), Gary has cooked in many acclaimed restaurants and none more so than the esteemed Gordon Ramsay Group. Gary's highest achievement to date is gaining his own Michelin Star when residing in the Channel Islands.

Gary not only aims to create traditional menus using locally sourced ingredients, but encourages his team to experiment with flavours and techniques. The Alnwick Garden Treehouse was inspired by The Duchess of Northumberland and is the largest wooden treehouse in Europe. Set 17 metres above ground amongst a leafy canopy of lime trees, inside, beset with fairy lights, is an award winning restaurant, which provides decadent dining at hand carved tables, and a range of specially designed 'poison' cocktails provides a nod to The Alnwick Garden's Poison Garden. Its wobbly rope bridges are all accessible to wheelchairs and pushchairs, and its lofty decking provides a calming vista of foliage. Constructed by a host of carpenters and joiners, each section of the treehouse walls are unique to the craftsman that built them and encircle a roaring log fire. The Alnwick Garden Treehouse is also a favourite of some famous diners and has played host to presenters Ant and Dec, the cast of Downton Abbey, and even Princes William and Harry.

Roots and Shoots Carrot Cake

INGREDIENTS

For the cake:

5 whole Eggs

250g Dark brown soft sugar

175g Veg oil

250g plain Flour

10g Baking powder

10g Ground cinnamon

100g Desiccated coconut

400g grated Carrot

150g soaked Raisins (remove from hot water before use)

For the spiced walnuts:

100g Walnuts

150g Castor sugar

100g Water

50g Ground mix spice

For poached baby carrot:

100g Baby carrot (any colour)

50g Castor sugar

50g Water

1 Star anise

For purple carrot puree:

200g Purple carrot

50g Castor sugar

100g Water

1 Star anise (can use same one from baby carrot)

For cream cheese topping:

100g Cream cheese

40g Honey

1 Orange zested and juiced

METHOD

Whisk the eggs, sugar and oil until the mixture has tripled in volume. Fold in the flour, cinnamon, baking powder and coconut until fully mixed. Now fold in the carrots and raisins being careful to keep the volume (so don't over work it).

Place mix into cake tin lined with grease proof paper and bake @ 160c for 20-22 minutes.

Cool on a wire rack.

Spiced walnuts

Put water and 100g sugar into a pan and bring to a quick boil. Add walnuts and simmer for 20 minutes. Pass walnuts through a sieve and discard liquid. When the walnuts are dry they are to be fried in hot oil at 170c until golden brown. Remove from oil and immediately toss in the remaining sugar and mixed spice. Allow to cool and keep in an airtight container until needed.

Poached baby carrots

Put the sugar, water and star anise in a pan and bring to a quick boil. Add the baby carrots and simmer for 7 minutes. Take pan off the heat and allow to cool naturally. Once cooled store in the liquid until needed.

Purple carrot puree

Slice the carrots as thinly as possible, then place all the ingredients in a large pan and bring to a boil as quick as possible. Cook for approx. 10 mins until carrots are fully cooked. Remove the star anise and blitz all ingredients in food processer until a smooth puree is made. Cool in an air tight container in the fridge until needed.

Cream cheese topping

Put the cheese, honey and zest in a mixing bowl and beat together. Add a small amount of juice at a time (you may not need all of the juice, you want a thick topping, not a liquid). When ready, store in an air tight container in fridge until needed.

To finish

Slice a portion of cake, smear puree across a plate, then put the cake in middle of the plate on top of the puree. Crush a few walnuts over the cake, place pieces of dry baby carrot around cake and quenelle a spoonful of the cheese topping over.

THE BURLINGTON AT THE DEVONSHIRE ARMS

BIOGRAPHY

Predicted as 'one to watch' by legendary chef Michel Roux Senior in 2012, Adam Smith is one of the most talented young chefs in the UK. Adam originates from Birmingham and started his life at the kitchen sink in a local restaurant. A lucky break gave him the opportunity to work with Chef John Williams MBE at The Ritz, London, becoming an integral part of the team for nine years.

In 2012 Adam won numerous awards, including the Roux Scholarship, offering him the opportunity to work in Le Meurice, Paris, which has 3 Michelin stars. 2013 saw Adam make the move to The Devonshire Arms, Bolton Abbey to head the Burlington Restaurant, which has since gained 4AA rosettes and won The Yorkshire Post Hotel Restaurant of the Year award. Adam's style of food echoes classical French combinations with his own very modern style, techniques & presentation.

His passion to create stunning dishes from the very best produce & stunning ingredients is what drives him to continue to develop his already remarkable culinary skills.

Yorkshire Rhubarb
white chocolate, lie and yoghurt

INGREDIENTS

Rhubarb Gel
585g Rhubarb skin
860g Rhubarb juice
150g Fructose
100g Caster sugar
Per litre of liquid 14g Agar
agar

Rhubarb Poaching Liquor
250g Sugar
75ml Water
4 Star anise
6 Cardamom pods
40g Ginger
75g Raspberries
400ml Water

White Chocolate Creeaux
250ml Milk
250ml Double cream
100g Egg yolks
1 Vanilla pod
4g Gelatine
500g White chocolate

White Chocolate Chip
110 Dark brown sugar
150g Caster sugar
180g Butter
5g Salt
105 whole Eggs
5g Baking powder
260g Plain flour
260g White chocolate chips

Carvetii Coffee Mousse
130g Yolks
130g Sugar (1)
90g Sugar (2)
325 Yoghurt
40g Yoghurt powder
325g Whipping cream
zest of 5 Limes
juice of 2 Limes
2.5g Gelatine
50g Cream
5g Gelatine
1 Vanilla pod
60g Egg yolk
100g Sugar
4 Tablespoons water
250g Whipped cream

METHOD

Rhubarb Gel
Mix the skin with the fructose and sugar and leave for 1hr
Add the juice to the mix and cook at 68oc for 1 hr
Pass and add the agar agar and allow to set
Once set blitz and pass

Rhubarb Poaching Liquor
Place the sugar water and spiced into a pan a cook until and nut brown caramel
Add the raspberries and allow to bleed out
Add the water and bring to the boil and simmer for 2 min
Pass and chill
Add the rhubarb to the liquor and sous vide cook at 680c for 12 min

White Chocolate Creeaux
Boil the milk and cream with the vanilla
Add the egg yolks to make an anglaise, add the soaked gelatine and pass
Melt the chocolate over a bain marie
Emulsify the anglaise into the melted chocolate
Allow to set for 4hrs in the fridge

White Chocolate Chip
Beat the butter until white then add the sugars and salt
Slowly add the eggs
Add the flour and baking powder
Then fold in the chocolate chips
Roll into a block and set in the fridge for 6 hrs
Cut to desired shape and bake at 175oc for 8min

Carvetii Coffee Mousse
White egg yolks until white and cook sugar(1) until 121oc and add to the yolks to make a bomb
Boil the lime juice and zest and whisk in the soaked gelatine, pass and add this to the bomb
Mix the yoghurt powder into the yoghurt and then add this to the bomb
Semi whisk the cream and sugar (2) then fold this into the bomb
Rest for 1hr the roll into desired shape and freeze

317

SEAHAM HALL

BIOGRAPHY

Richard is one of the uk's most celerbrated chefs and has two of the industry's most prestigious awards to his name- The Cateys Head chef of the Year award (under 250 covers), 2012 and the craft guild of chefs, Restaurant chef of the year award, 2012. He is also one of the only chefs to be named as one of Debrett's people of today. Over the years Richard has worked with some culinary heavy weights such as Martin Blunos, Michael Wignall and Robert Clayton as well as the Australasian master chef Cheong Liew and celebrity chef Peter Kuravita. Richard was eventually lured to the Channel Islands by Albert Roux to Head up the Tassili Restaurant kitchen in Jersey and In 2012 he was awarded a Michelin star for the Cuisine. Richard held on to the star until travelling to the North east to run the Orangery kitchen at Rockliffe hall resort and spa along with the rest of the team from Jersey. Richard is already putting his culinary mark on the northern circuit with the Orangery restaurant being awarded The Secret Diners 'Best Hotel Restaurant' When Away from the kitchen Richard loves to Go Carp fishing and spend time with his wife Leanne and two sons Jackson and Lennon.

Hazelnut Praline Sponge With Chocolate Ice Cream

INGREDIENTS

60g Polenta

280g Ground hazelnuts

50g Plain flour

5g Baking powder

zest of half a Lemon

125ml Olive oil (not extra virgin as the flavour is to powerful)

100g ready made/shop bought Caramel

3 Eggs

200g Caster sugar

For the Chocolate Ice Cream

600g full fat Milk

4 pasteurised Egg yolks

100g Milk powder

150g 70% Dark chocolate

For the Chocolate Ice Cream

600g full fat Milk

4 pasteurised Egg yolks

100g Milk Powder

150g 70% Dark chocolate

METHOD

Mix the Polenta, Ground Hazelnuts, Flour, Baking Powder and Lemon Zest ensuring all is well combined.

Next in a food machine whip the eggs and castor sugar until light and doubled in size.

Mix together the oil and caramel and slowly add to the egg and sugar mixture while continuing to whisk.

Allow to become light and doubled in size again.

Initially when you add the caramel and oil the mix will collapse but this is normal, don't panic.

Fold the dry mixture carefully into the mix and bake in a greaseproof paper lined tray measuring approximately 30cm by 15cm at 160 degrees centigrade for 40 minutes.

Allow to cool slightly and transfer to a cooling rack.

For the Chocolate Ice Cream

I've made this a one pot 'easy to do' recipe as many Ice Cream recipes involve messing around with thermometers and panicking about making scrambled eggs!

Boil the milk for one minute and pour over the egg yolks, milk powder and dark chocolate and whisk until melted.

Pour into your chosen Ice Cream machine and churn until the mixture is just set.

I prefer to eat the Ice Cream like this but you can freeze for 2 hours and serve on a piece of warm sponge!

For the Chocolate Ice Cream

Boil the milk for one minute and pour over the egg yolks, milk powder and dark chocolate and whisk until melted.

Pour into your chosen Ice Cream machine and churn until the mixture is just set.

I prefer to eat the Ice Cream like this but you can freeze for 2 hours and serve on a piece of warm sponge!

ROCKLIFFE HALL

BIOGRAPHY

Richard is one of the uk's most celerbrated chefs and has two of the industry's most prestigious awards to his name- The Cateys Head chef of the Year award (under 250 covers), 2012 and the craft guild of chefs, Restaurant chef of the year award, 2012. He is also one of the only chefs to be named as one of Debrett's people of today. Over the years Richard has worked with some culinary heavy weights such as Martin Blunos, Michael Wignall and Robert Clayton as well as the Australasian master chef Cheong Liew and celebrity chef Peter Kuravita. Richard was eventually lured to the Channel Islands by Albert Roux to Head up the Tassili Restaurant kitchen in Jersey and In 2012 he was awarded a Michelin star for the Cuisine. Richard held on to the star until travelling to the North east to run the Orangery kitchen at Rockliffe hall resort and spa along with the rest of the team from Jersey. Richard is already putting his culinary mark on the northern circuit with the Orangery restaurant being awarded The Secret Diners 'Best Hotel Restaurant' When Away from the kitchen Richard loves to Go Carp fishing and spend time with his wife Leanne and two sons Jackson and Lennon.

Chocolate Cigar, 'Cherry Black'

INGREDIENTS

270g Egg yolks

1 Whole egg

60g Water

500g Dark chocolate 72%

300g Whipping cream

300g Milk

275g Castor sugar

60g Cherry flavour heat stable

100g Kirsh

10 fresh Cherries (stones removed)

100g grated Chocolate 72%

METHOD

For the chocolate mousse, melt chocolate over a bain marie until it reaches 45 degrees c. Boil the water and 125g of the sugar until it reaches 121 degrees c. Meanwhile Whip 120g of the egg yolk and whole egg with an electric whisk and slowly add the sugar mixture. Semi whip the cream and fold into the egg mix, slowly pour over the melted chocolate and mix until a smooth mousse is formed, place the mousse into a piping bag and pipe cigar shapes onto cling film laid out on a work surface, roll the cigar shapes in the cling film and tie each end tightly forming a cigar, place in the refrigerator until needed, they can also be frozen for up to a week.

For the Cherry foam, bring cream and milk to a simmer, meanwhile whisk remaining sugar and egg yolk until white and light, pour over simmered cream mix and return to the heat stirring all the time until it reaches 72 degrees c. Cool the mixture. When cool add the flavour, blend in a food processor for 2 minutes and place in a cream whipper siphon gun and charge with 2 bulbs of gas. Use as required

To assemble the dish, remove cigars from cling film, roll in the grated chocolate (reserve some for plating) place the cigar in the middle of your chosen serving dish place 2 halves of cherries and pipe some of the mousse from the siphon gun, to finish sprinkle over some of the remaining chocolate

Wine suggestion - Maury, Masamiel

There's Seaweed & There's Mara Seaweed

"Why is no-one eating all this seaweed?" their friend asked. The rest is history.

It's now five years since a chance conversation during an afternoon stroll along the Fife coastline lead Fiona Houston and Alexandra (Xa) Milne to establish Mara Seaweed.

Since then they've developed the UK's leading seaweed company with a sea-to-shelf production facility, and an expertise in innovation, flavour, nutrition, sourcing and processing. Not bad for two women with no food industry experience - just passion and a crazy idea to build a premium Scottish export brand.

Back in 2003, Fiona and Xa met waiting for their kids in the school playground. They discovered a shared love of food and Scotland's natural landscape and decided to write a book, "Seaweed and Eat It – A Family Foraging and Cooking Adventure", as well as a family-friendly column in the Telegraph Weekend section called " Forage Rangers".

Through the book Fiona and Xa tapped into a trend for forgotten flavours. They unearthed natural, authentic ingredients. And they discovered Scotland's overlooked native seaweed resource.

Fascinated, they quickly taught themselves everything about seaweed and began to investigate how to develop products that would be easy-to-use in everyday modern menus. Fiona's entrepreneurial upbringing added to a shared love of natural organic food with Xa soon led to the creation of their business.

They took their ideas to chefs around Edinburgh and at the beginning of 2011, Mara (which means 'the sea' in Gaelic) was born. Its mission? To 'nourish body and soul' by harnessing goodness from the sea.

If it seems odd to be so passionate about that slimy green stuff that attacks you on your annual beach holiday, consider this. Seaweed is the most highly mineralised vegetable on earth. It thrives when languishing in cold nutrient-rich water, like the seas lapping the Scottish coastline, absorbing nutrients from the ocean and sunlight. It takes electrolytes, minerals and trace elements from the ocean and converts them into seaweed that we can eat. It doesn't need soil. It doesn't need fertiliser. It doesn't need machinery. Seaweed doesn't need to be farmed at all, because it's a completely sustainable future food that even helps ward off climate change by absorbing carbon dioxide and releasing oxygen. What's not to love?

But harnessing such goodness from the sea needs care and attention, so Fiona and Xa employed a dedicated Harvesting Manager, Rory MacPhee, to run harvesting teams. Mara hand harvests seasonally by the monthly moon cycle – about 12 days a month – to ensure the seaweed is at its nutritional prime and to guarantee its flavour. The seaweed is sourced from gathering wild stocks below "Mean Low Water Spring Tides". All land is owned by someone – and the seabed is land. Below Mean Low Water Spring Tides all land in Scotland is owned by the Crown Estate, so Mara has to work closely with them too.

Harvesting is tough, cold and physically demanding – but it's also extremely rewarding. The harvesters speak with admiration of the light and colours and how they get into an elemental rhythm dealing with the plants in their natural environment. They have to work fast in a window of just 2-3 hours when the tide is at its lowest, and Rory has to be careful to get them off the beach before the tide comes back in. All the seaweeds are always harvested in such a way as to ensure their re-growth – caring for the coast and its ecology is very important.

Once harvested, the drying process is as close to the natural cycle as possible, using heat and air outside and then in Mara's bespoke drying unit that mimics the natural process. From harvesting to drying takes no longer than 24 hours, so the seaweed is 'fresh' and all the flavours and nutrients have been captured.

In fact, the nutrients are 50% of the reason Fiona and Xa fell in love with seaweed – and they're why seaweed is considered a superfood. It's rich in essential everyday nutrition, containing protein, potassium, magnesium, calcium, iron and B12. It's also high in fibre, which is good for gut health and helps you feel fuller for longer.

Perhaps most importantly, seaweed is an excellent source of natural iodine. Around two thirds of British women don't have enough iodine in their diet and since 1992, the World Health Organisation has deemed iodine deficiency as a major health issue. Iodine is essential to healthy functioning of the thyroid gland, which regulates metabolism, brain function, sleep patterns, the nervous system and much more. Many common complaints – such as weight gain, headaches and sleeplessness – can be helped by boosting iodine intake. Or put another way, by eating more seaweed.

What's more, seaweed can be used instead of salt. Seaweed is a healthy flavour enhancer as it's natural umami - the fifth taste, which comes from "umai" delicious and "mi", essence. It's the other 50% of the reason Fiona and Xa fell in love with seaweed. It's a good tasting superfood.

So what did Fiona and Xa do with the seaweed, to make it easy to use in the modern kitchen? They created a range of seaweed seasonings. Milled into a flake to be used liked herbs, Mara seaweed can be shaken or spooned into dishes to add depth of flavour and a boost of nutrients. What's not to love?

North-North West

Starter
Main
Dessert

CHAOPHRAYA & THAIKHUN

BIOGRAPHY

Kim's true passion has always been food so in 1993 Kim opened a small Pad Thai Cart, whilst still running a garment Factory. It was tough for Kim working both of these but she kept going and went on to adding more noodle stalls to the collection and finally getting rid of the garment Factory. Kim then won an award for her Pad Thai which is the recipe still used in 12 restaurants to date.

Kim was working in Bangkok in 1997 when she met her partner Martin. It was around 2 o'clock in the morning and this charming Englishman and his friends came to buy some food from Kim's Street Stall. They were in Thailand on holiday, Martin was hungry but his friends were tired and wanted to go back to the hotel, he managed to convince them to come get some food...and that's when they met.

Kim moved to the UK in 1999 where she worked in a Japanese restaurant as a waitress and Kitchen porter then set up a new Thai restaurant with her twin sister in Leeds, this partnership soon came to an end.

So in 2004 Martin and Kim started their journey of bringing a vision and dream to reality – opening their first restaurant Chaophraya in Leeds, the home town of Martin. This was a tough year for Martin & Kim with family and friends helping a lot to set this restaurant up. Martin & Kim then went on to open in Manchester, Liverpool and Birmingham between 2007 and 2011. in 2012 Martin & Kim ventured to Scotland and opened Edinburgh and Glasgow.

It was at this time Kim decided she wanted to bring a truly authentic feel of her home country to the UK and recreate the dishes she learnt on the Streets of Bangkok to the Streets of the UK.

Chaophraya is high end luxurious restaurants, based on the likes of the Mandarin Oriental in Bangkok with leather seating, ornate statues and luxurious finishes. Kim & Martin love eating on the streets of Bangkok ordering various dishes from the street vendors and really tasting the true taste of Bangkok and this is what they want to bring to the UK with Thaikhun.

The name is pronounced 'Tycoon' which is meant to celebrate the work of the street hawkers back in Bangkok...they are the real foodie entrepreneurs. Thaikhun is like the younger, crazy and funkier sister to Chaophraya.

Dan Burns - Natural Selection Design

Papaya Salad

INGREDIENTS

Papaya Salad (per portion)

¼ Fresh red chilli (dependent of spice preference)

1 Tablespoon of tamarind sauce

½ Carrot

¼ Papaya

Handful of cherry tomatoes

Handful of fine beans

1 x Lime wedge

1 Clove of garlic

1 Tablespoon of fish sauce

1 Dessert spoon of peanuts

1 Teaspoon of Palm sugar

METHOD

First begin by washing and preparing all the vegetables, then shred the Papaya and carrot with a julienne peeler, giving you nice thin even strips of vegetable.

Then use a pestle and mortar to crush the garlic, tamarind sauce, chilli, palm sugar & fish sauce, once the consistency is that of a paste, then add the shredded vegetables, cherry tomatoes and green beans and further mix in the pestle and mortar to ensure all the flavours fuse.

The final step, prepare the salad on a decorative plate, garnish with the peanuts, lime wedge, best served with sticky rice or Pork skewers.

Perfect summer family dish

RESTAURANT ONE EIGHTY

BIOGRAPHY

Restaurant One Eighty at Best Western plus Pinewood on Wilmslow offers innovative dishes.

Colin Starkey Executive Chef strives to consistently champion & enhance current seasonal produce while maintaining maximum flavour. Colin sources all his produce from local suppliers such as H. Greaves & sons (www.hgreaves&sons.co.uk) & Neve Fleetwood (www.nevefleetwood.co.uk) who supply all Colin's meat & fish products.

Using both modern & classic techniques Colin brings exciting twists & classical flavours to the table at Restaurant One Eighty. Restaurant One Eighty has already achieved an AA rosette in its first year & is achieving excellent reviews from food critics, blogger's & press from all over the country.

Hand Dived Scallops & Lamb Sweetbreads
celeriac & truffle puree and fennel chutney

INGREDIENTS

Hand Dived Scallops & Lamb Sweetbreads, Celeriac & Truffle Puree And Fennel Chutney.

Ingredient's (Serves 2)

4 Large Hand Dived Scallops (Prepped & Cleaned).

2 Rectangle pieces of Cucumber

2 Small Cubes Of Butter.

Splash Of Olive Oil.

4 Pieces Of Trimmed Lamb Sweetbread's.

3 Floz Tempura Batter & Cornflour For Dusting.

½ Large Celeriac. (Finely Diced)

Milk To Cover.

Truffle Oil.

Salt & Pepper.

½ Bulb Fennel (Finely Diced).

60 Grm Castor Sugar.

60 Grm Water.

Burnt Onion Powder.

Edible Flower's To Garnish.

METHOD

Bring Fennel, Sugar & Water To Boil & Simmer For 20 Minutes, Remove From Heat & Allow To Cool.

Bring Celeriac & Milk To Boil, Simmer Until Celeriac Is Soft & Strain (Keep Milk).

Blend Celeriac Adding A Little Milk Until You Have A Smooth Puree – Season With Truffle Oil & Salt To Your Taste, Keep Warm For Serving.

Lightly Dust Sweetbreads With Seasoned Cornflour, Place In Tempura Batter & Lightly Coat, Blanch In Hot Fryer (185) Until Lightly Golden & Remove From Oil.

Heat A Non-Stick Pan, Lightly Oil Scallop's & Season, Place In Pan With The Cucumber Add Small Cubes Of Butter, Depending On Size Cook For 30-45 Seconds On Each Side.

Put Sweetbreads Back In Fryer To Finish Cooking, Remove Drain Oil With Kitchen Roll & Season With Salt.

To Plate - Warm A Plate / Bowl Under The Grill, Spoon Your Celeriac On To The Plate, Arrange Scallops & Sweetbread's On Top Of Cucumber, Top With Fennel Chutney & Garnish With Flowers & Onion Powder, Finish With A Little Truffle Oil.

THE MILLSTONE

BIOGRAPHY

The Millstone at Mellor is a hidden treasure in the heart of The Ribble Valley in Lancashire. Chef Patron Anson Bolton has been at the helm since 2002 and led the team to 2 AA rosettes for the 10th year in succession and the AA 5 Star inn award – one of just 29 in the country. Anson's food ethos is about keeping things simple – in his broad Bolton accent he'd say 'not mucked about with', working with the best quality ingredients and focusing on the flavours. It's an approach that has won many supporters locally and despite all the financial challenges of the last few years The Millstone food sales continue to grow year-on-year with glowing reviews from guests who just love the honesty of the offering and the relaxed professional service style.

Duck Spring Rolls & Chilli Jam

INGREDIENTS

Duck Filling

5 Duck legs

pinch of Cinnamon*

1/3 tsp Black peppercorns*

1/3 tsp Cardamom pods*

6 Cloves*

1 Star anise*

1/3 tsp Salt*

Chilli, Garlic And Ginger Paste Filling

1 heaped tsp of Garlic chilli & ginger paste (see method right)

8 Spring roll sheets

Batter to seal

(1 tbsp Flour & water mix to thick paste)

100ml Hoi sin sauce

Garnish

1 peeled Cucumber

4 peeled Carrots cut in to long strips - ideally on the mandolin

Chilli Jam

(makes approx 2kg)

250g Red chilli

8 plum Tomatoes

2 Red peppers

1/2 Onion

6 cloves Garlic

2 Star anise

2 cups Demerara sugar

2 cups Muscavodo sugar

1 tsp Chilli powder

4 cups White wine vinegar

2 tsp Smoked paprika

2 tsp Mustard seeds

1 tsp Salt

Dressing

2 tbsp Toasted sesame seeds

50ml Rice wine vinegar

200ml Rapeseed oil

1 handful chopped Coriander

Whisk together

METHOD

For The Duck Spring Rolls

Cover the duck legs with the water and the ingredients marked *. Bring to the boil and simmer for approx. 2 hours till the duck is ready to fall off the bone - but do not overcook as this will make the duck tough. Whilst still warm remove the skin, bone, cartilage and any of the cooking spices leaving just the duck meat. Place in a container and chill. Make the chilli, garlic and ginger paste by putting equal quantities of fresh chopped garlic, chopped fresh ginger and de-seeded chopped red chillies in a blender, cover with oil and then blitz till smooth. Lightly fry the garlic, ginger and chilli paste in a frying pan to release the spices and mix in with the cold duck then add the hoi sin sauce. Separate the spring roll pastry and cover - the pastry dries out very quickly so keep covered. Divide the duck mix into 8 equal portions and place one portion at the top centre of the pastry square, brush all the edges with a little batter, fold each lap over the duck mix then tightly roll, brush the end piece of pastry to seal. To cook deep fry at 180°C for 3 mins till golden and finish in a hot oven for approx. 3 mins. At 180°C.

For The Chilli Jam

In a food processor roughly chop the chillies, peppers, tomatoes, garlic and onion. Then place all the ingredients in a thick bottomed pan, bring to boil and simmer for approx. 60 - 90 mins till a thick sticky consistency. Remember the mix will thicken as it chills. Serve the spring rolls with a spoon of chilli jam and carrot and cucumber salad, drizzle with a little of the sesame dressing

THE LORD CLYDE

BIOGRAPHY

Ernst van Zyl is the owner and chef of The Lord Clyde in Kerridge – the only pub in Cheshire to hold three AA Rosettes and one of only four North West pubs to appear in the Top 50 UK Gastropub's list 2016.

Ernst has a pedigree culinary background having worked in some of the UK and Ireland's best hotel kitchens. Before opening The Lord Clyde, Ernst worked at Etrop Grange in Manchester as well as the Radisson Manchester and London's Park Lane Hotel.

Ernst opened The Lord Clyde with his business partner Sarah in 2014 and has more recently acquired two more properties – The Hanging Gate in Higher Sutton, Macclesfield and The Knott Inn in Rushton Spencer.

Known for his confident and creative flavour combinations, Ernst has a modernistic approach, injecting playfulness and seasonality into every dish. The Lord Clyde has earned itself an enviable reputation as a restaurant in a pub, offering accessible fine dining in cosy surroundings in the foothills of the Peak District.

Unrelenting in his commitment to creativity and learning new techniques and skills, Ernst regularly uses his spare team to complete placements at world renowned restaurants such as Noma in Copenhagen, Heston Blumenthal's The Fat Duck in Bray and Raymond Blanc's Le Manoir aux Quat' Saison in Oxfordshire.

Born and raised in Cape Town, South Africa, Ernst has lived in the UK since he was 21.

Cured cod cheek

with shallot, wild garlic, pancetta and a roasted onion and smoked bacon dashi

INGREDIENTS

Cured cod cheek
1kg Cod cheeks – cleaned
240g fine Salt
180g Sugar
20g Coriander seeds –
toasted and crushed
Zest from 2 Limes
Zest from 2 Lemons

Shallot puree
1kg Shallots
50g Butter
50g Oil
2 sprigs of Thyme

Shallot foam
80g Milk
½ tsp Xantham
½ tsp Agar agar
140g Shallot puree
60g Double cream

Shallot shells
10 small round Shallot

Wild garlic oil
100g Wild garlic
200g Oil

Roasted onion and smoked bacon dashi
1kg cold Water
25g Kombu
1 Onion
250g Smoked back bacon

METHOD

Cured cod cheek
Mix together the salt; sugar; coriander seeds and both zests and cover the cod cheeks. Place in refrigerator and leave for 4 hours. Wash off cheeks under cold running water and keep in fridge.

Shallot puree
Finely slice and sauté with the oil; butter and thyme and golden and caramelised. Puree immediately until smooth.

Leave to cool and refrigerate.

Shallot foam
Boil together for 1 minute.

Heat together and then mix with the milk mixture. Pour into an isi bottle and charge once; shake well and keep warm in the waterbath.

Shallot shells
Cook shallots in waterbath at 85C for 25 mins. Chill in ice bath. Cut in halve and scorch with a blow torch and then separate the onion to make shells.

Wild garlic oil
Blend together. Pass through a muslin cloth. Keep oil refrigerated.

Seal in a vacuum bag and cook at 60C for 1 hour.

Pass.

Seal all ingredients in a new vacuum bag and cook at 85C for 75 mins.

Pass and let cool.

Roasted onion and smoked bacon dashi
1kg cold water
25g kombu

Seal in a vacuum bag and cook at 60C for 1 hour
Pass

1 onion – roasted until very dark
250g smoked back bacon
The seaweed water from previous

Seal all ingredients in a new vacuum bag and cook at 85C for 75 mins.
Pass and let cool.

✓NORTHCOATE

25/8/12

BIOGRAPHY

Nigel Haworth, not only showcases his own gastronomic brilliance at Northcote, but sets the benchmark for fine dining across the UK. Nigel is now approaching his 30th anniversary at Northcote, with business partner Craig Bancroft, displaying an instinctive understanding of his region and a cultivated awareness for diners' needs.

Trained in his native county Lancashire at Rossendale Catering College, from there he embarked on a culinary journey which would take him to Switzerland, Gleneagles and the Grosvenor Hotel London, before returning to Lancashire to take a lecturer role at the same college he studied at. 1984 he was offered the Head Chef at Northcote, Ten years on and Nigel was celebrating Egon Ronay Chef of The Year Award, one year later a Michelin Star followed, successfully retained ever since.

In recent times, Nigel has appeared regularly on television, shows such as Saturday Kitchen; Market Kitchen; Paul Hollywood's Pie & Puds, also making a winning appearance on the popular Great British Menu series in 2009.

Wester Ross Seared Salmon Loin

with fennel pollen, sweet onion, garden hints

INGREDIENTS

Cured cod cheek
1kg Cod cheeks – cleaned
240g fine Salt
180g Sugar
20g Coriander seeds –
toasted and crushed
Zest from 2 Limes
Zest from 2 Lemons

Shallot puree
1kg Shallots
50g Butter
50g Oil
2 sprigs of Thyme

Shallot foam
80g Milk
½ tsp Xantham
½ tsp Agar agar
140g Shallot puree
60g Double cream

Shallot shells
10 small round Shallot

Wild garlic oil
100g Wild garlic
200g Oil

**Roasted onion and
smoked bacon dashi**
1kg cold Water
25g Kombu
1 Onion
250g Smoked back bacon

METHOD

Cured cod cheek
Mix together the salt; sugar; coriander seeds and both zests and cover the cod cheeks. Place in refrigerator and leave for 4 hours. Wash off cheeks under cold running water and keep in fridge.

Shallot puree
Finely slice and sauté with the oil; butter and thyme and golden and caramelised. Puree immediately until smooth.

Leave to cool and refrigerate.

Shallot foam
Boil together for 1 minute.

Heat together and then mix with the milk mixture. Pour into an isi bottle and charge once; shake well and keep warm in the waterbath.

Shallot shells
Cook shallots in waterbath at 85C for 25 mins. Chill in ice bath. Cut in halve and scorch with a blow torch and then separate the onion to make shells.

Wild garlic oil
Blend together. Pass through a muslin cloth. Keep oil refrigerated.

Seal in a vacuum bag and cook at 60C for 1 hour.

Pass.

Seal all ingredients in a new vacuum bag and cook at 85C for 75 mins.

Pass and let cool.

Roasted onion and smoked bacon dashi
1kg cold water

25g kombu

Seal in a vacuum bag and cook at 60C for 1 hour

Pass

1 onion – roasted until very dark

250g smoked back bacon

The seaweed water from previous

Seal all ingredients in a new vacuum bag and cook at 85C for 75 mins.

Pass and let cool.

THE LONDON
CARRIAGE WORKS

BIOGRAPHY

Being a chef was not the first thing I wanted to be in life, I love art and was studying a graphics and illustration course in North Wales whilst keeping the job I'd had in my local pub, working my way up to Sous chef. I fell in love with the kitchen, quit my course and started to train.

"Before I knew it I was 23 and head chef in Liverpool, 52 Lark Lane. I had my own kitchen, my own menus and the creativity to do what I wanted. Lark Lane was very much influenced by the amazing flavours of the Mediterranean, but I wanted to bring back the best of Britain. I wanted to be part of the movement to fresh and local and in particular the colours of the seasonal produce.

After going on to run some of the top restaurants in the city I eventually arrived as Head Chef at The London Carriage Works – sister to the eponymous boutique hotel - hope street hotel.

"After two years I feel well and truly settled, working with a great team at the best hotel and restaurant in the city. Alongside producers, farmers and growers we have been with since opening this recipe takes advantage of our new coastline forager, a rich seam for delicious ingredients.

Each menu I launch is tougher and more technically challenging than the last, we have some very exciting dishes in the pipeline complemented by our local produce and continuing to use colour to bring the dishes to life. I've been lucky to learn from some very talented people and have made so many friends along the way. I'm excited about the future of Liverpool's food scene."

Wild Liverpool Bay Sea Bass
with a razor clam and shellfish seabed, crab bisque and local sea herbs

INGREDIENTS

Tomato sponge 'coral'
400g Eggs
50g Olive oil
50g Flour
Salt and pepper
40g Tomato powder (freeze dried)

Olive oil 'sand' powder
80g Extra virgin olive oil
25g Tapioca maltrodextrin
3g salt

Crab Bisque
2 Tablespoons of rapeseed oil
1 Onion (sliced)
1 Fennel
1 Carrot (sliced)
2 Bay leaves
1 Garlic clove (crushed)
1 Teaspoon of tomato purée
1 Medium whole crab
1 Teaspoon of brandy
1 Pinch of saffron
1 Pinch of smoked paprika
Zest of one lemon

Sea bass
One whole Liverpool Bay Sea bass

Shell fish
1 Razor clam (per portion)
3 Clams
1 Baby squid
1 Teaspoon of Southport potted shrimp

METHOD

Tomato sponge 'coral'

Mix all ingredients with a hand blender.

Put the mixture in a siphon gun and leave in fridge.

Charge the siphon with 2 gas cartridges.

Fill a plastic cup with the mix.

Bake in microwave at max power for 40 seconds.

Leave to cool, remove from cup and tear to serve.

Olive oil 'sand' powder

Whisk together all ingredients in a bowl until it converts to a powder.

Pass through a tamis and keep sealed until plating.

Crab Bisque

Gently simmer the crab in 2 litres of water for 30 mins, remove from stock and cool. Pick meat from the crab // keeping the brown and white meat separate.

Strain the liquid and reduce to one litre. Heat oil in a large saucepan, add the onion, fennel, carrot, bay leaves and the crab shell, legs and body and cook for 10 mins until veg is soft. Add garlic and tomato purée and cook for 1 minute.

Add the brown crab meat, saffron, brandy and season.

Add the crab stock and lemon zest, stir, cover and cook for another 15 mins, then remove from heat.

Blend soup then pass through a fine sieve until

Sea bass

De-scale the wild bass and remove the fillets from both sides.

Portion into 5 x 6oz portions and score the skin.

Salt the skin and place into a hot pan with a little oil, cook for 5 mins until the skin crisps, then place under the grill with the skin facing down for a further 3-4 minutes until the flesh is white and firm.

Finish with a squeeze of lemon, foaming butter and season.

Shell fish

Remove the tentacles from the baby squid, slice body into rings, flour and deep fry.

Prepare razor clam by removing the 'foot' and intestinal tract.

Open razor clam with other clams in a small amount of crab stock over a high heat.

Remove from heat and add the shrimp.

Remove all of the clam meat from the shells and arrange onto the razor clam shell with the shrimp.

To Plate

Place the bass on the plate.

Add 2 dessert spoons of olive oil sand.

Lay the razor clam shell (with meat) onto the sand.

Add the crab white meat, tomato coral and fresh local sea herbs (samphire, salty fingers and fennel tips).

Froth up the crab bisque and sieve separately into a jug.

THE WOODBRIDGE INN

BIOGRAPHY

Mark Benson has been a senior chef to 2AA Rosette standard in some seriously busy establishments for some ten years, and has enjoyed considerable freedom in the direction of his food. Home smoking, charcuterie, bread making and ice-cream making are all part of his armoury, and when in December 2014 he joined the Woodbridge Inn to head up the kitchen crew, he found himself immediately in his element.

Mark has his roots in the Lake District where he developed a passion for fishing, and fresh seasonal fish has always formed an important influence on his menus, as they do at the Woodbridge Inn, sitting as it does on the banks of the River Severn at Coalport in Shropshire. His fish supplier, M&J Seafoods, voted the UK's Best Fish Supplier 2015 by Restaurant Magazine, delivers fresh fish to the Woodbridge's kitchens daily.

Pan-Fried Smoked Cod Loin
with samphire, clams, spring onion mash and saffron velouté

INGREDIENTS

Veloute
50g Butter

40g Plain flour

750ml Warmed fish stock

1 Pinch of saffron (soaked in water)

100ml Double cream

Spring Onion Mash
500g Potatoes, peeled and halved

125ml (4 floz) Milk

1 Bunch of spring onions thinly sliced

½ tsp Salt or to taste

25g Butter

Fresh ground pepper to taste

Smoked Cod
4 x 6/7oz Smoked cod loin

Mushrooms

200g Wild mushrooms

1 x tsp Butter

1 x tsp Chopped fresh herbs

Salt

Pepper

Pickled Mushrooms
75g Wild mushrooms

1 x Pinch of salt

1 x Pinch sugar

2 x tbsp White wine vinegar

1 x tsp Chopped chive

METHOD

Start with the velouté! Soak a pinch of saffron in two tablespoons of hot water for 10/15 minutes, heat the butter in a saucepan over a medium heat, add flour and stir well to combine and "cook out" for approximately 2 minutes.

Whisk in fish stock a ladle at a time to make a thick glossy sauce. Add 1 juiced lemon and saffron including water and season to taste. Finish with double cream.

Boil potatoes in a large pot for approx. 20 minutes or until tender, drain well and return to the heat for a few minutes to dry out.

Heat milk, butter and spring onions in a saucepan. Mash the potatoes with salt and add the milk butter and spring onion mix, season to taste with fresh ground black pepper.

Heat a pan on a medium high heat, season the cod with a little salt and fresh ground black pepper and leave aside.

Add 1 tablespoon of rapeseed/vegetable oil to the pan and place fish in skin side down and cook for 1-2 minutes or until the fish starts to turn golden brown.

Place the pan in the oven at 185 oc for 6-7 minutes, then take out and rest the fish. While the fish is resting poach the baby leeks and clams in a court bouillon for two minutes, season with butter, salt and pepper and keep warm.

Pan fry a handful of wild mushrooms in butter on a medium heat, finish with fresh chopped herbs, and finally blanch samphire for 20 seconds to keep a little crunch.

Garnish with lemon and a few pickled mushrooms.

ASKHAM HALL

BIOGRAPHY

Richard grew up in this area of Cumbria and has a deep understanding of the seasons, wild foods and produce that grows here from his childhood spent out shooting in the woods, fishing on the river Eden and looking after his own rare breed chickens which he has brought to Askham Hall. Having developed a passion for cooking at a young age he has spent the last 12 years working away from the area honing his skills and developing his cooking style.

He spent 4 years working with equally renowned chefs John Burton Race and Anthony Demetre In London. He also spent 2 Years in France and had various placements around the world including a stint at NOMA in Copenhagen and also with the famous 3 Michelin star French chef Marc Veyrat in Annecy who specialises in mountain plants and herbs.

Since then he has gone on to refine his style, and now back in Cumbria, settled in Askham, he is rediscovering his connection with the ingredients he grew up with. Using the techniques he has learnt on his journeys, he is now bringing out new interpretations on the way ingredients are used, something we are all very excited about.

West Coast Turbot, Macaroni
wild asparagus, brokali, mussels and ras el hanout sauce.

INGREDIENTS

Veloute
4 portions of Turbot

20 pieces of Wild asparagus

8 pieces of Brokali (Half kale half broccoli variety of the brassica family!)

12 pieces of Macaroni

20 Mussels

4 portions or Ras el hanout sauce

2 handfuls of Baby spinach

For the Macaroni Pasta Dough
125 g Pasta flour

1 Egg

1 small Egg yolk

12 ml Olive oil

For the Ras El Hanout Sauce
2 large Onions (diced fine)

2 garlic cloves (sliced)

1 Bay leaf

2 Lime leaves

1L White wine (reduce down 2/3)

3L Fish stock (reduce down)

1 tin Coconut (454ml)

1.5 table spoon of Ras el hanout

0.5 table spoon Turmeric

1 teaspoon of Lecithin

Lemon juice to taste + mussel juice from the precooked mussels

METHOD

For the Macaroni

Place all ingredients in a food processor and blend for 30 seconds or so adding a little water if needed so it starts to come together (you don't want the dough to be too wet). Tip the mixture out onto a work surface and knead for a few minutes then wrap in cling film and rest for 30 minutes. Once rested roll the dough out on a pasta machine to about number 2 and cut into small rectangles about 1 inch in width. Using a macaroni kit or a clean piece of dowel wood roll the pasta around until tubes are formed. Dry the pasta (on top of the oven) this will be cooked later.

For the Mussels

Heat a pan then add the mussels with a bit of white wine, quickly put a lid on and wait until the mussels open and the juices are released. Once open tip them out of the pan on to a tray (reserving the juices) and chill as quickly as possible, once chilled take the meat out of the shell and make sure you take off the beard (the string like bit attached to the mussel) set a side.

For the Sauce

For the sauce in a pan sweat off the onions and garlic in a little butter for about 4 minutes, add the bay leaf, lime leaves, Ras El Hanout, turmeric and cook for a further 5 minutes (be careful not to burn) next add the white wine and reduce by 2/3rds then add the fish stock and again reduce by 2/3rds once reduced pass off the liquid through a fine chinois and discard the onions etc., return the liquid to the pan add the coconut milk and mussel juice and cook out for around 5 minutes. Once finished blend in the lecithin with a hand blender and season with lemon juice and salt to taste.

To Assemble

In a medium hot non-stick pan add a little oil and seal the turbot until lightly coloured then place in the oven at 180 degrees for about 4 minutes (depending on size) whilst you're doing that cook the dried macaroni in salted water for 5 minutes. Once the turbot has had its 4 minutes take out from the oven flip the fish over add a knob of butter and baste for about 30 seconds, squeeze a little lemon juice over the fish and take out of the pan and let rest for a minute. Meanwhile warm the muscles in a little of the sauce adding the macaroni once cooked, wilt the spinach in a little butter, season. For the wild asparagus and the brokali blanch in boiling salted water until cooked, season and roll in a little butter.

ALDERLY EDGE HOTEL

BIOGRAPHY

Overlooking one of Cheshire's most desirable villages, the award winning Alderley Edge Hotel is renowned for its quality of service, luxurious accommodation and acclaimed cuisine.

With over ten years experience at Alderley Edge Hotel, it came as no surprise that when Sean Sutton was appointed Head Chef, he did it with style, flair and imagination.

Maintaining the hotel's impressive three AA Rosettes, Sean strives to create great British dishes with a twist. Overseeing two restaurants within the hotel, The Brasserie and Alderley Restaurant, his team are dedicated and keen to learn new cooking styles to keep up with Sean's impressive skills.

At just 30 years old and originally from nearby Macclesfield, Sean is just at the start of what promises to be a fantastic career as an innovative and exciting Head Chef.

Monkfish
with a chicken and sweetcorn noodle broth

INGREDIENTS

4 Monkfish portions (120g)

4 Chicken thighs (boned)

1 cooked Corn on the cob

4 Spring onions

800ml Chicken stock

350g Vermicelli noodles

1 head of Pak Choi

1 bunch of Coriander

1 Lime leaf

2 leaves of Gelatine (soaked in cold water until soft)

1 ltr Vegetable oil

METHOD

To Start
Cut the sweetcorn away from the cob
Chop approximately half of the coriander finely
Blanche Pak Choi in boiling salted water for 1 minute then shock in ice water

For the Chicken
Place Chicken in a saucepan and cover with Vegetable Oil
Cook gently on a low heat until tender
Remove from the oil and drain on cloth (make sure you keep the oil).
Allow to cool, then cut to a square shape (keep the trimmings).

For the Monkfish
Roll each portion in double layers of cling film and place in a saucepan with water.
Bring up to simmer and take off the heat.
Allow to cook for 20 minutes in residual heat.

For the Crispy Noodles
Take out around 50g of vermicelli and bring the pan of leftover Vegetable Oil up to 180°c.
Carefully drop the noodles into oil until crispy then quickly drain off onto a cloth and season to taste.

For the Chicken Stock
Pour chicken stock into sauce pan and bring to a simmer.
Add half the sweetcorn, half the chopped coriander, 2 spring onions and the lime leaf.
Simmer for 30 minutes – take off stove and pass through sieve.
Whilst still hot take out 300ml of stock and add the soaked gelatine.
Keep remaining stock for the broth.

For the Noodle Press (make in advance)
Place remaining noodles in boiling salted water for 1 minute, then drain.
Mince the remaining Sweetcorn, Spring Onions, Coriander and all the Chicken trimmings.
Lightly colour in a pan and mix through the noodles.
Place in a lined tray and pour over 300ml of Chicken Stock & Gelatine mix.
Allow to cool for 4 hours.

Assembly
Portion a square of noodle pressing and place in a bowl.
Arrange Chicken, Pak Choi and Sweetcorn around the plate.
Take the Monkfish out of the cling film and place onto noodles.
Finish with crispy noodles and Coriander leaves.
Pour broth over Monkfish at the table.

THE HANGING GATE

BIOGRAPHY

The Hanging Gate is the highest pub in Cheshire. The views stretch as far as Wales which has helped to earn The Hanging Gate a well- deserved reputation as a stunning destination. The pub was taken over by Ernst van Zyl, chef patron of Michelin rosette listed "The Lord Clyde" in October 2015, which altogether make an unbeatable team at The Hanging Gate. Ernst who has been working alongside Head Chef Tom Clarke to bring a relaxed approach to the finest quality dining. The Hanging Gate's menu is a great example of perfectly picked local ingredients, putting together creative modern plates, cooked to the highest of standards. During the summer, Al Fresco dining is a must, to make the most and enhance the magical outlook, there is no better place to compliment the sunset in Cheshire.

Pan Fried Wild Sea Bass
patatas bravas, lemon brown shrimp, greens, beurre noisette

INGREDIENTS

4 Sea bass (Wild or farmed)

2 Red chills

200grams of New potatoes

2 Red onions sliced

2 Garlic cloves chopped

3 Fresh tomatoes

1/2 tsp Tomato puree.

1 tsp Sweet paprika.

Pinch of sugar.

handful of Coriander

1 tsp Butter

100g Brown shrimp.

Micro coriander (to garnish)

2 Lemons

1 Lime (zest)

100g Samphire.

METHOD

Start by roasting new potatoes in oven @ 200'c for 20/30 mins. Drizzle olive oil, salt and pepper on the potatoes.

While potatoes are roasting, start by dicing red onion, tomatoes, chilli, garlic and coriander, zest 1 lemon and the lime into the mix, mix all together so evenly combined.

Wash samphire thoroughly under running cold water before use. Don't add salt when washing samphire as it's already salty enough.

Take seabass make sure it does not have any bones; trim the sea bass to remove the belly.

Score the skin on top, 4-5 times to stop it from curling up in the pan.

When new potatoes are cooked remove from oven and aloud to cool 5/10 mins, when cool to handle cut them in half, and add the raw mix which was prepped earlier to the oven tray. Mix well.

To cook seabass add to a cold pan skin side down, heat slowly to get skin nice and crispy. Checking on it every 1-2 minutes to make sure it is not burnt. When the skin is crispy flip over and cook for one minutes take out the pan and allow to rest.

While seabass is resting, heat another pan up; add new potatoes and samphire, salt and pepper.

In the pan you cooked sea bass, add butter, and allow to turn brown; just as the butter turns brown add the shrimps and lemon juice. Cook for 45 seconds – 1 minute. (until the shrimps have heated up)

To plate
Put new potatoes on the plate, crating height as you do, place seabass on top, then spoon brown shrimp and butter over the top of the seabass, for extra flavour put micro coriander around the dish, and add a wedge of lemon.

SIMON
RIMMER

BIOGRAPHY

When Simon Rimmer opened his first restaurant, Greens, in 1990, he did so with two cookery books, no idea how to cook, but a passion to create a great destination restaurant... and chat girls up!

He wasn't even supposed to be in the kitchen. His role, or so he hoped, was front of house lothario to the beautiful people of West Didsbury. However, financial reality got him into the kitchen (no money to employ anyone) - a decision that changed his life.

You will see Simon's face more and more on your TV screens, as host of Channel 4's Sunday Brunch alongside Tim Lovejoy they continue to cheer up the nation's Sunday mornings.

In recent times he has also appeared on BBC 2's Something For The Weekend, as well as appearing on BBC2's Great British Menu, Celebrity Mastermind, Grub's Up, Recipe for Success, BBC1's This Little Farmer, Saturday Kitchen, Richard and Judy on Channel 4, Cooking the Books and Breaking into Tesco for Channel 5.

He's also written 4 books – The Accidental Vegetarian, Rebel Cook and Lazy Brunch (with Tim Lovejoy) and his latest book Seasoned Vegetarian

Moroccan Spaghetti

INGREDIENTS

300g Spaghetti

1 finely chopped Onion

pinch Turmeric

8 fresh Tomatoes, stalks removed and finely chopped

2 cloves Garlic

100g toasted, Flaked almonds

100g cooked, washed Chick peas (tinned are fine)

Salt & pepper

100ml Olive oil

bunch each of Parsley and coriander, finely chopped

5g ground Cinnamon

5g ground Cumin

5g ground Coriander

METHOD

Cook the dried spaghetti to al-dente.

Gently fry the onion and garlic in the oil until it's soft.

Add the toms, cinnamon, coriander, cumin and turmeric. Cook over a medium heat until the toms break down, about 20 mins.

Season up the sauce and then add the almonds and chick peas, then fold the herbs through just before serving.

To serve – divide the pasta between 4 plates and spoon some of the delicious sauce on top.

LIME TREE
RESTAURANT

BIOGRAPHY

The Lime Tree Restaurant is a family run business set up by Patrick Hannity in Didsbury, Manchester in 1986. In 2012 Patrick launched The Lime Tree Restaurant and Wine Bar in Bollington, Cheshire. Overlooking Bollington Green and situated in two converted Victorian shops the restaurant offers a relaxed and welcoming dining experience in a stylish rural setting.

Chef Ric Bell heads the kitchen team. With many year's experience working in award winning restaurants Ric demands quality to be at the heart of his menus; "At the Lime Tree we're fortunate enough to work with some great quality produce -we like to support British farmers and artisan producers and our constantly changing menu reflects this. We love to use natural ingredients in their prime, with access to local game throughout the autumn, and spring lamb, rare breed pork and Aberdeen Angus beef from our own farm just a couple of miles away at Macclesfield Forest."

Hardingland Farm Pork
roast loin, wild mushrooms, baby spinach, shallot puree,
fondant potato, madeira jus

INGREDIENTS

Fondants

4 medium sized Potatoes

250g Butter

125ml Chicken stock

1 medium sized Shallot
(sliced)

2 Cloves

4 Sage leaves

1 Clove garlic, peeled

1 Bay leaf

Pork

800g Pork loin, skin on

good quality Olive oil

Salt

Mushrooms

300g mixed Wild
mushrooms

200g Baby leaf spinach

20g Butter

Shallot puree

20g Butter

300g Shallots, sliced

100ml Cream

Salt

Sauce – Madeira jus

25g Shallots, sliced

1 litre good quality
Chicken stock

100ml Red wine

50ml Madeira

good quality Olive oil

METHOD

Fondants

Peel and trim potatoes into desired shape.

Melt butter and stock together, add remaining
ingredients.

Colour one side of potatoes in a hot frying pan.

Turn potatoes over to have coloured side up,
immerse in the stock and butter mix and cook on
160°C for 15-20mins or until just soft when tested
with a knife

Pork

Remove skin, set aside. Cut loin in half
lengthways.

Roll in cling film and tie ends to shape, leave
overnight if possible

Remove cling film, season the pork, then sear all
sides in hot pan and roast in the oven on 180°C for
15mins or to desired taste, rest for 10mins.

For crackling, cut into shards rub with oil and salt,
bake in oven on 200°C until crisp and crunchy.

Mushrooms

Prepare mushrooms

Wash spinach

Sauté mushrooms in a hot pan with butter, add
spinach and wilt, season accordingly.

Shallot puree

Sauté shallots with butter, until golden in colour.

Add cream and reduce by half.

Blend until smooth, season to taste

Sauce – Madeira jus

Fry shallots, add red wine and Madeira jus.

Reduce by two thirds, add stock.

Reduce again until desired consistency and
colour.

Pass through muslin and season to taste

Build

Swipe the shallot puree across the middle of the
plate.

Place the fondant to one side, add the mushrooms
to the other side.

Slice pork, 4 slices each and lay across the
mushrooms at an angle.

Nape with jus and drizzle around the plate.

Place crackling on top of fondant.

THE YEW TREE INN

BIOGRAPHY

The Yew Tree Inn is a rather handsome village pub, built by The Earl of Crewe in the 19th century that has been lovingly refurbished to its former glory. Inside you'll find open fires, old beams and a great big bar plus the odd twist or two that befits the quirkiness of this beautiful corner of Cheshire. We've also added a wonderful summer terrace for al-fresco dining and watch out for future events, including farmers' markets and bespoke weddings, on our adjacent paddock.

We offer freshly made, locally sourced food from a menu with daily specials combined with informal service in a cosy and relaxed atmosphere. At the bar you'll find an eclectic range of spirits including an ever growing single malt collection, plus an extensive wine list and an award winning range of cracking real ales & craft beers.

Our team of chefs, led by head chef Rob McDiarmid, change the menu every eight weeks to reflect seasonal changes and you'll find a daily changing specials board in the pub.

We are so fortunate to be located in a county full of passionate, artisan producers. We use fantastic, award winning Red Poll beef from our neighbours at Oaklands, pork, vegetables, free range eggs & more from the Brosters farm on Bunbury Heath, cracking sausages from Burrows of Bunbury, we receive daily fresh fish deliveries and our cheese, yoghurt, ice cream and other dairy products are all locally sourced. Even our chips come from potatoes that are grown no more than 15 miles away, chipped on the farm before being delivered fresh in water everyday, ready to be double fried in dripping for that real pub flavour!

Roast Chicken Breast
parmesan gnocchi, pea & proscuitto

INGREDIENTS

4x Skin on chicken breast, ideally French trim

2x large Maris piper potatoes

30g Ricotta cheese

25g plain Flour

30g Semolina

40g Parmesan

1x Egg yolk

1x pinch Salt

2x pieces of Prosciutto

100ml quality Chicken stock

Double cream

Frozen/fresh peas

Pea shoots to garnish

METHOD

Boil the potatoes in salted water then put through a potato ricer/ mash using a masher

Beat the parmesan and egg yolks into the warm mash

Fold in the plain flour and semolina into it to form a dough

Shape the gnocci dough into small cylinders about 2cm wide and 3cm long

Place the gnocchi into the salted boiling water until they float on the surface for 30 seconds, take out and leave to cool

Using a hot pan, fry the chicken breasts, skin side down until golden brown then put on a baking tray into an oven at 180c for 10-12 mins

In a saucepan, add the chicken stock and reduce by half over a high heat then add the double cream and reduce further until the sauce coats and sticks to the back of a spoon. Add the peas.

On a baking tray lay out the prosciutto and bake until crispy

In the frying pan add the gnocchi until they are golden and brown

To assemble the dish, carve the chicken breast in two at an angle and leave to rest. In a bowl or plate place the gnocchi and spoon the sauce & peas around it. Place the carved chicken on top and garnish with the crispy prosciutto and pea shoots. Enjoy!

LUKES EATING HOUSE

Image & recipe from Luke's cookbook

BIOGRAPHY

At 18 years old Luke Thomas become Chef Patron of his first restaurant Luke's Dining Room which won Berkshire and Buckinghamshire Restaurant of the Year in 2013. At just 20 years old Luke opened Retro Feasts, an exciting pop-up social diner concept in Mayfair focusing on recreating childhood favourites into cleverly revitalised dishes for today's open-minded diners. 2015 has seen Luke launch Retro Feasts in Dubai as the diners first permanent residence and his first overseas venture. Founder of Luke's Broadway, Luke has partnered with Puma Hotels to create this Modern British Bistro in the heart of the Cotswolds. Luke's first book 'Luke's Cookbook' has recently been published by Penguin and has been very well received by the public. Luke doesn't stop there, his latest exciting project is a new restaurant Luke's Eating House & Gin Rickey's Bar which opened in 2014 in Chester.

Grilled Veal Chops, Tuna & Caper Sauce

INGREDIENTS

4 x 340g Rose veal chops
(around 3-4cm thick)

1 tablespoon Olive oil

Lemon wedges to serve

Salt and pepper

For The Sauce:

125g Salted butter

3 Garlic cloves, peeled and
sliced into slivers

2 Banana shallots, peeled
and finely diced

3 tablespoons small Capers

1 tablespoons roughly
chopped fresh Flat-leaf
parsley

juice and zest of 1 Lemon

250g fresh Tuna (centre
cut), diced into 5mm pieces

METHOD

To make the sauce, melt the butter in a saucepan over a low heat and add the garlic slivers and diced shallots. Leave to cook gently or 5 minutes so that the flavours can infuse - be careful not to burn the garlic. Preheat the oven to 160oc.

Season the veal chops all over with salt and pepper. Heat the oil in a frying pan over a medium to high heat and cook the chops for 2-3 minutes on each side, until they have taken on some good colour. Transfer them to a baking tray and finish cooking in the oven for around 5 minutes.

To finish the sauce, stir in the capers, chopped parsley, lemon zest and juice into the shallots. Add the diced tuna and mix well so that the hot buttery ingredients coat the fish. Remove from the heat.

Serve the cooked veal chops on warm plates and spoon over the tuna and caper sauce.

Garnish with lemon wedges.

HEATHCOTES

BIOGRAPHY

Paul has 2 restaurants: his original Olive Press Preston serving Italian grills, pizza and pasta, and Heathcotes Brasserie cooking French and British cuisine.

Paul has been awarded three Honorary Fellowships from Liverpool John Moores University, Lancashire University and his home town Bolton University in recognition of his achievements in catering. Paul has published two cookbooks, Rhubarb & Black Pudding and Heathcotes at Home, writes columns to a number of regional newspapers and magazines and also appears regularly on TV.

Paul chairs the North's Academy of Culinary Arts, Adopt-a-School, encouraging the traditions of his profession and is also a fundraiser for Childline and the NSPCC, Fashion Kicks and Youth Zone.

In 2009 he was awarded an MBE for his contribution to the Hospitality Industry.

Marmite roasted pressed Goosnargh Chicken

with crispy egg & soft sage & onion mash

INGREDIENTS

8 Chicken legs (boned, skin on)

Marmite

Olive oil

6 Eggs (soft boiled & chilled)

Flour

1 Egg (beaten with a good pinch of salt)

Breadcrumbs

1/4 Onion (finely diced)

6 Sage leaves (finely shredded)

Chicken jus

Salt & pepper

For The Crispy Egg

soft Boiled egg

1 Egg (beaten)

Flour (to coat)

Salt

Breadcrumbs

For The Sage & Onion Mash

4 Maris piper potatoes, approx 800g

150ml Milk approx

30g Unsalted butter

Sea salt & freshly milled pepper

4 leaves of finely shredded Sage

1 large Spring onion (or 2 small) finely sliced

METHOD

Courgette Puree

Slice the courgettes and shallots as thinly as possible. Melt the butter and oil in a heavy bottomed pan. Add the shallots and sweat until soft. Add courgettes stir and place tight fitting lid. Cook for 5 mins. Add the white wine and cook until dry. Place the contents in blender with the sprigs of rosemary and blend for 5 mins on the highest speed. Near the end of the process add the cold diced butter to emulsify. Cool quickly.

Roasted Baby Courgettes

Season the baby courgettes with olive oil, salt and pepper, place in a metal dish and roast in

a hot wood fired oven for about a min or until cooked, alternatively you could just grill the courgettes on a metal skillet.

Lemon Thyme Crumb

Chop the lemon thyme leaves, in a frying pan melt the butter. Add the lemon thyme. Then add the bread crumbs and slowly cook for a few mins until golden brown. Season with salt and pepper.

Lemon Thyme Dressing

Whisk all ingredients together let infuse for a week if possible.

To Assemble The Dish

Season the scallops with pomace oil and salt, fry in a hot pan until one side is golden then turn them over and add a good knob of butter. Place in the oven for a couple of mins, take out and squeeze a bit of lemon juice over each scallop. Take out of the pan and let rest for a min. Whilst you are cooking the scallops, warm the courgette puree, baby fennel and courgettes under the grill or in the

oven. Dress the leaves with the vinaigrette and place ingredients on the plate as you would like, sprinkle the roasted courgettes with a teaspoon of the thyme crumb.

BERTRAMS

BIOGRAPHY

Chef Spencer Burge and his team use international influences, traditional Lancashire recipes and a broad range of locally sourced ingredients to produce exciting dishes for Bertram's Restaurant.

Bertram's is a unique modern restaurant and cocktail bar affording exquisite panoramic views of the delightful rolling hills of Lancashire thanks to its elevated position. A restaurant with rooms and an impressive luxury apartment, it also boasts of its connection with the global winner of World Luxury Spa of The Year award – The Woodland Spa.

Chocolate Lime

INGREDIENTS

Chocolate, Ginger & Pistachio Truffles
1 tbsp Black treacle

300ml Double cream

150g Dark muscovado sugar

3 tsp Ground ginger

100g Crystallised stem ginger

400g Dark chocolate callets

200g White chocolate callets

100ml Water

50g Pistachio nuts blitzed to a powder

Lime Cheesecake
170g Sugar

570g Cream cheese

10 Limes (5 zest 10 juice)

710ml Whipping cream (semi whipped)

6 Leaves gelatine (soaked & rung out)

Red Velvet Cake
60g Unsalted butter at room temperature

150g Caster sugar

1 Egg

20g Cocoa powder

40ml Ced food colouring

½ tsp Vanilla extract

120ml Buttermilk

150g Plain flour

½ tsp Bicarbonate of soda

1½ tsp White vinegar

Honeycomb
165g Caster sugar

25ml Honey

60g Glucose

30ml Water

7g Bicarbonate of soda

Apple & Lime Semi Gel
750ml Apple juice

3 Lime zest

5g Agar agar

2g Xanthanum gum

METHOD

Chocolate, Ginger & Pistachio Truffles
Add the treacle, sugar, cream, water, ground ginger and stem ginger to a pan. Bring the mixture to the boil, simmer for 2 minutes. Stir & remove from heat

Pour the mixture into a blender, add the chocolate and blitz until the chocolate has completely melted. Leave to set in the freezer, at least 2 hours

Once the ganache has set, roll into balls before the ganache starts to melt and roll in pistachio powder.

Lime Cheesecake
Heat juice & rind
Once boiled, add gelatine, take off heat
Whisk sugar & cheese together
Add cheese mixture to lime slowly
Fold in whipped cream & set.

Red Velvet Cake
Preheat the oven to 170°C.

Cream the butter and sugar. Turn the mixer up to high & slowly add the egg. In a separate bowl, mix together the cocoa, food colouring and vanilla, add to the butter mixture and mix until evenly combined. Turn the mixer down to slow and slowly pour in half the buttermilk. Beat until well mixed, add half the flour and beat until everything is well incorporated. Repeat until all the buttermilk and flour have been added. Turn the mixer up to high speed and beat until you have a smooth, even mixture. Turn the mixer down to low speed and add the bicarbonate of soda and vinegar and mix.

Honeycomb
Boil all the ingredients except the bicarb to a light caramel, add bicarb and quickly whisk

Pour onto a tray lined with greaseproof paper and leave to set.

Apple & Lime Semi Gel
Reduce 500ml apple juice by half and top back up with remaining 250ml.

Add agar mixed with ¼ tsp sugar and stir to boil.

Pour onto a metal tray and set.

Put set jelly in a food processor along with a little more apple juice and switch on high.

Mix xanthanum gum with a bit of sugar and add to jelly. Allow to form a semi stiff glossy jelly.

THE COTTAGE IN THE WOOD

BIOGRAPHY

The chic restaurant with rooms, The Cottage in the Wood, is fast gaining a reputation as a 'foodie bolt hole'. Head Chef Chris Archer is behind the wheel in the kitchen. He draws on his experience to offer contemporary food that has its roots in classic cooking and makes the most of Cumbria's larder; putting Herdwick hogget, Lorton rare breed pork and other local seasonal delicacies such as Lythe Valley damsons, alongside other world class ingredients.

Chris, who is 27, has an impressive CV under his belt. His grounding was a three year apprenticeship at two Michelin starred Winteringham Fields under Chef patron Germaine Shwab. He went on to work at two Michelin starred Midsummer House under Chef Daniel Clifford and the Michelin starred The Yorke Arms at Ramsgill near Harrogate.

Chris was 'hooked' on cooking at an early age when he produced a batch of 'superb scones' (the quality of which he has never been able to replicate, apparently). Inspired by John Campbell's classic cook book, Formulas for Flavour, Chris organised his school work experience at the Vineyard at Stockcross, in John's Michelin starred Kitchen. He later went on to appear on Ready, Steady Cook.

The Cottage in the Wood is a 17th restaurant with rooms on Magic Hill, in the heart of Whinlatter Forest in the Lakes. It has gained a celebrity following for its exquisite cooking and complements its food offering with chic accommodation in a truly secluded setting. A genuine gastronomic retreat.

Palet D'or
carvetii coffee mousse - hazelnut ice cream

INGREDIENTS

Palet D'or

260g Dark chocolate
4 Egg yolks
4 Egg whites
75g Caster sugar

Hazelnut Base

125g Dark chocolate.
50g Feuilletine flakes
50g Crushed hazelnuts

Chocolate Glaze

75g Water
50g Cream
100g Sugar
50g Glucose
10g Dark chocolate
80g Cocoa powder
3 Leaves gelatine

Hazelnut Ice Cream

500g Double cream
500g Milk
150g Praline paste
12 Egg yolks
250g Sugar
100g Frangelico

Carvetii Coffee Mousse

250g Mascarpone
50g Rum
1 shot Espresso (Carvetii)
50g Cream
5g Gelatine
1 Vanilla pod
60g Egg yolk
100g Sugar
4 Tablespoons water
250g Whipped cream

METHOD

Palet D'or

Melt the chocolate gently over a bain marie (pan of steaming water).
Whisk the yolks until thick and creamy (ribbon stage).
Whisk the whites and sugar to make a glossy meringue.
Fold the melted chocolate into the egg yolk mix.
Beat half the meringue mix into the chocolate until smooth. Carefully fold in the remainder of the meringue.
Pour into 8 dome moulds, or rings and freeze.

Hazelnut Base

Melt the chocolate over a bain marie
Fold in the the feuilletine and hazelnuts
Pour onto greaseproof paper. Cover with another sheet and roll out till thin
Set in the fridge. Cut out 8 discs using a ring that correspond with the size of the Palet D'or moulds
Place a disc on each of the Palet D'or portions

Chocolate Glaze

Soften the gelatine in cold water
Warm all ingredients except the gelatine and chocolate
Stir the chocolate into the warm mix until smooth. Squeeze dry the gelatine and dissolve into the mixture
Allow to cool until a 'coating' consistency is achieved. Turn out the Palet D'or and coat with the glaze.

Hazelnut Ice Cream

Whisk egg yolks, sugar and praline paste until very thick
Warm the cream and milk close to simmering and whisk onto the yolk mixture
Cook the mixture gently to make a custard (coating consistency). Strain into a bowl or jug and add the frangelico. Allow to cool.
When cool, churn in an ice cream machine

Carvetii Coffee Mousse

Angharad MacDonald and Gareth Kemble of Carvetii Coffee Roastery in Cumbria strive to produce the best coffee possible. They achieve this through careful sourcing of beans, innovative roasting and an obsession with training their clients. We are very proud to work with them.

Mix the mascarpone rum and espresso. Soften the gelatine in cold water. Warm the 50g cream with the split vanilla pod. When soft, squeeze dry the gelatine and add to the warm cream/vanilla. Strain once the gelatine has dissolved. Now mix this into the mascarpone.

Whisk the yolks until pale. Boil the sugar and water to 110 degrees C then slowly whisk onto the yolk mixture. Continue whisking until cool.

Blend the mascarpone and egg yolk mixtures together. Finally, fold in the lightly whipped cream. Allow to set in a bowl in the fridge.

When set, beat to soften and pour into a piping bag. Store in the fridge.

Assemble the dish in a style that reflects your creativity. Pay particular attention to piping the Carvetii coffee mousse.

LAKESIDE HOTEL

BIOGRAPHY

Lakeside's Head Chef Richard Booth has a wide-ranging CV including stints at Michelin-starred establishments such as Le Manoir and Paris House, and cites his greatest influence as the larger than life John Benson-Smith. He has now been at Lakeside since 2005 and currently oversees a team of 20 servicing the hotel's two distinctly different restaurants; Lakeview and John Ruskin's Brasserie.

Over the past decade, Richard has developed an intrinsic understanding of the plentiful produce available in Cumbria and believes this endless supply of fresh, seasonal ingredients is the key to some mouth-watering menus. As well as having their own kitchen garden, the team can often be spotted foraging for the likes of wild garlic or local damsons in the Lake District landscape. The hotel even has its own herd of sheep and rare-breed cattle, underlining Richard's desire to make the most of the local eco-system.

Another important part of the food ethos at Lakeside is keeping the flavours honest and authentic, with a scattering of unexpected twists and taste sensations. The huge variety in Richard's culinary influences spans the continents, with recent inclusions ranging from Asian-influenced breakfasts to Peruvian-style and Swedish dishes.

Richard is equally committed to developing his talented team and working with the local community to inspire the next generation of chefs. As well as being a judge to Cumbria's Young Chef of the Year, he regularly runs workshops in schools and colleges to help get young people excited about food and instil a real sense of passion about what they put on their plate.

Pineapple Cheesecake
with green chilli ice cream

INGREDIENTS

Vanilla Cheesecake
500g Mascarpone
150g Caster sugar
200g Double cream
2 Oranges (zest only)
1 Vanilla pod de-seeded
60g Egg yolk
5 whole Eggs

Chilli Ice Cream
300g whole Milk
10g Milk powder
180g Caster sugar
5 Yolks
190g Double cream
1 Green chilli de-seeded
and finely chopped (leave
seeds in if you want it
hotter)

Poached Pineapple
1 Pineapple peeled
and cut into rectangles
(11cmx2.5cm)
130g Caster sugar
½ Vanilla pod de-seeded
50g White wine
50g Water
5 tbsp Pineapple juice

Sesame Seed Biscuit
152g Plain flour
88g Ground almonds
74g Icing sugar
120g Butter
220g Tahini paste
20g Sesame seeds

Banana Tuile
250g very Ripe banana
60g Granulated sugar
50g Plain flour
50g Milk
55g Praline paste
60g Butter (melted)

Coriander & Lemongrass Foam
1 stick of Lemon grass
150g Caster sugar
150g Water
½ Lemon (juiced)
70g Coriander
2.5g Hyfoamer
2g Xanthan gum

METHOD

Vanilla Cheesecake
In a food processor with the blade attachment, process all the ingredients together into a smooth creamy mixture. Then, place mixture in a rectangle baking tin approx. (30cm x 20cm), lined with cling film. Cook in the oven at 100C for 75 minutes. Leave to cool and place in fridge for 3 hours to firm up.

Chilli Ice Cream
Combine the milk, cream and chilli, bring to the boil in a thick bottomed pan. While that is on the stove, in a separate pan, whisk the sugar, milk powder and yolks to a creamy yellow texture. Pour the boiled milk over the sugar and eggs whisking all the time, so as not to scramble the eggs. Cook on the stove on a low heat until it coats the back of a wooden spoon, taste it, if it is not hot enough add another chopped chilli and leave to infuse. Leave to cool, then pass through a sieve and churn in ice cream machine.

Poached Pineapple
In a thick bottomed pan add sugar and water on a high heat, boil together until it starts to turn golden brown, at this point remove from the heat and add the white wine slowly and carefully as it is very hot. Add the vanilla and pineapple juice and return to the heat, boil to a syrup consistency, remove from the heat and place the pineapple in the liquor, cling film the pan and leave to infuse for 2 hours.

Sesame Seed Biscuit
In the food processor blitz all the ingredients together. Then, roll out between 2 pieces of parchment paper and chill in fridge for 1 hour. Bake straight from fridge between two flat baking trays for 12 minutes at 150C, until lightly golden in colour. When cooked portion the biscuit while still warm (11cm x 2.5cm).

Banana Tuile
Blitz all ingredients together adding the melted butter last. When smooth place in piping bag and chill for 1 hour. Once chilled pipe into long thin lines, as long as you can, onto parchment paper. Bake in the oven for 3-5 minutes at 150C, when dark brown in colour remove from the oven, work very quickly, peel the piping off the tray and mould into any shape you want.

Coriander & Lemongrass Foam
Bring water, sugar, lemongrass and lemon juice to the boil and then leave to cool. When cold add the coriander and blitz in a blender until pureed. Pass the combined lemongrass liquor through a tea towel. Weigh out 250g/250ml of the liquor, add 2.5g hyfoamer and 2g xanthan gum then whisk in blender until you get a light thick foam.

LAWNS RESTAURANT

BIOGRAPHY

Lawns Restaurant offers a menu for lunch and dinner of superb international cuisine, and we have an extensive selection of wines from around the world to accompany.

This beautifully styled room is the ideal venue for any special occasion or just a treat! Come along and have a look around the lounge is open from 11am until 11pm for non-residents.

Overseen by Executive Chef, Andrew Richards, Ben Mounsey, Lawns Head Chef, and his team, have a background working in of some of the most exclusive venues in the country. Bringing their experience to Thornton Hall, creating a selection of fantastic menus suited to all occasions, together with the ambience of Lawns, an unparalelled dining experience is created.

White Chocolate Dish

INGREDIENTS

Ganache Recipe
225g White chocolate
121g Double cream
pinch of Maldon

Ginger Oil Recipe
100g Ginger
300ml Rapeseed oil

Passion Fruit Soda Recipe
150g Passion fruit puree
Passion fruit flesh
70g Stock syrup
150g Soda
1g Xantham

Passion Fruit Mousse
300g Philli
80g Icing sugar
2 leaves Gelatin
200g Cream
50g Milk
50g Passion fruit
Citric acid

Passion fruit and Lemongrass Sorbet
400g Puree
150g Water
80g Caster
50g Glucose
½ fresh Ginger (sliced)
3 Lemongrass (chopped)

Caramelised Chocolate
250g White chocolate chips

Tempered White Chocolate Recipe
300g White chocolate

Garnish
Hung yoghurt
Lemon basil
freeze dried Passion fruit

METHOD

Ganache

Semi melt chocolate

Add salt to cream

Bring cream and salt to the boil

Pour over white chocolate and beat until it has a shine

Set in a container at room temp then chill

Ginger Oil

Warm oil to 60°

Add finely slice peeled ginger and mix in thermo @60 on 2.5 for 20 minutes

Remove from thermo and reserve for 10 days

Passion Fruit Soda

Mix all ingredients and taste

Pour into ice cube containers and freeze

Once frozen remove from tray and return to freezer

Melt 40% white chocolate to 60 % cocoa butter

Dip the soda cubes into liquid nitro then into choc mix

Repeat again

Place onto tray and seal whole left by cocktail stick

Leave in fridge to melt

Passion Fruit Mousse

Mix philli and icing sugar until smooth

Semi whip cream

Add passion fruit to philli

Warm milk and dissolve gelatin

Add milk to philli

Fold in cream and set in container

Passion fruit and Lemongrass Sorbet

Heat all ingredients

Remove from heat and cool/steep at room temp

Pass

Churn

Caramelised Chocolate

Bake chocolate on a non stick mat in the oven at 120°

Turn and stir occasionally for around 15 minutes until evenly golden brown

Remove from oven and let cool at room temperature

Once semi set crumble into smaller pieces

Chill in the fridge

Tempered White Chocolate

Heat 200g of white chocolate over a baine marie until melted and at 47°

Remove from the heat and fold in the remaining chocolate and stir continuously until the chocolate reaches 27°

Spread the chocolate thinly and evenly over acetate and finish with crushed freeze dried passion fruit and rock salt

Leave to set at room temp then chill in fridge

Garnish

For plating pull two swipes of ganache at adjacent angles, place your dipped soda on the most northern swipe.

Pipe five large dots of mousse around the chocolate followed by five dots of yoghurt.

Scatter the caramelised white chocolate diagonally from 2 o'clock to 7 down the plate and the passion fruit pieces diagonally opposite so the two rough lines cross.

Place two shards of tempered chocolate in the two biggest mousse dots and garnish with three lemon basil leaves.

To finish quenelle the passion fruit sorbet onto the middle of the dish and coat the items with ginger oil.

L20 HOTEL

BIOGRAPHY

L20 Restaurant is the training and commercial kitchen and restaurant of the L20 Hotel School, located in Merseyside, which was created by Hugh Baird College in 2013. The aim of the School is to shape the future of the hospitality industry, providing education, training, work experience and inspiration to those wanting to get into hospitality and those already in working in the industry.

The School is run slightly different to other parts of the college, it works with assessors and lecturers but has a general manager, a head chef, sous chef, restaurant manager and their own team of apprentices. This allows students on full time courses the chance to have valuable work experience in the various outlets of the Hotel School.

Head Chef Nick Boswell has been with L20 Restaurant since its inception in 2013, bringing with him years of experience working within kitchens of hotels and restaurants across the North West and London.

Nick contributes an immense amount towards the education of students at the L20 Hotel School, providing them with a real life working experience of the industry by working under his supervision.

Chocolate Pave, Peanut Butter Ice Cream, Peanut Brittle, Salted Caramel and Chocolate Soil

INGREDIENTS

Chocolate Pave
220g Dark chocolate
225g Double cream
1 Vanilla pod
2 Egg yolks
20g Butter

Peanut Butter Ice Cream
300g Milk
80g Peanut butter
200g Caster sugar
40g Ice cream stabiliser

Peanut Brittle
20g Salted peanuts
50g Caster sugar
12g Fondant paste
25g Liquid glucose
8g Water

Salted Caramel
50g Caster sugar
50g Water
40g Double cream
10g Butter
2g Maldon sea salt

Chocolate Soil
70 g plain cooking Chocolate
100 g Caster sugar
2 tbsp Water

METHOD

Chocolate Pave

In a heavy based pan, heat the cream and add the split vanilla pod and scraped seeds on a low heat for 5 minutes

Turn up heat to boil then remove the vanilla pod skin

Place chocolate in a large bowl and pour over the boiled cream and whisk

Whisk in the egg yolk then the butter

Pour into a clean 10 x 15 x 4cm mould lined with cling film and place in fridge until set

Peanut Butter Ice Cream

Place all the ingredients into the blender and mix until fully combined

Pour into ice cream churner for 40 minutes

Place into a clean tub and freeze

Peanut Brittle

Place peanut in a robot coupe and pulse until you have nib size pieces

Weigh the water, sugar, fondant paste and glucose into a small heavy based pan on a low heat until dissolved

Boil until it turns golden brown, remove from heat and add peanuts and pour onto a slipmat and smooth with a pallet knife and allow to cool

Once cool break into 5-7cm pieces and place into a sealable tub

Salted Caramel

Weigh the sugar and water into a heavy based pan, place on a medium-high heat and bring to boil until it turns a golden brown

Whisk in the cream, butter and salt and cook on a low heat for one minute

Chill and pour into a squeeze bottle

Chocolate Soil

Place the sugar and water in a heavy based pan over a medium heat

Cut the plain chocolate into small pellets about 1cm

When the sugar reaches 130 degrees (if you haven't got a thermometer wait until all sugar is dissolved and starting to change medium brown colour) then take off the heat

Add the chocolate bits and stir with the whisk

Make sure all the sugar coats the chocolate and stir for 2 minutes

Empty out onto a slip mat to chill, once chilled place into a sealable tub

To Plate

Place a sharp knife in to a jug of hot water to warm

Swirl the salted caramel on to a cold plate, place a tea spoon of chocolate soil off to one side of the swirl

Remove the pave from its mould and use the warmed knife to cut the chocolate into 2x 10cm slices

Place a slice of pave onto the caramel swirl, place a scoop off peanut butter ice cream onto the chocolate soil

Top with a piece of peanut brittle

Scotland

Starter
Main
Dessert

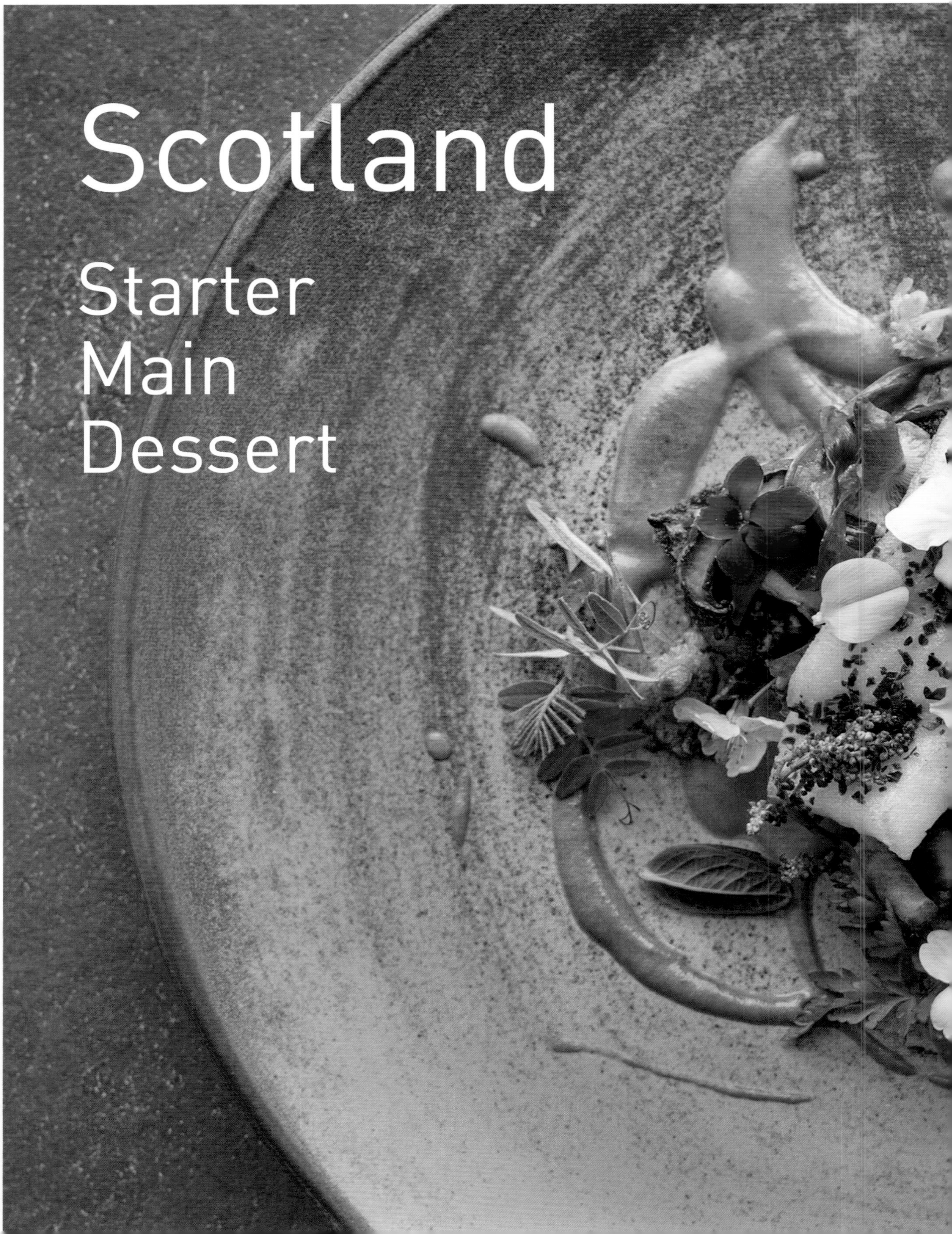

TOWER RESTAURANT

BIOGRAPHY

Since arriving in Edinburgh, Brazilian born Jose Dalto, has had the privilege of working with some very passionate Chefs who were happy to share their knowledge of cooking and instilled in Jose a respect for the produce Mother Nature provides, especially Scotland's bountiful larder. Named as Tower Restaurant Head Chef in 2012, Jose has continued to build on the reputation of Scotland's first and finest rooftop restaurant for fresh and locally sourced food from an inventive menu. You can expect dishes packed with flavour and impeccably cooked such as; haggis with spiced pineapple, briny-fresh Scottish oysters, pan-seared grouse breast with figs, lobster thermidor with chips and deer loin with baby beets.

Jose is passionate about Scotland's best food producers; so Isle of Mull scallops are hand-dived by Guy Grieves of the Ethical Shellfish Company, smoked salmon from Inverawe Smokehouse, happy chickens come from St Bride's farm, black pudding and haggis will be Dingwall's finest and the Tower is a proud member of the Scotch Beef Club buying only fully traceable Scotch beef from award-winning Borders butcher Shaw's of Lauder.

Heritage Tomato Salad
with bonnet goat's cheese

INGREDIENTS

Tomato Jelly

6 Mixed heritage tomatoes

300ml organic Tomato juice

3gr Agar agar

1 pinch Salt

1 pinch Sugar

2 drops Tabasco

1 clove Garlic

1 spring Thyme

Bonnet Goat's Cheese

200gr Bonnet goat's cheese

50gr Natural yogurt

Croutons

2 slices of White bread

METHOD

Tomato Jelly

Score the tomatoes and blanch in boiling water for 10 seconds , refresh with ice cold water and peel.

Cut the tomatoes in quarters, halves or any shape you like.

Arrange the tomatoes on your mould.

Bring tomato juice to simmer with rest of ingredients but not the agar agar, once simmering let infuse for 15 min.

Pass the juice through a fine sieve back into a clean sauce pan.

Bring back to simmer and add the agar agar, whisk until dissolved.

Pour in to the arranged mould and let it set.

For The Bonnet Goat's Cheese

Hand made on a small country farm in the damp lush pastures of Ayrshire. Matured for six months the cheese develops a thin rind and as it ripens the paste gets softer, smoother and creamier. It has a slightly nutty, herbaceous, sometimes smoky finish with a sweet lemony tang.

Place the cheese and yogurt in a mixing bowl and work it with a spatula until spreadable.

For The Croutons

Roll the bread to thin slices and cut to desired shape, rub some garlic to it and bake in the oven until crisp

To Serve

Spread the cheese on the slate, place the tomato jelly on top and dress it with some nice foraged leaves/flowers and the croutons.

"TOWER YOU ARE FAB!" Joanna Lumley

ULLINISH COUNTRY LODGE

BIOGRAPHY

Calum Montgomery is Head Chef at the exclusive Ullinish Country Lodge on the Isle of Skye.

A 17th Century lodge now operating as a restaurant with rooms boasting incredible views of the Cuillin hills and Oronsay island looking towards the Outer Hebrides.

Ullinish Country Lodge, following a major refurbishment, is a luxurious resting place in the midst of a lonely and wild landscape run by Pam and Brian Howard

A native of Skye, Calum was first inspired to take up professional cooking at the age of 14, while working part-time, as a Kitchen Porter. After working for 3 years as a chef in the Cuillin Hills Hotel, he attended the City of Glasgow College where he completed his professional training.

He spent 4 years developing his skills at the renowned One Devonshire Gardens, Glasgow, before taking up an invitation to work alongside Marcello Tully in the Michelin Starred Kinloch Lodge, where he remained for 3 years as senior sous chef. He received the Sous Chef of the Year award, at the Scottish Hotel Awards in 2015. Drawing inspiration from the stunning island landscapes and the abundance of fresh ingredients that are available on Skye, Calum attributes the Nordic influence in some of his dishes to his experience working in Denmark with Michelin star chef, Wassim Halal.

Roasted Wood Pigeon Crown
with baby beetroot, hazelnuts and brambles

INGREDIENTS

2 whole Pigeon crowns
(oven ready)

4 Baby beetroot

4 Baby golden beetroot

100g blanched Hazelnuts

20g fresh Rosemary

2 cloves of Garlic

250g full fat Milk

50g Hazelnut oil

10g Runny honey

3g White truffle oil

(Hazelnut oil soaked

bread)

8 Scottish brambles

METHOD

To prepare the confit legs, remove from the carcass, trim excess sinew and French trim the bone.

Place the legs in a small sauce pan and cover with 100ml chicken or pigeon stock, 100ml madeira, 1 tsp maple syrup, 1 tsp golden syrup, 1 tsp black treacle, 1 clove of garlic, and I sprig of thyme

Slowly cook the legs for 1-2 hours, remove from the pan and pass the jus through a fine sieve into a fresh saucepan. Season the sauce to taste and thicken with a small amount of diluted cornstarch. Place to one side.

To prepare the beetroot, wash by hand, remove the leaves and stalk and place in a pot of simmering seasoned water. Cook for 15 -20 minutes until the beetroot can be pierced with a knife without any resistance. Allow to cool then, using your hands, rub the skin and expose the flesh.

Prepare an emulsion by combining the honey, truffle oil and hazelnut oil. Season with a little sea salt (Isle of Skye sea salt is the best you can get!)

Toss the cooked beetroot in the emulsion to glaze and season.

To prepare the hazelnut puree, place the nuts in a suitable tray and roast in an oven set at 180'c for 5 mins until they turn a nice golden colour. Reserve a few chopped nuts for garnish., Transfer the remainder to a small saucepan and cover with 300g milk and 50g butter. Simmer for 30 minutes, being careful not to boil. Finally, transfer the mixture to a food processor and blend until smooth. Taste, season and set aside at room temperature.

Now, it's time to roast the wood pigeon.

Place a heavy bottom based frying pan on a medium heat. Allow the pan to smoke slightly then, add 1 tbsp sunflower oil. Season the pigeon gently with table salt and cracked black pepper and place gently in the pan, colouring all sides of the crown.

Then, add 50g of chopped butter to the roasting pan along with a sprig of rosemary and a clove of crushed garlic. Bring the butter to a bubble, then baste the pigeon a few times before placing it in an oven pre-heated to 180'c for one to two minutes. The core temperature of the crown should reach between 38'c and 45'c (Medium Rare)

Remove the bird and baste a few more times with the rosemary butter, then allow to rest for 10 minutes in a warm area of the kitchen on a cooling wire.

Add some raw beetroot trimmings to the sauce to enhance the colour and give an earthy flavour and reheat, slowly

Begin assembling the plate, starting with the beetroot, hazelnut puree, confit leg, roasted hazelnuts and some deep fried beetroot leaves.

At the restaurant we use our hazelnut bread lightly drizzled with hazelnut oil to dress the plate This can be substituted with any type of bread, served as a "crouton".

Finally, carve and plate the roasted pigeon. Garnish with a few brambles and decorate the plate with a plentiful drizzle of the pigeon jus.

BRIDGEVIEW STATION

BIOGRAPHY

Rory Lovie

HEAD CHEF @ Bridgeview Station

I've been Head Chef at Bridgeview Station in Dundee for two years now, sourcing local and Scottish produce for my menus. My Food is very simple with no more than five or six ingredients on the plate which allows the flavour of the fantastic produce shine through.

My Motto is Think Seasonal, Eat Scottish

I came to Bridgeview Station with a wealth of experience having worked under Tony Heath (Lets Eat) and latter Willie Dean before moving on to 2AA Opus One Restaurant in Perth were I was head chef for 3 Years maintaining the restaurants 2AA accolades

Dunkeld Hot Smoked Salmon
pickled pittormie kohlrabi, cucumber, radish

INGREDIENTS

Salmon
1 side of Hot smoked
Salmon
Crème fraiche to bind
1 tsp Wasabi
Salt and cracked black
Pepper to taste

Pickled Kohlrabi
1 small Kohlrabi
50ml White wine vinegar
100ml Water
25g Caster sugar
Few Thyme sprigs

Cucumber
1 Cucumber
Salt

Radish
100g Radish

Micro Coriander to garnish
cracked Black pepper

METHOD

Salmon
Take the skin off the side of the hot smoked salmon and flake up the salmon into a bowl.
Mix the salmon with crème fraiche and wasabi until it becomes bound together.
3Season to taste and put in the fridge.

Kohlrabi
Peel the outer skin off the kohlrabi then thinly slice it using a mandolin. Place it in to a bowl and leave to one side.
Place the vinegar, sugar, water and thyme sprigs in to a small pot and place on to the heat, bring it to the boil then pour it over the kohlrabi. Leave to cool.
Place the cooled pickled kohlrabi in to the fridge.

Cucumber
Thinly slice Cucumber on a mandolin lengthways until you get to the seeds.
Lay out flat on a tray with some J-Cloth on it.
Cover liberally in salt and leave for thirty minutes.
Once thirty minutes have passed, wash the cucumber very gently to get rid of the salt.
Place back on some J-Cloth to dry out the moisture.
Once dry, place into the fridge.

Radish
Thinly slice the radish using a mandolin.
Store in ice water in the fridge until ready to use them.

The Build
Take the salmon out of the fridge and place into a metal mousse ring to form a perfect circle in the middle of the plate.
Take out the pickled kohlrabi, cucumber and radish out of the fridge.
Place the three or four pieces of rolled cucumber, thinly sliced radish and pickled kohlrabi on top of the salmon.
Garnish with some cracked black pepper and few shoots of micro coriander.
Enjoy.

CARNOUSTIE

BIOGRAPHY

I have worked in the industry for 27 years starting of as a kitchen porter whilst I was a boy at secondary school, once I left school I did my apprenticeship and gained my 706/1 and 706/2.

After gaining these qualifications I went to London to work at The Tower Thistle, after about 2yrs went to Wentworth Golf Club, then onto Chester Grosvenor, after 1 year I went to Edinburgh were I met my wife, and where we both worked at the Sheraton Grand, then onto various privately owned businesses, then in 2013 worked at the Edinburgh Malmaison for 2 years.

Did a short spell at MacDonald hotels before coming to Carnoustie Golf Hotel and Spa back in March 2016, I'm looking forward to the challenges that lay ahead, along with the prestigious golfing events which the hotel will be hosting, The Seniors Open 2016, and The British Open in 2018.

The Hotel has 96 rooms situated on the edge of the world famous Carnoustie Golf Links, which regularly plays host to major golfing events, and enjoys views across the Links,

The Carnoustie also has meeting & events space for up to 200 guests, and Calders Bistro which serves locally sourced produce daily.

Ham Hock Terrine

INGREDIENTS

4 Ham hough

2 Onion

4 Carrots

3 sticks Celery

1 Leek

1 bulb Garlic

10 Black peppercorns

2 Bay leafs

5 sprigs Thyme

5g Parsley

8lt Water

Piccalilli

700ml Malt vinegar

2 tbsp Coriander seeds

500g Cauliflower, broken into 3cm florets

2 Onions, peeled and chopped

3 tbsp English mustard powder

3 tbsp Plain flour

1 tbsp Turmeric

2 tsp Ground ginger

150ml Cider vinegar

100g Red peppers, cut 1cm dice

1 Courgette, quartered lengthways and cut into 1cm slices

2 Garlic cloves, peeled and sliced

200g Granulated sugar

METHOD

Place all ingredients in a pan and bring to boil then simmer for 3hrs topping up with water if needed, and keep skimming as needed.

Once cooked, take out the ham then strain the stock and keep, while the hocks are hot, pick the meat off the bone and keep the meat separate.

Chop gherkins and flat parsley and mix in with ham, add some ham stock and then taste for seasoning.

Line a terrine mould with cling film, then add the ham mix and pack as full as possible till the mould is full, the fold over the cling film and then press overnight.

When serving, cut a slice and then serve with piccalilli and toasted sour dough bread.

Piccalilli

Place the malt vinegar and coriander seeds in a large preserving pan and bring to a boil. Add the cauliflower and onion and simmer for 5 minutes until slightly softened but still crunchy. Meanwhile, put the mustard, flour, turmeric and ginger in a small bowl and gradually whisk in the cider vinegar until smooth. Add the remaining vegetables, garlic and sugar to the pan and stir over the heat for 2–3 minutes until the sugar has dissolved. Drain over a large bowl to collect the vinegar.

Put the mustard mixture in the pan and bring to the boil. Gradually add the drained malt vinegar and simmer for 10 minutes, until thick enough to coat the back of the spoon. Add the drained vegetables and take off the heat. Spoon into sterilised jars – if they're not kilner jars, cover them with plastic discs and elastic bands rather than metal lids, which can sometimes react with the vinegar.

BLYTHSWOOD SQUARE

BIOGRAPHY

I grew up in the Southern part of Hungary where my family grew vegetables & fruits. We also kept a variety of farm animals.

I can still remember the taste of my Mother's delicious dishes and the smell of her freshly baked bread. The house was filled with the aromas of the air-dried ham that my Father carefully aged and the saucissons he made. I can still see my Grandmother at the flour dusted table stretching out her strudel pastry.

Today these memories greatly influence my cooking here at Blythswood Square Glasgow along with the culinary influence of Scotland and Scottish traditions.

Gently Roasted Breast of Quail
with glazed confit leg, golden raisins, pain d'epice, celeriac & sauternes sauce

INGREDIENTS

For the quail:

40ml Scottish rapeseed oil

20gr Unsalted Scottish butter

4 sprig of Garden thyme

2 clove of Garlic, crushed

2 jumbo Quail

100ml Duck fat

4 sprigs of Garden thyme

2 clove of crushed Garlic

1 medium Orange, zest only

Seasoning to taste

Sauternes sauce:

30ml Scottish rapeseed oil

20gr Unsalted Scottish butter carcasses of the above jumbo Quails 1/2 Banana shallot, peeled

3cm piece of Carrot, peeled

1 cloves of Garlic, chopped

3 sprig of Thyme

300ml light Chicken stock

150ml Sauternes

10gr Unsalted Scottish butter

40gr seedless golden Raisins

15ml -8 Vinegar

Celeriac remoulade:

1 medium Celeriac, peeled

2 lrg Scottish Free range eggs, yolks only

1 teaspoon Dijon mustard

150ml Scottish rapeseed oil

1 teaspoon White wine vinegar

1 teaspoon of Lemon juice

Salt and pepper to taste

Celeriac pure:

100ml Full fat milk

50 ml Double cream

120gr Celeriac trimmings, small dice

Seasoning to taste

To finish:

2 slice of Pain d'epice

15gr Unsalted Scottish butter

Red amaranth or daikon cress

Malden Salt

METHOD

Remove the legs from the quails then trim the drum bone. Sprinkle with salt, pepper, orange zest and set aside for 15 minutes. Heat up the duck fat with the thyme, crushed garlic and infuse for 5 minutes. Once the fat is infused, add the pat dried legs and cook slowly until tender. Once cooked, remove from the duck fat, pat dry, trim off the drum bone and gently remove the bone from the thigh being careful not to damage the meat. Warm under the grill and glaze with the sauce just before serving.

Prepare the crown by cutting off the lower back and than removing the wing tips. Remove the wishbone. Sprinkle the inside of the crown with salt and pepper, insert the thyme and set aside until needed. Sear the crown in hot butter and oil until golden then cook in hot oven (200C) for 4 minutes. Remove the crown from the oven and rest on a small tray upside down to allow the juices to flow in the breast meat, alternatively cook in 50C water bath for 50 minutes, then finish in a hot frying pan. Remove the meat from the bone, sprinkle with salt and pepper before serving.

To make the sauce, use the reserved carcasses and trimmings.

Heat the frying pan, add the oil and butter, then sauté the bones until golden. Remove the carcasses and drain off the excess fat; while, in the same frying pan sauté the shallot, garlic and carrots with the thyme until golden. Add the bones and de- glaze with 75ml sauternes, reduce by half then add the chicken stock. Simmer for 15 minutes then add the remaining wine. Pass through a super bag to remove all debris. Add the golden raisins and set aside. Adjust the seasoning with salt and pepper, and the acidity with -8 vinegar.

Make celeriac puree with the ingredients listed in a TM® - speed 3/90C for 12minutes, than blitz on speed 8 for 30sec. Then pass through a sieve, season to taste and keep warm.

For the remoulade, make mayonnaise with the ingredients listed, and then add the julienne celeriac, season to taste.

For the crispy gingerbread, heat the butter and fry the gingerbread. Once crispy and golden, pat dry.

CAFE CASSIS

BIOGRAPHY

This will be Denis second entry into the Great British cookbook after being rated very highly on his first entry and getting great feedback, Denis has decided to submit another dish this year. He hopes you enjoy his take on an amazing Scottish dish with a little bit of a French twist.

Born in the French town of Nantes, chef-owner Denis began cooking at home for his family aged 13, before training at "Les Sorbet" in Noirmoutier. He travelled to London in order to work at the Savoy Hotel for Anton Edelmen, and there honed his skills as a chef before refining these through work across France, Italy and the Caribbean. His enthusiasm and passion for what he does comes across in his dishes, which are often fresh takes on classics with a strong French influence. Denis' engaging personality and diverse menu has loyal customers coming back for more.

Denis and his wife Alison opened Cafe Cassis in June 2011 on the south side of Edinburgh. Alison and the front of house team provide a friendly yet relaxed service, whilst Denis provides quality fresh dishes made from local produce. Denis is 100% customer focused and after the service you can find him chatting to customers, passing on tips and advice or just making sure their Cafe Cassis experience was a memorable and enjoyable one. Denis and Alison have been married for 20 years and have two daughters Leora and Ellie, who sometimes come along and help out Mum & Dad.

Haggis Profiteroles
with a french twist with potatoes

INGREDIENTS

Choux Pastry

120g Butter

1 pinch Salt

25cl Water

2 pinch of Mixed spice

140g Plain flour

4 med. Eggs

50g Haggis

Puree

200g boiled Carrots

300g Mashed potato (as you like your mash, I add butter and a teaspoon of grain mustard.

55ml Chicken stock

25g Butter

200g Garden peas

30ml Chicken stock

teaspoon Olive oil

4 Basil or Mint leaves.

Haggis

450grms Haggis

5cl Chicken stock

2.5cl of Whisky

Shallot Jus

tablespoon Olive oil

1 large Banana shallot chopped

1 crushed Garlic clove

4cl Red wine

10cl Beef stock

Salt & Pepper to taste

METHOD

Choux Pastry

In a large saucepan add butter, water, salt & mixed spices, heat gently until butter has melted. Turn up the heat and add all the flour, stir well with a spatula for a couple of minutes, until the mixture starts to come away from the sides of the pan. Pour the mixture into a bowl to cool for 10 mins. Once cooled sprinkle the haggis over the mixture and mix together. Beat one egg at a time into the mixture until dough is smooth and glossy and a soft dropping consistency. Using a piping bag with a 1cm nozzle, pipe mixture onto a grease proof sheet approximately 3 cm (£2 coin) in diameter or if you prefer a main course size pipe the mixture for larger profiteroles. Rub the top of each profiterole with some milk; this will make the choux crispy and coloured.
Bake for 25 to 30 min until golden brown. Do not open oven while cooking, as profiteroles may not rise properly. Once cooked cool on a baking tray, do not put in the fridge.
Prep puree while profiteroles are cooking. I use three purees for 3 profiteroles but you can use any puree of your choice. Remembering the haggis has strong-spiced flavours.

Puree

To assemble your purees add your ingredients into 3 separate bowls and mash them together until a smooth puree or mix them together in a food processor. Keep warm until serving.

Haggis

In a saucepan heat up 5cl chicken stock add your haggis, stir on a low heat until haggis is hot, then add the whisky and stir together. Once whisky is mixed with haggis turn off the heat cover with a lid to keep warm.

Shallot Jus

Heat olive oil in a saucepan then add the chopped shallots and crushed garlic over a medium heat until soft and translucent, increase the heat then add the red wine and beef stock and salt and pepper to taste. Cook over a high heat until sauce reduces by half.

Assemble Dish

Assemble Dish Cut profiteroles in half (3 per person) place the base on a plate. Add a quenelle of haggis to each choux pastry. Make another quenelle of each puree in between your profiteroles. Pour a tablespoon of sauce over the haggis then place the tops of your choux pastry on top of each profiterole and sprinkle with chopped chervil or parsley to decorate and serve.

Et voila!!! Bon appetit

FOURTH FLOOR RESTAURANT

BIOGRAPHY

Stuart Muir has been Executive Chef at the Forth Floor Restaurant Harvey Nichols since opening in August 2002 where he has earned a reputation for producing constantly exciting dishes created from the very best, personally sourced British produce.

Stuart acquired his love of cooking from his parents, spending time with his father fishing and shooting on the local rivers and moors and with his mother preparing and cooking the fresh produce. Stuart has been cooking ever since.

Stuart was awarded a Michelin Star and 3AA rosettes at the age of 22 whilst Head Chef at Knockinaam Lodge, he was the youngest chef to win this prestigious accolade in Scotland at the time.

After a brief spell travelling the world gaining a wealth of experience from a number of other Michelin Star Chefs, Stuart joined the team at the Balmoral in Edinburgh as Head Chef at Number One and Hadrian's.

From here Stuart went to be executive Chef at the famous Old Course Hotel in St Andrews, before deciding to return to Edinburgh to launch the award winning Forth Floor Restaurant at Harvey Nichols.

Stuart uses a selection of locally sourced produce to create dishes that match modern flavours with classical technique.

Roast Mackerel
caramelised melon, homemade cream cheese, spring vegetable salad, candied pistachios and honey truffle dressing

INGREDIENTS

2x Mackerel fillets

Crispy filo tubes

100g Cream cheese

100g Pistachios

100g Sugar

100g Water

Honey and truffle dressing

1 Baby carrot

1x Navet (baby turnip)

1x Golden baby beetroot

150g Spinach leaf

100 Samphire

1x Watermelon

1x Honeydew melon

1x Cantaloupe melon

Honey Truffle Dressing

1tsp Honey

1tsp Dijon mustard

1tsp Truffle oil

100ml White wine vinegar

300mil Olive oil

Juice and zest of one lemon

Salt and pepper

METHOD

To make the filo tubes lay one sheet of filo pastry on a chopping board and brush with melted butter, slice the pastry in 1inch thick ribbons. Wrap around a metal tube and bake at 165 degrees c for 5 minutes.

Place the sugar and water into a sauce pan and bring to the boil. Once boiling add the pistachios and leave to cook for 20mins. Once the 20mins is up drain the nuts and place on a baking sheet. Place in the oven at 165 degrees c until slightly caramelised. Leave to cool.

For the baby veg simply peel and cook in salted boiling water along with the samphire.

Cut the melon into equal squares and char under the grill.

TO SERVE

In a hot pan add a drizzle of oil and fry the mackerel fillets skin side down until cooked half way through. Turnover, take off the heat and add a knob of butter.

Meanwhile in a separate pan, fry off the spinach in butter and season. Once cooked drain on a kitchen towel.

Using the same pan as the spinach add another knob of butter and add the baby veg once warm drizzle with the honey truffle dressing.

Fill the filo tubes with the cream cheese and place onto the plate.

Place the spinach in the middle of the plate and add the two mackerel fillets on top.

Arrange the baby veg and melon around the mackerel and drizzle with honey truffle dressing and candied pistachios.

GAMBA

BIOGRAPHY

Derek's love of cooking started when he was a young commis chef at The Fountain Restaurant in Glasgow. His drive to develop his talents took him to the Channel Islands, French Alps and Spain. He spent a year in Spain after leaving his position as Head Chef in Rogano, this was to enhance his knowledge in sourcing and cooking fish. On return again to Glasgow Derek secured the head chef role of Papingo, another classic restaurant in Glasgow's dining history. Then in 1998 Derek was appointed head chef and owner of Gamba, which saw his cooking earn the reputation of the finest seafood restaurant in the city. Caring about sustainability and a commitment for reducing waste, Derek is a three star sustainability champion for the Sustainable Restaurant Association. His exceptional cooking skills has gained recognition after recognition, year-after-year with two AA rosettes and most recently earning the title of Seafood Restaurant of The Year 2015 by the Caterer and Seafish Scotland under his leadership.

Seared Hand-Dived Isle Of Mull Scallops
creamed celeriac, apple and curry

INGREDIENTS

20 Hand dived king scallops

3 tbsp Olive oil

1 med Onion (chopped)

1 med Celeriac (chopped)

1 Granny smith apple (grated)

Thumb size piece of grated root ginger

2 Cloves of garlic (chopped)

1/2 a litre of Pressed apple juice

1/2 litre of Fish stock

1 dessert spoon Curry powder

1/2 dessert spoon Ground cumin

1/2 dessert spoon Ground coriander

1/2 Cinnamon stick

1 Cup of double cream

Salt and ground white pepper

Fish Stock
1.8kg Fish bones (turbot, lemon sole or monkfish are best)

2 litres of Water

1 Onion, finely chopped

1 Leek, finely chopped

½ Whole bulb of garlic, sliced horizontally

1 Lemon, sliced

2 sprigs Parsley

1 tbsp Vegetable oil

METHOD

Heat the olive oil in a thick-bottomed pan on a medium heat.

Sweat the onion, garlic and ginger till soft (do not colour).

Add the spices and cook on a low heat stirring occasionally. When the mixture starts to dry out, add the celeriac and stir into the onions and spices.

Slowly add the apple juice, fish stock, and cinnamon stick, and cook on a low heat and simmer until most of the liquid soaks into the celeriac.

Add in the double cream, salt and pepper to taste and check the seasoning (add more for taste.)

When the cream starts to reduce, remove from the heat along with the cinnamon stick.

Liquidise the celeriac mix to a puree texture, place in a bowl and leave to cool so the spices infuse the mixture.

Add the grated apple and divide the puree between the four plates evenly.

Sear the scallops in a non-stick frying pan till lightly browned in colour, then place the scallops on top. Garnish with some fine herb's or pea shoots.

Fish Stock
Wash the bones very thoroughly and chop up.

Cook the vegetables and garlic in the oil for a few minutes. Do not colour

Add the chopped fish bones and cook without colouring for about five minutes

Add the water and bring to the boil. Skim well, removing any froth.

Add the lemon and parsley. Simmer for 20-30 minutes.

Pass through the sieve and leave to cool

When cool, the stock can be frozen

RIVERHOUSE
RESTAURANT

BIOGRAPHY

Chef Ollie Quintin is originally from Britany in France when he was classically trained as a chef. He came to Scotland in the late nineties and after working in various top end hotel and 5 stars cruise liner, Ollie settled back in Scotland.

"The quality of the larder available on our door step is exceptional and it is all a chef can ask for. Incorporating Scottish products and big flavour into a balanced dish has been the basic principle of our menu at the River House. We aim to deliver our customer a tour of Scotland through our menu. "

Inverurie Rump of Lamb,

sweet potato fondant, pistachio granola, celeriac puree, port wine and rosemary jus

INGREDIENTS

4 x 7oz. Rump of lamb
2 x large Sweet potato
½ litre Chicken stock
10ml Port wine
75ml Veal jus
5g Rosemary
200g Sugar snap
20g Lamb lettuce

Celeriac Puree
1 x medium Celeriac head
75ml Whipping cream
25g Unsalted butter
Salt and pepper

Pistachio Granola
50g Rolled oats
25g Puffed rice cereal
25g Pistachios, roughly chopped
25g unsweetened Coconut chips
10g ground Flax seeds
25g Golden raisins
¼tsp Allspice
½tsp Cinnamon
½tsp Fleur de sel
30ml Extra virgin olive oil
25g Honey

METHOD

Cover the celeriac with water and add 1 tsp of salt. Boil until very soft, then strain through a fine sieve. Press with the back of a spoon to extract as much liquid as possible. Heat the cream and melt the butter to a nutty brown colour. The ingredients are best combined whilst they are still warm. Put the cream, butter and celeriac in a blender and purée until completely smooth. Season to taste. Reserve. –

Combine all ingredients together and bake flat on a tray for 10 min at 200 degrees Celsius. Until golden brown. Allow to cool, Pulse a couple of time in a food processor. Keep in an air tight container.

Peel the sweet potato and cut 4 disc of 1 cm thick, seared those in Oil for color on both side, add the chicken stock and cover of tin foil, bake until the fondant are soft .

On a hot pan, seared your seasoned Rump of Lamb, and bake them for 12 min at 180 degrees. Then rest the meat.

Deglaze your pan with the port, reduce and add the veal jus, reduce and finish with chopped rosemary.

Blanched the sugar snap, add a nut of butter and salt,

Assemble your dish, fondant on the plate, dots of celeriac puree, sugar snap, carved rump of lamb, sauce, finish with the granola and lamb lettuce.

Bon appetit!

THE RESTAURANT AT THE APEX GRASSMARKET

BIOGRAPHY

Leith-born chef, Tony Singh (45), is a leading personality in the Scottish restaurant industry. As chef director of a string of award-wining restaurants in Edinburgh – including Tony's Table, Roti and more recently Oloroso – Tony has pushed the boundaries of culinary innovation for over 16 years. Always open to new ideas, his approach to food is to 'keep it real and fun'.

After formal training at Telford College, his distinctive style soon developed, leading to positions with The Royal Yacht Britannia, The Balmoral Hotel, The Royal Scotsman Train and Skibo Castle. Today, Tony is known for his contemporary Scottish cooking, which combines his love of local produce with influences from his Sikh upbringing – both his Mum and Dad were great cooks! His menus feature all the very best seasonal ingredients, sourced right off his doorstep, with a spicy Indian/Asian twist. Awards for his culinary talents include: Drambuie Chefs Association Best New Restaurant of the Year; Scottish Chefs Award Scottish Chef of the Year; and SLTN Best Restaurant.

Roast Pork Belly
with chermoula

INGREDIENTS

1.5kg boneless Pork belly, with rind

4tsp Black peppercorns

1½ tbsp Sea salt

Chermoula

100g Coriander

50g Flat-leaf parsley leaves

10 Garlic cloves

2 tsp Cumin seeds (toasted until they change colour, then ground)

1 tsp Smoked paprika

1 Green Serrano chilli

¼ tsp dried Chilli flakes

100ml Rapeseed oil

zest and juice of 2 Lemons

½ tsp Salt

METHOD

Pop all the ingredients for the chermoula into a blender and whizz until you have a rough purée. Add more oil if it is too thick then check the seasoning. If you do any left over, the chermoula keeps well in the fridge up to 1 week, though you need to cover it with a layer of oil. It's normal for it to discolour slightly.

Score the pork rind with a knife at 5mm intervals. Pat it thoroughly dry with kitchen paper then leave for 2 hours until completely dried out. It needs to be really dry so that you get crunchy crackling.

Toast the peppercorns in a dry pan until they smell aromatic. Cool and grind in a pepper mill or mortar and pestle and mix with the salt.

Pat the pork flesh completely dry with kitchen paper. Rub the salt and pepper mixture all over the flesh, but not the rind. Leave for at least 1 hour, or as long as possible, to allow the flavours to permeate. When you're ready to roast the pork, preheat the oven to 230°C/gas 8.

Place the pork on a rack sitting above a roasting tray. Roast for 30 minutes, then reduce the heat to 160°C/gas 3 and roast for a further 1½ hours. The meat should be meltingly soft and will pull away easily if you try and pinch a piece. Remove from the oven and allow to rest for 10 minutes, loosely covered with a piece of tin foil to keep it warm.

To serve, hack off some crackling, slice the meat and serve with a dollop of chermoula.

THE THREE CHIMNEYS

26/09/05

Eamon McCabe

BIOGRAPHY

Scott Davies joined The Three Chimneys in June 2015 and is happily settled into his role, which he describes as a once-in-a-lifetime opportunity. Scott's ethos is to get back to the roots of what was always intended when the Restaurant was founded 31 years ago: the absolute best of Skye, Land and Sea, using a mix of Scottish and Nordic influences.

Scott grew up in the village of Caerleon near Newport in South Wales, the son of a Welsh carpenter and a Scottish pharmacist, who met in Mallaig, while sailing on the west coast of Scotland. When he left school he was determined to enrol at catering college and did so in Dundee, as his family returned to live in Scotland and settled in Carnoustie. From here, his ambition to become a leading Scottish Chef never left him, working and learning with a number of top names, such as Isle of Eriska Hotel, Glenapp Castle Hotel, plus a year spent in Australia at The Point Restaurant in Melbourne.

Scott became Senior Sous Chef at the well-known Russacks Hotel in St Andrews, where he took Rocca Restaurant to 3 AA rosettes within a year of being promoted to Head Chef in 2012 - a remarkable achievement for someone of age 26. From there he moved to The Adamson, a brand new up-market bistro establishment in St Andrews, where he built a new kitchen team and a great name for excellent food. While working there, Scott participated in the 2013 series of BBC TV's MasterChef: The Professionals. He was runner-up in the final of the competition and excelled in his performance, watched and supported nationwide.

Woodland Turbot
last and new season wild mushrooms – wild herbs – Orbost iron age pork

INGREDIENTS

Prepare in advance

Fermented Ceps
50g Cep mushrooms
Salt

Winter Chanterelles;
50g winter chanterelles
1 carrot
1 celery stick
1 shallot
1 clove of garlic
Cider vinegar, enough to cover the vegetables
A pinch of nutmeg and pinch of allspice
6 black peppercorns
1 bay leaf and sprig of thyme

Pork Belly;
400g pork belly, skinned and boned
30g table salt
350ml buttermilk
100ml water
2 parsley stalks
2 sprigs of thyme
1 bay leaf
1 tsp. black peppercorns
1 garlic clove, crushed
1ltr pork fat, melted

Prepare on the day

Potato Terrine;
1kg King Edward potatoes, peeled and thinly sliced
250g unsalted butter
Salt and pepper
1 clove of garlic, peeled and finely sliced
2 tsp. thyme leaves

Wild Garlic Puree;
50g unsalted butter
2 banana shallots, peeled and finely sliced

A pinch of salt
100g wild garlic leaves, washed
100ml double cream

Fresh Scottish Chanterelles;
50g fresh chanterelles
25ml water
25g butter
1 sprig of thyme

Sauce Vierge;
1 tsp. baby capers (not salted)
½ tsp. gherkins
1 tsp. wild garlic leaves
1 tbsp. parsley
1 tbsp. chervil
1 tbsp. chives
½ tsp. tarragon
1 tsp. white anchovies
½ tsp. Dijon mustard
50ml extra virgin olive oil
20ml lemon juice

Turbot;
2 x 300g turbot on the bone, skinned
Salt and pepper
A thumb sized piece of clarified butter
50ml 5-day aged silver birch sap
8 fresh silver birch leaves
25g butter
5g dried Kombu seaweed flakes

To serve;
Wild herbs, flowers and garlic leaves from land and sea

METHOD

Fermented Ceps; add 2% of salt to the weight of the mushrooms. Leave in a sealed jar for a minimum of 1 month. Turn the jar upside down after 1 week.

Winter Chanterelles; finely dice the carrot, celery stick, shallot and garlic. Cover with cider vinegar, nutmeg, allspice and peppercorns. Bring to boil, remove from heat. Add bay leaf and sprig of thyme. Leave to cool. Finally, add mushrooms and place in a sterilized sealed jar. Rest for a minimum of 1 week.

Pork Belly; boil the water, salt, parsley, thyme, bay leaf, garlic and peppercorns. Once boiling, take off the heat and cool. Add the buttermilk and pour over the pork belly. Cover and leave in the fridge for 24 hours. Remove the pork belly from the brine and wash it off. Place in a tray and cover with pork fat. Cover with a tight fitting lid and cook at 110°C for 6 hours, or until tender. Remove the pork belly from the fat and place on greaseproof paper. Cover with another sheet of paper and press between two trays in the fridge overnight. Cut into regular sized pieces, weighing approximately 50g each. Return to the fridge.

Potato Terrine; line a tray with greaseproof paper and cover with a layer of potato. Brush with butter and season with salt, pepper, garlic and thyme. Repeat until all of the potato has been used. Cover with another piece of greaseproof paper and cook at 170°C for 1½ hours until golden brown and tender. Leave to cool for 1 hour. Cover with a fresh sheet of paper, press with another tray on top, return to the fridge and leave overnight. Cut into four pieces, 12cm by 6cm.

Wild Garlic Puree; melt the butter in a pan and cook until a light brown colour. Add the shallots and a pinch of salt and cook gently for 10 minutes. Add the wild garlic and sweat down for 2 minutes. Add the cream and cook for 2 more minutes. Blitz and pass through a sieve. The result should be a loose puree. Season to taste.

Fresh Scottish Chanterelles; add the chanterelles to a hot pan with the water, butter and thyme. Cook for two minutes on a medium heat until the chanterelles are cooked and glazed.

Sauce Vierge; finely chop all the ingredients, mix together and season. Put to one side until needed.

Turbot; season and pan-fry the turbot fillets in clarified butter for 2 minutes, turn and cook for 2 more minutes, until a golden colour. Remove from the pan, place in the oven at 180°C for 4-6 minutes (or until the fish is 45°C at the core). Remove from the oven and rest for 4 minutes. In a pan, add the birch sap and leaves, butter, seaweed, and reduce for 1 minute or until you have a glaze. Add any juice from the turbot after it has rested. Remove the fillets from the bone and warm up in the glaze.

To serve; pan-fry the pork belly and potato terrine for 2 minutes on each side until golden. Spoon the sauce vierge over the pork belly and keep warm. Heat the wild garlic puree and spoon onto the plate. Place the pork belly and terrine on top of the garlic puree, followed with the turbot. Randomly place wild herbs, flowers and garlic leaves and mushrooms around the plate. Finish with sauce.

RED ONION

BIOGRAPHY

Award winning Red Onion is situated in the heart of Glasgow city centre. Chef/patron, John Quigley's roller coaster career started in London's West End where he quickly established himself and gained a reputation for excellent casual gourmet dining. He then took the opportunity to travel the world as a private chef to rock stars and celebrities such as Bryan Adams, Tina Turner and Guns n Roses.

Opened over 11 years ago, Red Onion is a contemporary casual dining experience with a menu that offers something for everyone. The kitchen produces new interpretations of classic Scottish cookery, serving dishes that people know and love. Its environment is modern and comfortable and the service relaxed and informal with the bustling feel of your local neighbourhood bistro.

Finnan Haddie Fishcakes
with baby gem, peas, poached egg and parsley cream

INGREDIENTS

700g Potatoes, diced

500g Finnan haddie

4 Spring onions fine sliced

1 Lemon zest and juice

1 tbsp chopped Capers

1 Egg yolk

pinch White pepper

100g Breadcrumbs

200ml Double cream

25ml Dry white wine

1 Chicken stock cube

juice of 1 Lemon

2 tbsp chopped Parsley

4 large handful Baby gem leaves

4 small handfuls defrosted frozen Peas

Oil for shallow frying

Eggs for poaching

METHOD

Pre heat oven to gas mark 7, 425°F (220°C).

Boil the potatoes for 10 -12 minutes until tender. Drain and mash. Allow to cool.

Place the fish on a non stick bake tray and cook for 7/8 min-should be very slightly under done. Remove and allow to cool.

Mix the potato, fish. egg yolk, capers, lemon zest, ½ breadcrumbs, remaining parsley and spring onions, season and mould into 8 fishcakes. Pat cakes into remaining breadcrumbs and fridge for 30 min.

Dissolve stock cube in 4/5 tbsp of hot water, Heat a small saucepan and add wine, let wine boil till reduced by half, add cream and stock cube boil, simmer till slightly thickened add parsley and lemon juice.

Heat oil on wide frypan over med heat, add fishcakes and fry for 3 min either side, turn occasionally if colouring too much.

In a separate pan poach eggs.

Add peas to boiling water and keep warm.

Arrange baby gem and peas on plate, place fishcake on top and place egg on top of cake, pour over sauce.

THE CASTLE
RESTAURANT

BIOGRAPHY

Graham Campbell wanted to be a chef from an early age. His first job as 'the lowest of the low' was at the Caledonian Hotel in his hometown of Oban, where he progressed to sous chef before moving down to Rochdale for a position at Andrew Nutter's eponymous restaurant. 'There was finely presented food – loads of produce and dishes that I had just never seen before,' says Graham. 'I had to make a lemon tart and I didn't have a clue how to do it.'

Moving on to Paul Heathcote's Longridge, he worked under head chef James Holah, previously sous chef at Claridge's, and it was here that his fine dining career began in earnest. 'That was a real eye opener,' he says. 'I got introduced to many new foods; I had never seen foie gras or mushroom ravioli, I had no idea that any of that existed. They put me on larder and asked me to make an amuse bouche – I had no idea what that was.' Within three months he was sous chef.

In 2008 he decided to move back to Scotland, taking up a position as head chef at The Ballachulish House near Fort William. Cooking a small menu for the restaurant's select clientele, he took everything he had learnt from Heathcote's and made it my own. In 2009 he was awarded a Michelin star for his food, much to his surprise, becoming the youngest chef in Scotland to receive a Michelin star aged twenty-five. Describing his cooking as 'precise, well presented and flavourful', Michelin highlighted in particular his velouté of artichokes with girolles and truffle, his roast duck, pomme dauphinoise, foie gras and cherry sauce, and his strawberry parfait and salad with raspberry sorbet. The restaurant closed shortly after, but this unexpected affirmation of his talents proved a huge motivator. 'That is when I started buying all the books and researching myself, and since then it has always been about me and what I do,' says Graham. 'I dabble and experiment with flavours.'

Wild Halibut
with cucumber textures, sea vegetables, smoked creme fraiche

INGREDIENTS

4x 170g portions of Halibut

Cucumber Textures

2 Baby cucumbers

1 + 1/2 large Cucumber

20g scottish Rapeseed oil

Agar agar

Salt

Sea vegetables

10g Sea sandwort

10g Orache

20g scottish Rapeseed oil

wash and pick all Vegetables and dress with Rapeseed oil

Radish to garnish

Puff wild rice

10g Wild rice

200g Vegetable oil

Smoked Creme Fraiche

100g Creme fraiche

1 Lap-sang souschon tea bag

METHOD

Cucumber textures

Take the baby cucumbers and cut them in 1/2 length ways.

Place them in a vac pack bag drizzle with oil and season with salt then seal on full.

Using the whole cucumber put through a juicer.

Take the juice and weight out.

Take that weight and using the agar match it to 1% of that weight so 100g = 1g.

Place all in a pot and bring to boil.

Place in a tub and allow to cool in the fridge until set.

Take set mix and blend until smooth pass through a fine chinois and put in a squeeze bottel.

Peal the 1/2 cucumber and cut in 1/2 length ways.

Take 1 1/2 of the cucumber and scrape the seeds out.

Using a blow torch char the rounded side of the cucumber then place in a vac pack bag.

Drizzle with oil and salt and vac on full power.

The other 1/2 of the cucumber using a mandolin slice thinly and then place in a vac pack bag. Drizzle with oil and salt and seal on full power.

Puff wild rice

Heat oil to 220°c in a pot

Add rice for about 3-5 seconds strain and. Place on a cloth to dry and season with salt

Smoked creme fraiche

Place the creme fruit in a bowl and using a smoke gun fill the gun and put the pipe into the bowl covering the tomb of the bowl with a loose fitting lid.

Start smoking the creme fraiche until the smoke is cooking out the sides then pull the pipe out and leave the more to infuse for 5 minutes.

Once infuse mix with a whisk season with salt and check if its smoky enough if not repeat process until happy.

Then transfer mix to a piping bag.

WEDGEWOOD

BIOGRAPHY

Paul Wedgwood is one of Scotland's leading chefs and restaurateurs. Since opening his eponymous restaurant on Edinburgh's famous Royal Mile in 2007 Paul has established himself as a prominent figure in Scotland's food scene as well as creating an award winning and much loved restaurant.

Praise for Paul and his restaurant have been consistently high, The Sunday Times named it one of the five best in Edinburgh and it has won a clutch of accolades in the years since it opened from Harden's Best New Restaurant in the U.K and several Scottish restaurant of the year titles.

Paul's innovative cooking uses fresh, local and seasonal ingredients with dishes such as Lobster Thermidor crème brulee and Isle of Mull cheddar and onion bread and butter pudding featuring on the menu. He is also a keen forager and always has a fresh daily foraged salad on offer as well as a variety of haggis from traditional to more unusual versions such as rabbit or venison.

What sets Paul apart is his enthusiasm to communicate his passion for food and his outstanding ability to impart his knowledge to others: He has appeared regularly on STV, BBC and many international tv channels. He participates in the Edinburgh Restaurant and Science Festivals, he has taught in schools and has represented his city and country abroad in Italy, South America, the Caribbean and Australia. He is also Head Chef of the annual Celtic Festival in Barbados where he co-owns a series of healthy cafes under the Relish brand.

Venison, Squash Purée, Black Pudding Mash, Savoy Cabbage, Elderberry Jus

INGREDIENTS

Squash purée

1x Squash - diced
Vegetable stock
100g Butter
Season to taste

Mashed Potato

4 large Roaster potatoes
100 ml's Cream
50g Butter
Season to taste

Savoy Cabbage

1x Savoy cabbage

Elderberry Jus

200mls Red wine
20g Redcurrant jelly
1x Onion
1x Carrot
1x Leek
1x stick of Celery
(all finely chopped)
2l Veal stock
100g Elderberry chutney

METHOD

Squash purée

Roast squash until soft, add to thermomix.

Add stock a little at a time until you have the right consistency.

Add butter and season to taste

Mashed Potato

Steam the potatoes whole until cooked through.

Cut in half, scoop out the potato and put through a ricer.

Heat the cream and butter, add to potato.

Season to taste

Savoy Cabbage

Finely slice the cabbage removing the roots as you go.

Steam for two minutes

Season to taste

Elderberry Jus

Reduce red wine to a glaze, add jelly.

Caramelise the veg and add to the wine.

Add veal stock and reduce until it's the consistency you require.

Add chutney

399

THE STOCKBRIDGE RESTAURANT

BIOGRAPHY

Jason Gallagher is chef / patron of The Stockbridge Restaurant in the heart of Edinburgh's New Town. The restaurant is nestled below the cobbles of charming St Stephen Street in the Stockbridge area of the city where it has become a firm favourite amongst locals and visitors alike since Jason and his partner Jane Walker took over 12 years ago. In that time Jason has been awarded two AA Rosettes and been named City Chef of the Year at the Scottish Chef of

The Year Awards, as well acquiring numerous other accolades. Priding itself on providing a fine dining experience without the pretentious association, this family-run restaurant has managed to maintain a traditional dining experience for its clientele – white table cloths and polished silver – while putting a creative and modern flare on the Scottish dishes served.

Classically trained, Jason cooks the very best Scottish food with a French influence. As a member of The Slow Food UK Chef Alliance he ensures that ingredients are all locally and sustainably sourced and whilst he takes his lead from classic dishes Jason likes to keep things fresh with an imaginative take, always making the food the star of the show.

Smoked Haddock Chowder With Sea Bream

INGREDIENTS

1lb Smoked haddock

1 fillet of Seabream or seabass

1pt Milk

1 Bay leaf

Thyme

10 Peppercorns

1pt White stock

1lb Shitake mushrooms (or button mushrooms)

2 small Butternut squash or 1 large (peeled and cut into 1cm dice)

2 Onions (diced)

2 cloves Garlic

2 Yellow peppers (diced)

Butter

fine shredded Spinach leaf

METHOD

Place the smoked haddock, white stock, peppercorns, bay leaf and milk into a deep pan and bring to a simmer, slowly adding the thyme. Afterwards, poach the haddock for five minutes before removing it and allowing it to cool until it flakes.

Next, sweat off the vegetables in butter in a deep frying pan at a high heat until they have started to soften. Strain the milk and stock broth over the vegetables and bring to the boil. Reduce the heat, add the flaked haddock and the shredded spinach and simmer for 10 minutes until the vegetables have softened. Before serving be sure to check the seasoning of the dish.

For that extra touch, season and score the skin of a fillets of Seabream or Seabass, place it skin side down in a hot pan with a small amount of vegetable oil and cook for a couple of minutes (depending on the thickness of the skin). Turn it over and cook on the other side for one minute. Serve on the top of a bowl of your delicious chowder.

TOM KITCHEN

23/11/12

BIOGRAPHY

Tom Kitchin, one of Britain's leading chefs, was born in Edinburgh, Scotland and his culinary CV extends from early training at the five-star Gleneagles Hotel to experience garnered working with some of the world's most renowned chefs and restaurants including Pierre Koffmann and the 3 Michelin-starred La Tante Claire, London, 3 Michelin-starred restaurant Guy Savoy in Paris and Alain Ducasse's 3 Michelin-starred restaurant Le Louis XV in Monte Carlo.

The Kitchin's philosophy 'From Nature to Plate', is a true reflection of Chef Tom Kitchin's passion for the finest, freshest Scottish seasonal produce and the cooking at his Michelin star restaurant The Kitchin reflects Tom's training under some of the world's best chefs, blended with his own Scottish heritage.

Tom has become well-known on television, having appeared on BBC's Saturday Kitchen, UKTV Food's Market Kitchen, The Great British Menu as well as headlining BBC series, The Chef's Protégé in 2013. Tom has also joined some of the UK's most renowned chefs as a judge at the MasterChef Chef's Judging Table on a number of occasions.

Strawberry & Yoghurt Panna Cotta

INGREDIENTS

Panna cotta

125g Cream

125g Yoghurt

60g Caster sugar

2 ½ leaves bronze Gelatine - soaked in water until soft

Strawberry consommé

600g Strawberries hulled

60g Caster sugar

Lemon juice to taste

Strawberry jelly

¼ pint Strawberry consommé

1 ½ leaves of Gelatine-soaked in water until soft

Orange confit

2 x Oranges

200ml stock Syrup

Juice of one Orange

Strawberry crisps

100g Caster sugar

100g Water

100g Strawberries

Strawberry coulis

100g Strawberries hulled

10g Icing sugar

Lemon juice

Meringue ingredients

6 large Egg whites

1½ teaspoons White wine vinegar

250g Caster sugar

1 teaspoon Cornflour

Strawberry sorbet:

500g Strawberries hulled

112g Caster sugar

38g Glucose powder

Lemon juice

METHOD

Panna cotta method (done before service):

In a heavy bottom pan warm the cream and sugar on a low heat until the sugar dissolves

Add the gelatine and stir before adding the yoghurt

Whisk together until smooth

Strawberry consommé method (done before service):

Place all the ingredients in a bowl. Wrap the entire bowl in tin foil and place over a pan of simmering water.

Allow 2 hours of cooking, topping up water if required.

Add lemon juice to taste

Pass liquid through a muslin cloth

Strawberry jelly method (done before service):

Warm half of the consommé and add the gelatine leaves and mix

Once the leaves have dissolved, add the rest of the consommé

To Build the Panna Cotta ((done before service):

Taking four to six moulds, alternate a layer of panna cotta and a layer of jelly allowing each layer to set (45 minutes) before adding the next

Store in the fridge to keep chilled

Juice of one orange

Orange confit method (done before service):

Peel and remove the white from the skin

Take the orange skin, and cut it into triangles before blanching three times

Cover the skin triangles in sugar syrup with the juice of one orange and cook slowly

Strawberry crisps method (done before service):

Boil the water and sugar for 4 minutes to the boil

Slice the strawberries thinly, dip in the cooled syrup

Place on a greaseproof tray

Dry overnight in a low oven at 70 degrees

Strawberry coulis method:

Blend all the ingredients together and pass through a fine sieve

Meringue method (done before service):

Heat the oven to 100°C. Line a large baking sheet with baking parchment. To make the meringue, using an electric mixer or electric hand whisk, whisk the egg whites with the white wine vinegar until they begin to froth and increase in volume. Now whisk in two-thirds of the sugar, a little at a time. When stiff peaks form, add the remaining sugar and sift in the cornflour. Fold in, using a large metal spoon, until just incorporated.

Spoon the meringue into a piping bag and start to pipe small kisses on the baking sheet. Place these into the oven and let the meringue kisses dry out for 35 - 45 minutes. Turn off the oven but leave them in there with the door open to cool completely.

Strawberry sorbet method (done before service):

Blend all the ingredients together

Add the lemon juice to taste so it's not too sweet

Pass and churn in an ice cream machine

To serve (prepared during service):

- Carefully remove the panna cottas from their moulds and place in individual bowls
- Place panna cotta in the middle of bowl
- Cut strawberries into nice pieces and coat in some coulis and place around the panna cotta
- Place 3 orange confit nicely
- Place 3 meringues around
- Put 1 crisp on top the panna cotta to hold the sorbet
- Place 2 more crisps nicely
- Dress the strawberries in nice flowers or herbs, maybe use lemon thyme
- Put a small quenelle of sorbet on top the panna cotta and serve consommé in a jug to be poured at the table

21212

BIOGRAPHY

Paul began his career in catering at the age of 20. Since that time he knew instinctively that being a chef was for him.

After completing three years of catering studies, Paul secured roles at various Michelin-starred restaurants including Canterbury's 74 Restaurant and Gidleigh Park. He later moved to Nunsmere Hall Hotel in Cheshire as Head Chef where his partnership with Katie O'Brien began. Glowing reviews followed. Paul answered an ad in Caterer & Hotelkeeper which read "Wanted; an artistic person with an open mind, flair and imagination for new concept in cooking." This led to his collaboration with Juniper in Greater Manchester.

While his creations yielded unexpected combinations the deep thought given to the balance of each dish ensures flavours that complement rather than compete and meals that are memorably exciting. Juniper received accolades and praise from fellow chefs and reviewers alike and became the North West's only 4AA rosette restaurant and Greater Manchester's only Michelin-starred restaurant as well as ranking in the top 20 restaurants in The Good Food Guide and England's Restaurant of the Year in 2003.

Paul and Katie relocated to Edinburgh and opened 21212, a restaurant with rooms, in May 2009. The restaurant received numerous awards immediately after opening including winning the Best New Restaurant in the UK in 2009 at the National Restaurant Awards. In January 2010, only eight months after opening, 21212 received a Michelin Star. At the Catering in Scotland Awards 21212 has scored a hat trick with Best Newcomer in 2010, Paul Kitching as Best Chef in 2011 and Best Restaurant in 2012. In 2013 it was the only restaurant in the UK to be awarded four AA rosettes.

Lemon Tart
glazed curds, blueberry puree, innis & gunn beer

INGREDIENTS

Sweet Pastry
250g Plain flour

50g Butter

50g Icing sugar

1 Whole egg

1 Tablespoon water

Lemon Curd
750ml Double cream

4 Lemons

100g Caster sugar

4 Eggs

Blueberry Puree
25g Dried blueberries

250g Fresh blueberries

100ml Stock syrup

Stock Syrup
100g Caster sugar

100ml Water

1 x Vanilla pod
(split & seeds scraped)

Other Ingredients
1 Bottle of innis & gunn
beer

Dried fruit of your choice

Tart case size – 4 x 3"

METHOD

To make the stock syrup. Put water, sugar and vanilla in a pan. Bring to the boil and simmer for five minutes. Take off the heat and leave to cool.

Next make the sweet pastry dough. Put flour, sugar and butter into a bowl. Rub together until it resembles a bread crumb consistency. Beat the egg, add to flour mix. Add water until the dough is bound together. Roll into a ball. Refrigerate and leave to rest for at least 30 minutes. Line tart cases and blind bake for 10 – 12 minutes at 170°c, leave to cool.

Lemon Curd Method:
Zest and juice lemons, place in a pan with the syrup. Heat until the sugar has dissolved.
Mix the eggs and cream. Add to the sugar and lemon.
Return to the heat. Cook out stirring continuously to avoid the egg from scrambling. Once thickened and bubbles start appearing on the surface pass through a fine sieve and refrigerate.

Blueberry Puree Method:
Heat the stock syrup.
Add blueberries, heat through to break up the fruit. Blitz in a blender until smooth. Then pass through a fine sieve.

TO ASSEMBLE AND SERVE

Take the tart case add a spoon of puree to the bottom then cover with the cooled lemon curd using a pallet knife smooth it until level. Sieve icing sugar generously on top caramelising with a blow torch. Place on a plate and dust with icing sugar, serve the tart with a selection of dried blueberries or Scottish dried fruit of your choice.

Place a shot of Innis and Gunn in a glass. Heat a little milk then froth and spoon the foam on top of the beer - serve.

PEEBLES HYDRO

BIOGRAPHY

Proud Fifer, Chris Hazelton Head Chef at Peebles Hydro in the Scottish Borders. Chris served his time in some of Fife's premier establishments under both Ian MacDonald and Craig Millar.

In May 2015 he joined the Peebles team, finding a perfect match with many of his beliefs and ideas. From the chickens in the gardens, bee hives on the grounds and the herb garden within touching distance of his kitchen. Chris believes these are invaluable tools for his team and young guests alike – a chance for them to see food in its truest form as it comes through the seasons naturally.

As Chris says "It really doesn't get any more local than this, in the grounds of your own hotel, utilising and incorporating ingredients into the menu whenever possible".

Vanilla Panna Cotta

Scottish raspberry consommé, raspberry & micro coriander salad, pistachio & demerara tuille

INGREDIENTS

Panna cotta

Double cream 450ml

Whole milk 450ml

Caster sugar 75g

Vanilla pod 2

Gelatine 5 sheets

Consommé

Scottish raspberries 500g

Water 500ml

Caster sugar 25g

Salad

Scottish raspberries 18 (large)

Micro coriander 10g

Tuille

Puff pastry 100g

Pistachio 50g

Demerara sugar 20g

Egg yolk 1

METHOD

For the panna cotta

De seed the vanilla. Bring the vanilla (pod and seeds), cream, milk and sugar to the boil, remove from heat. Soften the gelatine sheets in cold water, add to the mixture and dissolve. Pass through a fine sieve. Allow to cool slightly. Pour into glass, place in fridge to cool fully and set.

For the consommé

Slowly bring the water, berries and sugar to a light simmer, allow berries to poach for 15 minutes. Remove from heat pass through fine sieve and allow to cool.

For the tuille

Cut the pastry into fine strips, brush with egg yolk. Coat the strips with demerara and crumbed pistachio. Bake for 15 minutes at 140'c

To assemble

Pour the consommé into the glass to cover the top of the panna cotta, place the raspberries in the centre of the consommé and garnish with micro coriander. Finally place the tuille in the glass and serve.

KNOCKINAAM LODGE

30/08/14

BIOGRAPHY

Tony's career path first began in his home city of Manchester at the Brittania Hotel. The Head Chef quickly noticed his talents and encouraged him to head up to Gleneagles Hotel where he could develop his skills further. From there he went on a journey through Michelin Star establishments including Mallory Court, The Box Tree and Inverlochy Castle and then onto his first Sous Chef position at Llangeod Hall.

Arriving at Knockinaam Lodge by chance back in 1994 as Head Chef, Tony fulfilled his dream of winning his own Michelin Star which he retained for a record 20 years. Tony was awarded the prestigious Scottish Chef of the Year 2008.

Knockinaam Lodge is situated in its own cove in the South West of Scotland and has 10 ensuite bedrooms, five of which have fabulous sea views over to Northern Ireland. The lodge is steeped in history, Winston Churchill met General Eisenhower during WW2 and the area was the setting for John Buchan's 39 Steps.

Hot Apple Crumble Soufflé
with double vanilla bean ice cream

INGREDIENTS

4 Granny smith apples

4 dsp Crumble topping

4 tbsp Crème patisserie

8 Egg whites

2 tbsp Caster sugar
(1 tbsp for apple purée and
1 tbsp for soufflé)

Crème Patisserie

1 pt Milk

1 Vanilla pod
(split lengthways)

100g Caster sugar

25g Cornflour

25g Flour

4 Egg yolks

Crumble Topping

100g Plain flour

50g Caster sugar

50g Butter

1 dsp Porridge oats

Pinch of mixed spice

METHOD

Line four ramekins with melted butter and chill until the butter has hardened. Reline the four ramekins with melted butter then coat in caster sugar. Leave in a cool place.

To make the crème patisserie place the milk in a pan. Scrape seeds from the vanilla pod and add into the milk. Boil. In a bowl cream sugar, egg yolks, flour and cornflour. Pour the hot milk onto the sugar mixture while whisking. Once combined pour back into a clean pan and cook over a medium heat for approximately 3 minutes until it thickens. Cool and store until required.

To make the crumble topping rub the flour and butter together until it resembles fine breadcrumbs. Stir in the sugar, porridge oats and mixed spice. Sprinkle the mixture thinly over a baking tray and bake in a pre-heated oven at 170ºC until lightly golden. Leave to cool.

Peel, core and dice the Granny Smith apples and place into a small pan with 1 tablespoon of caster sugar and 1 tablespoon of water. With a lid on the pan cook on a gentle heat until the apples are tender. Purée with a hand blender while the apples are still hot. Keep warm.

In a mixing bowl whisk the egg whites with the remaining caster sugar until it forms soft peaks. Warm half of the apple purée with the crème patisserie and mix together.

Whisk in one third of the egg whites to the apple purée and crème patisserie mixture. With a spatula fold in the remaining two thirds of the egg whites making sure you retain as much air as possible.

Fill the ramekins half full with the soufflé mix. Add a teaspoon of the remaining apple purée to the centre of each of the ramekins. Fill the ramekins with the remaining soufflé mixture. Level and then run the tip of a knife around the edge to break the seal and let the soufflé rise evenly. Sprinkle the crumble mixture on top.

Bake in a pre heated oven (170ºC) for 6-7 minutes. Dust with icing sugar and serve immediately with a scoop of double vanilla bean ice cream. You could either have a go at making your own ice-cream or use a luxury alternative. Enjoy.

MONACHYLE MHOR

BIOGRAPHY

Marysia is originally from Gdansk in Poland and moved to Scotland in 2006. She trained at Forth Valley College, Falkirk. Marysia has been working at Monachyle Mhor with Tom Lewis, chef and owner, since 2010 becoming head chef in 2013. In the same year Marysia was also a quarter finalist on BBC Two's Masterchef – The Professionals.

Monachyle Mhor Hotel is a family run hotel. The family have grown the businesses to include a bakery, a fish restaurant/ chippy, a farm and a motel. All of the businesses are branded under the name of Mhor.

The hotel's cooking style is seasonal and they use local produce at every opportunity. The Mhor farm supplies the beef, pork and lamb to the restaurants. The venison used is also shot on the 2000-acre estate. Mhor have their own gardens where they also grow their own vegetables, herbs & salads.

Garden Rhubarb Bavarois
Poached Rhubarb, Pine Head Oatmeal Praline, Origin Honeygar Ice Cream

METHOD

Rhubarb Bavarois:

Bring milk and rhubarb puree to boil, stirring it occasionally. Meanwhile soak gelatine in cold water until is bloomed.

Whisk egg yolk and caster sugar until pale and thick. Pour rhubarb mixture into the egg yolks, stirring with the whisk. Pour the mixture back to the sauce pan , add lemon juice and cook gently until is thick enough to coat the back of the spoon.

Strain it through chinois, squeeze water out of gelatine and add to rhubarb mixture, stir until dissolves. Let it cool down completely.

Make the Italian meringue and fold with rhubarb 'custard' , in another bowl semi whip cream and fold with the rest. Pour it into lined tray or individual moulds. Place it in the fridge for at least 8hrs to set completely.

Poached Rhubarb:

Put the chopped rhubarb, butter, sugar, vanilla pod and brandy into a small saucepan. Bring to the boil, then reduce the heat to gently poach the rhubarb until it has softened. Add more sugar if the rhubarb is too sharp.

Origin Honeygar Ice Cream:

Bring milk , double cream and vanilla gradually to boil. Meanwhile whisk egg yolks, caster sugar, liquid glucose till pale white, pour boiled milk over whisked eggs yolk and stir fast.

Pour back the mixture to the pot and on medium heat, stirring constantly, let the mixture to thicken up until covers the back of the spoon. Add reduced apple juice and honeygar.

Pass through fine chinois into a bowl and let it cool over iced water.

 Pour the mixture to ice cream machine, and churn ice cream. Place in the freezer.

Pinehead Oatmeal Praline:

Place the sugar and oatmeal into a saucepan over a medium heat and caramelise gently, stirring to coat the oatmeal.

Once browned, pour the mixture out onto a non-stick baking sheet, spread out and leave to cool. Once cooled and set, smash the praline into pieces with a rolling pin.

Bitter Orange Puree

Heat orange, sugar, and 2 cups of water in heavy-bottomed saucepan set over medium-high heat, stirring to dissolve sugar; cook until orange is very soft; remove from heat.

Place orange in a blender, blend until smooth, adding cooking liquid as needed. Gradually add 1 tbsp. of Cointreau blend well.

INGREDIENTS

Rhubarb Bavarois:
200g Rhubarb puree
40ml full fat Milk
4 Egg yolks
25g Caster sugar
3 Gelatine leaves
200g Double cream
125g Italian Meringue
juice from 1 Lemon

Poached Rhubarb:
2 sticks Rhubarb (chopped into even pieces)
30g/1oz Butter
4 tbsp Caster sugar
1 Vanilla pod (split)
splash of Brandy

Origin Honeygar Ice Cream:
150ml full fat Milk
350ml Double cream
1 pod of Vanilla (cut in half, scrape seeds out)
25g Caster sugar
5 Egg yolks
10g Liquid glucose
500ml of Apple juice (reduce to 75ml)
100ml of Origin honeygar

Pinehead Oatmeal Praline:
100g Pinehead oatmeal (toasted)
100g Caster sugar

Bitter Orange Puree:
1 Orange
200g Granulated sugar
1 tbsp of Cointreau

Macmillian Cancer Support

Macmillan's ambition is to reach and improve the lives of everyone living with cancer and to inspire millions of others to do the same.

For a long time, cancer meant a death sentence. But the story of cancer is changing. There isn't just one cancer, but over 200. We're getting better at diagnosing it earlier and treatments are improving. While some people will still die of their cancer, more people are living longer with it, and some are surviving it.

This means that more people than ever need our support. There are 2.5 million people living with cancer in the UK and by 2030 that number will rise to 4 million. That's equivalent to the population of Leeds, Liverpool, Bristol, Birmingham, Belfast, Edinburgh, Cardiff and Plymouth.

When you're facing cancer, it can feel like you've lost control. Macmillan is here to help you take it back.

Whether it's a nurse being there from the moment you're diagnosed; a helping hand with your everyday chores, advice about money worries or just someone ready to listen when you need to talk.

Cancer isn't going away, but we can all help make sure no one faces it alone, by donating or volunteering, campaigning or raising money in whatever way you choose.

Together we are all Macmillan cancer support.

For support every step of the way, call the Macmillan Support Line Free on 0808 808 00 00 or visit www.macmillan.org.uk

We couldn't provide all the support we do without you.

If you want to get involved, in whatever way you can, call us today on 0300 1000 200

Hospitality Action

Offering grants, counselling and advice, Hospitality Action provides a real lifeline to thousands of hospitality industry workers in need.

Angela was heartbroken as she very bravely underwent a mastectomy followed by multiple courses of chemo and radiotherapy.

The treatment left Angela feeling tired and weak and caused her to gain weight meaning her clothes no longer fitted. As she spent more time at home the heating bills rose. Mother to two daughters and relying on her husband's wages the family began to struggle.

It was here that Hospitality Action stepped in.

We were able to provide a grant for better fitting clothing and a contribution towards the increased heating bills. The money also went towards a much-needed family holiday.

Angela Tanner
Bar Manager -
Edinburgh

Angela says: "Your help has been invaluable. I cannot put into words how much we benefited from some time away together, I didn't once think of cancer. I was in hospital for more surgery recently and we all enjoyed looking through the holiday photos together, that says it all."

Please support our work so we can help even more people suffering with life changing illness Angela was forced to give up her job as a Bar Manager having been in the role for nearly ten years, when she was diagnosed with breast cancer.

For more information and ways to support the charity please contact:

Hospitality Action
62 Britton Street
London
EC1M 5UY

Tel: 020 3004 5500 | Fax: 020 7235 2094 | www.hospitalityaction.org.uk | info@hospitalityaction.org.uk
facebook.com/HospitalityAction | Twitter: @HospAction @HospActionNorth

Northern Ireland

Starter
Main
Dessert

MERCHANT HOTEL

BIOGRAPHY

John Paul Leake
Executive Chef, The Great Room Restaurant at The Merchant Hotel

John Paul Leake's career began in 1997 in his native city of Belfast, where he worked in a number of well-established restaurants before travelling to Asia and Australia. Upon his return, he moved to London to further enhance his culinary skills and worked at the Michelin star Mirabelle restaurant for Marco Pierre White before joining the world-renowned two Michelin star restaurant, The Square, under Phil Howard. He then moved on to the Orrery restaurant before returning to Belfast to pass on this world class experience. John Paul has been working at The Merchant Hotel's Great Room Restaurant for more than six years. The five-star hotel is situated in the heart of Belfast city centre and The Great Room is undoubtedly one of Northern Ireland's most extraordinary restaurants with its stunning Victorian interior complete with Ireland's largest chandelier. John Paul has worked tirelessly to ensure the food matches its magnificent surroundings. The Great Room Restaurant delivers elegant, contemporary incarnations of classical dishes using only the finest seasonal ingredients. The restaurant has been awarded 2 AA Rosettes and John Paul has been at the helm of a number of unique events - from Opera evenings to MTV award dinners - and has cooked food for everyone from high-profile dignitaries to the biggest artists in the world such as Madonna, Robbie Williams and Kylie.

Dressed Kilkeel Crab
cucumber jelly, prawn beignet, soft egg, avocado puree and water cress

INGREDIENTS

3 medium Crabs (approx. 800g each)

1 Lemon

100g chopped Chives

30g chopped Flat leaf parsley

3g Cayenne pepper

3g Celery salt

100ml Mayonnaise

Avocado puree

4 ripe Avocados (flesh only)

100g Crème fraiche

1 Lemon juiced

Pinch of salt

little cold Water (to slightly loosen)

Cucumber jelly

3 medium Cucumbers (chopped)

10ml Sherry vinegar

Pinch of salt

2.5 g of soaked Gelatine for every 100g of cucumber juice.

Prawn beignet

50g Self-rising flour

Pinch of salt

90mls sparkling Water

2g Lemon juice

METHOD

Cooking the crab

Fill a deep pot with water and bring to the boil. Place the crabs inside and cook for 16 minutes on a medium heat. Once cooked place into the fridge until cold then take out and remove the legs, pick out the white meat and place into a medium bowl. Zest the lemon into the crab and add the cayenne pepper, celery salt, herbs and mayonnaise. Mix very well then taste the mixture and add extra seasoning to taste. Place mixture into round moulds, top with chives and serve.

Cucumber jelly

Blend the cucumbers with a pinch of salt and sherry vinegar until smooth, then add the gelatine and pass through an extra fine sieve into a 3cm deep tray. Leave to set in the fridge for 4 hours then cut into small square pieces.

Quail eggs

Boil the quail eggs for 2 minutes 30 seconds then place into ice water. Peel and serve by cutting in half and sprinkling with a little cracked white pepper (caviar optional).

Prawn beignet

Mix all ingredients together and leave to set for 30 minutes. Lightly flour the prawns and deep fry until golden.

This dish can be served with picked watercress, sour dough Melba, dill pickled cucumber and caviar.

CORICK HOUSE

BIOGRAPHY

Chef Aaron Duffy joined the team at Corick House Hotel & Spa in 2015 bringing with him a passion, flair and natural talent for all things food. Having travelled and worked in Austrailia, London and Belfast, Aaron developed his knowledge and skills. Having competed in Young National Chef of the Year for the UK, Craft Guild of Chefs Graduate Award, IFEX, Euro Toques Young Chef of the Year to name a few, Aaron shows his commitment and appetite for the industry.

After a significant investment of over £4 million within the last four years, Corick House Hotel is the only 4* hotel in Co. Tyrone, bringing you back in time with period style, where you can escape from the hustle and bustle of everyday life with breath taking views of the valleys and mountains.

Aaron's ethos is to source ingredients close to home that are seasonal and sustainable. His love of classical dishes, techniques and flavours combined with a quirky, modern twist are evident in his food. "For me flavour is key, we work on dish and ingredients thinking how can we incorporate as much flavour in this ingredient as possible, then we work on mouthfeel, textures and presentation"

Silverhill Duck Breast
with apple and elderflower, blackberry ketchup,
glazed carrots, baby turnips, fondant potato and duck jus

INGREDIENTS

Duck
4 Duck breast
200g Duck bones
4 Duck skin

Duck jus
200g Duck bones
2 Star anise
1 Cinnamon stick
250ml Red wine
1 Carrot
2 Shallot
3 cloves Garlic
1 washed Leek
1 sprig Thyme
500ml Duck stock
50g Red currant jelly

Apple and elderflower
2 Granny smiths
250ml Elderflower cordial
100g Castor sugar

Blackberry ketchup
100g Blackberry's
50g Castor sugar
1 Cinnamon stick
50g Ultratex

Vegetables
8 Baby carrots
4 Baby turnip
50g Sugar
1 sprig Thyme

Fondant potato
4 Maris piper potato
250g Butter

Apple crisp
1 Granny smith
Stock syrup

METHOD

Duck jus

Roast the bones and the vegetables together until golden brown then add to a large surface pot. Using the red wine de glaze the roasting tray and add the wine to the pot and reduce. Now add the duck stock and reduce for around 2 – 3 hours. Pass the jus through a fine chinois then reduce and season until you're happy with flavour and consistency. Once happy pass the jus through a muslin cloth.

Apple and elderflower puree

Peel the apples and then cook in the elderflower cordial and add sugar. Once cook blitz to a fine puree and pass.

Blackberry ketchup

Toast the cinnamon stick then add the fresh blackberry's and sugar. If you need to add liquid you can always add a little water to thin. Blitz to a fine puree and pass. Then add in the ultratex which will thicken the puree to give a beautiful mouth feel.

Fondant

Peel the potato and square of, using a round cutter cut through the potato but leave the cut out potato in the whole potato. Now heat the butter until foaming. Add the potato and cook in the oven for at 180°c for 30 mins. Once cooked pop out the cut potato which will reveal a beautiful white potato with a golden brown top.

Vegetables

In a sauce pot using thyme, salt, garlic and boiling water cook the turnip for 12 minutes then sauté in foaming butter. For the carrots bring the sugar and water to the boil and add the carrots then cover with a cartouche and cook for 10 minutes until caramelised.

Apple crisp

Thinly slice the apple and dip in stock syrup then place into dehydrator until crisp.

Crispy skin

Take the duck skin from the legs and place onto a roasting tray. Season well with sea salt and cook for 10 minutes at 180°c. then place onto a jay cloth to take away any excess fat.

Duck breast

For the duck breast slice the skin with a sharp knife being careful not to go into the breast and season well. Place onto a cold frying pan with no oil and onto a low heat gradually increasing the temperature. This will render the skin down. Place in the oven for 6 minutes at 190°c. Once the breast is out of the oven add in a knob of butter, sprig of thyme and a clove of garlic. Baste the breast in the butter and then allow to rest for 6 minutes.

For the plating of the dish keep a circle around the plate with the centre free and assemble each element.

CULLODEN ESTATE & SPA

BIOGRAPHY

Chef Paul McKnight started working for Hastings Hotels at 17 years of age and worked his way through the ranks. He attended Portrush Catering College prior to joining the Hotel Group.

During his 35+ years of culinary service he has completed culinary stages at The Ritz Hotel, London and also gained experience in the Grand Hyatt, The Palace, Aquavit, The Mark Hotel and the world famous Plaza Hotel at Central Park, New York.

For the last 10 years Paul has been lucky to have some of the most world famous Chefs from the UK and Ireland join him and his brigade at the Culloden. These have included Gordon Ramsey, Phil Howard, Raymond Blanc, and Derry Clarke.

One of the keys to his success is his pledge to give all guests a taste of what makes his local menus so special. The island of Ireland has a proud heritage of farming and fishing, resulting in an abundance of sensational produce and he wants to give every diner a true taste of this in every dish he serves. Local food provenance is very important to Chef Paul and this is particularly true with 2016 being Northern Ireland's Year of Food and Drink.

Five Mile Town Goats Cheese Curd Comber Beets
& broighter gold rapeseed oil

INGREDIENTS

200g of Fivemile town rindless goats cheese

150mls of Double cream

1 red Beetroot

1 Golden beetroot

1 packet Popcorn shoots

2 Comber sorted radishes

tea spoon of Boighter gold rapeseed oil

Viola flowers (optional)

tea spoon of Honey

White truffle oil

A couple of sprigs of Thyme

Maldon sea salt

4 large Apples

1 litre of Apple juice

10.3 of Agar Agar

a taste of Balsamic vinegar

1 Torpedo shallot

25gs of Butter

METHOD

Goats cheese cured, thinned down with double cream until consistency of a light puree.

Cook beets until slightly firm middle, peel and cool.

Cut purple beetroot into inch and a half batons.

Cube golden beetroot

Melt tea spoon of honey, a splash of white truffle oil, toss golden beetroot in.

For red beets, roast in oven with thyme and sea salt for 5 minutes.

To make apple gel, peel 4 large green apples and 1 litre of apple juice. Bring to 86 degrees and add 10.3g of Agar Agar. Whisk in and cool to set. Once set, blitz and pass through chinois. Once done gel ready.

For beetroot puree, boil until soft, remove from cooking liquor. Peel, add to food processor with 2 table spoons of balsamic vinegar. Season. Pass through chinois.

Pan roast torpedo shallot until golden brown and season with butter.

Dress plate as photo with trimmed popcorn shoots and rainbow radishes.

At Culloden Estate & Spa we present on a green plate to showcase colours.

MOURNE
SEAFOOD BAR

BIOGRAPHY

Andy Rea is one of the most prolific and experienced chefs working in Northern Ireland today. From his roots training in catering at the Belfast Institute, Andy went on to work throughout America before returning to Belfast to work as Head Chef for Paul Rankin at his one Michelin star (Northern Ireland's first) restaurant Roscoff, latterly Cayenne, scooping numerous national accolades along the way, firmly cementing his name in culinary history. In 2006, in partnership with seafood farming duo Joanne and Bob McCoubrey, Andy opened 'Mourne Seafood Bar' in the heart of Belfast to critical acclaim for its no nonsense affordable approach to fresh local seafood. A plethora of industry awards followed and the trio have gone on to open a Dublin branch in the Grand Canal basin in April 2014.

Asian Noodle Cakes
with mango salsa

INGREDIENTS

400g mixed Seafood, prawn nest, scallops, cod, salmon etc. (No skin or bones)

1 Egg

1-2 tsp Thai green curry paste, more if you like it hot

25g fresh Coriander chopped

1/2 bunch Scallions, chopped fine

100g fine Egg noodles (follow cooking instructions) cooked and dried

Mango Salsa

1 large ripe Mango, diced

1/2 Red chilli, finely diced

15g Coriander, finely chopped

2 Scallions, finely diced

1 tsp. pickled Ginger, finely diced

zest of 1/2 Lime

juice of Lime

METHOD

Take 100g of the seafood and cut into small dice (1/2 cm). Transfer into a large bowl, then add coriander and scallions. Season with sea salt and black pepper.

In a food processor, blitz the rest of the seafood with curry paste, egg, sea salt and black pepper.

Add the processed seafood to the diced seafood and mix. This is the base of your fish cakes. Mould into 8 small equally sized patties.

Roll patties in cooked egg noodles, squeezing noodles into the cakes.

Pre-heat fryer to 160°C, fry noodle cakes until light golden colour and lift fry basket for 1 minute and then re-fry until golden.

Mango Salsa

Mix all of the above ingredients together and season with a little Thai fish sauce. This can be made the day before. Keep refrigerated.

LOUGH ERNE RESORT

BIOGRAPHY

Noel McMeel, one of Ireland's top chefs and a man who has dedicated his life to the obsessive pursuit of food excellence. If that makes him sound like a culinary recluse, the good news is that he's anything but. Noel encapsulates a wonderful combination of charisma, charm and wit, with a hint of self- effacement that makes him instantly likeable, qualities that are backed up by his formidable cooking talent. "My father always said, "...never forget the field you were foaled in..", which simply means to never forget where you come from. And I haven't. My roots are still firmly set in the Irish soil of my family farm and the values I learned there about the quality and integrity of foodstuff are probably more relevant to me now than ever before." Mind you, Noel's cooking style has moved on somewhat from the days when he helped his mother make soda farls in the working kitchen. Today he's just as likely to be found preparing a celebrity gourmet bash in Washington, introducing a new television audience to the secrets of fine food or creating a menu for diners at the Lough Erne Resort in county Fermanagh, where he is head chef. Indeed, with celebrity credentials which include Paul McCartney's vegetarian wedding extravaganza, and no less than five invitations to cook celebration dinners at the world renowned James Beard Foundation, Noel's culinary reputation is now firmly established on the international scene.

Lobster, Sea Bream & Salted Squid
with buttered asparagus, spring onions & citrus foam

INGREDIENTS

Sea Bream

4 fillets Sea bream, skin on (scaled)

1 tbsp Extra virgin olive oil + extra to finish

juice of 1/2 Lemon

Sea salt and freshly ground pepper to taste

1 Lobster

2litre (2 quarts/8 cups) boiling salted Water

500g / 18 ounces melted Butter

1medium Squid, cleaned and sliced

2 Limes

Extra-virgin olive oil

1/2 teaspoon Salt

Citrus Foam

1 1/2 cups Orange juice

2 tbsp Sugar

½ pt / 1 ¼ cups Heavy cream

1/2 Lemon

1 1/2 sheets Gelatine

Court-bouillon

½ lit / 2 cups White wine

1litre / 1 quart / 4 cups

Water

2 tbsp White vinegar

3 stalks Celery, roughly chopped

1 Carrot, peeled and roughly chopped

1 Leek, rinsed and roughly chopped

1 Yellow onion, peeled and roughly chopped

2 cloves Garlic

1 Fennel bulb, roots and green top cut off, sliced in thick wedges

METHOD

Bring a very large saucepan of salted water to the boil. Using long tongs, quickly but carefully lower live lobsters into the boiling water. Simmer for about 10 minutes, or until lobsters are bright red. Remove and leave to cool

Sea Bream:

Cut each fillet on top of the skin, 3 times with a sharp knife (this allows the heat to penetrate more easily). Season with 4 pinches of salt and 2 of pepper.
Over a high heat, in a large, ovenproof frying pan, heat the oil. Sear the fillets on the flesh side for 30-40 seconds in the hot olive oil. Turn the fillets over and cook for 2-3 minutes. Transfer to the oven and cook for 2-3 minutes longer, depending on thickness. Taste and correct the seasoning, if necessary, then sprinkle the lemon juice over the fillets.

Court-Bouillon:

Bring all court bouillon ingredients to a boil in a medium sauce pan, lower to a simmer, and cook 15 to 20 minutes.

Place squid in medium saucepan. Strain hot court bouillon over the squid. Turn heat on low so that liquid steams but does not simmer, for 1 minute. Taste a squid ring: it should be just opaque and tender. If still chewy and translucent, cook for another 30 seconds to 1 minute but no longer. Also add the Asparagus into your stock for less that 1 minute.

Citrus Foam:

Combine orange juice and sugar and reduce over medium heat by half. Add the juice of half lemon. Add gelatine in cold water until soft, about 5 minutes, then squeeze gently to remove excess water and add to warm juice reduction. Add juice to heavy cream and strain through a sieve. Shake and refrigerate for 2-4 hours before using. I use it into a thermo pack but when using it you can add it to a blender and mix for 1-2 minutes, and always make sure that the foam is warm when serving.

To serve, put all of the ingredients neatly onto a warm serving bowl and pour foam around the sides of the fish. SERVES 4

THE IVORY

BIOGRAPHY

The Ivory Restaurant & Bar is a chic and contemporary restaurant located in the heart of Belfast City. The Ivory offers fantastic food, excellent service and breath-taking views in stylish surroundings. Situated on the third floor of House of Fraser in Victoria Square. The Ivory has quickly grasped the hearts of food lovers and is making its mark on the Belfast dining out scene.

The Ivory has the largest outdoor dining space in Northern Ireland offering a unique al fresco experience. A favourite amongst locals and celebrities, The Ivory has something for everyone!

Kieron Donnelly has been Head Chef of The Ivory Restaurant since 2009 and since he has made his stamp with signature dishes that our clientele know and love. Ever since a young age Kieron started to feed this passion and dedicated his younger years working and learning under the best of Northern Irish chefs, whilst developing his unique culinary skills.

Seared Saddle of Irish Venison
celeriac fondant & puree, red wine figs & chocolate sauce

INGREDIENTS

200g of Venison saddle loin

1 head of Celeriac

2 Figs

25g Sugar

25ml of Cabernet sauvignon vinegar

500g Butter 400g of which should be clarified

250ml Red wine

250ml of Venison stock

30g Pearl onions

5g Chocolate buttons

500ml Vegetable stock

Olive oil & watercress to garnish

METHOD

Sauce
Mix the pearl onions & the red wine & reduce until the wine has becomes syrupy, add the venison stock and the chocolate buttons, reduce until the sauce becomes dark and glossy.

Figs
Cut the figs in half put the sugar into a small pan & place figs flesh side down. On a low heat gently caramelize the sugar and figs, once caramelized deglaze with the cabernet sauvignon vinegar, reduce until the wine becomes a syrup.

Celeriac fondants and puree
Peel the celeriac and cut it in 4 cm slices, on average you would get three slices, the middle one is probably the best one to use for the fondants. So using a round cutter, cut out three cylinder pieces of celeriac, place the cylinders into a pan add all the clarified butter cook on a low heat until they have softened.

Dice the remainder of the celeriac, then into a pan add the chicken stock and the diced celeriac, boil until there is no bite. Pass the diced celeriac and blend with the butter.

All of the above ingredients can be prepared prior to the cooking of the venison.

Venison
Sear the saddle in hot pan with pomace oil until all sides are caramelized, once caramelised baste the venison for a few minutes with the remaining 100g of butter let it rest for ten minutes. Put into an oven at 190oc for two minutes rest again for 4 minutes. Use these 4 minutes the regenerate the other ingredients. Now its time to plate up.

DEANES EIPIC

BIOGRAPHY

Chef Danni Barry is one of an elite group of female Michelin starred chefs in the UK and only the second female chef ever in Ireland to gain a star.

Danni hails from the Mourne country in Northern Ireland. Her cooking career began in 2003 in the then Michelin starred Deanes in Howard Street with chef Michael Deane.

Four years later Danni went on her travels to South Africa, Australia, New Zealand and mainland Europe, garnering knowledge from the high end restaurants in which she worked along the way.

After a spell at Simon Rogan's l'Enclume, in Cumbria, now the number one restaurant in the UK, she was appointed to head up the kitchen at Rogan & Co in Cartmel, where she remained until Michael Deane persuaded her to come back to Belfast to take the helm at Deanes EIPIC.

Danni is driven by her passion for only the freshest and most seasonal produce being cooked to perfection. Her style is progressive, honest, flavoursome, light, visual, balanced and modern.

Scorched Cod
roasted & pickled cauliflower, bone sauce & costal greens

INGREDIENTS

Cod

1 x 700g - 800g
Sustainably farmed cod
fillet

10g Sea salt

Bone Sauce

1kg White fish bones

500ml White fish stock

100ml White wine

2 cloves Garlic

1 small White onion

1 bulb Fennel

1 Leek

1 sprig Thyme

4 tbsp Double cream

50g Unsalted butter

Cauliflower Purée

1 head White cauliflower

30g Unsalted butter

50ml Double cream

Pickled Cauliflowers

50g Caster sugar

100ml White wine vinegar

150ml Water

1 Shallot

1 sprig Tarragon or thyme

1 Purple cauliflower

1 Romanesco

Coastal Greens

10g Salt

100g Water

20g Butter

METHOD

Cod

Use a sharp, preferably flexible, knife to remove the skin from the cod fillet. Using tweezers remove any pin bones that run along the centre of the fillet. Ask your fishmonger to do this if unsure.
Cut the fillet into 4 even slices weighing around 120g each.
Place each fillet individually on a square of baking foil season with sea salt, drizzle with a little oil and fold up the edges to make a parcel.

Bone Sauce

Wash the bones in cold water, place on a roasting tray and cook in an oven at 180°C for 10 - 12 mins until a deep golden brown.
Dice the vegetables and cook over a low heat with a little oil, stirring often for 10-15 mins until they begin to caramelise. They should be soft and brown in colour.
Add the white wine and fish stock to the vegetables with the thyme and simmer for 10 minutes.
Pass the stock through a fine sieve into a clean saucepan to reduce.

Cauliflower Purée

Trim all the florets from the head of cauliflower. Cut down until approx. 1-2cm in size.
Melt butter in saucepan, add the florets and cook until soft and evenly golden brown in colour.
Add cream and bring to the boil.
Transfer to a blender to make a smooth purée. Add salt to your taste.

Pickled Cauliflowers

Place all the ingredients aside from the cauliflower in a pan and bring to the boil allow to cool slightly.
When lukewarm add small florets or fine slices of the purple cauliflower and romanesco.

The Build

Reduce oven temperature to 160°C
Reduce the roasted bone stock to 300ml, add the cream and reduce until it begins to thicken. Whisk in butter for a glossy finish. Keep warm.
Warm the purée in a small pan, wilt the greens in a little butter until soft.
Place the cod parcels into the oven for 8 mins.
Remove and open the parcel to reveal the top. Use the blowtorch to get an even dark crust on top. Taking care to work quickly and not overcook the fish. You can use a toothpick to check when the fish is ready. It should slide in the centre of the fillet with no resistance.
Spoon over the fillet the juices collected in the foil then remove cod from parcel onto warm plates.
Add a spoonful of the bone sauce. And small spoonful's of the cauliflower purée.
Dress as you wish with the pickled florets, slices of romanesco and greens.
And serve.

OYSTERS

BIOGRAPHY

Oysters Restaurant Strabane was established in 2007 by local husband and wife team, Kevin & Caroline Clarke. In the intervening period, this couple have successfully made their mark on the Northern Ireland stage with a reputation for imaginatively designed cuisine and superb customer service. In turn, Oysters is now acclaimed as one of Northern Irelands finest cuisine gems, having captured the attention not only of their dining clientele but also that of several award bodies and publications which have recognised them on many levels for food, customer service and wine experience. Notably Oysters has been acclaimed "Best Restaurant in Northern Ireland" by License & Catering News both in 2010 and again in 2014. "We are passionate about all aspects of our offering," enthuses Kevin, "with the local provenance of our foods key to our success". Check out Oysters website (www.oystersrestuarant. co.uk) and the corresponding social media platforms to explore blogs delving into the provenance of our suppliers and producers. Only the freshest, seasonal and premium products sourced from local suppliers are acceptable to Oysters, with time and endurance afforded the task of sourcing and approving same. Add to this the refreshingly innovative style of our Head Chef, Niall Gorham, who is equally driven by the same ardour for fresh, seasonal, locally sourced product, including personally growing, hunting, foraging for many of his fresh ingredients and the end result is truly enticing." Round off the package with a reputation for exceptional (albeit unpretentious) customer service and this family-run restaurant provides a veritably exquisite dining experience.

Pan-fried John Dory
with fivemiletown goat's cheese potato cake, tomato, chive & chervil beurre blanc

INGREDIENTS

4 x 100gms John dory fillets

50gms Shallots

3½ floz White wine vinegar

3½ floz White wine (dry)

200gms Unsalted butter

50gms Tomato concasse

15gms Chervil (chopped)

15gms Chive (chopped)

500gms Potatoes

100gms Butter

100gms Goat's cheese

100gms Rocket

Salt & pepper

Flour for dusting

Chervil to garnish

METHOD

Cooking Method - Goat's Cheese Potato Cake

Peel and cut potatoes into pieces of similar size. Place in salted cold water, bring to the boil and simmer gently for 20mins until tender. Drain and mash well. Add butter and seasoning. Leave to cool. After 20/25mins cooling, fill a 2/3 inch cutting ring half way up with the potatoes. Place 25gms of goat's cheese in the middle and top up the ring with more potatoes. Lightly dust with flour and place in fridge.

Cooking Method - Beurre Blanc

Place the shallots, white wine dry, white wine vinegar into a small pan and reduce by ¾. Remove from direct heat, whisk in the butter little by little but don't allow to become too hot. Check for seasoning. Add the tomato, chive and chervil. Leave aside in a warm place.

Cooking Method - John Dory Dish (complete)

In a large to medium size pan, heat up some oil and fry off your potato cake, cooking both sides until golden brown. Remove from pan and place on a tray and remove to a heated oven at 180°C. Allow 8/10mins to heat through.

Heat a medium pan, season the John Dory fillets. When the pan is hot but not smoking hot, place the fillets in the pan skin-side down first. Cook for 2/3mins until the skin is nice and golden. Turn over and cook for another 3mins. Place on a tray and into the oven for about 3/4mins. Aim to have the potato cakes and fish ready at the same time.

Plating Up

Place the potato cake in the centre of the plate, place 25gms of rocket on top of the potato cake and drizzle the sauce around the plate. Place fish on top of the potato cake. Garnish with 3 chervil leaves around the plate(one at 12 o'clock, one at 5 o'clock, one at 7 o'clock). Ready!

JAMES ST SOUTH

BIOGRAPHY

James St. South offers a modern dining experience with great food and an exciting wine list in Belfast city centre.

Originally opened in 2003 by chef Niall McKenna, the interiors have been refurbished by Aidan McGrath (McGonigle and McGrath Architects) transforming the restaurant to give a modern, contemporary feel with its extensive pass and bar area running the length of the restaurant making it glamorous and unique; the perfect place for that pre dinner drink.

The menu served up by Head Chef David Gillmore focuses on classic cooking using the best of locally sourced produce.

Antrim Beef Fillet
ox cheek lasagne & English asparagus

INGREDIENTS

4 x 160 Fillet steaks

4 x 40g Braised beef cheek pieces

1litre Beef stock

1 bunch x Asparagus spears

12 x Wild asparagus spears

fresh Truffle

Pasta

250g OO Pasta flour

170g Egg yolk

Salt

For the sauce

50g Butter

200g Shallots

200ml Red wine

400ml Beef stock

1 Bouquet garni

Salt and pepper

METHOD

Braise the ox cheek in beef stock at 150°c for 3 hours.

To make the pasta, mix the flour and salt with the yolk until incorporated and then knead for 5 minutes. Allow to rest in the fridge before rolling. Once rested, roll until thin and blanch in boiling water. Remove and cut into squares 8cm x 8cm.

For the sauce heat the butter in a large pan and add finely chopped shallots and sauté until golden brown.

Add in the red wine and simmer until the liquid is reduced by three quarters. Add in the bouqet garni and the beef stock and return to the boil and simmer until reduced by half. At the restaurant we add butter at this stage to the sauce to get a nice gloss to it, for the same effect add 20g butter and whisk until melted.

Trim the asparagus and reserve 4 spears for garnish. Chop the rest and sweat off in butter until soft. Once soft, season with salt and pepper and blend until smooth.

Place the beef fillets in a hot pan and colour on all sides. Place in a pre heated oven on 180°c and cook for 4 minutes on each side. Allow to rest for 5 minutes in a warm place before serving.

To serve place the asparagus puree on the plate and top with the beef cheek. Top with the past square and top with blanched green and wild asparagus. Carve the beef and present on the plate. Serve with grated fresh truffles and some of the reduced ox cheek stock.

LINEN HILL

BIOGRAPHY

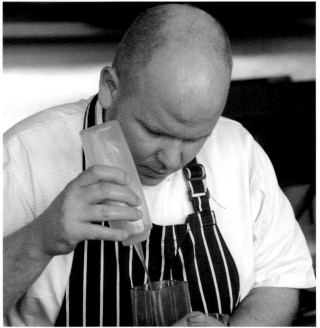

Shaun Hanna, grew up the busy fishing port of Kilkeel, Co. Down, and studied at Southern Regional College, Newry, Northern Ireland, before starting work at the acclaimed Hastings's Slieve Donard Hotel, Newcastle, Co Down.

From there Shaun progressed to the Hilton St Anne's Manor Berkshire, before returning to Ireland during the Celtic Tiger boom, where he began his first role as head chef at The Oarsman in Carrick on Shannon.

Shaun enjoyed a season on the Yachts of Seabourn, under the direction of Charlie Palmer before returning to the UK to work under Chris Marshall at Panoramic 34, Liverpool.

He returned to Northern Ireland in 2011 to open Canteen at The MAC in the award winning MAC theatre, in the bustling Cathedral Quarter of Belfast. Shaun then opened his own restaurant with business partners John and Fiona Robinson at The OUTLET Village, Banbridge, Co. Down. Since opening in 2013, Shaun has gained the title of NI Chef of the Year 2014, and has been awarded several 2014 Great Taste Award stars for his products they sell under the Linen Hill brand. Whether, it's locally shot wild venison, home grown vegetables or the freshest daily catch - Shaun's menu will always reflect his favourite phrase 'keeping it local'.

Beetroot Cured Glenarm Salmon
pickled vegetables, carlingford oyster fritter

INGREDIENTS

Cured Salmon

1 side Glenarm salmon – skin on & pin boned

4 whole Beetroot – peeled & grated

100g Caster sugar

60g Sea salt flakes

1 tsp Fennel seeds

Zest & juice 1 Lemon

Zest & juice 1 Lime

Pickled Vegetables

1 Carrot

1/2 Cucumber -peeled

1/2 bulb Fennel

2 Radish

200g White wine vinegar

200g Water

25g Sugar

1/2 tsp Coriander seeds

1 Bay leaf

Oyster Fritter

4 Carlingford Oysters

150g Self raising flour

1/2 tsp Salt

300ml Whitewater
Belfast black (stout)

METHOD

Cured Salmon

Check salmon for any bones, trim belly fat, and any white. Combine all ingredients together.

Line bench with 3 layers cling film place salmon in centre, skin side down. Cover with beetroot mixture, fold over the cling film tightly so none leaks out or air gets in.

Place salmon on a baking tray. Place another tray on top of the salmon and place on some weights.

Chill for at least 7 days. After 7 days, remove salmon and scrap of mixture, pat dry and wrap until needed. Slice with a sharp carving knife as you would smoked salmon.

Pickled Veg

Thinly slice carrot, fennel and radish and using a small parisienne spoon ball the cucumber.

Prepare the pickling liquor - heat water, vinegar and sugar until dissolved. Add the coriander seeds and bay, keep on a low heat and add vegetables, carrot first then fennel cucumber and radish, remove from heat and allow to cool.

Oysters

In a bowl mix the flour and salt, whisk in the stout to form a light batter, shuck the oysters and rinse in cold water to remove any grit.

Toss in a little flour the dip into batter and deep fry in hot oil 180°C until crisp and golden, drain on kitchen paper and season.

THE RIVER ROOM

BIOGRAPHY

The River Room Restaurant at Galgorm Resort & Spa offers a unique and intimate dining experience. Enjoy modern Irish dishes prepared by Chef Chris Rees whilst taking in the breathtaking panoramic views of the River Maine and lush parkland of the Resort's 163 acre estate.

Born and raised in Belfast, local boy Chris Rees has certainly earned his culinary stripes when it comes to excellence in cooking. Having worked his way up through the cooking ranks in many of the city's top restaurants, Chris joined the Galgorm team in 2009. Promoted to Head Chef in 2013 Chris has proven himself to be a highly dedicated and skilled Chef with true flair and creativity for fine dining cuisine.

He offers diners at the River Room dishes that are true to the ingredients, showcasing local artisan producers and helping to promote Northern Ireland as a serious food destination. His menu focuses on seasonal ingredients sourced from carefully selected local suppliers and the Resort's very own kitchen garden. He believes in 'honest food' that delivers maximum taste and isn't swayed by trends but always makes the ingredients the star of the show.

Chris's work ethic and passion for his craft means his sights are set high, with ambitions to be recognised as one of the top chefs in the country. He continues to innovate and create inspiring food that will bring with it accolades for both himself and The River Room at Galgorm Resort & Spa.

Stuffed Crown Of Partridge
with chestnut gnocchi, butternut squash, smoked bacon & savoy cabbage

INGREDIENTS

2 Partridge (whole)

4 slices of Dry cured streaky bacon

The meat of one Pork sausage

1 Shallot (finely chopped)

1 Butternut squash

1 packet Chestnuts

1 Savoy cabbage

100g dry Mashed potato (no butter/ cream)

20g Breadcrumbs

25g Flour

1 Egg

Olive oil

Salt & pepper

small bunch of fresh Sage (finely chopped)

METHOD

For The Partridge

Remove the legs from the bird. Roast the legs at 160°C for 10-12 mins until the meat falls from the bone. Reserve the leg meat. Remove the breast from the crown with a sharp knife, being careful to keep them as one piece. Mix the breadcrumbs, leg meat, sausage meat, shallots and sage, season and stuff inside the breast. Roll the stuffed crown in cling film and leave aside.

For The Gnocchi

Mix the potato, egg and flour together and add a pinch of salt, add 20g of grated chestnut. Separate into small even pieces (depending on what size you want the gnocchi). Using a fork or gnocchi board, form into ridged pieces by flattening small pieces of the dough onto the board or base of the fork then gently roll off to create each individual piece. Blanch in boiling water until it floats then remove and refresh in iced water until cool.

For The Squash

Peel and cut the squash into slices then dice into cubes (or use a small pastry cutter for rounds). With the trim, boil in a little water until soft, transfer to a food processor and blend to a puree add seasoning. Cook the cubes or rounds in boiling water until soft and set aside.

To Assemble The Dish

Poach the partridge crown in the cling film for 10-12 mins in simmering water until cooked through and slightly firm. Remove from the cling film and add to a hot pan with a little olive oil, the bacon slices, pieces/rounds of squash, gnocchi and remaining chestnuts and roast until golden (10-12 mins) at 160°C. Remove from the pan and set aside. Cook the sliced savoy cabbage in a little butter until soft.

Slice the crown and lay on the cabbage. Dress the plate with the puree, chestnuts, roast squash, bacon and spoon over some of the reduced pan juices.

SAPHYRE

BIOGRAPHY

Patrick James Rowan credits his mother with his passion for cooking as she always encouraged him to try new things, flavours, ingredients and dishes.

He started his career in a busy gastro pub in his home town Donaghadee. After 2 years he moved to Michelin starred Paul Rankin in Cayenne Belfast. Through working with Paul, Patrick realised and decide that cooking was definitely the career for him. Patrick moved to London for six months to further enhance his skills and working for Jason Atherton in the Michelin starred Pollen Street Social.

Under Jason, Patrick took his cooking and skills to another level. Upon returning back to Ireland he worked for Danny Millar in his fine dining restaurant Balloo House. After 2 years working under

Danny, Patrick then took the step into his first Head Chef position in SAPHYRE Belfast. Approaching the end of the first year in SAPHYRE, the restaurant has achieved the LCN Newcomer of the Year 2014 and is highly respected for its contribution to the food industry within Northern Ireland.

Glamour elegance and refinement are the qualities that characterise both the dishes and the dining space within SAPHYRE. Set within an architecturally stunning converted church, the layout and bespoke dining room translates beautifully whether it's a romantic evening for 2, a night out with friends or a private party be that a christening, wedding or a special celebration.

Hay smoked goose
parsley root & quince

INGREDIENTS

4 Goose breast

10 Quince

10 Parsley roots

1 bunch of dried Hay

1 bunch Cavolo nero

METHOD

FIRSTLY SMOKE THE GOOSE

We use a smoke gun in the restaurant to cold smoke the goose as this gives a better end product. If a smoke gun is unavailable a traditional hot smoking pan can be used. The goose is smoked six times with smoke gun, waiting for the smoke to subside each time before repeating the process.

FOR THE PARSLEY ROOTS PUREE

Take six of the parsley roots and slice them very finely covering with chicken stock and a cartouche. Cook until tender and until the chicken stock has reduced and intensified in flavour. Transfer to a food processor and blend until smooth, adding in a knob of butter and a splash of double cream. Adjust the seasoning and pass through a fine sieve.

FOR THE QUINCE REDUCTION

Peel and halve the quince. Place in a pot and cover with water Add the zest of one orange and two star anise. Poach gently for two hours until the liquid takes on a red colour. Pass the liquid through a sieve lined with muslin cloth, discard any solids. Use 500g of sugar to 600g of the quince liquid reducing slowly until a syrup consistency is gained.

TO ASSEMBLE

Blanch the remaining four parsley roots in salted boiling water until tender, refresh in ice water. Sauté the parsley roots in a pan of foaming butter, turning constantly for an even colour. Glaze with some jus and keep warm. Season the goose and lay skin side down in a cold pan and cook on a low heat to slowly render the fat out of the skin to make it golden and crispy (approx 5 mins). Transfer to the oven and cook for a further five minutes. Remove the goose from the oven and let rest for 5 mins, it should be pink when carved. Swipe some of the parsley root puree across the base of the plate. Arrange the blanched cavolo nero on top of the puree. Place the glazed parsley root vertically on the plate.

Carve the goose and arrange on top of the glazed parsley roots. Drizzle the quince reduction around the edge of the plate followed by some jus.

For added theatre, we present the finished plate under a smoke filled cloche.

HOWARD STREET

BIOGRAPHY

For Head Chef Marty Murphy what started out as a holiday job set him on an unexpected path, travelling around the world, experiencing new and exciting flavours. At the age of 20, while on holiday, Marty got a kitchen porter job in a florida restaurant. What was to last a few weeks turned into a career. Igniting the flame within, Marty returned to Belfast to study. Form there he went to work for Michael Deane, amongst others. Marty started off on a two year trip around Thailand and Australia. In Thailand, he spent time with locals, teaching him the basics of thai cooking, and an understanding and importance of fresh ingredients. Australia brought Marty back into the kitchen, working in top restaurant, ARIA. After a brief period back at home, Amsterdam called next, michelin 2-star Vermeer. There Marty realised the idea of how high the standard can be taken and how hard the push is needed to reach it. Returning home again, Marty spent 3 years as Head Chef of The Potted Hen, where he met business partner Niall Davis, who both shared the vision of creating something new for Belfast. In 2013 the pair opened up Howard Street. The emphasis, good local produce with Thai and asian flavours, and wine and cocktail menu to compliment. The industrial feel and decor of the restaurant is a nod to the 100 year history of the building, with an original terrazzo floor and dobbins from textile manufacturing hanging on the wall. Situated in the heart of Belfast city, it could easily be at home in any other city of the world.

Szechuan Roast Monkfish
with bok choi, spiced crab spring roll and hot & sour prawn broth

INGREDIENTS

300g Monkfish

2 Spring roll wraps

100g fresh White crab meat (picked to ensure no shell fragments)

6 whole Bok choi leaves

50g Prawn shells

25g Tom yum paste

1 Lemongrass stalk (chopped)

10g Basil stocks

20g sliced Shallot

20g sliced Onion

20g slice White cabbage

10g diced Red chilli (deseeded)

10g sliced Ginger

1 split Red chilli

25ml Red wine vinegar

5g grated Palm sugar

250ml good quality Vegetable stock

30g good quality Mayonnaise

10ml Light soy sauce

20g crushed Szechuan pepper

5g toasted Sesame seeds

METHOD

Ask your local fishmonger to remove the monkfish from bone and remove skin. Cut into 2 x 150g portions and set aside.

To make broth, put Tom Yum paste with a splash of oil onto an oven tray and place in oven at 180°c for 10 minutes until dark red in colour. Roast prawn shells at the same temperature for 10 minutes.

In a saucepan gently fry off sliced shallot, lemongrass, basil stalks, ginger and split chilli for 10 minutes, without colouring. Add roasted Tom Yum paste and cook for a further 10 minutes on a low heat. Add red wine vinegar and palm sugar, reduce to a syrup. Add roasted prawn shells and veg stock, simmer for 20 minutes and strain.

To make spring roll, in a bowl add picked crabmeat, diced chilli, cabbage, sliced onion, soy sauce and mayonnaise. Mix well until combined. Place spring roll wrapper on a dry surface, take half the crab mix and place it 1/3 of the way up the wrapper in a rough sausage shape. Tuck in the ends and roll up sealing the top of the wrap with a little beaten egg.

Blanch bok choi in boiling salted water for 1-2 minutes and refresh in iced water.

To assemble

First heat a heavy based pan and add olive oil. Roll the monkfish in the crouched szechuan and season with salt. Place fish in pan and cook over a medium heat, turning once or twice before placing in oven at 170°c for 10-12 minutes depending on thickness of fish. Set aside in a warm place.

Place broth back on the heat and reduce by 1/3. heat a deep fryer to 180°c and cook spring rolls until nice and golden. remove and cut on an angle. Heat bok choi in broth and add toasted sesame seeds.

Arrange in a shallow bowl, with first sliced monkfish, then spring roll. Arrange the bok choi around the spring roll, finally pour the hot broth around the outside.

THE OLD SCHOOL HOUSE

BIOGRAPHY

Will Brown started his cooking career in London with Marco Pierre White at the Mirabelle in Mayfair aged 17. He then returned to Belfast were he worked in the well established Roscoff under Paul Rankin. He then moved to London and during a 3 year stint he worked at The Square a two Michelin star restaurant in Mayfair and The Glasshouse.

The fundamental backbone of his dishes remains unchanged. Impeccable seasonal ingredients are accurately cooked and brought together on the plate in a harmonious, elegant, yet satisfying manner.

Restaurant is listed in "Good Food Guide 2013" and John & Sally McKennas' Guides 2013.

Seabream
stuffed with a crab and scallop mousse, served with foraged sea herbs

INGREDIENTS

4 fillets Seabream

5 Scallops

100g Crab meat, picked

1 Egg white

50ml Cream

Salt

juice of ½ Lemon

foraged Sea herbs – goosetongue, fat hen, samphire, sandwort

1tsp Lemonzest

splash of White wine

1knob unsalted Butter

METHOD

Take 4 fillets seabream, pinbone and descale. Set aside

Scallop and Crab Mousse

Remove the row and membrane from scallop, put on cloth and absorb moisture from the scallop

In a food processor, blend scallops until smooth, add egg white, then cream. Add lemon juice, pinch of salt and blend to a smooth consistency.

In a mixing bowl mix together freshly picked white crab meat with scallop mousse until well combined

Put a layer of clingfilm on the worktop, place seabream fillet on top

Put the scallop and crab mousse into a piping bag and pipe mousse into the centre of the fillet

Wrap in cling film and steam for 11 minutes

To make a very simple sauce while the seabream is cooking

Add a splash of white wine to a hot pan, reduce the wine, stir in a little unsalted butter and add foraged sea herbs for 30 seconds

To finish the dish, open the parcel of seabream and remove cling film

Place on the plate and spoon over sea herbs and butter emulsion

443

GRAZE

BIOGRAPHY

Two award winning friends with a passion for creating exceptional dining experiences look forward to welcoming you to a new casual dining experience in the heart of East Belfast.

We have a passion for flavour, quality ingredients, and for creating an atmosphere that is comfortable, affordable and a haven for people who simply love food and drink. Graze is located in the heart of East Belfast serving seasonally-inspired cuisine with a commitment to using local and sustainable foods.

Smoked Lough Neagh Eel

textures of beetroot, pickled heritage carrots, rainbow radish, local samphire, horse radish aioli, micro leaf

INGREDIENTS

1 whole Eel, filleted

1 white Beetroot

1 golden Beetroot

1 purple Beetroot

1 white Carrot

1 purple Carrot

1 orange Carrot

3 rainbow Radish

200g fresh Horse radish

3 Cherry tomato

3 yellow Cherry tomato

1 Granny Smith apple

1 Clementine orange

1 small bunch of Wild rocket

25g dehydrated purple Beetroot

10g fresh blanched Samphire

Salt & pepper

Micro leaf

Selection-

Coriander leaf, red stem Radish, red Armatha, Sorrel

PICKLING INGREDIENTS

100ml of White wine vinegar

100ml White wine

100ml Olive oil

1 tbsp Maldon salt

Juice of 1/2 Lemon

SMOKE

1 bag Whiskey oak wood chips

1 large Deep tray

1 resting Rack

4 Dario moulds

AIOLI INGREDIENTS

1 Egg yolk

100ml veg oil

25ml Rapeseed oil

1 tbsp White wine vinegar

1/2 tsp English mustard

1/2 tsp Coarse grain mustard

1/2 Lemon juice

200g fresh finely grated Horse radish

METHOD

PICKLING

Combine all of the ingredients together in a bowl.
Peel and quarter each of the rainbow radish.
Peel carrots and make 3 ribbons of each carrot.
Place in bowl and cover with pickling juice and leave for 30 mins.
After time remove and place in the fridge.

BEETROOTS

Cook and peel your 3 coloured beetroots.
Finely slice the purple beetroot. Cut the remaining beetroot in 1/2 inch cubes to garnish dish.

SMOKING

In a deep tray place a dario mold in each corner. Scatter whiskey oak chips onto the base of the tray.
Place resting rack on top of dario molds. Add your eel fillets.
Place tray over a flame burning ring until wood starts to smoke.
Leave to smoke for about 6 mins for a light smoke. Then remove fillets of eel and allow to cool.

AIOLI

Whisk the egg yolks in a bowl, then add the mustard and whisk together. Gradually add about half the oil, very slowly at first, whisking continuously for around 3-5 minutes, or until thickened. Once you've added about half the oil, whisk in 1 tbsp of vinegar – this will loosen the mixture slightly and give it a paler colour. Continue to gradually add the remaining oil, whisking continuously. Season with a pinch of salt, a squeeze of lemon juice and a little more vinegar, if needed. Now add your finely grated horse radish to complete your aioli

APPLE & CLEMENTINE

Wash your apple and orange. Cut the apple into batons.
Segment your clementine and place apple and orange aside until later.
Have fun plating all of the ingredients on a plate to make a perfect picture - we hope you enjoy.

WINE AND BRINE

BIOGRAPHY

Chris McGowan's inaugural venture, Wine and Brine in Moira, County Armagh, aims to showcase the region's wealth of local produce through traditional cooking methods that wouldn't have been out of place in your great granny's kitchen.

Fermenting, brining and curing all take centre stage at Wine and Brine, hence the name, yet this unpretentious restaurant offering is designed for people who, quite simply, love food, and want to enjoy it with friends and family in a relaxed atmosphere.

Despite having worked for some of Europe's most admired chefs and in fine dining establishments in London, McGowan has worked hard to create an environment that is as comfortable to patrons as a pair of warm socks on a cold day – a 'local' in the true sense of the word and one which prides itself on its hands-on relationship with customers. McGowan can be seen in the open plan kitchen six days a week and strives to make customers feel at home. In fact, almost 90 per cent of Wine and Brine's custom is return.

This trust in, and acceptance of, the food on offer is important to McGowan as he is keen to help diners come to appreciate these traditional cooking methods and make them as accessible and normal as they would have been way back when.

Gooseberry, Custard, Elderflower Beignets

INGREDIENTS

Custard

x8 Egg yolks

150g Sugar

handful fresh Elderflower

500ml Double cream

250ml Milk

Gooseberry

300g fresh Gooseberries

200g Caster sugar

Batter

150g Plain flour

150g Cornflour

75g Icing sugar

140ml Sparkling water

METHOD

For the custard, combine the cream and milk in a pan and bring to a simmer. In a bowl, whisk egg yolks and sugar. Pour over hot cream and whisk again.

Transfer back to the pan and stir continuously until mix coats back of a spoon.

Add elderflower, place a lid on top and leave to cool. When cool, pass through a fine sieve and refrigerate.

Combine gooseberries and sugar in a pan and cook down to a compote. Leave to cool.

Combine all dry ingredients in a bowl for the batter and gradually add the sparkling water to make a thin batter.

To serve:

Place a spoonful of compote in each bowl. Warm and pour custard.

Lightly flower elderflower heads, dip in batter and fry at 180°C until golden. Drain and dust with icing sugar. Serve immediately

BROWNS IN TOWN

BIOGRAPHY

Tipped as one of Ireland's top talents, Ian Orr trained under the late Robbie Millar at Northern Ireland's formative Michelin-starred restaurant Shanks before moving to London's River Cafe and then to Head Chef at Rathmullan House Hotel in Donegal.

Since opening Browns Restaurant in 2009, Ian has opened Browns in Town, Browns on the Green and, in 2014, Browns at Ardtara Country House   --all with the help of his business partner Marcus Roulston plus his personally trained and highly talented team.

In 2015, "Browns" became the only restaurant in Northern Ireland to be invited into the prestigious "Ireland's Blue Book" association of hotels and restaurants and his newly acquired Ardtara Country House Hotel won the Best Hotel Restaurant in Northern Ireland (RAI). In 2016, Ardtara was awarded four Gold Stars by the AA and two Rosettes for food in 2016 and "Best Guest Accommodation in Northern Ireland 2016/2017.

Ian Orr's Hot Chocolate Fondant

INGREDIENTS

100g Plain flour

120g Caster sugar

100g Butter

100g Dark chocolate
(70% minimum cocoa
solids)

2 whole Eggs

2 Egg yolks

METHOD

Melt the butter and chocolate together in a glass or metal bowl over a pan of gently simmering water. Ensure the water in the pan doesn't touch the base of the bowl.

Beat the sugar and eggs together in a separate bowl until pale and creamy, then add to the chocolate and butter mix.

Gently fold through the flour until it is fully combined with the chocolate and butter.

Butter 6 ramekins and pour the mixture evenly into them.

When needed, bake in the oven at 180° for 10 minutes. Timing is crucial at this point as you want the centre of the fondant to be a pool of chocolate sauce. Invert each ramekin onto a serving plate and serve immediately.

In Browns we serve this with homemade milk ice cream but a good quality vanilla ice cream works well too. For a simple raspberry coulis, gently heat 300g of fresh raspberries with 75g of caster sugar and 1 star anise in a small pan until the raspberries have collapsed and released all their juices. Remove the star anise and push the mixture through a sieve to get rid of the tiny seeds. Leave it to cool before drizzling the coulis over the plate alongside the fondants.

THE POACHES POCKET

BIOGRAPHY

Originally established in the 1800's as an old coaching inn, The Poacher's Pocket is situated in the heart of picturesque County Down. With the exposed oak beams, stone floors and leather upholstered booths, this charming country pub and restaurant boasts a cosy, traditional feel with a touch of contemporary flair. The menu features hearty dishes with classic flavour combinations as well as traditional pub favourites and sumptuous daily specials using the best of local seasonal ingredients. The recently refurbished pub and restaurant includes an artisan food and wine farm shop open every day from 9am. Serving freshly baked breads, premium dry-aged steaks, fresh local fish and The Poacher's own home-cooked sauces, chowders and soups, diners can now take-away some of their gastro-pub favourites and enjoy them at home.

Sticky Toffee Pudding

INGREDIENTS

55g/2oz Butter (plus extra for greasing)

170g/6oz Demerara sugar

1 tbsp Golden syrup

2 Free-range eggs

2 tbsp Black treacle

200g/7oz Self-raising flour (plus extra for flouring)

200g/7oz pitted Dates

290ml/10fl oz boiling Water

1 tsp Bicarbonate of soda

½ tsp Vanilla extract

For the sauce:

110ml/4fl oz Double cream

55g/2oz Butter (diced)

55g/2oz Dark muscovado sugar

2 tbsp Black treacle

1 tbsp Golden syrup

Vanilla ice cream (to serve)

METHOD

Preheat the oven to 200°C/400°F/Gas 6. Grease and flour 6 individual pudding moulds.

Cream the butter and sugar together in a food processor until pale and fluffy. Add the golden syrup, treacle and eggs, a little at a time, and blend until smooth. Add the flour and blend, at a low speed, until well combined. Transfer to a bowl.

Meanwhile, blend the dates and boiling water in a food processor to a smooth purée. Stir in the bicarbonate of soda and vanilla.

Pour the date mixture into the pudding batter and stir until well combined.

Pour the mixture into the moulds and bake for 20-25 minutes, or until the top is springy and golden-brown.

To make the sauce, heat all of the ingredients in a pan, stirring occasionally, until boiling.

To serve, remove the puddings from the moulds and place onto each of 6 serving plates. Pour over the sauce and serve with a scoop of vanilla ice cream.

VANILLA
RESTAURANT

BIOGRAPHY

Darren opened Vanilla in 2009 where he quickly built a reputation for serving exceptional dishes using quality local and homegrown produce. This reputation is compounded by our No. 1 rating on Trip Advisor for both Newcastle and County Down, as well as our inclusion in the Michelin and Good Food Guides.

After 25 years in the Hospitality Industry, Darren is still as driven as he was watching his grandfather Tommy (former Head Chef, Slieve Donard Hotel) cook all those years ago. It's this drive that ensures that Vanilla will continue to provide it's customers with a fantastic dining experience.

Chocolate Fondant

INGREDIENTS

120g White Chocolate

3 Whole Eggs

3 Egg Yolks

160g Caster Sugar

160g 82% Dark Chocolate

160g Butter

120g Plain Flour

METHOD

Take six pudding moulds, grease well with butter then dust heavily with coco powder & set aside

Melt white chocolate and pour into 20g moulds, (ice cube trays usually work perfect), Chill until hard

Place butter and chocolate over a Bain Marie, in a heat proof bowl; allow to melt fully and slowly whilst mixing occasionally, Note: do not allow mix to over melt and get to hot as this will destroy the chocolate

Whilst the chocolate and butter mix is melting, place sugar, eggs and egg yolks in a clean electric mixing bowl and beat until trebled in size and light thick (note: the best way of telling that it is at the correct stage is if you lift the whisk and draw a figure of 8 with the whisk and it should be visible for a few seconds after)

Now combine the chocolate and butter mix with the egg and sugar mix, Note it is important not to knock the air out of the egg and sugar mix, its best to add half the egg mix into the chocolate first, to lighten it up, then continue with the rest

Sieve the flour on top of the chocolate mix, fold in thoroughly again being careful not to knock the air out of the fondant mix

Divide the fondant mix evenly between the six moulds, push 1 white chocolate cube into the middle of each one, ensuring that the white chocolate is not touching the bottom and is not visible from the top either, as if it's floating in the middle of each fondant

Bake in preheated oven, 220c for 9 minutes, allow to rest for 2 minutes before turning out and serving

THE OX
BELFAST

BIOGRAPHY

Chef owner Stephen Toman started his career in his home-town of Belfast before being bitten by the travelling bug. With experience gained over years of travelling, from 5-star resorts in America to the Michelin starred kitchens of Paris, including Taillevent, L'Astrance and the iconic L'Arpège, Stephen eventually returned home. Annual trips back to stage in the kitchens of Paris allowed a wealth of ideas to percolate and mature, culminating in the opening of OX in 2013 with friend and former colleague Alain Kerloc'h.

Stephen shows his creativity with an enthusiastic approach to seasonal produce, bringing fresh ingredients alive on your plate, with a delicate emphasis on vegetables. Each dish leaving the kitchen is thoughtfully designed so every element on the plate plays an integral role in showcasing the best quality produce. Since opening Stephen, Alain and their team have secured a number of awards Including; Best Newcomer at the Irish Restaurant Awards 2013, Best Restaurant - Ulster at both the Irish Restaurant Awards 2014 and FOOD&WINE Magazine Restaurant of the Year Awards 2014 and Best Chef - Ulster 2013 and 2014 at the FOOD&WINE Magazine Restaurant of the Year Awards.

Lemon Polenta Cake
with coconut sorbet and crème anglaise

INGREDIENTS

Lemon Polenta Cake

3 Lemons (puree the flesh; reduce it with juice to half)

185g soft Butter

210g Caster sugar

3 Eggs

155g fine Polenta

150g Almonds

1/2 tbsp Baking powder

Coconut sorbet

500g Coconut puree

75g Sugar

150ml Water

Crème anglaise

125ml Cream

125ml Milk

50g Yolk

50g Caster sugar

5g sprigs of Thyme

METHOD

Lemon Polenta cake

Mix lemon reduction, butter and caster sugar.

Beat in eggs slowly then fold in polenta, almonds and baking powder. Pour mixture in lined rings, and bake at 160°C for 15-20 mins.

Coconut Sorbet

Boil the sugar and water, then mix in the coconut puree.

Place the content into Pacojet canister. Freeze until solid then use Pacojet to churn.

Crème Anglaise

Scald milk, cream and thyme. Mix egg yolk with sugar. Pour liquid over yolk and sugar mixture and whisk. Return to pot and cook, stirring continuously until it coats the back of a wooden spoon then pass

Plating

Turn out warm polenta cake onto bowl. Pour crème Anglaise around cake. Scoop coconut sorbet and garnish with chopped pistachio.

World Leading Cookery School Sponsor the Great British Cookbook.

The Great British Cookbook which raises money for Macmillan Cancer Support and Hospitality Action, are delighted to announce that Le Cordon Bleu London, leading culinary arts, wine and management school are sponsoring the cookbook.

Founded in Paris in 1895, Le Cordon Bleu has grown from a popular culinary magazine to one of the most prestigious global networks of culinary arts and hospitality management institutes.

In 2012, Le Cordon Bleu London moved from its base on Marylebone Lane to its new state-of-the-art premises, 15 Bloomsbury Square.

Offering a range of industry relevant cuisine, pâtisserie and wine Diplomas alongside a variety of engaging short courses taught by their team of high calibre Master Chefs, students are often considered to be synonymous with outstanding ability across the globe.

Although traditional French culinary techniques remain at the heart of Le Cordon Bleu, the school's academic programmes continue to be pioneered as a response to consumer and industry demands, which as a result has seen the introduction of the Diploma in Culinary Management and the Diploma in Gastronomy, Nutrition and Food Trends within the last two years.

Le Cordon Bleu's place in the industry plays an integral part in the success of the hundreds of students who graduate each year. With such a respected reputation, Le Cordon Bleu London also host a number of industry competitions from National Chef of The Year to Bocuse d'Or, which benefit from the professional facilities and equipment.

The Master Chefs at Le Cordon Bleu can often be found on the judging panel at culinary competitions, or sometimes actively competing in their own right. This maintains the vital connection the school has to the industry, and opens a unique opportunity for students to witness first-hand the dedication and passion that chefs require to become and remain successful.

Chef Alan Swinson, Culinary Arts Director at Le Cordon Bleu London: "The book is supporting two very worthy cause and we are delighted to be sponsoring this collection of recipes from Britain's best chefs. With the evolution and transformation of British food over the last two decades The Great British Cookbook brings together and demonstrates the culinary excellence we have to offer today."

Gary Allen Founder of the book: "We are delighted to have the support from such an iconic cookery school who have no doubt had so many chefs involved with the book come through their school. The book will certainly inspire people who want to be part of the hospitality industry and Le Cordon Bleu are a great organisation to provide the training."

Proceeds from the book sale are going to Macmillan Cancer support and Hospitality Action

To find out more about Le Cordon Bleu you can visit www.lecordonbleu.edu/london

Thank You...

We would like to thank all of the chefs and venues for helping to make the book a reality with their generous support and the amazing recipes

Le Cordon Bleu London
The All About Tourism Team
Gossama Design and Marketing
Andy Whyles – Founder and Director – All About Tourism
Adam Simmonds – Chef – Consultant
Petra Medley and Warren Tait

A special thank you to all the agencies and various publishers who helped

Dedications

I would like to dedicate the book to all of the team at All About Tourism
To my good friend and business partner – Andy Whyles, my amazing wife - Sarah Allen and all my friends and family who helped me through the book when I was diagnosed with Cancer very early into the project.

Without you all I would not be here to have finished the book

Thank you to Macmillan Cancer Support - Your support was incredible